P9-CFY-725

THE GHOSTS OF
CANNAE

THE GHOSTS OF
CANNAE

Hannibal and the Darkest Hour

of the Roman Republic

ROBERT L. O'CONNELL

RANDOM HOUSE

New York

Published in the United States by Random House,
an imprint of The Random House Publishing Group,
a division of Random House, Inc., New York.

RANDOM HOUSE and colophon are registered trademarks
of Random House, Inc.

LIBRARY OF CONGRESS CATALOGING-IN-PUBLICATION DATA
O'Connell, Robert L.
The ghosts of Cannae: Hannibal and the darkest hour of
the Roman republic / Robert L. O'Connell.
p.   cm.
Includes bibliographical references and index.
ISBN 978-1-4000-6702-2
eBook ISBN 978-0-679-60379-5
1. Cannae, Battle of, Italy, 216 B.C.   2. Hannibal, 247–182 B.C.
3. Rome—Army—History.
4. Punic War, 2nd, 218–201 B.C.—Campaigns.
5. Carthage (Extinct city)—Relations—Rome.
6. Rome—Relations—Tunisia—Carthage (Extinct city).   I. Title.
DG247.3.O25 2010   937'.04—dc22   2009040006

Printed in the United States of America on acid-free paper

Random House website address: www.atrandom.com

Title-page image © 2010 Jupiterimages Corporation

2 4 6 8 9 7 5 3 1

First Edition

Book design by Jo Anne Metsch

To Harry Dell, who taught me about
Greeks and Romans and even had
some sympathy for Carthage

CONTENTS

LIST OF MAPS

CAST OF CHARACTERS

Agathocles of Syracuse—Invaded Carthaginian North Africa in 310 B.C. and subsequently won a victory in the field, which prompted the revolt of native Libyans before Agathocles was forced to withdraw. This invasion revealed how vulnerable Carthage was at home.

Antiochus III—Basileus of the Seleucid Empire, he made the mistake of hiring Hannibal as a military consultant after the Second Punic War, and then allowed himself to be drawn into a disastrous war with Rome that ended with defeat at the Battle of Magnesia in 189 B.C.

Appius Claudius—Roman survivor of Cannae who helped Scipio Africanus put down the mutiny at Canusium and who later joined Marcellus at the siege of Syracuse.

Archimedes—The great Greek mathematician who organized the defense of Syracuse against Rome.

Hamilcar Barca—Hannibal's father, and a commander during the First Punic War. Hamilcar later established the family empire in Spain and is thought to be the source of his son's hatred of Rome.

Hannibal Barca—Instigator of the Second Punic War, invader of Italy, and among the most capable generals in history.

Hasdrubal Barca—Brother of Hannibal. He was left behind in Spain to guard the family holdings during the Second Punic War. He later invaded Italy over the Alps and was subsequently killed at the Battle of the Metaurus in 207 B.C.

Mago Barca—Brother of Hannibal. He played a vital role at Cannae and later returned to Spain, where he struggled against the Romans. He too invaded Italy in 206 and subsequently died from a wound he received there.

Cato, M. Porcius—A Roman politician and soldier. He was an archetype of conservatism and was a lifelong enemy of Scipio Africanus, not to mention Carthage.

Q. Fabius Maximus—Roman consul and dictator who devised the unpopular strategy of avoiding battle with Hannibal and relying on attrition instead.

Cn. Fulvius Flaccus—Brother of the consul Q. Fulvius Flaccus, and the losing general at the First Battle of Herdonea. He was tried for treason, and his surviving troops were exiled to join the *legiones Cannenses*.

Q. Fulvius Flaccus—Roman consul and important commander in the Second Punic War. He was one of the key participants in the siege of Capua.

Flaminius, Caius—Roman consul and general who made a career of assaulting the Gauls and giving their conquered lands to Roman colonists. He was ambushed by Hannibal at Lake Trasimene and was killed along with much of his army.

Flaminius, T. Quinctius—Roman general and victor at the Battle of Cynoscephalae, which effectively finished Philip V. Flaminius later was sent to Bithynia to hunt down Hannibal.

Hanno "the Great"—The leader of the Carthaginian opposition to the Barcid agenda. He was the Barcids' opponent during the Second Punic War and appears to have spoken for the interests of commercial agriculture.

Hasdrubal (cavalry commander)—Brilliantly led the Celtic and Spanish cavalry at Cannae.

Hasdrubal Gisgo—Longtime Carthaginian commander, first in Spain and then in North Africa during the Second Punic War. Not a great soldier, but extremely persistent. Also, the father of Sophonisba.

Hasdrubal the Handsome—Carthaginian politician and Hamilcar Barca's son-in-law. He took over the Barcid holdings in Spain after Hamilcar's death. Hasdrubal the Handsome was assassinated in 221 and replaced by Hannibal.

Hippocrates and Epicydes—Carthaginian brothers of Syracusan descent whose maneuvers proved to be the catalyst for Syracuse's revolt against Rome.

Indibilis—A powerful local Spanish chieftain whose shifting loyalties came to epitomize the treacherous political environment in Iberia during the Second Punic War.

Laelius, Gaius—Longtime military subordinate to Scipio Africanus. A talented commander in his own right, he played an important role in securing the North African countryside during the Roman invasion that would lead to Carthage's surrender.

Laevinus, M. Valerius—Capable Roman commander in Greece during the first of Rome's wars against Philip V. He later served in Sicily.

Sempronius Longus, T.—Roman consul defeated at the Battle of the River Trebia in 218 B.C.

Maharbal—Opportunistic Carthaginian cavalry commander who challenged Hannibal to march on Rome after Cannae.

Marcellus, M. Claudius—One of the key Roman generals during the Second Punic War, and conqueror of Syracuse. Marcellus was an extremely belligerent commander who was killed in one of Hannibal's ambushes in 208.

L. Marcius, Septimus—Roman commander in Spain who rallied the survivors after the defeat of the elder Scipio brothers.

Masinissa—Numidian prince and later king of Massylia in North Africa. He was an excellent cavalry commander who first served with the Carthaginians in Spain and later switched sides to join the Romans. He would prove a potent force in Carthage's defeat and later destruction.

Muttines—Talented Numidian cavalry commander who went over to the Roman side in Syracuse and subsequently became a citizen.

Nero, C. Claudius—Roman general in the Second Punic War in both Spain and Italy. It was his surprise march to the Metaurus that probably sealed Hasdrubal Barca's fate.

Paullus, L. Aemilius—One of the two consuls defeated at Cannae. Paullus was killed there.

Philip V—King of Macedon who after Cannae made an alliance with Hannibal and subsequently fought two wars with Rome.

Pleminius, Quintus—A Roman legate whose brutal behavior at Locri toward the town's citizens and toward his fellow Roman commanders almost brought about the disgrace of Scipio Africanus.

Prusias II—King of Bithynia who employed Hannibal during the 180s as a city planner and admiral. Prusias ultimately betrayed Hannibal.

Pyrrhus—Epirote king who invaded Italy and fought the Romans in a series of three costly battles between 280 and 275 B.C.

Regulus, M. Atilius—Roman consul who invaded North Africa during the First Punic War and subsequently suffered defeat and capture. His example was later cited by Romans wary of staging an analogous invasion during the Second Punic War.

Salinator, M. Livius—A Roman consul who came out of retirement and disgrace to lead (with Nero) the Roman armies at the Battle of the Metaurus, which ended the invasion by Hasdrubal Barca.

Scipio, Cn. Cornelius—Brother of Publius Cornelius Scipio, who was also known as Scipio the Elder. Like his sibling, Cnaeus died fighting in Spain.

Scipio, P. Cornelius—Father of Scipio Africanus. He and his brother led the Roman effort in Spain until they were defeated and killed.

Scipio Africanus, P. Cornelius—Victorious Roman leader in Spain, and the conqueror of Hannibal at Zama in North Africa.

Sophonisba—Heroic daughter of Hasdrubal Gisgo. She was also the wife of Syphax, whom she influenced deeply and kept loyal to Carthage until he was defeated and captured.

Syphax—The Massaesylian king who provided much of the opposition to the Romans during Scipio Africanus's invasion of North Africa.

Torquatus, T. Manlius—Hard-core Roman who denounced the prisoners that Hannibal took at Cannae. He subsequently consolidated Roman control of Sardinia.

Varro, C. Terentius—Roman consul defeated at Cannae. He survived to be given other commands, somewhat inexplicably.

Xanthippus—The Greek mercenary who organized the Carthaginian defense in 255 B.C. in the face of the Roman invasion led by Regulus.

THE GHOSTS OF
CANNAE

I

TRACES OF WAR

[1]

Polybius of Megalopolis peered down from a pass high in the Italian Alps and caught sight of the rich green Lombard plain far below. It was exactly the same inviting panorama Hannibal had shown his half-starved, half-frozen, thoroughly discouraged army seventy-three years before, exhorting them to stay the course on what would prove to be an amazing path of conquest. Quite probably enough bits and pieces of that weary host remained visible for Polybius to be sure he was in the right spot; a certitude denied future chroniclers, and giving rise to one of ancient history's most enduring and futile controversies: Where exactly did Hannibal cross the Alps?[1] Polybius, for his part, was free to concentrate on questions he found more important.

It was his aim—an endeavor that would eventually fill forty books—to explain to his fellow Greeks how a hitherto obscure city-state on the Italian peninsula had come to dominate, virtually in the course of a lifetime, the entire Mediterranean world. But if Rome stood at center stage in Polybius's inquiry, Hannibal and Carthage were his foils. Each in their own way had nearly put an end to Rome's ambitions. Both by this time were dead, obliterated by Rome, but it was the challenges they had posed and the disasters they had inflicted that Polybius found most compelling. For no matter how bad things had gotten, Rome had always responded, had picked itself up out of the dustbin of history and soldiered on. And it was in defeat more than victory that Polybius saw the essence of Rome's greatness.

It never got worse than Cannae. On August 2, 216 B.C., a terrible apocalyptic day in southern Italy, 120,000 men engaged in what amounted to a mass knife fight. At the end of the fight, at least forty-eight thousand Romans lay dead or dying, lying in pools of their own blood and vomit and feces, killed in the most intimate and terrible ways, their limbs hacked off, their faces and thoraxes and abdomens punctured and mangled. This was Cannae, an event celebrated and studied as Hannibal's paragon by future practitioners of the military arts, the apotheosis of the decisive victory. Rome, on the other hand, lost—suffering on that one day more battle deaths than the United States during the entire course of the war in Vietnam, suffering more dead soldiers than any other army on any single day of combat in the entire course of Western military history. Worse yet, Cannae came at the end of a string of savage defeats engineered by the same Hannibal, Rome's nemesis destined to prey on Italy for another thirteen years and defeat army after army and kill general after general. Yet none of this would plumb the depths reached on that awful afternoon in August.

It has been argued that Polybius, aware of Cannae's enormous symbolic import, deliberately structured his history so as to make the battle appear as the absolute low point in Rome's fortunes, thereby exaggerating its significance.[2] Yet, not only do sheer numbers argue the contrary, but also Rome on this day lost a significant portion of its leadership class, between a quarter and a third of the senate, the members of which had been anxious to be present at what had been assumed would be a great victory. Instead it was a debacle by any measure, so much so that a case can be made that Cannae was even more critical than Polybius believed, in retrospect a true pivot point in Roman history. Arguably the events of this August day either initiated or accelerated trends destined to push Rome from municipality to empire, from republican oligarchy to autocracy, from militia to professional army, from a realm of freeholders to a dominion of slaves and estates. And the talisman of all of this change was one lucky survivor, a young military tribune named Publius Cornelius Scipio,* known to history as Africanus. For at the end of many more years of fighting, Rome still would need a general and an army good enough to defeat Hannibal, and Scipio Africanus, with the help of what remained of the battlefield's disgraced refugees, would answer the call and in the process set all else in motion.

---

* Typical Roman names of the late republican period had three elements: a praenomen, or given name (in this case Publius), chosen from a limited list and having no family connotation; a nomen, referring to the *gens* or clan name (Cornelii); and, finally, the cognomen, or family within the clan (Scipio).

[2]

Two questions spring to mind: How do we know? and Why should we care? For this is, after all, ancient history, among the dimmest and potentially most obscure of our recollections. Putting relevance aside for a moment, it is still necessary to concede a point made by Cambridge classicist Mary Beard: "The study of ancient history is as much about how we know as what we know, an engagement with all the processes of selection, constructive blindness, revolutionary reinterpretation and willful misinterpretation that together produce the 'facts' . . . out of the messy, confusing, and contradictory evidence that survives."[3]

In other words, what we know for sure is entirely limited, and all the rest is basically opinion. This point is driven home by the single sliver of archaeological evidence purporting to show that Hannibal ever actually invaded Italy—an inscription thought to commemorate Fabius Maximus's capture of the port city of Tarentum and containing the name Hannibal but not a word about Tarentum or Fabius.[4] After all those years, all those battles, that's it. Speaking of battles, military historians are prone to muddying their boots walking the fields on which mayhem once took place, seeking all manner of insights from the terrain, revelations that they maintain it is impossible to derive from the flat pages of a book. With Cannae and virtually all the other battles of the Second Punic* War, this exercise is, well, just an exercise when it becomes apparent that it is impossible to locate the battle sites with any degree of precision; during twenty-two hundred years, rivers change course, lakeshores advance and retreat, contemporary sprawl steamrolls the landscape.[5]

All we really have are words, preserved for us in the most haphazard fashion out of a much larger body of literature. So the study of ancient history is roughly analogous to scrutinizing a badly decayed patchwork quilt, full of holes and scraps of material from earlier work. Central to understanding the process of study is an awareness that, besides an occasional fragment liberated from the desert by archaeologists, there will be no more evidence. The quilt is it; everything must be based on a reasoned analysis of the fabric at hand. Plainly the quality

* "Punic" is derived from the Latin *"punicus"* and refers to Carthage and Carthaginians.

and integrity of some of the patches greatly exceed those of the others, so they will be emphasized and relied upon whenever possible. Yet, because of the limited nature of the material, there is always the temptation to fall back on a truly outlandish polka dot or a monumentally garish plaid, if only to figure out where it came from and what it might have meant in its original form. In the end, even among otherwise tasteful and scrupulous ancient historians, something is almost always better than nothing.

Fortunately for us, that "something" generally includes things military. Ancient historians were united in their belief that force was the ultimate arbiter of human affairs, and almost without exception wars and their outcomes were at the center of their works. Printing presses were nonexistent, and literacy was the possession of a tiny minority generally clustered around the ruling classes. Military history was not only dramatic and entertaining; it could be highly instructive for those in charge.

To Polybius, plainly the best of our sources, command in battle was "the most honorable and serious of all employments" (3.48.4) and he wrote knowing he had the ear of some of war's most enthusiastic practitioners. He was not in Rome by accident, or by choice. Polybius was a hostage, a *hipparch,* or master of cavalry, brought there in 167 B.C. along with a thousand of his countrymen to ensure the future good behavior of the Greek region of Achaea, part of the grinding, half-unwilling process by which the Romans eventually stifled Greek freedom. In a city where patronage meant everything, Polybius managed to attach himself to the clan and person of Scipio Aemilianus, grandson of one of the two losing consuls at Cannae, a perch that gave Polybius unparalleled access to the sources he needed for his great project of explaining Roman success. Besides trekking the Alps, he visited the state archives and read old treaties between Carthage and Rome, examined the personal papers and correspondence of important players, traipsed across battlefields, and journeyed to other pertinent locations. He even examined a bronze tablet Hannibal had had inscribed, enumerating his sanguinary achievements before leaving Italy. Polybius also interviewed a number of Cannae's participants, including two of Scipio Africanus's key henchmen, Gaius Laelius and the Massylian prince Masinissa, and he possibly even spoke to some of Cannae's survivors, although they would have been very old.

He also read a lot of history—contemporary or near contemporary accounts that are now lost to us. Key here was the work of Fabius Pictor, a distinguished Roman senator, who after the defeat at Cannae had been sent on a mission to the Delphic oracle to try to figure out what had gone wrong soothsayer-wise. Fabius Pictor is interesting in part due to his kinship with Fabius Maximus, the savvy architect of the strategy of attrition and delay that at least cut Rome's losses to Hannibal, and also because Fabius Pictor's history seems to have revealed deep fissures in the Carthaginian government's support of Hannibal's invasion.[6] We know that Polybius used the work of L. Cincius Alimentus, a moderately important Roman soldier and politician who had been captured by Hannibal and had struck up a relationship with the Carthaginian invader. Polybius also used the work of Aulus Postumius Albinus, who was consul in 151 B.C. There were probably others on the Roman side.

Remarkably—given the truism of history being written by the winners—Polybius had available to him a substantial body of work that told the story from the Carthaginian, or at least Hannibalic, side. Two historians in particular, Sosylus the Spartan and Silenos from Kaleakte, accompanied Hannibal to Italy and stayed with him "as long as fate allowed."[7] While Polybius is dismissive of Sosylus as a gossip, the Spartan knew Hannibal well enough to have taught him Greek, and a surviving fragment of his seven-book history indicates some competence. This is significant since some believe that Polybius's account of Cannae may have actually come from Hannibal himself speaking to Sosylus or possibly Silenos.[8]

Even skeptics concede Polybius a place, along with Herodotus, Thucydides, and Tacitus, in the first tier of ancient historians. Without his single-book account of the First Punic War, we would know very little about this conflict, the longest in ancient history. His lost recounting of the Third Punic War is thought to have provided the basis of the historian Appian's narrative, who here is far better than elsewhere. Yet it was Polybius's rendering of the second war with Carthage that made and preserves his reputation as a great historian,[9] even though the account has a gaping hole in the middle. Fortunately for our purposes, the narrative ends right after Cannae and—with the exception of a few fragments mostly on campaigns in Sicily and Spain—picks up just before the final climactic battle of Zama. Nevertheless, the absence of the middle narrative clouds many issues and leaves us reliant on a single source, Livy, who is more the storyteller and less the analyst. Polybius

above all sought the truth, weighing the facts carefully, and characteristically looking at both sides of things controversial; he is the rock on
which our understanding of the period is anchored. Still, as scrupulous
and fair as Polybius was, his affiliations, sources, and purpose left him
with some biases—Scipios, Fabians, and their friends are generally
made to look good, and others may have been scapegoated to cover for
their mistakes. And ultimately it is his view that Rome and not
Carthage deserved to survive. He was also not very good with numbers.
His armies are smaller or larger than they should be; at Cannae his
dead outnumber those who could have taken part in the battle.[10] There
are other incongruities. No one is perfect.

Certainly not Livy, or, more formally, Titus Livius. Recently a
prominent classicist joked that Herodotus, historiography's eternal
tourist, sported a Hawaiian shirt.[11] In this vein it is possible to imagine
Livy as an ancient version of a Hollywood mogul, capturing the sweep
of Rome's history with a notably cinematic flair. Of Livy's original 142
books only 32 survive, but luckily ten of those are devoted to the Second Punic War, and it is almost possible to hear marching across those
pages the faint thunder of the original score—cymbal, kettledrums,
and trumpets—the clatter of short swords striking Gallic shields and
the impassioned Latin of senators debating what to do about Hannibal.
In all of historical literature it is hard to match the ghastly clarity of
Livy's Cannae battlefield the morning after, as he pans the wreckage
strewn with dead and half-dead Romans, shredded survivors begging
for a coup de grâce. The man knew how to set a scene. This is also the
problem. Livy's history looks better than it actually is. Verisimilitude is
not truth, just the appearance of truth.

A native of what is now Padua, Livy was born in 59 B.C., his life span
almost exactly bracketing that of Augustus Caesar, Rome's first
emperor—or *princeps*, as the main man preferred. Livy began writing at
thirty, or approximately 190 years after Cannae; so there was nobody
left to talk to. He pretty much stayed put, avoiding battlefields and
archives, instead relying exclusively on literary sources. He used Polybius but seems to have derived him, at least in part, from an intermedi-
ary. Livy probably based his depiction of Cannae and the war's early
years primarily on the now lost seven-volume history of L. Coelius
Antipater, who had used many of the same sources as Polybius, particularly Fabius Pictor and Silenos. This commonality helps explain why
Polybius's and Livy's renderings of events basically track in parallel.

Yet unlike Polybius, Livy had absolutely no experience as a soldier or as a politician, being unique in that regard among important Roman historians.[12] Because he was an amateur writing for amateurs, his battle descriptions focus on clarity and take place in distinct stages.[13] Given the chaos of actual combat, this helps make the mayhem more coherent, but it definitely warps reality.

An analogous criticism can be leveled at Livy's treatment of political decision-making. He was a fierce patriot and partisan, and despite the success of the Augustan regime, the conservative oligarchic senate remained his ideal. Meanwhile, those perceived as "popular" politicians—Flaminius, Minucius, and above all Terentius Varro (the star-crossed supreme commander at Cannae) came in for what is likely more than their fair share of abuse. Livy is also in his element setting up a forensic dustup, with rivals artfully framing the issues and relentlessly undermining opposing positions—logical tours de force until it is realized they are utterly artificial. How could he have known, beyond the barest outline, what was said?

This speaks to a larger point. Ancient history is replete with such speechifying, useful in delineating issues, dramatic, and at times rhetorically elevating (think Thucydides's Melian dialogue or Pericles' Funeral Oration), but it is not to be taken literally. There were no voice recorders or stenographers. Most speeches were extemporaneous. Consider also the obligatory harangues given by commanders to their troops before battle. Livy and Polybius are full of them. Here the problem is not only accuracy but transmission; even generals blessed with the most basso profundo of voices would, without amplification, have had trouble being heard by more than a fraction of their armies, numbering in the multiple tens of thousands. And in Hannibal's case, he would have had trouble being understood by his soldiers, who undeniably spoke a polyglot of tongues and dialects. The words we have are plainly not the words that were said.

Still the Second Punic War is remembered far better than most events this far back in time, blessed not just with two sources, but two historians at or near the front rank. Our good fortune becomes almost embarrassingly obvious when the competitors—foot-draggers progressively removed from the drumbeats of war—are considered. Most important is Appian, an Alexandrian Greek who made his mark in Rome and then settled down in the middle of the second century A.D. to write a twenty-four book history that is more a cluster of monographs than a continuous chronicle. The quality varies with the sources, which are often hard to identify. When he uses Polybius for the Third Punic War, he is fine, but his account of the Second Punic War is bastardized and garbled—so much so that the great German historian Hans Delbrück quotes Appian's entire version of Cannae just to show how lucky we are to have Polybius and Livy![14] Appian's rendering of the battle of Zama reads like something out of *The Iliad,* with the principals Hannibal, Scipio Africanus, and Masinissa all engaging in individual duels. The Romans, as we shall see, did have a penchant for single combat, so this might have happened, but it very probably didn't. They were all too busy being generals. That's the way it is with Appian; things that appear ridiculous on average just might have happened, so they cannot be entirely dismissed. Unlike Polybius's, Appian's numbers do generally add up; the size of his armies and his casualty figures are as good as anyone else's. Even Appian's nonsensical take on Cannae has a redeeming feature—a carefully plotted ambush, more dimly recalled by Livy and something never to be entirely discounted when dealing with Hannibal, the proverbial trickster.

It's much the same with the others. Still further removed in time, Dio Cassius, a Roman senator whose family hailed from Bithynia in Asia Minor, wrote an eighty-book *History of Rome* in the third century, of which only about a third still exists in fragments, but it is supplemented by a continuous summary composed by Zonaras, a twelfth-century Byzantine monk. Dio Cassius was reported to be a thorough researcher, but also a fancier of rhetoric, so his account is often a matter of style over substance. The net effect is something like sedimentary rock, earlier stuff compressed and distorted to the point where it is hard to make out much that is cogent beyond a few interesting details. There is an accounting of Cannae and it does contain an ambush, but it is impossible to tell if Dio Cassius used sources independent of those we already have.

Besides narratives, there is also a body of biography—but a slim one. Most famous and useful is Plutarch, who assembled in the late first century A.D. a series of parallel lives of famous Greeks and Romans. While his aim was to delineate the character and personality of his subjects, he still managed to include lots of useful historical bits and pieces. Regrettably, Hannibal and Scipio Africanus are not covered, but the biographies of Fabius Maximus, Marcellus, and Titus Quinctius Flaminius all provide information that either corroborates or enlarges upon the fabric of reliable knowledge. Cornelius Nepos, a Roman biographer from the first century B.C., also composed lives of both Hannibal and his father, Hamilcar, which contain information not otherwise available, but they are short to the point of being cursory.

The rest of the quilt amounts to a collage of snippets from the geographer Strabo; the scholar Pliny the Elder; and the historians Diodorus, Pompeius Trogus, Justin, Eutropius, and Timagenes of Alexandria. All refer to one or another item of interest. Finally, there is one very large and unsightly patch, so homely it mocks the entire process of preservation. That would be the *Punica* of Silius Italicus, a monumentally bad epic on the Second Punic War, which at twelve thousand verses remains the longest piece of Roman poetry still available to us. Wading through this monstrosity of simile and bloodletting in search of something useful, the reader is reminded of the sheer randomness by which all but a scrap of the *Annales* by Ennius (a far better poem that some argue had an impact on Polybius) was lost, while Silius was conserved. Still, as bad as was his art, Silius was a political survivor in the time of Nero and seems to have grasped two critical aspects of the Second Punic War—that Cannae was a pivotal point in Roman history, and that the need to develop a general who could fight Hannibal on something approaching even terms was the genesis of Rome's slide toward civil war and eventually despotism.[15] Was this the poison pill that Hannibal slipped Rome? This in turn brings us to the second of the two questions asked earlier: Why should we care?

[3]

In the ancient world and most epochs that followed, history was viewed as the preceptor of princes. And behind this was a faith in fate, a fear of manipulative deities, and a belief that if only prior mistakes could be learned from and their repetition avoided, good fortune might smile on the protagonist. We have a far different view today. Physicists tell us that nothing is preordained. Consequence is highly contingent, so sensitive to small perturbations at the start of an event sequence that virtually any outcome within the range of the possible can become reality. Prediction may be on the skids, but those same physicists also tell us that unfolding events have a way of mysteriously self-organizing. So is the past really such a misguided flashlight on the future? Long before the science of complexity stuck itself between fortune's spokes, Mark Twain seemed to have gotten it about right when he concluded that although history doesn't repeat itself, it does sometimes rhyme.

There is much about the clash between Rome and Carthage that seems hauntingly familiar. The physical magnitude, the very scale and duration of the Punic Wars—particularly the first two—remind us of our own recent past. Like World Wars I and II, the Punic Wars were conflicts waged overseas and on a giant scale. The showdown between the Roman and Carthaginian fleets off Cape Economus, for instance, remains in terms of the number of participants the largest naval battle ever fought.[16] Similarly, the loss of life in these two ancient conflicts was proportionately as massive and unprecedented as their equivalents in our own era.

And as with the great wars of the twentieth century, the outbreak of the Second Punic War followed logically from the unfinished business of the first. More to the point, perhaps, is that in both cases the loser of the first conflict seems to have been dragged into the second largely by the actions of a single man, Carthage by Hannibal and Germany by Hitler. And both men enjoyed an initial string of stunning victories that drove their opponents to the very brink of collapse; yet neither Britain in 1940 nor Rome after Cannae succumbed. They stared down the odds and somehow retrieved victory from the ashes of disaster.

There was, of course, a Third Punic War, fueled by revenge and waged with the calculated intent of Carthage's utter destruction—genocide by any other name. We have avoided such a fate, but had there been such a thing as World War III, there is little doubt that much of what we call our civilization would now lie in ruins. At last we may have learned there is and must be a limit to war.

We can also detect the reflection of these ancient conflicts in matters far more personal. The conscience of a nation is often revealed by the fate of its veterans, particularly veterans of defeat. Belatedly we Americans have done what we can to rehabilitate our Vietnam vets and expunge the memory of their lonely return, vowing it will not happen again to those coming back from Iraq. Rome's example argues that this is not simply a matter of compassion but a matter of prudence.

After Cannae the senate didn't just turn its back on its survivors; it stigmatized them, banishing them to Sicily for more than a decade. These soldiers were joined only by the refugees of other armies similarly pulverized by Hannibal. Those more fortunate in battle would, for the most part, be deactivated and allowed to rejoin their families and farms after a campaign or so. Life was hard in the countryside, and a family's survival demanded the soldier's presence. But the notorious victims, known collectively as the *legiones Cannenses,* were left in limbo as their lives at home disappeared. They became quite literally the ghosts of Cannae, and in large part their story will be the story of this book. For now it is necessary to know only that while commanders came and commanders went, only one man was willing to give the survivors of Cannae a shot at redemption, and he was Scipio Africanus. They would follow him to Africa and wreak terrible vengeance on their original tormentors, and being human likely underwent a very fundamental transition in their loyalties. Scipio and the senate had set a dangerous precedent. Soon enough, Roman armies would look to their commanders and not the state to ensure their future. And should the commander choose to march on Rome, they would follow him. This is a lesson that should never be forgotten.

The lethal brilliance of Cannae was of such an order that the encounter became one of the most studied and emulated battles, casting a long shadow over military history and the profession of arms even to this day. Yet the battle's true place in mind and memory turns as much on the paradox it poses for the basic premises of what we call the Western way of war—that armed conflict is fundamentally about massing great armies to contest and achieve crushing victories, which in turn will reliably lead to the infliction of defeat and successful conclusions overall. A good case can be made that as long as Hannibal was on the Italic peninsula, he never suffered a significant tactical defeat. In 216 B.C., after Cannae and the string of drubbings that preceded it, Hannibal had all but destroyed Rome's field forces. Subsequent to that, though less famously, he persisted in exterminating entire Roman armies. Yet overall victory continued to elude him.

"It is in Italy, our home-land, that we are fighting," Fabius Maximus had advised the doomed Lucius Aemilius Paullus shortly before Cannae. "Hannibal, on the contrary, is in an alien and hostile country. . . . Can you doubt then that if we sit still we must gain the victory over one who is growing weaker every day?" (Livy, 22.39.11ff) Time was Rome's ally, and what the crafty stalwart was proposing was something akin to a national insurgency—small war, harassment of Hannibal's sources of supply, and savage reprisals against those misguided enough to throw in their lot with him. The Romans, being Romans, were never satisfied with such a strategy. But until they could come up with someone capable of beating Hannibal at his own game, this strategy sufficed to keep them in the war, gradually restricting his freedom of movement and eventually isolating him in the toe of the boot of Italy. In the end he was forced to leave, having proverbially won all the battles but lost the war.

Today Americans face an analogous situation, both specifically in conflicts with Islamic extremists and more generally. We have reason to question whether our very violent and sudden way of war matches the military problems we now face, whether our views of what organized violence can accomplish should be supplemented or replaced by strategic alternatives, the most developed being the Eastern approach exemplified by the writings of Sun Tzu. It can be argued that along with the Battle of Trafalgar, Cannae provided the template for tactical success in the corpse-ridden first half of the twentieth century. Now in the twenty-first, who is willing to face us in open battle when they can do us more harm at less cost by attacking asymmetrically? Perhaps some, but many will choose insurgency.

The Romans did. But it is important to remember that it was not a matter of preference. They leveraged their weakness into strength because it worked—until they could land a crushing blow. At best, the past only rhymes. The Romans and Carthaginians fought as they did because of who they were and where they came from. Their assumptions, not our own, ultimately engendered reality during the Second Punic War.

[4]

What happened at Cannae, even the decision to have a battle on that day, was as much a result of ritual and tradition as it was a result of choices made by the participants. Hence, an understanding of the battle demands that we step back in time and take account as best we can of the origins and implications of those factors. By the time Cannae was fought, humanity had been waging something we would recognize as organized warfare for a bit more than five thousand years.[17] For a long time before, though, we had engaged in other violent pursuits, aggressive activities that had cumulatively provided us with the behavioral and tangible assets that would enable us to become true military creatures—what amounted to the raw materials for war.

Hunting had been central. Our evolutionary ancestors were killing and eating other animals long before we evolved into humans.[18] To do this required not just effective strategies; our forebears needed weapons; but both were largely a matter of the size of the quarry.

On the one hand there were the problems and possibilities associated with stalking and killing small game. Many were already prey for other animals and had developed avoidance strategies dependent upon stealth and speed. Being slower afoot, our ancestors needed some means of striking from a distance, and that meant velocity and accuracy. Accomplished bipeds since splitting off from the great apes, hominid arms were free to throw and hominid hands were able to grasp and direct sticks and stones. For a long time that was probably our best trick. Then, sometime far down the evolutionary track, perhaps beginning around five hundred centuries ago, behaviorally modern humans came to understand and exploit the possibilities of mechanical advantage. They began fashioning bolas, throwing sticks, boomerangs, and eventually and most important, slings and bows.[19] The last two would become persistent handmaidens not just of the chase, but also of war. For they were efficient killers, and they also provided a measure of physical and psychological safety by dispatching the victim at some distance. But as with other strategies aimed at minimizing risk, there was a cost in terms of potential gain, and this would prove to be a major factor—not just in hunting, but in the kind and motivation of armies that eventually evolved in the ancient world.

Much earlier, when modern humans marched out of Africa and moved north, they found a host of really big animals waiting for them, many congregating in huge herds. This was the tail end of the Pleistocene, a period when the back-and-forth march of mile-high glaciers had stimulated genetic ingenuity and the evolution of a lavish array of megafauna—beasts whose very size was their central advantage in an environment that paid big dividends for heat retention. Together such fauna constituted a movable feast for human predators with the cunning and courage to help themselves at Mother Nature's groaning board. But it was very dangerous, and slings and arrows would not get the job done.

These beasts were not used to being chased, especially not by bipedal newcomers. This meant you could get in close, but also that you had to get in close. To kill such thick-skinned, thick-skulled behemoths demanded direct confrontation, either deep penetration with a spear or heavy blows to the head with a club or ax. But doing this alone would have been suicidal. So big and lethal were these prey that human males had to hunt together in groups. Evidence shows that earlier humans had hunted big game, but now we had the advanced language skills, imagination, and memory to plot coordinated strategies, and an increased capacity for social cohesion. Over time, the experience of confronting big, lethally aroused animals forged hunting parties into teams specialized to face danger, bonded to risk everything in pursuit of a mutual objective and in protecting members in peril. Hunting parties became brotherhoods of killers, prototypes of the squad-size small units that one day would form the basic building blocks of armies.

Meanwhile, when recounting and celebrating their kills back among the band, it is likely the hunters indulged in dance, and as they shared rhythmic and intricate patterns of big muscle movements, they further welded themselves together. Those dances were choreographic prototypes of the marching and drill that would one day unite armies and create the tactical dynamics of the battlefield.[20]

In the meantime these fraternities of death-dealing were absolutely without precedent in terms of hunting efficiency, as is evidenced by the excavated bones of a hundred thousand horses driven over cliffs in Germany and by similar finds elsewhere.[21] Such epic acts of killing seem to fly in the face of a considerable body of evidence that portrays hunter-collectors as parsimonious killers by inclination, true game managers.[22] But there is no real contradiction. Herding is a defense mechanism animals use to make themselves scarce. Contacts between predator and prey will be fewer, and when contacts do come, the predator will be overloaded, having only a limited time and ability to kill. This is why hunting animals at times becomes wantonly destructive. They are just following one of the iron laws of the jungle: kill all you can while you can. It was a variation on this rule that Hannibal's army would apply to the trapped Roman legions at Cannae many centuries later. But that would require a far different environment and considerable psychological conditioning.

For the time being, aggression among humans was likely to have been mostly much more personal and discrete—concerned primarily with the tangle of issues surrounding mating, dominance, and, when it mattered, territory.[23] There is little direct evidence of how this played out, but our own residual behavior along with the behavior of other animals gives us some good leads. Since much of animal behavior hinges on reproduction, confrontations characteristically center on individual competitors, and in most species they are males. And while war as it evolved in the ancient world would become essentially a matter of men acting in groups, the proclivity for individual combat was always present, and in the case of the Romans it was brilliantly exploited.

Given the basic motivation of aggression of this sort, there was also no necessary advantage in going to lethal extremes. Strong, though definitely rescindable, human inhibitions against killing our own are well documented[24] and are paralleled by similar disinclinations in other animals. Who would kill, who would not, who killed easily—these are matters not much explored in military history, but they are arguably vital issues, particularly in close combat. Hannibal's invading army was at its core composed of case-hardened veterans. Freeze-dried in the Alps and then tempered by the blood of countless legionaries, they had learned to kill without qualm or hesitation. This was something the Romans could not duplicate so long as they persisted in fielding armies filled with inexperience.

In any case, this killing without qualm or hesitation was so inherently frightful that it had to be enfolded, disguised, and regularized, and once again characteristic forms of aggression within species seem to have provided the context. Among mammals we see a clear pattern of ritualization in combat, with opponents normally following rules—or at least stereotyped behavior—and employing their defense mechanisms symmetrically—antler versus antler in deer and moose, for instance. Noise, visual impressions, and particularly size are important, with dueling animals reacting in ways that make them appear louder, bigger, and more frightening. Ritualization also has a temporal and a spatial dimension, with combat normally being staged at regular intervals synchronized to the female reproductive cycle and sometimes at a habitual venue. So too the human armies of the Second Punic War would often gather at a certain time to fight by mutual consent on fields carefully chosen for battle. Trumpets would blare, drums would pound, and within the ranks soldiers would don crested helmets to make them appear taller, uttering their most horrible war cries, fortifying their spirits to close face-to-face and match sword against sword to confront at last war's terrible reality. Now, these patterns do not extend across all species, nor did they characterize all the forms of ancient warfare, but they do represent recurring themes and are clearly different from the characteristics of predation, which is far more pragmatic, spontaneous, and indiscriminate.[25] Logic points to us having enlisted both the characteristics of predation and the aggression associated with reproductive dominance, along with the weapons we developed and the attitudes we accumulated through participation in each, and then enfolded them in the institution we invented and now call war.

[5]

It's hard to put a finger on exactly when true war started—not just occasional group or individualized mayhem but regularized societal violence. The best bet is that it ignited initially to protect one of several rich but temporary food sources, and eventually took off in a sustained way several millennia after people first settled down in the ancient Middle East to raise crops and domesticate animals.

Briefly put, the logic of this agronomy pushed nascent shepherds and their flocks out away from the farmers and their crops and into the beginnings of an independent existence. Life was tough out there, though, and the magnet of stored grain seems to have drawn the herdsmen into an intensifying syndrome of raiding agricultural settlements, a syndrome that reached a crisis point around 5500 B.C. This makes sense, because around this time the farming communities dotting the region began building walls around dwelling areas, stone shields against hostile outsiders.

At a later date in the timeline, pastoralism got a true leg up when shepherds learned to mount horses, which enabled them to move out onto the Inner Asian steppe. Out there they would continue to live a life of riding and rustling and raiding that would periodically lead them to spill off the high plains and descend on settled societies both east and west, with temporary but devastating effect, all the way up through the thirteenth century A.D. and the epic advances of Genghis Khan's Mongols.

These Inner Asian steppe horsemen were truly men apart, well away from the main military thread of our story. But they raise an important point. As frightening and bewildering as were their attacks to the victimized, they were not without purpose, mere random violence. They were acts of organized theft, specifically addressing a societal short-coming, the periodic collapse of their flocks. All the other forms of warfare that sprang up in the ancient world were also motivated by some kind of societal shortcoming; it was just too costly to fight for any other reason.

Back down on the farm, the seeds of war had taken hold independently, and agricultural communities had begun fighting regularly among themselves for territory and dominance. We get an excellent picture of how this evolved among the competing Sumerian city-states on the flatlands bordered by the Tigris and Euphrates rivers, in what is now still contentious Iraq. In particular we have two very suggestive relics, the first of these being a fragmentary victory monument carved around 2500 B.C., known today as the Stele of the Vultures.[26]

It is a stone snapshot of the Sumerian order of battle, and it reveals a basic split. Out front, armed for single combat, is Eannatum, ruler of Lagash, symbolically looking forward to a day in the Middle East when elite warriors would seek out and fight equals while a host of lightly armed underlings would do their best to stay alive. But in the Stele of the Vultures, Eannatum is backed up by something entirely more lethal—an infantry column, all wearing helmets, advancing shoulder to shoulder behind a barrier of locked rectangular shields and presenting a hedgehog of spears—a full-fledged phalanx. Military historians have mostly overlooked the implications of this early depiction of a pha-lanx, and have focused instead on the development of this presumably advanced infantry formation by the culturally resplendent Hellenic Greeks almost two thousand years later. Actually, the technical and tactical requirements for a phalanx are simple. What's needed is a will-ingness to confront adversaries at close quarters and to face danger in a cooperative fashion—the big-game hunter mentality. This is where our second relic becomes telling.

We have preserved on clay tablets the written chronicle of a ruler thought to be roughly contemporaneous with Eannatum. The ruler is Gilgamesh of Uruk, humankind's initial literary hero. Among the ac-counts of Gilgamesh's exploits is a suggestive tale of a war with the rival city of Kish over water rights. The action opens with Kish having warned the men of Uruk to stop digging wells and irrigation ditches on disputed territory. Gilgamesh wants war but plainly lacks the power to make the decision stick. Instead, he must go before a council of elders, and when they rebuff him, have their decision reversed by an assembly of all the city's fighting men.[27] Those who would bear the brunt of combat had a clear and direct interest in the outcome, and it stands to reason that they might willingly have taken their place in the danger-ous but decisive phalanx. War at this time and place was a cooperative endeavor all about preserving and enforcing the balance of power among multiple independent political entities; but that was not the fu-ture in the Middle East, nor was the future of the region's infantryman to be found in the tight-knit ranks of the phalanx.

The sheer drudgery involved in irrigated agriculture, combined with the massive populations it was able to feed, meant that the dynam-ics of governance were heavily weighted in the directions of compul-sion and rigidly enforced pyramids of power. Meanwhile, the balance among the competing city-states of Sumer proved transitory and was overturned in the middle of the twenty-fourth century B.C. by a single player, Sargon, who proceeded to implement a blueprint for imperial tyranny. His agents fanned out across the alluvium, framing the struc-ture with tax lists, trustworthy locals, garrisons, royal governors, and, kept close at hand, a picked body of heavily armed retainers.[28]

As time passed, similar cadres of elite warriors would provide the cores of the ancient Middle East's armies, fleshed out by a multitude of temporarily dragooned and highly expendable foot soldiers. Lacking the motivation and sense of common purpose necessary to advance onto what amounted to ground zero, about the best that could be done with such troops was to provide them with a long-range weapon—typically a bow—to support the leadership and their retainers as they fought it out hand to hand in and around chariots, or later on horse-back.

Though large and superficially impressive, such force structures were not inherently very effective; paradoxically, being effective was only partially the point. Looking beneath the rapacity of rulers reveals that armies of this sort addressed the inherent instabilities of societies that were driven by more people digging more ditches, to grow more grain, until natural disaster, crop failure, and epidemic disease sud-denly reversed the spiral and dictated retrenchment. The demographic roller coaster was impossible to escape, but the bumps could be smoothed by military action. Imperial forces might lurch forward to capture new laborers, or in times of overpopulation they might capture more land—or simply self-destruct, leaving fewer mouths to feed. Be-cause such armies and the tyrannies they served enlisted the fundamental loyalties of so few, they were brittle and prone to collapse. So the history of the ancient Middle East came to be littered with military disasters, and empires and dynasties in Egypt, Mesopotamia, Anatolia, and Persia came and went with dramatic suddenness. Still, their logic was compelling. So new tyrannies arose on top of the old and few eluded their grasp.

One group that tried with some success inhabited a string of independent little cities along the coast of what is today Syria, Lebanon, and Israel; this group came to be known collectively as the Phoenicians. Literally backed up against the sea by the aggression of imperial behemoths, the principal Phoenician centers—Berytus (modern Beirut), Byblos, Sidon, and Tyre—transformed themselves into commercial dynamos, thriving not just on trade but on the concept of value added, turning murex snails into royal purple dye, the cedars of Lebanon into ornate furniture, and, much more commonly, glass into trinkets, beads, and gewgaws.[29] For the Phoenicians were among the first to produce and trade manufactured goods in truly huge quantities. And they did so by virtue of a key invention, the ancient sailing vessel, capable of transporting goods measured by the ton, rather than the pound, the entire length of the Mediterranean basin.

The sea was not simply an avenue to wealth; it was a refuge from imperial land power. This standoff was inadvertently depicted in an Assyrian inscription describing King Luli of Tyre slipping a five-year siege, escaping literally out his city's back door, to join the fleet and go elsewhere.[30] Partly to avoid Assyrian pressure and partly in anticipation of the Hellenic Greeks, who also were starting to move into these waters, Phoenicians in the late ninth century B.C. began to plant colonies dotting the shores of the western Mediterranean, the most famous being Tyre's settlement of Carthage. Unlike the Greeks, the Phoenicians did not care to control the hinterlands, and confined themselves instead to enclaves that served as trading posts and havens for shipping. The posts were placed at intervals of around one day's sailing time and were set on sites that sought to duplicate the small coastal islands, rocky promontories, and sheltered harbors of the Levantine cities. The key to survival and prosperity—besides fending off and buying off land power at home—was to keep the trade lanes open out there.

War for Phoenicians became a matter of expedience, a necessary part of doing business in an increasingly competitive environment. Phoenicians certainly fought a number of massed battles at sea—most memorably at Salamis—but formalized naval combat was arguably less important than the suppression of piracy through relentless coastal patrols, more of a policing than a military role.[31] This is important to our story, because it was this focus on policing rather than on warfare that was inherited and instinctively practiced by one of our two protagonists, the doomed city of Carthage.

The military outlook of the other protagonist, Rome, was deeply conditioned by the Phoenicians' maritime rival, the Greeks, but by the Greeks at home, fighting on land. For there had emerged on the Hellenic mainland a patchwork of city-states, each one dedicated to its own self-determination, and all engaged in an eternal melodrama of war, alliance, and betrayal. This balance of power, like the earlier one in Sumer, spawned between 675 and 650 B.C. a tactical reliance on that characteristic formation of the martially enthusiastic, the phalanx. For the citizen-soldiers of Hellas, this battle formation was a profound expression of their sense of social solidarity; fighting together, risking it all shoulder to shoulder, was at the heart of their civic existence. But if asked who best defined their fighting spirit, those in the rank and file would have almost certainly pointed to a blind poet several centuries earlier, who recounted the deeds of heroes still four centuries further back in time, Mycenaean aristocrats who were anything but corporate combatants.

The story of Homer's *Iliad* is a tale of rowdy individualists engaged almost exclusively in single combat, as much for personal prestige as for military advantage.[32] But the poet portrayed them and their deeds in such a compelling manner that he not only convinced Greeks how to act when they fought one another; his words transcended time and place to cement the foundation of war in the West. Above all, combatants were aggressive, matching arms symmetrically, first taking turns casting spears, then moving closer to stab with an extra spear, then still nearer to finish things with their swords—he "who fights at close quarters" was a frequent and positive Homeric epithet.[33] The greatest of the heroes—Achilles, Hector, Diomedes, and Ajax—are among the biggest, loudest in their war cries, fleetest afoot, and inevitably armored—characteristics that would be deeply admired and highly influential throughout the course of Western armed combat.

Anything less confrontational was disdained. Diomedes speaks the mind of the Homeric warrior when he addresses Paris, the adulterer and the only major figure in *The Iliad* to place principal reliance on the bow: "You archer, foul fighter, lovely in your locks, eyer of young girls/If you were to make trial with me in strong combat with weapons, your bow would do you no good at all."[34]

All of this the Hellenic Greeks mainlined, injecting its essence into their phalanx, where, armed as individual combatants, they fought collectively but with the same confrontational willingness to close, an aggressive zeal that would one day cut like a knife through the bow-based armies of the East. Meanwhile, this spirit spread westward.

Beginning in the eighth century B.C. the Greeks began settling along the coasts of Sicily and southern Italy, an area the Romans would come to call Magna Graecia. *The Iliad* being the Greeks' favorite story, they almost certainly brought it with them. (It appears that the first literary reference to the poem was scratched into a clay drinking vessel, circa 730 B.C., that was excavated from a grave on the island of Ischia in the bay of Naples.) Plainly, the military institutions of the Greeks had an influence farther north. Whether indirectly, from contact with their deeply hellenized neighbors the Etruscans, or from actual observation of Greek fighting techniques, by around 550 B.C. the Romans adopted their own version of the heavy-armored phalanx, a change recorded in the so-called Servian reforms.[35] While the ups and downs of their subsequent military adventures would lead the Romans to move dramatically away from the phalanx, the style and substance of the changes they made give every appearance of a continuing Homeric orientation, still fighting in formation but as individual combatants, in a routine notably similar to that followed by the heroes of *The Iliad*.

The impetus for that transformation began in 390 B.C., when a truly shattering event occurred. A band of thirty thousand Gauls, an amalgam of the tribal peoples living to the north, crossed the Apennines in search of plunder and descended upon the Romans. Physically much larger and wielding long swords with frantic abandon, these Gauls literally engulfed the Roman phalanx at the River Allia. To compound the trauma, the marauders then swept down on Rome, thoroughly sacking the place. Livy (5.38) pictures the refugee Romans watching forlornly from a nearby hill, "as if Fortune placed them there to witness the pageant of a dying country." Yet their resolve was unbroken, and with all else lost they looked "solely to their shields and the swords in their right hands as their only remaining hope."

The episode on the hill may have been apocryphal, but the sentiment was real enough. Also, from this moment the Romans nurtured a

nearly pathological fear and hatred of Gauls, a dread brilliantly exploited by Hannibal. By the time of Cannae, after a long string of
Roman reprisals and incursions into the Gauls' tribal areas, the feeling
was certainly mutual. Despite Roman portraits of them as a bunch of
drunken louts and fair-weather warriors, the Gauls were formidable
combatants and were imbued with a berserker's aggressiveness. It's a
stretch to imagine the Gauls reciting Homer around the campfire, but
their penchant for single combat, their theatrical acts of courage, and
their sheer bloodlust would have made them right at home on the
plains of Troy. Basically, this was the fighting profile of their tribal
cousins stretching all the way to Spain. All of them would be at Cannae
fighting for keeps. Was it any wonder that battle ended so decisively?

[6]

By 216 B.C. the Mediterranean basin had coalesced into what amounted
to a single strategic environment, composed of a relatively small number of powerful state entities. While there were some economic overtones, this was largely a political and military phenomenon, with the
leadership of the major players diplomatically in touch and aware of
basic power relationships, though these were certainly subject to mis-
calculation. Like its East Asian analogue, which had been unified just
five years earlier under China's first emperor, Ch'in Shih Huang Ti, the
Mediterranean system was ripe for further consolidation. But in the
West this was only dimly apparent, nor was it in any way clear who
might emerge preeminent.

A Greek, or rather a Greek from Macedon, was probably the best
bet. More than a century earlier, an astonishingly talented father-and-
son team from this unlikely backwater at the northern edge of Greece
had set the wheels of change in motion. First, the father, Philip,
through a combination of ruthlessness and military brilliance, had
managed to temporarily consolidate the ever fractious mainland
Greeks, and then had been promptly assassinated. At this point his son
and collaborator, Alexander, seized opportunity by the throat and led
Greeks and Macedonians all on a great crusade to avenge Persia's two
invasions of Hellas a century and a half earlier. By the time Alexander
died in Babylon in 323 B.C., he had proved himself to be an even greater
soldier than his father. Using an updated, extended-spear Macedonian

version of the phalanx and a wickedly effective heavy cavalry, he had managed to obliterate a series of bow and elite dependent Persian hosts and in the process had brought the entire ancient Middle East under his sway.

Unity, however, did not prove the order of the day. Instead, a pack of successors grabbed what they could, and then battled one another for more in an epic series of internecine struggles, which a century later left Egypt under the Ptolemys; most of the remainder of the Persian empire in the hands of the Seleucids; and left Macedonia, phalanx central, ruled by the descendants of one of Alexander's original generals, Antigonus the One-Eyed. Because Alexander's successors were all Macedonians, they basically fought alike, depending on a steady supply of phalangites and cavalrymen. They also needed full-time men-at-arms to maintain control, and this basically put a premium on military professionals, particularly in the east but also elsewhere in the Mediterranean. The century of fighting had prompted Greeks in general to think seriously about war, to expound upon tactics and strategy, to work out the possibilities of siege craft, and to elaborate naval warfare. Greeks and Macedonians, officers and underlings, military men for hire, they were considered state of the art.

This imparted a cynical "great game" mentality among many of the players, particularly the Hellenistic states and their martial offspring. Dramatic rises and falls, sudden desertions, and transfers of allegiance littered a military landscape where war-hardened mercenaries were the coin of the realm. For the most part the system bred a certain pragmatic restraint. Battles were rarely waged for any strategic purpose greater than as a test of strength.[36] A single decisive victory was usually sufficient to determine a war's outcome in an environment where nobody in his right mind remained on the losing side for long. Because troops were basically interchangeable, it was plausible for the defeated to hope for a place in the ranks of the opposite side. On the other hand, the system's very cynicism might lead the victor to conclude that the vanquished were worth more on the slave market, a possibility attested to by the practice of keeping plenty of chains and manacles handy.[37]

This was very much a world where, to paraphrase Thucydides,[38] the strong did what they could and the weak did what they must. There has been a recent interest in ancient history by conservative scholars, in part, it seems, because they find today's post-cold-war world deceptively dangerous and see parallels with the earlier period. But the time we are talking about was far crueler, one in which force was essentially its own justification, and the consequences for weakness were utterly threatening. For instance, the prospects presented to fortified towns and cities when besieged were: surrender and suffer, or resist, and if you fail, suffer much worse. Citizens of places that fell might expect to be subjected to indiscriminate slaughter and rape initially, and later quite possibly sale into slavery. This did not always happen, but it was frequent enough. For soldiers, fate was simple and stark—win, and so long as you weren't wounded badly or killed, you prospered. Lose, and you might very well lose everything. Still, if your alternatives were drudgery and victimization, the soldier's life might be short and dangerous, but at least it was exciting.

For this was also a time of military adventure and larger-than-life adventurers. The example of Alexander the Great should not be underestimated; he personified to the age's soldiers of fortune all that was glorious and might be achieved by a general with sufficient courage, audacity, and skill. If Homer's Helen was said to have launched a thousand ships, then Alexander's memory set many an army marching down destiny's road.

Archetypical among Hellenistic condottieri was Pyrrhus, surnamed Eagle, the sometime king of Epirus and full-time opportunist. At seventeen he fought at the battle of Ipsus, the swan song of Antigonus the One-Eyed; spent time with Ptolemy, becoming his son-in-law; meddled in Macedon until, having overstayed his welcome, he was forced back to Epirus and boredom—but not for long. It was at this point, 281 B.C., that he discovered a place for himself in Italy. The Greek city of Tarentum, hard-pressed by the Romans, had extended Pyrrhus an invitation to help them and the rest of Magna Graecia. Within a year the Eagle had landed with twenty-five thousand professional infantry and cavalry, along with twenty of what were considered to be the game-breakers of the Hellenistic force structure, war elephants. As we shall see, the whole concept of a panzer pachyderm was vastly overrated, but for the uninitiated they were truly terrifying. Horses were repelled by their smell, and foot soldiers without special training were terribly vulnerable.

Nonetheless, Pyrrhus appears to have understood he was in for hard fighting, commenting after reconnoitering the Roman camp: "The discipline of these barbarians is not barbarous" (Plutarch, Pyrrhus 16.5). He was right. At the ensuing battle near Heraclea, the Romans stood up well to Pyrrhus's phalanx, but their cavalry was driven off by his elephants and their wings collapsed, leaving seven thousand dead on the field. It had been costly, but Pyrrhus had clearly won a victory and plainly expected the Romans to seek terms. He even made a dash toward Rome, perhaps expecting some of their allies to desert; none did.[39] Still, he was prepared to be generous; but in the end the Romans rebuffed him. So the next year, 279, he fought them again. This time the Romans held out for two days before Pyrrhus's phalanx and elephants prevailed, but his losses numbered thirty-five hundred. "If we are victorious in one more battle with the Romans, we shall be utterly ruined" (Plutarch, Pyrrhus 21.9), he was heard to say. But there were no signs of surrender, and at this point he did something very Hellenistic.

The Eagle took wing, answering the call of the Greeks in Sicily, where the Carthaginians appeared to be on the verge of taking over the whole island. In short order Pyrrhus's army routed the Carthaginians, who characteristically tried to buy him off. He would have none of it. But then he made the mistake of executing two prominent Greeks from Syracuse, and he quickly lost favor. Pyrrhus would return to Italy, where the stubborn Romans finally defeated him near Beneventum (modern Benevento) in 275, and then die two years later in street fighting back in Greece. Pyrrhus's Alexandrian dreams of conquest had come to nothing. Unlike his foes in the West, he'd lacked staying power. But before he'd departed Sicily, he'd said something very prophetic: "My friends, what a wrestling ground for Carthaginians and Romans we are leaving behind us!" (Plutarch, Pyrrhus, 23.6.) One of them, not a Greek, would inherit the future.

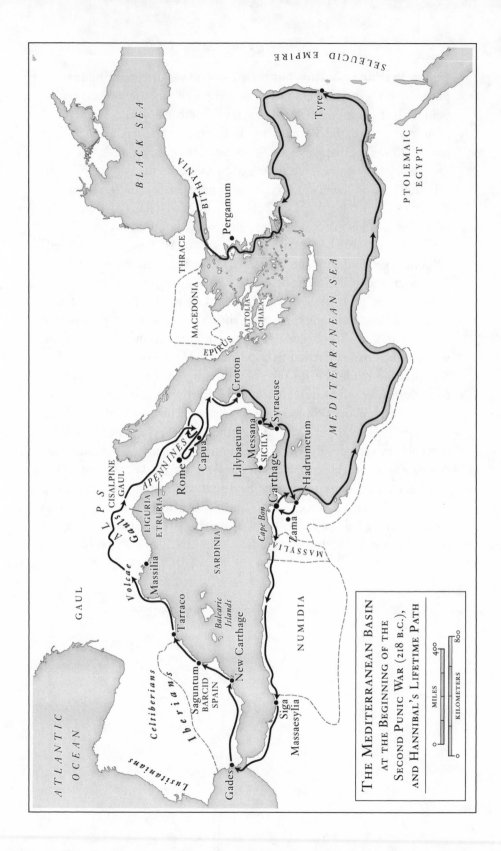

THE MEDITERRANEAN BASIN
AT THE BEGINNING OF THE
SECOND PUNIC WAR (218 B.C.),
AND HANNIBAL'S LIFETIME PATH

II

ROME

[1]

The first sign of them coming would have been a high thin dust cloud characteristic of cavalry on the move. This would have been followed by a lower, far denser particulate envelope thrown up by the infantry and its supply transport.[1] The huge army moved slowly southeast toward the flatlands of the Adriatic coast, wary of the kind of ambush that Hannibal had laid for Flaminius and his army at Lake Trasimene. Polybius implies in his history that the Roman leadership had reports that the Carthaginians were already at Cannae, but bitter experience had taught them that Hannibal could show up anywhere.

Not that they were expecting to lose. Despite a string of three shocking defeats, the Roman mood from consul to lowliest of foot soldiers was probably one of grim determination. Setbacks were at the core of their history, but always these setbacks had proved the triggers for eventual victory. If you were a Roman, there was every reason to believe this unfortunate chain of events was but a prelude to success.

Corrective steps had been taken. If anything, during the earlier clashes, Hannibal had held the numerical edge; that was far from the case now. For this occasion the Romans had raised a multitude: a force basically four times larger than a standard consular army, consisting of super-size legions pumped up to five thousand men apiece. Modern sources agree with Polybius's (3.113.5) estimate that, when cavalry and allied contingents were added, around eighty-six thousand Romans were on their way to Cannae.[2] The very size of this juggernaut said a good deal about its intent. In previous defeats the Roman center had broken through, but too late to prevent the wings from being crushed

by Hannibal's cavalry. This time sheer momentum was intended to
carry the day much more quickly—it was not an elegant plan, but it
was certainly a reasonable one, given the Roman way of thinking about
war. Having drifted into southern Italy, Hannibal was not only far from
Carthage and his family's base in Spain, but he was now hundreds of
miles removed from the tribes of Gaul that had proved to be his best
source of fresh troops. One significant setback would put an end to his
invasion of Italy.

The command structure the Romans had put in place left every impression that the intention was to meet Hannibal and crush him. Fabius
Maximus's strategy of delay and harassment had plainly been rejected
in the most recent set of elections, and the consuls put in place, Caius
Terentius Varro and Lucius Aemilius Paullus, were (despite Livy's
protestations to the contrary in the latter's case) committed to a battlefield confrontation.[3] The military tribunes, or legionary commanders,
assembled for this army have been shown to be considerably more numerous and experienced than was normally the case.[4] Perhaps most
telling of all, between a quarter and a third of the Roman senate had
joined the army, and most other senate members had close relatives
serving. While some may have been there purely to enhance their careers, many had valuable military experience to impart, and as a whole
there is no denying that a very considerable portion of the Roman
leadership class had staked their personal futures on the fate of this
army.

To drive the point home, through the ranks an unprecedented step
had been taken; Livy (22.38.2–5) tells us that for the first time the military tribunes had formally administered an oath to the Roman soldiers
and their Latin allies, legally binding them not to "abandon their ranks
for flight or fear, but only to take up or seek a weapon, wither to smite
an enemy or to save a fellow citizen." Win, or die in place; there was to
be no alternative. This was a hard message and a very Roman one; for
the survivors of Cannae, it would shape the next fifteen years of their
lives. For the great majority of the army, however, it was less complicated, since they had less than a week to live.

But for now the Romans could reject the notion that they were
marching toward disaster, that their plan and the very nature of their
army would be turned against them. They were Romans, and the nature of Rome's society and Roman history had to reassure them that
they were heading down the path to victory. So it's worth looking into

these matters in more detail, for it will clarify why these Romans allowed themselves to be ensnared in the trap Hannibal set for them. Looking more closely will also help explain how they could learn from this bitterest of lessons and eventually overcome him.

[2]

The Rome of 216 B.C. was a mass of contradictions, a jumble of paradox, but instead of incoherence its contrariety generated strength and flexibility. Rome was at once stubborn but adaptable. It placed great emphasis on tradition, yet was empirically disposed to change. It was governed by an oligarchy, but cloaked itself in democratic forms. Its state structure was an edifice of jerry-built institutions, which were, nonetheless, functional and resilient. Devoted to the law to the point of legalism, Rome was at heart a society held together by a web of personal patronage—patron-client relationships that stretched far beyond the city walls. For although Rome retained the consciousness of a city-state, it was already something much larger and more expansive. And despite being bound by fetial law, which forbade aggressive war, it was rapaciously devoted to conquest. For those who were defeated, Rome's startling cruelty coexisted with equivalent acts of magnanimity. And among the defeated, Rome forged a hegemony based on the fiction of alliance, but in the process generated real and tenacious loyalty on the part of the subjugated. Still, in one area Rome was not the least bit conflicted, and that was in its devotion to military power. At rock bottom Rome was a place made by war; warfare was in essence the local industry.

Rome's economy reflected both the clarity of its military intentions and the ambiguity of its soul. At one level it is safe to call Rome a nation of farmers,[5] not the drudges of irrigated agriculture but small freeholders working the land largely on a subsistence basis. Surpluses were generated and there was some commercialization of agriculture, but the business aspect, especially at the level of symbology and public discourse, was not emphasized. Small farms were valued as morally elevating, and in large part this was because they bred good soldiers and helped the state exert control over conquered territory. Rome had consistently sent out colonies of its landless, and as they had reached into the sophisticated economic environment of Magna Graecia, this migration probably had the effect of lowering economic development. But expanding in this way had made strategic sense and, in theory at least, had increased military manpower—the right kind of manpower, troops toughened by a life of heavy work in the fields.

But as with many things Roman, the story was entirely more complex. In the mid-1960s famed historian Arnold J. Toynbee[6] put forth the thesis that Hannibal's depredations in southern Italy ruined the rural economy and depopulated the area, paving the way for latifundia, or large estates, worked by cheap and abundant slaves. This short-circuited Rome's cycle of rural virtue. Further inquiry, though, has revealed that Rome was already far down the road to becoming a slave-dependent society at least a century earlier.[7] And as Rome's success in war accelerated through the period of the three Punic Wars and beyond, so did the number of war captives who were enslaved and sold, the number possibly reaching into the low hundreds of thousands.[8] This was plainly highly lucrative for both the commanders and the state treasury. Meanwhile, among the ranks, the potential for plunder seems to have been an important motivator for erstwhile farmers to turn from their plows and take up their swords.[9] And while it is difficult to estimate what percentage of Rome's metalworking capacity was devoted to the implements of war, we can probably rest assured that the city's forges were more likely to beat plowshares into swords than vice versa. There were also profits to be made at home from victualing the army, but this was somewhat beside the point. For the senate customarily expected vanquished adversaries to defray a substantial portion of the cost of the campaigns waged against them, generally in the form of food and matériel.[10] For Rome at least, there is little doubt that war was the health of the state.

Leadership and governance was a similarly deceptive skein of motivation. Earlier, Rome had undergone a complex process of constitutional development, a struggle of the orders in which plebeians (commoners) had gradually gained rights and power from the patriciate (first families), at least formally. In fact, by 216 "plebeian" and "patrician" no longer meant very much; Rome was really ruled by a combination of powerful families from both orders. Just as in George Orwell's *Animal Farm,* where all pigs are equal, but some are more equal than others, in Rome the people were supreme in all branches of government, but the few and the influential called the shots.[11] Thus in the three major assembled bodies besides the senate, the Comitia Centuriata, the Comitia Tributa,* and the Concilium Plebis,† the popular membership could only vote for or against a measure, not debate it. Plus, in the first of these, the Comitia Centuriata, which had the key roles of voting to declare war, to accept peace terms, and to elect the major magistrates (consuls, praetors, and censors), the membership was stacked in a way that reflected an archaic military order that allowed a relatively few wealthy members to have a near majority. Further entrenching the roots of privilege was the patron-client system that underlay so much of Rome's social order: if you were wise, you did not vote to bite the hand that fed you. This is significant to our story because Livy in particular seeks to tag some of Hannibal's most notorious consular victims—Caius Flaminius and Terentius Varro—as somehow "popular leaders," elected over the good judgment of Rome's betters.[12] Contemporary sources view this as hogwash; given the electoral mechanisms at the time, neither Flaminius nor Varro could have been voted into office without the support of powerful elements of the nobility.

Real decision-making resided elsewhere, and that was in the senate. But as was characteristic of Rome, the senate's clout was based on influence, not formality. This body governed through custom, not law; it had seized preeminence on its own initiative rather than through constitutional enactment.[13] Normally senators served for life and numbered around three hundred, regulated by censors, who periodically revisited the rolls. Drawn mainly from the rural gentry, members also comprised all former key magistrates elected to administer the Roman republic.

This was important because some senators were plainly more equal than other senators. Power here was a matter of central position, and at the core was an inner circle of families that possessed ancestors who had risen to consular rank. These *nobiles* were the true movers and shakers and they belonged to an exclusive club—between 223 and 195 B.C., only five new families managed to climb to this highest rung. Meanwhile, Fabii, Cornelii, Claudians, Aemilii, Atilii, and a handful of

---

* The Comitia Tributa was composed of citizens, including patricians, though membership was based on ancestry. It was presided over by a consul and sometimes by a praetor or curile aedile. This body elected curile aediles, quaestors, and special commissions, and also passed legislation.
† Befitting of its name, the Concilium Plebis included only plebeians in its membership and was presided over by a tribune of the plebes. The council elected the ten plebeian tribunes, along with the aediles of the plebes and special commissions. It too voted on, but did not debate, legislation.

other great houses continued to dominate the senate, which in turn dominated the state, particularly in the areas of finance and foreign affairs.

But how and in what direction? This is controversial. Until recently, historians tended to believe that specific policies could be associated with factions grouped around certain key families, and that these associations were consistent over several generations. While this concept was attractive analytically, it was not supported by the ancient sources and has lost favor.[14] Still, while senatorial politics were likely more fluid than earlier assumed, it remains possible to see policy factions coalescing around key figures over the short term, who likely represented a great family with numerous supporters. Hence it is plausible to think of Fabians, led by Fabius Maximus, as being consistently disposed toward caution, while the Cornelian element, personified by Scipio Africanus, can be viewed as predisposed toward aggressively confronting Hannibal.[15]

In more general terms senatorial dominance is easier to explain. Unlike the other assembled bodies, it met continuously and not just when the powers that be decided it was time to vote on something important. Not only was discussion ongoing, but the senate was Rome's abiding repository of leadership. Unless disgraced or otherwise disqualified, all senators serving in a specific office, such as the consulship, would eventually go back to the general membership of the senate. Thus it became customary for consuls to refer all important matters back to their predecessors. Similarly, magistrates were expected to follow the body's advice, particularly when it was formally expressed in a senatus consultum, even though, in typically Roman fashion, the senate did not have the power to legislate. It would have taken a bold magistrate to cross an institution where he would have to serve for life after his term of office ended.[16]

Finally, it is important to emphasize that the senate was all about things military. More often than not issues of foreign policy devolved into questions of "Who are we going to fight?" Despite characteristically couching its campaigns in defensive terms, scholarship points to the senate consciously and continuously looking for new opponents to conquer.[17] And while the people retained the final say on matters of war and peace, the decision was profoundly shaped by the senate, which kept an iron grip on diplomacy. Similarly, although consuls were elected by the Comitia Centuriata, it was the senate that decided where they would serve or, more realistically, fight—and what they would fight with, since the senate also determined the size and composition of the forces allocated for each campaign.

This was highly functional and appropriate. For within the body itself, leadership, experience, and prestige largely translated into *military* leadership, experience, and prestige. When it came to warfare, the corporate wisdom of the Roman senate was impressive. As we shall see, Roman commanders made numerous tactical missteps during the war against Hannibal, but the overall strategic direction—the province of the senate—was hard to fault. Stripped to its essentials, the senatorial approach consisted of three principles: take the offensive whenever possible, keep the pressure on, and never give up. With rare exception, and even when Rome was plainly losing, the senate refused to negotiate with a hostile combatant, except on the basis of the adversary's submission. During the Punic Wars, the worse things got, the more adamant and determined the senate became. The senate laid out a hard set of rules, and was a stern taskmaster, but it was not necessarily out of sync with those it directed.

[3]

Whatever the discordance between rhetoric and reality, between belief and actual conditions, Romans drank deeply from the fountain of patriotism, and, unlike the proverbial Kool-Aid, it made them stronger. This was a society on its way to becoming something entirely more complex, on a path that would lead eventually to civil war and the end of the republic. But at the point when Hannibal descended upon it, Rome was a unified and resilient entity, as tenacious as any other society on the face of the earth. Romans, and to a slightly lesser extent Rome's allies, believed in Rome and, more to the point, were ready to die for it. They faced defeat after defeat at the hands of a military genius—not with passive endurance but with a grim determination to prevail, a determination epitomized by the survivors of Cannae but emblematic of the entire society.

At the upper echelons, Romans had a passion for public service in the form of elective office—an urge that in the later stages of the republic would reach maniacal proportions and become a key factor in the system's collapse. But during the struggle with Carthage, political ambition, while intense, remained within traditional bounds. Personal success in Rome was defined by the *cursus honorum*—literally "course of honors"—the progressive election of an individual to a series of increasingly important magistracies. Polybius (6.19.4) tells us that in order to begin the process young members of the elite had to have participated in ten annual military campaigns (almost always in the cavalry). This is telling. It was a commonplace that Roman generals were politicians, but this also says that the politicians were militarized.

Given Rome's size, the number of higher offices was remarkably few, and turnover was notably fast—basically one year, following the Warholian rubric and maximizing the number who got to be famous, if not exactly experienced. Other than the ten plebeian tribunes elected to serve as an independent check on power through their capacity to veto any official act, and the four aediles, who were mainly responsible for administration and festivals, the other key elective offices entailed some sort of soldiering. Each year twenty-four military tribunes were voted in and then assigned, six to a legion, to act as a rotating staff of commanders.[18] There were eight quaestors, who were mainly financial officers but who also served on the consul's legionary staff and could undertake independent military duties. The next set above were the praetors, by this time four of them. These officials were originally meant to take over the consuls' civil duties at home but instead were increasingly detailed for provincial administration and military command.

At the pinnacle of the elective rat-race were the consuls, in positions that not only ratified individual success but ensured their continuing familial influence. There were only two of them—by this time normally a patrician and a plebeian—and during their twelve months in office they were expected to wrestle with the state's most important problems, which almost always meant they were fighting Rome's most dangerous enemies. The basis for their power was the imperium, the right to command troops and administer justice. So that no one would miss the point, consuls, and the other few magistrates vested with the imperium, were accompanied by a designated number of lictors—attendants armed with axes bundled with rods called *fasces,* a badge indicating their chief's capacity to inflict both capital and corporal punishment.[19]

As we have seen, the consul's power was circumscribed by the senate when the consul was within the city, but out in the field he had absolute command. Ordinarily this worked well, but in the emergency of the Second Punic War, consular armies were combined on several key occasions, raising the fundamental question of who was in charge. Cannae was one of those occasions. Perhaps because of a bitter experience with monarchy earlier in their history, Romans were deeply committed to the principle of collegiality and redundancy in their leadership, but they were also a practical people.

So, possibly as far back as 500 B.C.[20] they had created the dictator, which at least mitigated the problem of dual authority. A single official, appointed for six months by the consuls, on the basis of a *senatus consultum*, the dictator had absolute power even within the city, a status symbolized by his twenty-four lictors to a consul's twelve. Nominated in the dead of night and customarily forbidden to serve on horseback, the dictator had the right to name an assistant with roughly the power of a praetor and named, logically enough, master of horse.[21] Dictators were designated to perform electoral and religious duties, but basically the office was a means of focusing military power in the face of disaster. As the frequency and intensity of Rome's wars increased during the third and fourth centuries B.C., so did the reliance on dictators, culminating in the office's archetype, Fabius Maximus. Dutifully he stepped down after six months, as was expected of dictators. But ultimately, as the careers of Cornelius Sulla and Julius Caesar would later demonstrate, the power vested in dictators would prove fatal to republican government. For at the heart of the system, even in a time of political stability, military power and glory trumped just about everything else.

As Rome expanded, the wealth and landholdings of its great families grew apace, as did their networks of clients. But all were a means to an end, and that end was prestige, which in turn was a function primarily of military reputation. This was the central motivation of the Roman aristocracy, the universal solvent to nearly any career obstacle, the essence of success on the Tiber. For those holders of the imperium who had won a significant victory over a foreign enemy, the senate might vote a triumph, the veritable crowning achievement of a Roman politico-military career. (Those not meeting these exacting standards might be given an ovation, the bellicose equivalent of a consolation prize.)

The triumph ceremony involved the victorious general, his face painted the same shade of terra-cotta red as statues of Jupiter, riding a chariot preceded by the senate and magistrates, along with the captured enemy leader (frequently on the way to being strangled). This procession was followed by the general's troops in a grand march through Rome's streets, lined with cheering crowds pelting the triumphant one with flowers. Meanwhile, within the chariot a slave held a golden wreath above the general's head and whispered in his ear that he was not a god. The general might have wondered, since there was only one higher Roman honor, the *spolia opima,* given to a general who managed to kill an enemy leader in single combat and then strip his armor. Although the *spolia opima* was awarded only three times (once in 222 B.C. to Marcus Claudius Marcellus, of whom we will hear more), it is still worth mentioning, since it serves to illustrate the importance Romans placed on individual combat in their tactical approach. For at a certain level, every man was meant to be a heroic warrior.

If the life of an ordinary male Roman citizen was not exactly the life of a soldier, as was the case among Spartiates, his life was certainly deeply conditioned by things military and especially by military obligations. All able-bodied property holders had to serve—ten years for cavalry and sixteen for infantry—states Polybius (6.19.2–4) who adds, "in case of pressing danger, twenty years' service is demanded from the infantry." While military operations were seasonal, and only a minority of citizens were required for the army in a single year, this was still a substantial burden. Even before recruitment, youth were trained by drillmasters to march, run, swim, carry heavy loads, and wield weapons[22]—which is worth mentioning, since Polybius (3.70.10; 3.106.5) attributed Rome's early defeats at the hands of Hannibal to legions filled with raw recruits without training. They may have been inexperienced, but they were not likely to have been simply civilians. It is common to refer to Rome's army as a citizen militia, and this is probably an accurate representation of earlier armies. But by the time the Carthaginians arrived, the army better resembled the great conscript armies of World Wars I and II,[23] perhaps even the American version, filled as it was with rural draftees whose prior existence had preconditioned them for combat, with useful skills like hunting and shooting.

But the militarization of Rome was far more pervasive culturally, and even religiously. Basically the Romans worshipped the same fractious warlike gods as the Greeks, but they were particularly given over to divination. When it came to warfare, they were virtually obsessed with the proper taking of auspices and obedience to various portents. To the modern eye there is an unadulterated weirdness in reading Livy as he chronicles the hardheaded Roman moves in the Second Punic War, and then just as seriously runs on about rocks falling out of the sky, two-headed calves, and ravens pecking at the gilding on a god's statue. Flaminius in particular is viewed as impious, and Livy all but blames the Roman disaster at Lake Trasimene on the consul's pigheaded disregard of the gods' obvious displeasure, such as tent standards that were hard to pull up (22.3.12–13).

As the fortunes of war continued to spiral out of their control, the Romans demonstrated a willingness to go to practically any lengths to propitiate the gods, including, after the catastrophe at Cannae, human sacrifice and even outsourcing. Thus, as noted earlier, the historian and statesman Fabius Pictor was sent to Greece to consult with the Delphic oracle as to what had gone wrong with the gods and how specifically they might be appeased. The Romans were still attempting to divine the gods' wishes fifteen years later, with Hannibal continuing to lurk in the south of Italy. When it was brought to the senate's attention that a prophecy in the sacred Sibylline Books indicated that a foreign invader might be driven from the peninsula by bringing the image of the Idaean Mother from Asia Minor to Rome, a delegation was dispatched to King Attalus of Pergamum to arrange the transfer (Livy 29.10.4ff). Again following the advice of the Delphic oracle, the Romans chose "the best man in Rome," Publius Cornelius Scipio Nasica, to receive the cult figure. While his cousin Scipio Africanus likely played a greater role in ultimately getting rid of Hannibal, the Roman people were presumably reassured.

If the sacred in Rome was soaked in blood and battle, so was the profane. This brings us to the controversial subject of gladiatorial combat. Introduced in 264 B.C. as part of funeral ceremonies, the contests quickly took on a life of their own, and are conventionally seen as exemplifying the cruelty and perversity of Roman social life.[24] Disregarding the later excesses of the games, gladiators may well originally have had a more serious purpose. Tactically the Roman army fought as individual swordsmen, psychologically the most demanding kind of combat, in its essence sheer human butchery.[25] Participation and success demanded extraordinary conditioning; training helped but it was also necessary to remove the veil of mystery from manslaughter. Gladiators showed Romans how to fight and die at close quarters, quite literally to confront mortality.[26] To modern sensibilities this must seem cruel, unnecessary, and ultimately criminal; for at a certain level it is simply impossible to bridge the gap that separates us in time and psychology from the Romans. But it may help our understanding to suggest that gladiatorial combat was, at least initially, in part a matter of instruction and not just popular entertainment. What they were seeking to instill was *virtus,* or individual martial courage, the quality one scholar calls "the root value of the Romans of the middle Republic."[27]

[4]

Accentuating the warlike stature of Rome may seem excessive or even irrelevant, since a number of other contemporary societies were also highly militarized. Yet most, particularly those dependent on irrigated agriculture, were basically tyrannies, and their armies were as much a mechanism of social control as they were implements of belligerence. Other societies, such as the Hellenic city-states, had sufficiently managed to enlist the loyalty of their citizenry to create effective and broad-based fighting formations. Yet the Greeks were forever fighting among themselves, and even the later Hellenistic coalitions forged by the more politically ecumenical Macedonians were brittle and ultimately transitory. The Romans were different.

As a matter of policy the defeated were certainly subordinated, but they were not subjugated; in the ancient world this was revolutionary. Rome forged a uniquely sturdy confederation based on the twin principles of incorporation and alliance, always informed by the rubric of "divide and rule."[28] Most remarkably, for peoples in the first category (generally incorporated in central Italy) Rome proffered a complex array of enfranchisements that led up to full citizenship. The rest were allies, not of one another, but of Rome only—each city and state was bound by a separate treaty and granted a customized range of options. Only one provision was standardized: all peoples were required to provide troops to serve under Roman command.

And to ensure they could and did, Romans attempted to literally cement their alliances with a remarkable network of highways, a web of paving stones. One day the empire would be interlinked by a system of more than fifty thousand miles of such roads, but at the time of Hannibal's invasion this network was limited to the Italic peninsula and struck out in four key directions. The first, the Appian Way (roads were named after the censors who built them, in this case Appius Claudius

Caecus), was begun in 312 B.C. and headed south, making the connection to Capua. Later, once the Romans had moved into Magna Graecia, they extended the road into Apulia all the way to Brundisium on the Adriatic at the top of the heel of Italy. To cover the northern flanks, in 241 they constructed the Via Aurelia to the key port of Pisae (modern Pisa) on the west coast facing the Ligurian Sea. Finally, Flaminius, seeking a quick means of reinforcing the northeast against Gallic intrusions, drove an eponymous highway all the way to Ariminum (modern Rimini) far up the peninsula on the Adriatic side.[29]

Now, in the actual conduct of the Second Punic War, the roads would prove something of a two-edged sword, since the Carthaginians could use them too. But these highways sent a psychological message to Rome's junior partners that was hard to miss. Expensive and laborious to build, often straight as an arrow, the highways allowed armies to move quickly to trouble spots. (The roadbeds actually were primarily useful for logistics carts; soldiers generally marched along the shoulders.[30]) These highways made it clear the Romans were building their coalition to last. Once in Rome's camp, always in Rome's camp.

Yet this merely diagrams the skeletal structure of the confederation. For as the Romans expanded, they very naturally and almost unconsciously transferred their domestic fixation on patron-client relationships to the dependencies they created through conquest. This was done not just as a matter of state policy, but also through networks of individual linkages between key Romans and their families with equivalents abroad, creating a vast web of personal loyalties and mutually beneficial relationships that resulted in a mass of social rituals and guest friendships.[31] What emerged was far stronger and more resilient than the basically parasitic empires characteristic of the ancient Middle East. The confederacy was no commonwealth; Rome was very much the dominant partner. In typical Roman fashion there was an element of ambiguity to the entire scheme, but inclusiveness was not just a façade, and it generated real fidelity.

However, not all were equally loyal and satisfied with their status. When Hannibal crossed into Italy, certain areas to the south of Rome—Samnium, the recently incorporated Greek cities, and Capua, the second city of the peninsula—were restive and prone to secession. But many localities here held firm, as did the Latin heartland and the regions to the north. Because the Carthaginian applied conventional standards of empire to the deceptive Romans, he thought that once he had thrashed them on the battlefield, their allies would fall away like ripe fruit. But in assuming this, he missed a great deal; his analysis was that of seeing an X-ray showing only bare bones, blind to much of the personal connective tissue that held the Roman body politic together.

Hannibal also may not have fully understood what a large body it was. Rome's wars, particularly the first one with Carthage, were very costly, and keeping so many men under arms would eventually lead to reproduction problems.[32] But when Hannibal arrived, the situation was far from acute; quite the opposite. One of the key advantages of Rome's alliance system—perhaps the key advantage, considering the huge number of casualties the Carthaginian would inflict—was the vast reserves of manpower it provided.[33] Polybius (2.24.1–17), who gives us a detailed and plausible accounting, estimates "the total number of Romans and allies able to bear arms was more than seven hundred thousand foot and seventy thousand horse, while Hannibal invaded Italy with an army of less than twenty thousand men." The historian neglects to add the Carthaginian's six thousand cavalry, but his point still stands. Taking on such a behemoth, no matter what Hannibal's fighting capabilities, was a Sisyphean task.

[5]

Empiricism, not originality, made Rome. The evolution of Rome's institutions was ultimately driven by what worked; this helps explain the ramshackle cast of what emerged. Romans did not proceed from theory, nor were they too proud to learn from others—even their enemies. They took what they saw, tried it out, and if it was successful, it became Roman. They also learned from their mistakes and their disasters, which brings us to what Romans themselves would have considered most important—the engine of their expansion, the backbone of the state . . . the legionary army.

The force described in Polybius's famous section on the Roman military system (6.19–42) was in many ways different from the one overwhelmed by the Gauls at the River Allia in 390 B.C. The Roman military would continue to evolve, and some even maintain that Polybius's description is actually of the force as it existed in his own time and not at the time of the Second Punic War—although most don't.[34] But only the most radical reinterpretation would attempt to argue that by the time of Hannibal's invasion one key aspect of the force had not already changed.[35]

At the core of the army was now the individual foot soldier. This might seem to be a truism; but it is actually critical to understanding why the system was so lethally effective and also how it could be literally crushed at Cannae. That most Roman heavy infantrymen fought in the style of a single combatant has been alluded to earlier; now it is time to go into detail.

This is not meant to imply that the infantryman was a loner, a tactical outlier. He was very much a constrained part of a larger formation, but his combat responsibilities were individualized.[36] In Roman terms *virtus* was balanced by *disciplina,* which was seen primarily as a brake on excessively aggressive behavior. Together the two operated as the yin and yang of combat comportment for foot soldiers.[37]

Romans had originally fought as part of a phalanx not much different from that of the Greeks. A densely packed mass protected by shields and armed with thrusting spears, the phalanx moved relentlessly forward seeking to break a rival formation through cumulative pressure and wounding. In other words, the violence it inflicted was that of the group. But as the Romans found at the River Allia, such a formation could be enveloped, and once penetrated from the flanks and rear, its inmates became utterly vulnerable. So over the space of time (the sequence is hard to pin down chronologically) the infantryman was transformed into something much more flexible; the phalangite became a legionary and his lethality was personalized.

It was largely a matter of weapons, or at least how they were employed. Rather than using his spear as a pike, most infantrymen (roughly four out of five) now threw their spears as javelins and then acted primarily as swordsmen—the same sequence followed by Homer's warriors in *The Iliad.* They were choreographed not as soloists but as a sanguinary corps de ballet across the forward edge of battle. But if the spirit was Homeric, the details were Roman, worked out mainly through observing their adversaries and figuring out what worked best.

As his formation approached the enemy, for most legionaries the first offensive act was to cast his *pilum,* borrowed, some Roman historians believed, from the Samnites, among his most indefatigable enemies.[38] Polybius maintains that an infantryman carried two types of *pila,* a thick and a thin version, one being lighter than the other. It may be that one was for longer ranges, but it is difficult to see how he could have held the spare while charging.[39] Besides, penetrating power was maximized at around fifteen feet, which would have limited our rapidly closing Roman to one really effective throw. For the *pilum* was essentially a manually delivered armor-piercing projectile—a four-foot wooden shaft attached to a long slender iron shank tipped with a barbed pyramid-shaped point, which effectively concentrated all the weapon's momentum at the point of impact. The target could be an exposed appendage or armored body but was more likely to be a shield, which says a good deal about the thought that went into the weapon and its use. Modern experiments have shown the *pilum* capable of penetrating about an inch of pine.[40] If that happened to be your shield, you were instantly in deep trouble, since it would have been nearly impossible to remove the weapon quickly. Designed to bend on impact (so it couldn't be thrown back), a protruding *pilum* was clumsy and heavy enough to marginalize your most important item of protection from the murderous infighting that was bound to follow.

Once in close to an opponent, a legionary was doubly dangerous. First, he wielded the *gladius hispaniensis,* a hefty but well-balanced double-edged short sword something over two feet long, tipped with a long triangular point. Probably adopted from Spanish mercenaries serving with the Carthaginians during the First Punic War,[41] the sword was easily capable of tearing away entire limbs with a single blow.[42] Yet the *gladius* was most lethal when inflicting puncture wounds, the ever observant Romans having recognized that a penetration of but two inches anywhere on the trunk was generally fatal.[43] Hence the legionary is often pictured in a slight crouch with his right or sword arm farthest from his opponent (the opposite of a modern fencer), poised to deliver an upward thrust at the belly or perhaps at an exposed thigh. But he had a basic problem. His short sword, while versatile and lethal, was still short, meaning that a determined thrust or slash could leave the legionary vulnerable to a devastating counterblow. This has led some to surmise that normally Romans attacked in a deliberate probing way, trying to score a number of lesser wounds.[44] Given individual differences in courage and aggressiveness, this is plausible, but the legionary had another means of creating an opening that is often overlooked, his shield.

All Roman heavy infantrymen carried a massive buckler, at the time of Cannae still oval-shaped and approximately four feet long and two feet wide. Also thought to be of Samnite origin, this *scutum* was care-fully constructed of three layers of plywood, each lined up with the grain at right angles to the others for strength. Thicker in the center and flexible at the edges, it was highly resilient to blows but also very heavy. (Reconstructions appear to peg it at about twenty pounds).[45] This was compounded by being carried in the left hand with a horizon-tal handgrip, which, when compared to a vertical handle, made it par-ticularly difficult to wield on the defense. But with an overhand grip this arrangement did enable the user to exert the full force of his shoul-der to deliver what amounted to a *scutum* punch likely to unbalance or even fell an opponent, which might leave the opponent open to a fatal short sword follow-up.

This routine would not have looked much like fencing or the fren-zied hacking of cinematic reconstructions, but more like a lethal sword dance, the adversaries darting and executed from multiple angles of at-tack. It is important to understand that unlike the closely packed pha-langites, legionaries were given a considerable patch of personal space to exploit and defend. Sources disagree as to spacing, with Polybius (18.28–30) giving each legionary a six-foot-by-six-foot box, while Veg-etius (3.14, 15) reduces his frontage to three feet and adds slightly to the depth; possibly it varied with circumstances. But in any case these dimensions affirm that the legionary was basically on his own, and that he needed room to fight. When robbed of this space in which to ma-neuver, as happened at Cannae, he was in trouble. This was a demand-ing form of combat, but with sufficient training, and when operating within the tactical and strategic schemes the Romans devised, it turned legionaries into extraordinarily deadly warriors.

But by the time of the Second Punic War the system was still in transition. Eventually, all legionaries would be armed alike, but at this point the methodical Romans still kept an element of the phalanx in their formations. The oldest and presumably the steadiest one fifth of the heavy infantry, the *triarii*, brought up the rear and retained the thrusting spear—the idea being to form a barrier of last resort should things not go well with the others.

There were also some variations in defensive equipment, but these were primarily reflective of differences in wealth, not tactical roles. Most important was the differential in upper-body protection, with common soldiers wearing a small nine-inch-square heart protector, or *pectorale*, while the richer could afford a Celtic-style ring-mail cuirass, likely worn over some sort of padding. Also, Polybius (6.23.12–5) tells us that legionaries employed a single greave, but richer ones might have added a second. Line infantry uniformly appear to have had good helmets, most commonly adaptations of a Gallic design, or Montefortino-type, basically a hemispheric bowl with a neck protector and often equipped with cheek pieces—all topped with an eighteen-inch-tall crest of feathers.[46]

All told—*pilum, gladius, scutum,* helmet, greave, chest protection—this adds up to a lot of stuff. The legionary was a heavy infantryman in fact as well as in name. At the high end—if mail was worn—his arms and accoutrements would have amounted to a nearly eighty-pound burden, around fifty pounds if only a *pectorale* was included.[47] This is of some significance to our story; not only did the trapped legionaries who attempted to swim for it at Lake Trasimene sink like stones, but Cannae was fought in the south of Italy in the middle of summer. Heat prostration was bound to have played a role in the slaughter, with, ironically enough, the best-protected Romans suffering the most. Nevertheless, the legionary of the Second Punic War was still very well equipped to do his job, a judgment endorsed by no less of an authority than Hannibal himself, who outfitted his best troops with Roman accoutrements captured at the Battle of the River Trebia and at Lake Trasimene.[48]

When it came to heavy infantry, the Romans took good care of their soldiers and closely attended to their needs. This is further illustrated when we take the individual legionary and place him in formation. As we saw earlier with the *triarii,* the Roman military's transition from the phalanx was only partially complete, and the tactical scheme at Cannae plainly needed further development. Still, the infantry fighting formations that the Romans had evolved—as best as we can figure them out—appear to reflect considerable insight into how fighting[49] among large groups of men really took place.

Basically the phalanx was meant for the flat battlefields. Its central problem was keeping together as it moved forward. Unless the men slowed virtually to a crawl, even slight terrain irregularities bent and eventually broke it, as some phalangites got out ahead and others fell behind, leaving fatal gaps for an enemy to plunge into. When the Romans moved into hill country in their attempts to conquer the upland tribes, they solved the problem, as Hans Delbrück famously stated, by giving the phalanx "joints."[50] In essence they sliced and diced it, breaking the formation into small groups or maniples (handfuls), formed by stacking two of the basic administrative units, or centuries (each made up of seventy-two men and led by a centurion), one behind the other. Between the maniples a space was left exactly the width of a century. This way the units could be detoured around obstructions, and confusion within the ranks contained within the maniple.

Of course this left a lot of gaps, which gets us to the second innovative aspect of the so-called manipular order, the slicing part. The Romans lined up their maniples in a *triplex acies*, cutting the phalanx latitudinally to create three separate formations lined up one behind the other, with some considerable space left between each. At the rear were the *triarii*, next came the maniples of *principes*, and at the front were the *hastati*, the latter two being armed with *pila* and short swords. When deployed for battle, the maniples of each type were placed directly behind the intervals between the maniples of the line in front, creating a checkerboard pattern, or *quincunx* (like the number five on dice). This only partially covered the gaps, but it allowed for something even more important and astute.

Nothing is more exhausting than close combat. Driven by a desperate combination of aggression and fear, supercharged with adrenaline, bouts of hand-to-hand fighting are estimated to have an upward limit of about fifteen to twenty minutes before the participants become utterly sapped.[51] Therefore, modern sources visualize ancient battles as having been basically episodic, begun with a frenzy of mayhem and then, if neither side broke initially, being paced over a period of hours by a series of time-outs for rest, reorganization, and recommitment, followed by repeated rounds of more fighting. The geometry of the manipular order exploited these physical and emotional limitations by allowing for the replacement of exhausted fighters with fresh ones, while at the same time providing shelter for those recuperating.

Here is how it might have worked. Once deployed in the *triplex acies*, a legion would approach the enemy in checkerboard fashion at a measured pace until reaching the outer edges of the anticipated combat zone. At this point tactical mitosis would have occurred, with the rear centuries of the first maniples, the *hastati*, moving to the left and then forward to join the front centuries in the space between each maniple, to form a solid line of fighters half as deep as the original formation. These groups then moved rapidly forward to engage the enemy, throwing their *pila* and weighing in with their short swords. Within the ranks of the *hastati*—made up of younger and more eager fighters—legionaries would move forward to replace fallen or exhausted comrades, until the adversary showed signs of breaking or was at least fought to a standstill. Taking advantage of this lull, the rear *hastati* centuries might resume their original positions behind, and the second line of maniples, the *principes*, would move through the re-formed gaps of *hastati*, repeat the mitosis, and confront the flagging foe with a line of fresh fighters, a tactical one-two. Meanwhile, as the fighting proceeded, the *hastati* could rest and the entire process could be renewed several times more. If things went really badly or the swordsmen of both of the two front lines became totally exhausted, the maniples of *triarii* could advance and break apart into a solid line of spears, behind which the others could take refuge. Or so it seems.

Plainly, there are differing interpretations and also questions as to how well the manipular order might have worked in actual battle. A minority of authorities question the intricacies of forming solid lines of fighters, and maintain that the Romans engaged with the original checkerboard pattern.[52] This is plainly simpler but seems fatally flawed, since it would have allowed adversaries to rush through the gaps and attack the flanks of the maniples, especially on the sides without shields. Still, close combat is confusing and desperate, and the kind of martial minuet outlined above would have demanded a tremendous amount of discipline, training, and tactical leadership to maintain over the course of an extended battle. It would have been especially so if and when centuries and maniples were asked to retreat in order to perform the necessary rearrangements.[53] This meant either marching backward or turning away from the enemy, difficult in the first instance and positively dangerous in the second. This could have been minimized by always moving the lines ahead so that even the maniples could have been re-formed without retrograde motion; but unless the fighting had gone very well, this was likely to have had the unwanted effect of breaking the necessary lulls in combat prematurely. Still, this serves to illustrate that the manipular order was basically for moving forward, not backward. In this way it had not changed fundamentally from the phalanx.

There was the potential for more flexibility. The subdivided nature of the system suggested the possibility of using lines or groups of maniples independently to flank or even swing behind an adversary. But it would require a military genius, Scipio Africanus, to make this flexibility apparent. In the meantime the Romans remained as Hannibal found them and as Polybius (34.9.9) described them, "disapproving of every kind of deceit and fraud, and considering that nothing but direct and open attacks were legitimate for them." Roman commanders and Romans in general were proverbially offensive, and their style of fighting and their past successes gave them confidence that they could chew through any adversary.

Yet the system itself made it difficult for the Romans to live up to these expectations. The formations demanded a great deal from the soldiers, not only individually, but also corporately in terms of precise coordination. This meant relentless drilling and unit continuity, but typically legions were discharged after a campaign season and new ones raised. Many of those called up would have had previous military experience, but as far as is known, they would not have served together, nor were their immediate commanders the centurions yet professionals.[54] So the process was necessarily one of building and rebuilding. Even if we assume Roman troops were individually capable, organizational performance lagged until desperation led to further systematic change.

Then there were the allies. When a legion deployed, it was normally accompanied by an *ala* of *socii,* or allies, commanded by Roman citizens. This unit seems to have been around the same size as a legion, but with triple the cavalry. Historical sources are mainly silent as to their military nature, which some believe indicates they were organized and equipped much like Romans.[55] But this remains open to conjecture, as do the allies' levels of training. We do know there were chosen allied troops—a third of the cavalry and a fifth of the infantry—known as *extraordinarii,* who appear to have been at the general's disposal, possibly indicating that the rest were less reliable. After all, most of the allied units were made up of those the Romans had already defeated, so how can we assume they were equally effective? When a consular army lined up for battle, typically two Roman legions took the center, with the two *alae* forming the wings. This position could imply that the *alae* had a lesser tactical role—holding the flanks while the Romans moved forward and carved the heart out of the adversary. Hannibal characteristically attacked the wings. There were a number of reasons for this, but one may be that he expected less resistance there. Thus while the larger message of the Second Punic War was one of allied loyalty, there is reason to believe that the allies may have been a weak link tactically.

While heavy infantry lay at the core of Roman fighting power, light troops and cavalry also formed an integral part of the legionary system; yet both also fell short in terms of effectiveness. For example, skirmishers played a vital if unsung role in ancient warfare, preying on enemy foragers and exposed infantry, supporting cavalry, and screening heavy formations as they deployed. They were especially effective on broken terrain, and during the fourth century B.C., light troops among the Greeks had assumed an increasingly important tactical role. Subsequently they had become more specialized and professional, until by Hannibal's day they formed a large pool of available mercenaries, a resource he employed to great effect.

Roman light troops, on the other hand—mostly known as *velites* ("fast men")—were plainly less developed at the time of the Carthaginian's arrival. Originally just a very lightly armed throng, the *velites* described by Polybius (6.22) were still the youngest and poorest troops in the army. Some historians argue that the *velites* were really more military servants than soldiers at the time of Cannae, and it was only in 211 that they were reorganized into true light infantry.[56] Most disagree, but the *velites'* persistent reverses early in the war are also telling. Although a quarter were probably too poor to afford anything much in the way of weapons, the remainder appear to have been fairly well equipped, with a sword, javelins, a decent circular shield, and a helmet sometimes topped with a wolf's skin for identification. They seem to have had their own officers, and there is evidence that they trained cooperatively with cavalry, but their organization remains a matter of speculation. Most likely they fought in an open order, perhaps attacking in waves.[57] But not with very much success.

Velites were pretty clearly the least prestigious class of fighters in the Roman army. For most it seems to have been an apprenticeship, the first step on the way to joining the heavy infantry. Because they were young, they were brave and enthusiastic but also impulsive. Worse for them, in facing Hannibal's light troops, they would be facing experienced killers, professionals of varying nationality—Balearic slingers, javelin-throwing Libyans, Ligurian lancers, Spanish spearmen—all fighting in their own unique ways, a grab bag of tricks, a miscellany of lethal potential. For *velites,* one style fit all: throw the javelin and then either retreat or draw near to fight at close quarters with swords as junior *hastati.*

Also worth noting is the virtual absence of the bow, an ideal weapon for skirmishers bent on harassment. While Hiero of Syracuse report-

edly sent the Romans a small contingent, including some archers, before Cannae, nothing more is heard from them.[58] Otherwise, the Romans eschewed the bow, as did the Carthaginians, a remarkable
occurrence given the usefulness of the implement and the desperation
of the conflict. Evidently, Homer and his admonition against archers as
"foul fighters" cast a long shadow in the western Mediterranean.

But if the Roman *velites* were "one-trick ponies," the Romans were
also, quite literally, reluctant riders. No one disputes that the republican Roman preferred to fight on foot. But the very strength of the
heavy infantry seems to have retarded the development of an effective
cavalry—a strange situation, given that the cavalry membership was
recruited from the upper classes and service with the horse provided
the path to higher office and thus command. While the ethos was probably not that of an adolescent romp, as one critic opined,[59] the enterprise seems lacking in serious military purpose. Since combat
distinction was the basis of a Roman political career, it has been argued
that members of the cavalry were prone to impulsive acts of bravura
and had a proclivity for single combat rather than for working together
as a disciplined unit.[60] Granted, they were organized—into *turma* of
thirty, ten to a legion—but just how well they followed direction is
open to question. Restraint was important with horses, since the chief
tactic of the headlong charge could quickly lead to stampeding a unit
of horses right off the battlefield and into irrelevance. Not only that,
but Roman cavalry, being heavily armed and made up of Romans, had
a proclivity to jump off their horses and fight it out on foot, thereby
sacrificing their central advantage.

This was important, since one of the chief roles of cavalry is reconnaissance; ancient armies were compact in comparison to the territory
they covered, and the need simply to find the enemy—preferably before he found you—was not to be dismissed.[61] But Rome's young aristocrats plainly preferred fighting to scouting. Since the allies provided
most of the horse, presumably much of this vital scouting was left to
them. Yet the monotonous frequency with which Roman armies fell
prey to ambushes during the third and second centuries strongly implies that the allies were not much better at reconnoitering than their
senior partners. If Rome's legions were not exactly blind, they were at
least nearsighted.

Finally, the fact that the route to command among Romans was
through service on the back of a horse raises questions about the lead-

ership of what was essentially an army of foot soldiers. Surely commanders studied and understood infantry tactics, and being mounted
provided some advantage in mobility and getting a better view of the
battlefield. Still the maniples were the territory of the various grades of
centurions, officers fairly low on the totem pole, and everybody above
the centurions had a background in cavalry. Other ancient armies were
similarly led, but few other armies were so dependent on the success of
their infantry. So the potential disconnect between Roman commanders on horseback and their troops on foot in terms of experience is
something to be considered, especially since Hannibal was thoroughly
schooled in all forms of warfare.

[6]

Having looked at the Roman military system in detail, it remains to
consider how the different components operated in concert. To explore this, it makes sense to gather up the Roman military's most characteristic product, a legionary battle force, and take it out for the
conceptual equivalent of a test drive, a short notional military campaign.

During this period the Roman combat model of choice was the standard consular army.[62] This was most efficient and responsive when configured to be about a quarter the size of the doomed big rig we saw
heading for Cannae at the very beginning of the chapter. Its basic en-
gines of destruction were two specifically Roman legions. Each one
consisted of six hundred *triarii,* twelve hundred *hastati,* twelve hundred
principes, and twelve hundred *velites,* for a total of forty-two hundred
foot soldiers, plus an additional three hundred cavalry. These were
joined by two *alae* of allied troops, each roughly of legionary size, along
with two associated contingents of cavalry, numbering nine hundred
horse respectively. When optional supernumeraries were added, the
total force added up to around twenty thousand. While Roman legionaries were notable for carrying heavy loads of their own equipment, it is hard to conceive of each legion needing less than a thousand
extra animals to carry and cart necessary equipment and baggage.[63]

Figuratively speaking, this was a big vehicle with a lot of horse (and
mule) power. Out on the *via* as the force made its way forward, it likely
measured in excess of a mile in length, so its road manners were some-

what questionable. It has been argued that prior to the big ambush at Lake Trasimene the legionary order of march was a careless shambling procession, only to be reined in by the firm hand of Fabius Maximus.[64] Polybius (6.40.3–14), however, outlines a much more regular procedure, with the *extraordinarii* placed at the head of the column, followed by the right allied wing and pack animals, then the first legion with its baggage behind it, trailed by the second legion, which had with it both its own pack train and also the baggage of the second *ala*, which normally brought up the rear. The cavalry was stationed either behind their respective infantry units or on the flanks of the pack train, to keep the animals together. In times of imminent danger, Polybius adds, the *hastati, principes,* and *triarii* formed three parallel columns for quick deployment.

Our consular army was basically an all-terrain vehicle, but the distance it covered was very much subject to the kind of surface it was traversing. On the best roads it was probably capable of a maximum of seventeen to twenty miles a day, with these numbers shrinking progressively as the route deteriorated and the obstacles increased.[65]

One thing was invariable, however. While there was still plenty of daylight, military tribunes rode ahead to choose and lay out not just a suitable rest area, but the legionary equivalent of a full-service truck stop. Having arrived at the designated spot, the army then spent the next three hours digging a carefully surveyed rectilinear perimeter ditch, forming a rampart, studding it with a palisade, building gates on each side, and then setting up within the enclosed area a precisely configured tent city predetermined to match exactly the army's organization. Polybius gives us a virtual blueprint of the facility, sparing us few details in a scheme that appears to have left nothing to chance. There was a designated space for nearly every function an army might need to perform in the cause of preventive maintenance—room to eat, sleep, train, assemble, store booty, march in and out, with traffic flow in all circumstances being carefully considered. But the camp was far more than a service center.

Both ancient and modern commentators agree that the methodical construction of a marching camp was among the most characteristic features of the Roman approach to warfare.[66] It was a center of motivation, a place of rewards and punishments for a system fervently committed to both. Here, before the rest of the army, men who had deliberately exposed themselves to danger received the decorations so coveted by Roman soldiers and so effective in leading them to risk their lives. Alternately, it was where those who had stolen from comrades, had slept on watch, had disobeyed, had tried to desert, or had proved less than courageous fell prey to savage and generally fatal chastisement, inflicted either by the lictors—flogging with their fasces and beheading with their axes—or by the soldiers themselves.

As much as anything the camp was a state of mind, a psychological weapon—both defensive and offensive. On the one hand it provided the legionary with an orderly bit of home territory, a familiar haven from what was often a very hostile and dangerous outer environment. It was also the nest of the *contubernium*, the squads of eight men who ate and tented together, reinforcing the small-unit bonds that are at the heart of any successful army. But looked at from the enemy perspective, the marching camp sent an entirely different message. By habitually fabricating a nearly identical fortification at the end of each day's progress, the Roman army signaled its irrevocable advance and the collective will pushing it forward.[67] The Romans were as relentless as their camps were inevitable.

But physically the camps were far from invulnerable. Any palisade of posts and tree branches thrown up in a matter of hours was bound to be fairly flimsy and capable of stopping only small-scale assaults. This inherent weakness has caused some to question the worth of the whole enterprise. There are numerous examples of Roman camps being overrun; yet this almost always occurred after a debacle in the field.[68] If an army was sufficiently degraded and demoralized, as happened at Cannae, no camp was likely to protect the survivors.

Still, this misses the point. The camp was essentially a staging area and potential rallying point. This was why Roman commanders customarily accepted battle only a short distance from their base. Their army might take the field rested and in good order, and if worse came to worst they still had a place to escape to. Troops on the run are at their most vulnerable. Any means of cutting short this pursuit and providing time for regrouping was a potential lifesaver. Camps did fall, but many a Roman army reemerged to snatch victory from defeat.

For our own army this is entirely premature. Dawn has broken. The sentries have remained alert beyond the perimeter, and there have been no attempts at harassment to disturb our sleep. Still, the enemy is near, and one glance at the consul's tent and the red vexillum staked outside it makes it apparent this will not be a day of marching. Before sunrise the consul met with his military council (quaestor, tribunes, and the senior centurion—the *primus pilus*—of each legion, plus the prefects of the allied brigades),[69] and the decision to do battle has been made and orders have been given. Almost immediately the shriek of the horns controlling the *velites* breaks the morning air as they filter out of camp to set up the screen behind which the heavy infantry will assemble. The cavalry follows almost immediately to join them.

By this time the legionaries have finished their breakfast and are making last-minute preparations—sharpening the edges of their short swords, burnishing their helmets, dressing for battle. They join their centuries and find their place in the avenues between the tent rows, gradually building three great columns of *hastati, principes,* and *triarii* in the broad space behind the ramparts, each maniple, legion, and *ala* positioned where it will belong in the battle line. The individual columns then march out different gates and reassemble in parallel, proceeding lengthwise toward the planned battlefield until reaching a point foreseen to be the Roman left flank. At this juncture all three columns make a ninety-degree turn right, marching parallel to the enemy until the other flank is reached by the head of the respective columns, whereby the *triplex acies* is in place.

The process sounds simple enough but was likely time-consuming and very difficult, with tribunes racing back and forth on horseback, attempting to keep the columns straight and marching at roughly the same speed. The process finished with the centurions redressing the maniples and attending to their vital spacing—geometry with a cast of thousands. Assuming all went according to plan, the *velites* would then withdraw through the gaps in the line and the cavalry would take up their positions on the extreme flanks, the allies on the left and the Romans on the right.[70] What was left was approximately one mile of death-dealing potential stretching menacingly across the horizon, a serried barricade of sharp instruments, determination, and bad intent. Many armies who faced this spectacle would not live out the afternoon, unless of course you happened to be led by Hannibal. For him it spelled opportunity.

The Roman army described here was like a modern vehicle we might take on a test drive in one more respect; it was replaceable. Should it be wrecked, another just like it could be ordered up and put together. This was at once its great strength and its weakness. Because both its leaders and its fighters were, if not amateurs, then at least temps, many more of roughly the same quality could always be found, promising a numbing succession of legions and near-endless Roman resistance. But when faced with a true virtuoso legion wrecker, about the best that could be achieved was more akin to a stalemate than victory. To rid itself of the succubus of Hannibal, Rome required a general as good as he, and a truly professional army. Both were to be found among Hannibal's victims at Cannae, but in taking up the general and the professional army, the republic drove the first few miles down the road to republican ruin.

III

CARTHAGE

[1]

He was waiting for them. His spies in Rome had told him of the great army's formation, and over the last few days the interrogation of prisoners and deserters had kept him up-to-date as to its plans and progress.[1] Despite having captured the Romans' grain stores, he had supplies to feed his army for only about ten days. It didn't matter; he was ready to make a stand. He meant to destroy them here at Cannae; afterward his men could forage unmolested. Hannibal was that kind of leader. Always cagey, but when the odds were with him, he never turned his back on a fight.

His every instinct told him this was the moment and the place. He had been over the ground repeatedly, to the point of understanding that if he deployed with his back to the wind Vulturnus, the dust might blind them. (Livy 22.46.9) He knew the Romans, could read them like a book. He understood how they would line up and that their aim was to break through at the center. He would let them try, taking them on at the point of attack, distracting them so they would not realize he was deployed in depth on both flanks. When they had been lured far enough forward, he would spring the trap, clamping them in, like the jaws of a vise. It was the most audacious of battle plans. If the timing went awry and the Romans broke through prematurely, disaster would inevitably follow. Success, on the other hand, demanded not just a masterful general, but a veritable "band of brothers" as subordinates to carry out not just the substance of his plan but its intent. The final piece was an army so schooled and experienced in Hannibal's way of fighting that it almost instinctively reacted to circumstance and opportunity.

All of this was most un-Carthaginian. Hannibal had not set foot in the city since he was nine years old, and would not return for another fourteen years. He had grown up instead with the army, a force carefully crafted over a space of nearly twenty years in Spain, not Carthage. Arguably, the general, his forces, and his war in Italy were aberrations, products of his family's desire for revenge against Rome, and a generalized image of the Alexandrian military hero, more than they were products of Carthage itself.

Carthage was a different kind of place, one that initially stumbled (the First Punic War) and then was dragged (the Second Punic War) into a disastrous confrontation with a society built to fight and conquer. If Rome marched to the drumbeat of the god Mars, Carthage was beguiled by mammon. If Rome fed on blood and iron, Carthage took sustenance at the table of commerce. If Rome made war, Carthage made money. It was that simple and that elusive.

What is there to say of a people whose legacy was recorded by enemies? A victim of the most thoroughgoing sort of genocide, Carthage is barely mourned even today. Consider these words, quoted with apparent approval by one of the modern world's leading ancient historians: "Bearded Orientals in loose robes, covered with gaudy trinkets, often with great rings of gold hanging from their nostrils, dripping with perfumes, cringing and salaaming, the Carthaginians inspired disgust as much by their personal appearance as by their sensual appetites, their treacherous cruelty, their bloodstained religion. To the end they remained hucksters, intent on personal gain, careless or incapable of winning the good will of their subjects."[2] Granted, the source is a historian of Rome, but even those devoted to understanding their lives conclude: "On the whole Plutarch was probably right to describe the Carthaginians as a stern people, hostile to pleasures and amusements.... The melancholy and barbaric temperament which made the Carthaginians so odious in the eyes of other nations was the result not of avarice alone, but of another feeling which appears to have dominated their entire being, namely, superstition."[3] Rest assured that whatever they were in actuality, posterity knows them from the perspective of a chronically bad press.

As such, much is made of what they were not. They were not very artistic. Their aesthetic, such as it was, remained steadfastly derivative, first of the Egyptians and then of their longtime enemies, the Greeks. They have left almost nothing in the way of literature. With the exception of one brilliant text by Mago on agronomy that the Romans thought to translate, the rest was burned or lost. Besides, their written language remained a consonantal skeleton devoid of vowels and really best at recording transactions, not thoughts. In the ways that we value, they do not appear to have been very spontaneous or interesting. Theater and sports were missing from their lives, their products were poorly designed and cheaply made, and their inscriptions were repetitive and ritualistic. They were hardly stylish, especially the men, inevitably clad in long straight woolen robes lampooned by the Roman dramatist Plautus. "Hey, you without a belt!" Their very names lacked variety. No binomial nomenclature for Carthaginians, just a single appellation, and many so tongue twisting to Latin speakers that for Livy, everyone was reduced to Hanno or Hannibal, Hamilcar or Mago.[4]

One thing they were was religious—obsessively and, as it turned out, murderously so. Possibly more than any other society in the Mediterranean world at the time, Carthaginians were enthralled and bound together by a pantheon of somber, rapacious, and ultimately bloodthirsty gods. Practically everything we have left of them, including their very names ("Hannibal," "he who enjoys Baal's favor"; "Hasdrubal," "Baal is my help," etc.) reeks of their devotion, one and all, rich and poor. Theirs was a cosmology, it seems, forever threatening to implode, presided over by gods demanding propitiation in the face of misfortune. In both myth and history the story of Carthage is one punctuated with flaming self-immolations, beginning on the pyre of the founder, Elissa, and ending on the city's final day in 146 B.C. with the fiery suicide of the wife of its last ruler, Hasdrubal.[5] But there was another more ominous legacy, one apparently missed by Polybius and Livy, though not by the more flamboyant and less reliable Diodorus, and that was infanticide. This was verified in 1921, when the excavation of some of the first truly Carthaginian sites unearthed urn after urn containing the charred bones of newborn children. Not only has further investigation revealed that the practice continued until the city's destruction, but the substitution of other animals for children apparently decreased over time.[6] While there are likely to have been underlying causes having to do with population control, in the minds of the participants, bad times and angry gods demanded the most extreme sort of sacrifice. One thing is certain: this grisly backdrop has not encouraged the rehabilitation of Carthage and its inhabitants in the modern historical consciousness.

So the image propagated by their enemies the Greeks and Romans persists, and that image for the most part views Hannibal as an agent of Carthage. Certainly there are undertones of discord, particularly in Livy's portrayal of the Barcid's political rival Hanno "the Great," but in the main the ancients saw the Second Punic War as a conflict between Carthage and Rome and not between Hannibal and Rome. Arguably this is because Carthage remained not simply alien and mysterious to them, but virtually unfathomable. History in the ancients' eyes was fundamentally heroic, but Carthage was not heroic. Had the ancients understood this, they might have grasped why the motives of Hannibal, a figure virtually carved out of the epic tradition, were so profoundly incompatible with those of his homeland. But this requires further explanation.

[2]

The Romans called them "Poeni," and with reason. Carthaginians were at heart Phoenicians. We might even call them Phoenicians on steroids—not in the muscular sense but in terms of their effectiveness. Traditionally thought to have been settled in 814 B.C. by Tyre, Carthage (or Kart-Hadasht, Phoenician for "new city") differed from entrepôts established by Phoenicians in the western Mediterranean by having an elaborate foundation myth featuring Elissa escaping from her evil husband-slaying brother, King Pygmalion of Tyre, with a group of fellow citizens, recruiting more settlers in Cyprus, and then landing on the North African coast on a promontory on the eastern side of Lake Tunis. Upon arrival she supposedly bought from the reluctant natives a plot of land that could be covered by the hide of a bull, and then promptly cut it into strips so fine that it encompassed a neck of land about two and a half miles in circumference. Besides earning them a reputation for driving a hard bargain, this myth also implied something very un-Tyrian, a hunger for land.

Carthage's initial development was what might be expected from Phoenicians, a reliance on seaborne trade and a resort to value added, so that the archaeology of the eighth and seventh century B.C. time horizons clearly reflects the presence of industrial and artisanal quarters.[7] Meanwhile, Carthaginians looked beyond their own confines for food and for an outlet for their surplus population, setting up for business on the wheat-growing Syrtic coast near Tripoli in Libya and sending out the first colony to Ibiza in 654 B.C.[8] Others would follow.

A century later Carthage was plainly thriving. Colonies and emporiums had been established along much of the coast of North Africa, southeastern Spain, Sardinia, and in western Sicily. The mother city, Tyre, had fallen on hard times at the hands of the Assyrians; so whatever control it might have exerted was no longer a factor. Also, Carthage had broken out of its original confines and now occupied the hinterlands of modern Cape Bon, an area of around twenty thousand square miles.[9] This was highly significant, because it set up the beginnings of a rural economy based on great estates and intensive cultivation.

All the while, Carthage's expansion was observed by its enemies from essentially an agrarian-imperial perspective. Hence it was remembered in almost exclusively military terms. At the core of Carthaginian power, according to this view, was its navy, and this perspective is accurate enough as far as it goes. In 535 B.C., Carthage in alliance with the Etruscans won an apparently decisive fleet action over the Phocaeans off Alalia in Sardinia, thereby establishing the reputation of maintaining a thalassocracy dominant in the western Mediterranean. Granted, the Carthaginians did build a substantial navy with excellent ships and crews renowned for their seamanship. But its purpose was primarily to protect Carthage's merchant marine from piracy, for which the Phocaeans were notorious. In fact, with the exception of a few references by Diodorus (13.54.1; 80) to actions off Sicily, and the defeat of Pyrrhus in 276 B.C., Alalia was the only fleet engagement the Carthaginians are known to have fought prior to the First Punic War. Naval vessels of the period were oar-propelled rams, requiring large crews and retaining relatively little space for food or water—more like racing shells than battleships. Their strategic range was very limited, in part because they normally had to be beached each night, and also because they were unable to ride out a heavy sea. At best this was a fragile asset, vulnerable to land attack and even more susceptible to getting swamped in a sudden storm. Carthage's navy served the city well in scaring off marauders—far less well as a tool of war. But to Carthage's enemies the force was intimidating, at least until the Romans built a fleet.

Then there was the memory of Carthage as a terrestrial aggressor, mostly defined by a two-hundred-year-long back-and-forth struggle for control of Sicily. By Greek accounting this was a hegemonic soap opera featuring the Carthaginian barbarian repeatedly at the gates, endless Punic perfidy, and sudden dramatic reverses, all epitomized by the Battle of Himera in 480, when the generalissimo Hamilcar, seeing the rout of his army of three hundred thousand (an absurdly inflated figure), cast himself onto the proverbial sacrificial fire. For an adversary supposedly bent on steamrolling the Sicilian Greeks, Carthaginian behavior has impressed some modern historians as suspiciously quixotic.[10] At the moment of imminent victory they seem to have stepped back. Rather than the Greek explanations—cowardice, plagues, and Pyrrhic fecklessness—it has been suggested that the Carthaginians marched to the beat of a different drummer, and at least initially fought in league with other Phoenician entities simply to maintain themselves and their commercial presence. Later, when they do seem more aggressive and anxious to formalize power relationships, it appears to be largely in reaction to the rise of Syracuse and its obvious ambition to consolidate the island under its own rule. In all cases, the basic instruments of Carthaginian assertiveness were mercenary armies, which appeared and disappeared with startling rapidity. Disposable force-structures-for-hire were emblematic of Carthaginian land power, at least until Hannibal and his father created something entirely more permanent and professional.

[3]

The best explanation for the paradox of Carthaginian power is economics. Unlike in Rome, where military power and glory lay at the root of everything, it was money that mattered in Carthage. This is understandable in the modern context; it was lost on the ancients. So they persisted in misjudging the Carthaginians, and the Carthaginians reciprocated—a fatal error, as it turned out. For they all lived in a world where war trumped commerce, a time when, if things got bad enough, you could not strike a deal. But if that was their fate, they made remarkable progress right up until the end.

Carthage was famously rich, but the nature and degree of that wealth remains obscure. In part this is because in a traditional business environment, concepts such as diminishing returns are buried beneath personal and political relationships. But this does not mean that they cease to operate, or that through a gradual accumulation of empirically derived information they can be implicitly understood and used to advantage. As far as we know, there was no abstract understanding of economics among the ancients, but they knew what worked and what didn't—especially the Carthaginians.

It is generally acknowledged that Carthaginians excelled as traders, and also in manufacturing and selling things made from simpler materials ... value added. But here the historical analysis frequently stops or is short-circuited by what appear to be some fundamental misunderstandings.

The first misunderstanding has to do with the nature and consequences of Carthage's expansion into the North African interior. Traditionally, this has been interpreted in a political context, landed nobility seen as an antipode to the aristocracy of trade, or in terms of those favoring internal as opposed to overseas expansion.[11] Recently, however, there has been a growing understanding of just how integrated Carthaginian agriculture was into the larger sphere of business enterprise.[12] By 300 B.C. the lands around the city had been turned into a vast food factory, an inner zone devoted to grapes, figs, olives, almonds and pomegranates, along with an outer band generating huge quantities of wheat—Punic latifundia worked by slaves and restive Libyan peasants and providing a massive component of total exports. This was why the Romans thought to preserve Mago's text on agronomy; it constituted the state of the art in turning plants into money. Still, the fecundity of Carthage amazed and even frightened the Romans. Livy (31.19.2) tells us that in 200, just a year after the Carthaginians were defeated in the Second Punic War, they nevertheless managed to send four hundred thousand bushels of wheat to Rome and to her troops in Macedonia. Ten years later, much more, including five hundred thousand bushels of barley for the Roman army, was offered as a gift by the obliging Carthaginians, but the Roman senate, plainly put off by such ostentation on the part of the vanquished, insisted on paying.

But there was more to Carthage as an economic powerhouse than simply a green thumb. Archaeological finds have led commentators to make note of the apparently high volume of imports to Carthage. This is usually viewed as a weakness—Carthaginian artisans are seen as lacking the skill and artistry to satisfy anyone other than the "unsophisticated western barbarians."[13] The fact that Carthaginians preferred Rhodian wine to African, that they favored Campanian ware and persisted in bringing in whole boatloads of Greek art and vases *de luxe,* is seen as an economic drain, a surrender to style over self-sufficiency. It was probably a sign of neither, but instead a sign of something much more sophisticated. Through a process of trial and error Carthaginians seem to have stumbled upon the principle of comparative advantage— the idea that even if a place could produce everything it needed more efficiently at home, it was still better off concentrating on what it did best and trading with others for the rest. This is not to say there existed a Punic David Ricardo[14] or that Carthaginians had a firm grasp of exactly what was going on, only that they tried it and it worked. And it kept on working until they grew incomprehensively wealthy.

The Carthaginians were good at business and bad at war. Paradoxically, their beatings at the hands of the Romans had the net effect of making them richer—less bellicose and more businesslike. This became most evident after the Second Punic War, when Carthage accepted near total subordination to Rome—literally outsourced warfare—and quickly reached new heights of prosperity, offering to pay off its huge war indemnity (nearly six hundred thousand pounds of silver) after only ten rather than fifty years.[15] This sort of thing infuriated the Romans, and because military power was their bottom line, it also frightened them. It was no accident that Cato the Elder, the man who ended every speech with *"delenda est Carthago"* ("Carthage must be destroyed"), held up as evidence of Rome's vulnerability a fresh fig reputedly picked in the Punic capital just three days earlier, saying, "Ah yes, we have an enemy this close to our walls!"[16] To Roman eyes a Carthaginian fig could never be just a fig; money would inevitably be turned to the ends of Mars. So the city's doom was sealed.

The Carthaginians should have known better, that their wealth could not protect them in a world ruled by war. Their cash machine was by its nature vincible. The city itself was protected by massive defenses, perhaps the most elaborate in the ancient world,[17] but the manicured countryside practically invited an invader to set up camp and live off the fat of the land. As far back as 310 B.C., Agathocles of Syracuse, besieged at home by Carthage, turned the tables on the Carthaginians and landed in Africa, bringing the city to the verge of ruin before he was forced to withdraw. Not only did he defeat the defenders in the open field near Tunis, thereby isolating the city from its inland empire, but the native Libyans greeted him as their liberator.[18] This was critical; the Libyans had already rebelled twice in the preceding century, and would do so again and again subsequently.[19]

Carthaginian expansion had been driven by the logic of economics, and as long as these ties were based on trade and merchandising, they appear to have been loose and not very onerous. Penetration into Africa, however, brought with it the usual mechanisms of territorial control—governors, provincial organization, taxes—and in general the grip of Carthage tightened with time.[20] While the population controlled by the middle of the third century was likely as large as, or perhaps even larger than, the Italian confederation's, Carthage was characteristically more interested in tribute than soldiers.[21] Unlike with Rome, there was no compensatory attempt to enlist the loyalty of the subject populations, much less to grant citizenship. This was an empire by and for Carthaginians; everybody else was just an economic input. It's no wonder Hannibal assumed Rome's allies would desert; loyalty among subordinates was not something Carthaginians cultivated or much understood.

Among themselves, though, they did stick together. While it is difficult to call a place that periodically relegated large numbers of its offspring to a fiery death a healthy society, it did at least give the appearance of being cohesive and well governed. Carthage was a place of merchant princes and presumably vast economic inequalities, but compared to the vicious internal strife evident in contemporary Greek cities, class conflict here remained muted if not exactly nonexistent. Twice during the fourth century would-be strongmen had tried and failed to stage putsches, and had received little support from the urban proletariat or even the city's slaves.

As it happens, a good deal is known of Carthage's governmental structure, Aristotle having had a good opinion of the scheme, which combined, he said, the best features of monarchy, oligarchy, and democracy (*Politics* 2.11). He also appears to have understood that it was an evolving system and had changed considerably since the beginning of the fourth century. The center of gravity when he wrote lay with the oligarchic element—a council of elders of several hundred long-term members, perhaps controlled by a body of 104 judges, or by another group of 30 key councilors. The exact relationship among the three is subject to some uncertainty, but with nobody denying they collectively embodied the city's wealthy.[22] The state's senior executives by the third century were two annually elected suffetes, whom Aristotle doesn't specifically mention but who were derived from an original monarchy with strongly religious overtones. They too were creatures of the plutocracy, holding supreme religious and civil authority but no command role over the military. Should the suffetes and the elders agree on a proposal, they could implement it without further consultation. But if they did not agree, they had to refer it to the assembly of the people, where any citizen could speak and even make a counterproposal—the democratic component.

Carthaginian politics are hard to track with any precision; we have only fragmentary references from the various Greek and Roman sources. But clearly there were factions and basic disagreements over policy, especially during the crisis period that began with the end of the First Punic War in 241 B.C. Some historians have attempted to characterize this time as part of a "democratic revolution,"[23] which seems overstated; but it does appear that power was shifting in the face of oligarchic failure, and what went on in the assembly of the people took on added significance. For one thing, it is apparent that during the first of the wars with Rome the assembly was electing Carthage's military commanders.[24] But this simply ratified what had always been true: in Carthage, unlike in Rome, politicians and soldiers had very different career paths, and the former basically saw the latter as employees.

The number of male citizens in Carthage was always small (probably never exceeding 120,000),[25] and consequently the city stopped relying on its own soldiers early in its history. Only in dire emergencies were its citizens called to arms, and even then the forces were limited (during the Mercenary War, 241–238 B.C., a desperate conflict, only ten thousand troops could be raised to fight with Hamilcar[26]) and not very capable, taking the field as a phalanx, the best formation for amateurs. But until Agathocles retaliated by invading Carthage, the city remained secure in its isolation in North Africa, and could afford to dispense with a standing indigenous ground force. Overseas, it made entirely more sense to rent rather than own, to hire and fire mercenaries as circumstance dictated.

Consequently, the number of Carthaginians who specialized in soldiering remained very small, limited to those who officered the hirelings, a cadre probably derived from a narrow group of noble families.[27] Since there didn't seem to be any specific time limit on a military commander's service and he was normally left to his own devices on campaign so long as he avoided defeat, it might seem that accumulated experience would add up to a high degree of professionalism. This was not necessarily so; for one thing, generals seem to have owed their positions as much to wealth and social standing as to competence.[28] And if they were given considerable autonomy, this could amount to enough rope to hang—or, more properly, crucify—themselves.

Corporate Carthage expected positive results from its military managers, and defeat was more than frowned upon. Unsuccessful generals were subject to a strict accounting before the executive board of 104 judges, and the results of a negative performance review could find the recipient mounted on a cross. Crucifixion, it seems, brought an end to more than a few budding military careers, four commanders having met their fate in this manner during the First Punic War alone.[29] This sort of negative incentivizing seems emblematic of the segregation of civilian and military expertise in Carthage. The Roman senate, filled with former soldiers thoroughly familiar with the friction and fog of war, proved much more forgiving of unsuccessful commanders, even of Terentius Varro, Cannae's biggest loser. Lacking any equivalent corporate understanding of land warfare, Carthage instead applied the stick, or rather the cross.

This brand of military disconnect also helps explain another characteristic Punic military delusion, a reliance on war elephants. Like the Romans, the Carthaginians got their first dose of panzer pachyderms from Pyrrhus, military history's favorite Epirote, when they fought him in Sicily during his short sojourn there in 278. Unlike the Romans, who simply learned to deal with the elephants, the Carthaginians had their own by 262 and soon became addicted.

This proved to be a bad habit. Elephants can be panicked easily, not a good quality during warfare.[30] When this happened, they tended to treat friend and foe alike, flailing wildly and stepping on anyone in the way, which was often the Carthaginians themselves. Granted, the elephants were terrifying to uninitiated enemy troops, and could disrupt cavalry, since horses found their scent repulsive. But there were simply too many ways they could be thwarted, and their net effect was to add another uncontrolled variable to the battlefield. They do appear to have played some role in defeating the Roman general Regulus when he invaded Africa in 256, but it is hard to find another comparable Carthaginian success with pachyderms. And this must be weighed against the elephantine expense of capturing, training, and transporting them, a negative cost-benefit result by any realistic accounting.

But Carthage was plainly struck by their jumbo size and power—an ancient ultimate weapon—a mirage the possession of which might render all other military shortcomings irrelevant, a particularly beguiling notion to an acquisitive people not much used to fighting on the ground. Also, elephants were available. Carthaginians, after all, lived in Africa, and so-called forest elephants (*Loxodonta africana cyclotis*) were likely to be found north of the Sahara. Although they were smaller than the Indian models ridden by the Hellenistic Greeks, they were still plenty impressive, standing nearly eight feet tall at the shoulder.[31] Even Hannibal was fooled, making a heroic effort to herd some over the Alps, only to have them die well before he ever reached Cannae. Still, he remained interested, and his disastrous last stand at Zama in 201 featured eighty of the giant beasts. But war is not a circus, and they panicked as usual, marking Hannibal as the last and greatest of the Punic pachyderm true believers.

Militarily, Carthage was on firmer ground at sea. Shipborne trade was the city's lifeblood, and the necessary skills and experience were likely to have been widely shared by a whole class of mariners. Undoubtedly many crewed in commercial transports. It also appears probable, though not certain, that Carthage's navy was largely, if not exclusively Carthaginian manned.[32] Since Hellenic navies were rowed by their own nationals, Polybius, a Greek, likely would have mentioned it had it not been the case with Carthage. It has also been suggested that naval service helps explain the political stability of the city, since it would have given the poorest elements steady employment.[33]

This was no minor proposition. By 256 B.C. the basic Carthaginian warship, a quinquereme (named after the arrangement of its oars), required a crew of around three hundred to row.[34] Archaeological excavation of the famed circular military harbor at Carthage indicates berthing space for around 180 first-line warships. Together this amounts to a requirement of fifty-four thousand oarsmen, a substantial percentage of the total male population. All signs point to Carthaginians taking great pride in their fleet, and this in turn points to wide participation. (Livy reports that when Scipio Africanus burned the Carthaginian fleet at the end of the Second Punic War, the sight caused grief as deep as if the city itself had been aflame.[35])

Arguably this pride and this participation were at the heart of

Carthage's tragic fate. The fleet, as noted above, was a fragile asset, and its military power was hard to apply, but that would not have been apparent, either to Carthaginian or to other eyes. During the first portion of the third century B.C., the force's squadrons swept around the waters of the western Mediterranean, showing the flag and looking very formidable. In 276, Plutarch tells us, the Carthaginians caught Pyrrhus in the Strait of Messana (modern Messina) and destroyed most of what was probably a convoy of merchant vessels carrying his soldiers.[36] When Carthage later went to war with the Romans, the admiral Hanno boasted that he would not even let Romans wash their hands in the sea. Given the circumstances, it sounded realistic, but instead the Romans would turn the waters around Sicily red with Carthaginian blood. For they would fight as if they were on land, and Carthage would find itself locked in a struggle that would consume huge quantities of its wealth. This is generally conceded, but there is something entirely more demoralizing that has been largely overlooked: quite probably large numbers of the citizens who manned the oars of Carthage's war galleys were killed.

[4]

Carthage and Rome had a long and not necessarily unfriendly relationship, with Polybius (3.22 ff) citing three treaties between the two states going back as far as 508–7 B.C. There is a lot of scholarly debate over the contents of the first two pacts, yet most agree they were largely about carving out spheres of influence for trade. The Carthaginians were interested in keeping the Romans clear of Libya and Sardinia, but they yielded primacy in Latium and granted the Romans commercial rights in Sicily—fair enough, considering the status and motivation of the parties. The final agreement in 279–8 was specifically concerned with mutual support against Pyrrhus, though nothing much came of it, except perhaps bad feelings. There is a confusing story that had a Carthaginian fleet descending on Pyrrhus's erstwhile ally, the city of Tarentum, in 272, just as the Romans were besieging it by land. The Carthaginians were offering their help, but this left the Romans suspicious, since no aid had been requested. At any rate, relations continued downhill.

A group of Campanian mercenaries, who had earlier worked for

Agathocles, seized the city of Messana in Sicily sometime during the 280s.[37] Calling themselves Mamertines, after the war god Mars, the Campanians took advantage of the confusion engendered by Pyrrhus's short stay to plunder the surrounding area and generally make a nuisance of themselves for upward of fifteen years. Then, hard-pressed by the new and vigorous ruler of Syracuse, Hiero, the Mamertines appealed to both Carthage and Rome for help. Both responded, which put them in a competitive position and eventually on a collision course. Many contemporary historians agree with Polybius that the Roman decision to take up the sword in 264 was basically opportunistic, driven by Rome's fundamental motivators—the potential for military reputation and plunder—Romans acting like Romans.[38] Still, it is interesting to note that in the years just prior to the first clash with Carthage, families of Campanian origin were on the political ascendancy in Rome (the Atilii, who held the consulship seven times between 267 and 245, were from Campania), and products from this district—pottery and wine—were in direct competition with Punic wares.[39]

The Carthaginians, for their part, had been wrangling over chunks of Sicily for three centuries; in that regard this was nothing new, a continuation of business by other means. But Carthage very likely had no idea what to expect or, in Livy's words (31.34.6) "what men they had to fight." After all, Sicily was an island, and Carthage was a sea power.

Actually, Carthage was at the precipice—the immovable object faced with Rome, the irresistible force. The first struggle would last twenty-three years, the longest continuous war in ancient history. Less than a century later there would be nothing left of Carthage, save smoldering ruins.

The First Punic War began inconclusively. The Carthaginian fleet proved unable to keep the Romans off the island, but the Romans had trouble making progress once they got there, since the rough topography did not favor massed land battles. (There would be only four in the entire conflict, two of them in Africa.) Also, most of the population lived behind walls, which made it hard for the Romans to get at and control the civilians. After the arduous though successful siege of Agrigentum, the Romans realized that the only way to win was to exclude the Carthaginians from the entire island, and that meant building a fleet.[40]

It was an audacious proposition. Romans did not take to the sea naturally, and apparently no one in Italy had experience with quinqueremes. Polybius (1.20.10) tells us that to fill the gap they used a Carthaginian warship that had run aground early in the war, and duplicated it one hundred times in sixty days—ancient reverse engineering. Meanwhile, oarsmen were trained on stages, sitting in the order they would assume at sea. Even if, as is likely, these rowers were joined by *socii navales,* naval allies, from Italian coastal towns with seafaring traditions, the Roman armada—its men and its timber—were bound to be green in comparison to Carthage's. They proved it on their first mission when the crews of a seventeen-ship squadron panicked and were captured, earning for their commander, an ancestor of Scipio Africanus, the nickname Asina ("she-ass"). This initial loss was deceptive, however. Almost immediately the Carthaginians ran into the main Roman fleet and lost a number of ships, and this was only their first unpleasant surprise.

The Romans had a secret weapon. Realizing their quinqueremes were outclassed, someone had suggested turning them into delivery systems for marines by mounting pivoting boarding bridges, which Polybius calls "crows," on their bows. As a Carthaginian vessel approached to ram, the crow from the Roman ship would slam down, embedding itself with an iron beak, whereupon a file of *gladius*-wielding Romans would storm aboard to wreak havoc on the helpless oarsmen. In the war's first massive fleet action off Myle on the north coast of Sicily, the Carthaginians were puzzled by the strange devices but sailed confidently ahead, and were thus impaled, losing around forty-five ships and ten thousand men, many of whom were killed.[41] If the crow was sort of the reductio ad absurdum of naval warfare, allowing the Romans to turn seaborne encounters into infantry battles, the Carthaginians were plainly slow to react, suffering a string of defeats off Sulci and Tyndaris, and then a huge one at Cape Economus. The latter, which involved almost three hundred thousand participants— more than had fought in a naval battle before or since—has been compared to Cannae in the way the Punic center collapsed inward; but certainly with different results. According to Polybius (1.28.10–14), the Carthaginians had over thirty ships sunk, and sixty-four captured by the Romans and their crows.

Rome now went for the knockout.[42] Refitting their fleet, they headed to Africa in the late summer of 256, disembarked near Cape Bon, and ravaged the rich agricultural district, just as Agathocles had done. At this point messengers from Italy ordered most of the fleet back with the spoils, leaving the consul Regulus with forty ships and two legions. He almost immediately met and defeated the Carthaginians at a place called Adys, plundering their camp and leaving them despondent and faced with the threat of a native revolt. But Regulus overplayed his hand. He offered peace terms so harsh that his opponents decided they had little to lose by continuing.

With their backs quite literally to their city's wall, the Carthaginians were open to suggestions. A Greek mercenary named Xanthippus, who was familiar with Spartan training methods, took command and drilled a scratch force of civilians into an effective phalanx. In the spring of 255 he led them onto a chosen field, accompanied by a strong cavalry element and approximately a hundred elephants. Rather than wait for reinforcements, Regulus, whose horse were heavily outnumbered, engaged and soon found himself engulfed and then captured, with only about two thousand Romans managing to escape to their original camp near Cape Bon. This disaster would cast a long shadow over Scipio Africanus's plan to take the Second Punic War to Africa a half-century later.

The Carthaginians, who had suffered negligible losses, were undoubtedly elated, but only temporarily. The Romans had readied a fleet to blockade Carthage at sea while Regulus invested it by land. Events having overtaken that plan, the fleet was now sent to rescue the remnants of the Roman invasion force. The Carthaginians intercepted the armada off Cape Bon,[43] only to lose 114 ships, many of them driven ashore and captured by the Roman grappling tactics—their fifth naval defeat of the war.

Carthage had not done well; nearly a decade of fighting had brought little but futility. The city was no longer under threat, but the fleet was shattered and it would be five years before we would hear of renewed operations at sea.[44] Carthaginian warships and seamanship were plainly superior, but in the massed engagements close to shore that had been typical of this conflict, there was little opportunity to apply these advantages. Instead the Carthaginians found themselves boarded and their vessels captured, and in such circumstances it can be presumed that the Roman marines were not gentle. This along with drowning must have led to many thousands of casualties. All aboard were probably not citizens, but the toll on the city's male population must have been heavy. It was fortunate for Carthage that, unlike during much of the war with Hannibal, prisoners of this conflict were frequently ransomed; therefore, many men were probably able to return to their homes. Still, the city's demographics must have been significantly affected. Carthage remained enormously wealthy, and could afford to reinforce and rebuild its mercenary land forces in Sicily at least five times during the war.[45] Yet the naval fleet was a precious asset, and if it were decimated, Carthage could not win this type of conflict.

Meanwhile the Romans were also being swamped by fate, discovering that while at sea, seamanship did matter. After picking up the remnants of Regulus's Afrika Korps, they ran into a sudden storm off Camarina on the south coast of Sicily. Probably already riding low in the bow from the weight of their crows, the war galleys didn't stand a chance against the heavy seas and rocky shores. Of 364 ships, Polybius (1.37.2) says, only 80 survived, and he calls it the greatest naval catastrophe in history. His words still stand; there is simply no modern equivalent. More than one hundred thousand Romans and Italians likely drowned—twice the number of dead at Cannae. That number may have amounted to 15 percent of all the military manpower in Italy.[46]

But if the Romans were discouraged, they didn't show it. Instead, they voted the two consuls in charge triumphs for the victory at Cape Bon, and set about rebuilding the fleet. By the spring of 254, they may have had as many as three hundred ships and were looking for trouble.[47]

They found it. After establishing superiority in Sicilian waters, they were back in Africa raiding the coast. While the Carthaginians failed to challenge them, the tides did, beaching the fleet until they managed to break free by jettisoning everything heavy, including presumably their spoils. Disconcerted, the Romans left in a hurry, and the commander Sempronius Blaesus compounded his problems by attempting an open sea return to Italy, during which he ran into another storm off Cape Palinurus in Lucania that cost him more than 150 ships. He too was voted a triumph, but for the next few years Romans cut back their operations and regrouped.

The year 249 found them blockading Lilybaeum, one of the last Carthaginian bases in Sicily, but none too successfully, since elements of the renascent Punic fleet stationed nearby at Drepana had repeatedly relieved it. The new consul, Publius Claudius Pulcher, rashly intent on eliminating this nuisance, sailed north at midnight aiming to surprise the Carthaginian commander Adherbal. The Punic fleet

barely cleared the harbor, but once in open waters was at last able to effectively apply its superior crews and equipment against the Romans,
who appear to have given up their crows and who ended up losing 93
out of 123 of their ships. And that was just the beginning. The other
consul, L. Iunius Pullus, was leading a convoy of eight hundred transports and 120 warships to resupply the troops at Lilybaeum, when he
was intercepted by a smaller Carthaginian squadron under Carthalo.
Without ever actually engaging, the Carthaginian admiral forced the
Roman fleet's two detachments close to the rugged shore, and then, an-
ticipating a storm, he ducked behind Cape Pachynon, leaving the Romans facing the full fury of the squall. Before the storm was over the
Roman navy had virtually ceased to exist.

Carthage had found an ally in Mother Nature, and she proved by far
the more effective killer, probably accounting for in excess of two hundred thousand Roman and allied drowned in the three great storms off
Camarina, Cape Palinurus, and now Cape Pachynon. Too exhausted to
reconstitute the fleet, the Romans were still not about to quit. Instead
they appointed a dictator, resumed ground force operations in Sicily,
and bided their time. Their adversaries, on the other hand, seemed to
have reached a strategic fork in the road.

Back home, beginning around 248, the Carthaginians appear to have
dealt directly with native unrest, waging war against the Numidians
and Libyans until the Carthaginians controlled a band 160 miles
deep—an Africa-first policy that came to be associated with the general and politician Hanno "the Great."[48] Just what this said about
Carthage's willingness to continue the war with Rome is hard to specify, but the effort is bound to have drawn resources away from it. Meanwhile, Hanno would remain in the eyes of the ancient sources the focal
point of those who believed that Carthage's best future was in its agricultural heartland. As such, Hanno became the great antagonist of
Hannibal's family and the skeptic of their subsequent overseas adventures.

Both were taking shape toward the end of 248, with Hannibal's own
birth and his father's arrival in Sicily.[49] Sometime earlier Hannibal's father, Hamilcar, had picked up the nickname Barca ("Thunderbolt"); it
certainly suited him and the rest of his clan. Unpredictable and lethal,
that is the way they would be remembered by history, as Barcids, carrying a last name in a society without them.[50] Hamilcar's aggressiveness made him a most un-Carthaginian general. He was sent to relieve

the more cautious Carthalo, and his first operation was a raid on Italy, ravaging the coast around Locri. This was the first installment in what would become a family saga of bringing war to the enemy's doorstep.[51] Back in Sicily, he established himself at Hercte, a high promontory above the sea, and began waging a guerilla campaign, striking like summer lightning the northwest coast of Sicily, and Italy as far up as Cumae. After three years he suddenly shifted thirty-five miles farther west to Eryx, where he held out for two more years between two Roman forces, resisting their every attempt to get rid of him. Polybius considered him the best commander on either side, but Hamilcar was plainly just holding on, starved for resources, hoping the Romans would give up first.

That was not about to happen. In late 243 the Romans decided to break the stalemate by building another fleet. But since the state lacked the cash, the endeavor had to be financed by leading private citizens— one, two, or three to a ship—asking to be reimbursed only if things went according to plan. This was an impetuous but characteristic act of faith and determination, especially considering the fate of previous Roman armadas.[52] All two hundred of the new quinqueremes were modeled on a particularly fast captured Carthaginian galley, and the Roman crews were exercised relentlessly in Sicily during the year 242 by the consul in charge, C. Lutatius Catulus. They had plenty of time to train, since the Carthaginians were slow to send out a fleet against them, a laggard nine-month response that points to trouble in raising the oarsmen necessary to crew their fleet of 250 warships.

At last the Carthaginians sailed in early March 241, intent on joining up with Hamilcar, who had been cut off from resupply by the Roman fleet. Instead Catulus intercepted them in heavy seas off the aptly named Aegates (Goat) Islands. Their ships weighed down with provisions and rowed by inexperienced crews, the Carthaginians were swamped, quite literally. Polybius (1.61.6–8) puts their losses at 120 ships, with 50 sunk, but refers to only ten thousand actual prisoners. (Diodorus 24.11.1–2 puts the figure still lower, at six thousand.) Given the weather conditions, this implies that at least fifteen thousand drowned, and possibly a great many more. It is also conceivable that their fleet was simply undermanned. In either case, it is apparent that the Carthaginians had reached the end of the line in terms of human resources.

Almost immediately the authorities at home gave the now hopelessly marooned Hamilcar full authority to negotiate a peace with the Romans. It was a mistake. Anxious to distance himself from any admission of defeat, Hamilcar worked through his subordinate Gesgo, who then bargained with Catulus to avoid having Hamilcar's army disarmed, which was another mistake.[53] Catulus, anxious to end the war on his watch, not only agreed to these terms, but imposed rather light conditions in other respects. Basically, Carthage had to evacuate Sicily; give up all Roman prisoners, while ransoming their own; and pay an indemnity of around 112,000 pounds of silver during the next twenty years. (This indemnity was later raised to 163,000 pounds over ten years, with 51,000 payable immediately.) The deal having been struck, Hamilcar marched his forces to Lilybaeum, abandoned his command, and promptly sailed for home, leaving the hapless Gesgo with the unenviable task of demobilizing twenty thousand mercenaries long without pay. This was the biggest mistake of all. For Carthage the war may have been over, but the fighting was far from finished.

The First Punic War had been an epic struggle. As was the case with World War I, at the outbreak of hostilities neither side had had any idea what they were getting into. Both wars were also contests characterized by immense tactical futility and huge losses. The Roman death toll is remembered as proverbially huge by historians, but less attention is paid to the price Carthage paid, in large part because its fleets avoided the kinds of storms that probably killed almost everyone involved.[54] Still, Polybius (1.63.6) estimates that Carthage lost five hundred quinqueremes during the conflict. Even if most of these ships were captured and their crews were not entirely made up of its citizens, Roman marines were swordsmen trained to kill, and many of the survivors may have been sold into slavery rather than ransomed. Altogether, it adds up to a lot of potentially missing Carthaginians.

And this was not a society well suited to warfare. During the long course of the conflict it had been the Romans who had taken all the initiatives to actually win—building a fleet and invading Africa. The Carthaginians, it seems, had fought mostly to persevere. With rare exception, they had failed to effectively apply their fleet, and from this point, Punic naval power would remain permanently depleted.[55] Wealth had bought endurance in the form of successive mercenary forces, but in the end this beast would turn upon its master in the most disastrous way, not simply biting the hand that fed it but going for the throat.

[5]

Forsaken by Hamilcar, who had apparently filled their heads with empty promises, the twenty-thousand-man force he left in Sicily can be presumed to have been in a foul mood, one only temporarily mollified by Gesgo, who at least had the sense to send them back to Africa in small groups on a staggered schedule to be paid off.[56] Had this been done promptly, each element might have been repatriated safely. Instead, apparently hoping to strike a better deal, the Carthaginians refused to put up any cash until all the mercenaries had arrived, a blunder of the first order. Having congregated and once again been put off, this time by Hanno "the Great," all twenty thousand marched on Carthage. Upon realizing just how frightening they were to their former employers, the mercenaries raised the ante repeatedly.

Worse followed, much worse. When the Libyan contingent became enraged and seized the unfortunate Gesgo, who had been trying to pay them, the whole force went into open revolt. This in turn led the Libyan peasantry, whose taxes had grown ever more burdensome during the war with Rome, to join the mercenaries. Many of the Numidian princes, who had been struggling against Punic domination over the previous decade, followed, and very soon Carthage faced an army many times the size of the one that had been led by Regulus. Once again the city revealed its terrible vulnerability on home soil.

This conflict would last more than three years until at least the end of 238 B.C., and in the words of Polybius (1.88.7), this struggle "far excelled all wars we know of in cruelty and defiance of principle." Beset by a sea of mercenaries, Carthage had trouble hiring more but eventually managed to put together a combination of Punic citizens and loyal local hirelings with no affinity to the veterans from Sicily, though the force was heavily outnumbered and lacking in experience compared to their adversaries. The imbalance was compounded by a leadership struggle at the top. Hanno, who proved to be a good organizer but was less competent in the field, found himself sharing command with Hamilcar Barca, a far better soldier. The two, already likely to have been political antagonists, did not play well together, and eventually Hanno would be forced to resign, but not before operations had been compromised.[57]

Fortunately for Carthage, the enemy was a body without much of a brain, and Hamilcar, applying his martial skills in ways not evident even in Sicily, consistently flummoxed the larger rebel forces, who responded with senseless acts of cruelty like dismembering Gesgo and his fellow hostages. At times Barca used diplomacy, winning over the Numidian Navaras and his forces, then rewarding him with marriage to his daughter. But for the most part he showed himself every bit the rebels' equal in atrocity, ordering captive mercenaries stomped to death by his elephants, and crucifying their leaders once their forces collapsed.

Observing from across the Mediterranean, the Romans, who disliked deserters even more than they disliked Carthaginians, were initially scrupulously fair, banning their merchants from trading with the mercenaries, and even returning the remaining Punic POWs free of charge. Then, around 240 B.C., temptation appeared on the Carthage-held island of Sardinia, where a group of Carthage's foreign hirelings seized the chaotic moment, murdered their officers, and Mamertine-like petitioned Rome for help. The Romans had wanted the island since building a fleet but had played coy until the locals ousted the mercenary mutineers, who fled to Italy and again propositioned the senate.[58] This time the Romans cast their scruples aside and voted to send an expedition to Sardinia, and when the Carthaginians protested, declared war on them. In no condition to fight, acquiescence cost Carthage not only Sardinia but an additional sixty-one thousand pounds of silver.

It was a defining act and a defining moment. Rome in effect had kicked Carthage when it was down. Few modern historians disagree with Polybius's (3.10.4) judgment that this episode did not simply further embitter Carthaginians but was a principle cause of the second war with Rome. The circumstances argue that Hamilcar and the Barcid clan were particularly outraged and held the grudge as long as they could hold a sword.

Conjuring what must have been the tumultuous political atmosphere of Carthage in 237 B.C. is a problematic endeavor, based essentially on scraps. Yet certain elements do emerge from the mists of time looking more like realities than apparitions. There was bound to have been widespread dissatisfaction concerning the events of the recent past, with the fingers of blame pointing in more than one direction. Also, we can make out two distinct factions, one led by Hanno the Great and the other by Hamilcar Barca.

Our own vision of the former has been clouded by Gustave Flaubert's portrait in the flamboyant historical novel *Salammbô*. Hanno is portrayed as ulcerous, obese—eating flamingo tongues and drinking viper broth, a repulsive creature whose cowardice is exceeded only by his cruelty. The real Hanno was no caricature. Granted, Livy plainly uses him as a foil to Barcid ambitions, but Hanno does seem to have had a good sense of power realities. His vision of "Africa first" and commercialized agriculture was a plausible future for the state. Still, he plainly represented the oligarchy that had presumably mismanaged the lost war with Rome, and he was personally associated with the policy of heavy taxation that had caused the Libyans to join the mercenaries in rebellion.[59] At this point, both his reputation and his style of government must have been open to challenge.

Yet skepticism of Hanno did not necessarily translate into approval for Barca. After all, it was Hamilcar's original abandonment of his forces that had led directly to their disastrous mutiny. Nor were his earlier desire to continue resistance in Sicily and his general intransigence toward Rome necessarily popular with an exhausted and depleted Carthage. Indeed, Appian tells a story of Hamilcar threatened with being brought to trial over his conduct in Sicily.[60] Still, of the two, Barca seems to have been the more resourceful and resilient.

It stands to reason that opposition to the oligarchy's recent record would have been located in the assembly of the people, and here one Hasdrubal the Handsome seems to have held sway—"the lord of the Carthaginian streets," Diodorus (25.8) calls him. It was this politician with whom Hamilcar forged a tight alliance, making him his son-in-law and possibly his lover.[61] Some have seen the stirrings of democracy in this pairing, but this seems like a stretch. More likely, it was motivated by a general dissatisfaction with contemporary events and, in the case of these two, mutual self-interest. Hasdrubal was young and apparently ambitious. Hamilcar had a plan and needed a command. The people elected the generals.

It was a marriage made ... if not in heaven, at least in Carthage, and then the happy couple would honeymoon in the south of Spain, the fabled land of silver mines, and make everybody rich—or at least rich enough to pay off the Romans. Compared to this scenario, Hanno and agribusiness must have sounded pretty stodgy, and the scenario's appeal is testified to by Hamilcar's apparently having left for Spain almost immediately, bringing his son-in-law with him.[62]

Before departing, however, Barca did several things that had immense significance for the future. No doubt careful to follow the rituals of a very religious place, Hamilcar performed a customary sacrifice,
probably to Ba'al Shamim, after which he requested a moment of pri-
vacy with his nine-year-old son. Hamilcar asked him if he would like
to come to Spain. The boy begged to be included, at which point the
father took him to the altar, placed his hand on the sacrificed carcass,
and made him swear an oath of eternal enmity toward the Romans.[63]
The son, of course, was Hannibal, and he told the story to Antiochus,
the Seleucid emperor, four decades later as evidence of his loyalty and
commitment to fighting the Romans. It's a melodramatic tale, but none
of the ancient sources, and few modern historians, doubt its veracity. If
there was one thing that bound the Barcids, it was a hatred of Rome.

The recent struggle with the mercenaries also seemed to have encouraged Hamilcar to value fidelity. The army he brought to Spain was
no Carthaginian rent-a-force; instead, the timing argues that he never
disbanded the elements he'd used to destroy the rebels. More to the
point, it appears he marched the army across North Africa, crossing to
Iberia at the Pillars of Hercules.[64] Possibly Carthage simply lacked the
ships to transport the force, but this is unlikely. It was a trek nearly as
extended, though probably not as difficult, as Hannibal's eventual
march over the Alps, the kind of long haul that hardens and bonds an
army, a training exercise by which—like Hamilcar's earlier proclivity
to directly attack Italy—the father provided a precedent for the son.
The march also serves to illustrate what one historian calls the Barcids'
"landlubberly preference for action on terra firma," strangely at odds
with their country's maritime tradition.[65] In a very un-Carthaginian
way, the Barcids were all about land power, and this army, tempered on
the long march to Spain in 237 B.C., was to remain their personal implement of aggrandizement, a professional rather than a mercenary force,
continuously under arms until Scipio Africanus finally shattered it
nearly forty years later.

[6]

Southeastern Spain had been influenced by Phoenicians since the first
millennium B.C., when they had established emporiums on the shores
of Andalusia, but subsequent Greek pressure, particularly from the

city of Massilia (today's Marseilles), had narrowed the Phoenicians' sway. Gades (modern Cádiz) at least remained Punic-friendly, and it was here that Hamilcar landed within easy reach of the gold and silver mines of the Sierra Morena. It appears that among the first things he did was arrange for a steady supply of these precious metals to be sent back to Carthage, a move that must have bolstered his political standing at home.[66]

The next eight years were occupied with almost continuous campaigning as Hamilcar worked his way east, occupying the coast of southern Spain, and then penetrated up the valley of the Baetis River (modern Guadalquivir River) to seal this band of territory on the inland side. The Massiliotes watched this expansion with increasing distress, and Hamilcar finally drew the attention of their allies the Romans, who sent a delegation in 231, only to be blandly told that he was simply fighting to pay off Roman war indemnities. A clever answer, delivered far from their sphere of control, but the Romans were unlikely to have departed convinced of his goodwill.

Two years later he was dead, ambushed by a Celtiberian tribe, the Oretani. According to one tradition, he sacrificed himself so that Hannibal and his brother might escape. There is an anecdote recounted by Valerius Maximus (9.3.2) of Hamilcar, years earlier, watching his three boys—Hannibal, Hasdrubal, and Mago—engaged in rough play, and noting proudly, "These are the lion cubs I am rearing for the destruction of Rome!" Perhaps, but not yet. Hannibal, the oldest, was not yet twenty, too young to take over the family business; instead Hasdrubal the Handsome was elected by the army to run things in Spain, and then his position was ratified at home.

Exactly what was the nature of this enterprise in Spain—was it Barcid or Carthaginian? It's impossible to say definitively; the evidence is just too fragmentary. Those who argue that it was planned and directed as a matter of Carthaginian state policy can dismiss as inconclusive any indications of Barcid independence, especially in the face of a larger strategic vision of outflanking Rome and developing a replacement for lost holdings in Sicily and Sardinia.

Yet in detail this story looks unconvincing; what clues remain are covered with Barcid fingerprints. Polybius (3.8.1–4) cites Fabius Pictor as saying that Hasdrubal the Handsome, after Hamilcar's death, journeyed briefly to Carthage and tried to take over the government, and when this failed, he returned to Iberia and ruled "without paying any attention to the Carthaginian Senate." The trip may be in doubt, but the management style rings true.

Diodorus (25.12) tells us that the Spanish tribes proclaimed Hasdrubal *strategos autokrator,* the same title conferred on Alexander by the League of Corinth. This may not simply have been because Diodorus was a Greek and was used to such terminology. There was a very Hellenistic cast to the Barcid operation in Spain; after all, this was the Mediterranean basin's most successful model of how to move into a hinterland and rule. The Barcids were essentially soldiers and conquerors of a more traditional sort. As such, they represented an order of power different from what had been prevalent in Carthage, and more akin to the Greek despotism of the east. Then there is the matter of the money. We have two double shekel pieces attributed to Barcid Iberian mints of the era, depicting what are possibly Hamilcar and Hasdrubal. Both are represented as Hellenistic monarchs crowned with the royal diadem and laurel leaves.[67]

Hasdrubal certainly behaved like a contemporary *basileus,* marrying a local princess (as Alexander had in Asia and as Hannibal would do in the future), and scrupulously playing divide and rule among the local tribal chiefs. He also set up a metropolis, New Carthage (modern Cartagena), a huge palace-cum-fortress complex on a peninsula three hundred miles east of Gades, a site that commanded one of the best harbors in the world and was in the vicinity of rich silver mines. It would become Barca central—an arsenal, a treasure chest, and the nerve center of an operation that by all appearances bought the Barcids independence and assuaged the more timid souls at home through a steady stream of precious metals. All the while charting a course dictated by family priorities.

These priorities led east, for now only toward the river Ebro, with Hasdrubal advancing along the coast from New Carthage. The Romans, worried that he might try to link up with rebellious Ligurians and Gauls and always with a good sense of who was in charge, chose to deal directly with the Barcid rather than with the Carthaginian senate, sending out their ambassadors in 226.[68] They struck a deal. Hasdrubal would not cross the Ebro, and he may have been assured that the Romans would not interfere to the south.[69] At any rate it was a line in the sand, and apparently Hasdrubal spent the next five years consolidating behind it. Then he was dead, handsome Hasdrubal assassinated by an angry Celt; ironic, since he'd always been more the diplomat than the soldier. This would not be said of his successor.

By acclamation the army chose Hannibal, now twenty-six, as their leader. Livy (21.4.2) tells us "the old soldiers thought that Hamilcar had been restored to them . . . the same lively expression and piercing eye, the same cast of countenance and features." And, it might be added, the same agenda.

IV

HANNIBAL'S WAY

[1]

Hannibal is at the center of our story ... at the center of anybody's story of the Second Punic War. Yet historians complain that we are left with but the shadow cast by his deeds, that his character eludes us.[1] Besides the paternal compact against Rome, there are no revealing childish anecdotes—little Hannibal tricking his playmates, beguiling a stallion, or concocting something equivalently brave and enterprising—the kind of homey palaver the ancients typically used to delineate their subjects. Still, it is the province of a certain kind of genius to remain forever ineffable. In the modern idiom, think Ronald Reagan, FDR, Thomas Jefferson; being indescribable may have been the touchstone of Hannibal's endless tactical wizardry.

The personal details that do remain mostly form an image of a generic martial workaholic. Livy (21.4.1–8), eying him through the lens of his own country's military conventions, depicts him as a good man with a sword, fearless in combat, oblivious to physical discomfort, sleeping on the ground amidst his men, sharing their hardships, eating for sustenance, not pleasure. In other words, Hannibal was an ideal Roman commander, with an obligatory dose of villainy, being Rome's bête noire. Livy describes "inhuman cruelty, more than Punic perfidy, no truth, no reverence for things sacred, no fear of the gods ... etc." In fact, for a Carthaginian, Hannibal does not seem very religious. None of the Barcids do, though this may be partly a function of the evidence, or rather the lack of it. As far as cruelty, he did crucify one or more guides who misled him at critical junctures, and there was at least one instance when he may have ordered prisoners slaughtered,[2] but there is more than a little irony in any Roman claim of enemy cruelty. This was to be a brutal war, and there is little evidence that Hannibal was any less humane than his opponents. Rather, there is evidence that he treated his dead foes—or at least their commanders—with some chivalry, giving them decent burials, an approach starkly contrasted by C. Claudius Nero delivering to Hannibal the head of his brother Hasdrubal to announce the result of the Metaurus campaign.

Clearly Hannibal was no monster. Even Livy concedes that, and certainly Polybius does, indicting Hannibal with only avarice—a quality not necessarily a glaring vice for a man far from home with an army to feed. Sex was no apparent preoccupation. He married once, a Spanish chieftain's daughter named Imilce, and Pliny the Elder credits him with a later liaison with a prostitute in the southern Italian town of Salapia, an item of some civic pride even three centuries later.[3] There is no record of other lovers, either female or male. He appears to have had friends, albeit almost all of them soldiers. He was also approachable and willing to be criticized, most famously by the cavalryman Maharbal after Cannae: "You know how to win a victory, Hannibal, but you don't know how to use one."[4] But he could give as good as he got, and his gallows humor shines through many of the anecdotes told about him. Thus, before Cannae, when an officer named Gisgo fretted over how amazingly numerous the Roman army appeared, Hannibal replied that there was something even more amazing: "In all this multitude there is no one who is called Gisgo." On the occasion of Tarentum's surprise fall, though nonplussed he remarked to the effect that the Romans must have gotten their own Hannibal.[5]

There is little doubt that this was a sane, even psychologically healthy, individual. A comparison to the murderous paranoia of Alexander, or to the incestuous dynastic scheming of the Hellenistic monarchs of the day, makes this still more apparent. Rather than manifesting jealousy at his brother-in-law Hasdrubal's succession, Hannibal gave every appearance of having won his complete trust as a subordinate.[6] Nor was there the slightest hint of sibling rivalry among the Barcid boys; without exception, to the day of their deaths both Hasdrubal and Mago pursued the interests of their brother—a family monolith, indivisible, in effect "all the fine young Hannibals."

Culturally, however, Hannibal was something of a changeling; for he was deeply Hellenized, and this is a real point of comparison with Alexander. Like the Macedonian, Hannibal had been tutored by Greeks, he spoke the language fluently, and he had a deep knowledge of their contemporary military practices and battle history. And also,

like the conqueror of the Persians, Hannibal embarked on his great expedition armed with Greek historians to capture what transpired. This
is suggestive. Alexander the Great was not simply the age's most brilliant captain; he exemplified heroic achievement in the Mediterranean
basin. The ancients—or their rulers, at least—lived in order to be remembered, and of all pursuits, military glory was the most indelible. If
there was a romantic side to Hannibal, it is to be found here. His epic
journey across the Alps, his vengeful pursuit of Rome, his brilliant set-
piece victories, his seemingly endless anabasis on the Italic peninsula,
all find their symbolic analogue in the Macedonian's payback for the
Persian invasion of Greece and in Alexander's subsequent adventures
in Asia. It makes sense that this was the emotional wellspring from
which Hannibal gained sustenance and endurance, especially as the
years passed and the goal grew ever fainter.

But if ultimately the source of Hannibal's strategic imagination
must remain a matter of speculation, his operational and tactical skills
are beyond dispute. At this level Hannibal was among the best military
commanders who ever lived. For sixteen campaigning seasons in Italy
he demonstrated an ingenuity and consistency that has never been sur-
passed, losing not one significant battle, and on five separate occasions
effectively obliterating major Roman field forces.[7] His capacity for
trickery was endless. Whether escaping from an apparently hopeless
trap, or springing one on a hapless foe, he always seemed to concoct the
unexpected and employ it to his own best advantage. In the case of the
Romans, he proved particularly adroit in maneuvers prior to battle,
turning their instinctive aggressiveness against them and fighting only
when and where he, not they, chose.[8]

Without doubt he possessed the best army that ever fought under a
Carthaginian standard, but his troops won in large part because Hannibal was their leader. Not only was he a master at using each combat
component to maximum advantage, but it is evident that his inspirational example was central to elevating the performance of all. During
the entire time they were together in Italy, immersed in what frequently must have amounted to a litany of privation, there was not a
single incident of truly mutinous behavior—an amazing record for any
Carthaginian army, and one that Scipio Africanus and the notoriously
well-disciplined Romans could not match.

He had their complete trust, but he'd earned it. It has been argued
that Hannibal lacked the patience for sieges, but there was seldom an

occasion in Italy when he could have sat down to wage such an attack without jeopardizing the safety of his troops. They were always his most precious asset, essentially irreplaceable, so he never allowed himself to be pinned down, never wasted them in fights without purpose, never relied on sheer force of numbers when there was an alternative. At one point Livy has him say: "Many things which are difficult in themselves, are easily effected by contrivance."[9] This was the tactical Hannibal in a nutshell. In the Middle Ages the phrase might have graced his escutcheon. One of his best modern commentators, J. F. Lazenby, compares Hannibal to "a boxer, faced by a heavier opponent he feinted, weaved and dodged, and kept out of range—but his punch was devastating when he saw his chance."[10] If anybody could make an army "float like a butterfly, sting like a bee," it was Hannibal.

But it was not enough. Talented he may have been, but taking on Rome was a far different proposition from Alexander taking on Persia. And had his strategic intellect matched his tactical wits, he would have grasped this critical point in an instant. Twenty-three years of the First Punic War was a stark monument to the magnitude of Rome's determination and resources. Meanwhile, Carthage, militarily at least, was exhausted; realistically the best Hannibal could have hoped for from this quarter was lukewarm support bought with Spanish silver. At least at the beginning of the first contest, Carthaginians had had reason to hope that in a war fought for an island, their fleet might prove decisive over a state without one; but now Hannibal proposed to attack Rome literally on home turf, trying to overcome the source of the city's greatest strength, land power. Hannibal had reason to believe in himself and his army, and he can be excused for underestimating the strength of Italy's alliance structure, but this invasion had no logical end to it. We shall see that there was a single moment after Cannae when he might have seized victory, but he couldn't have known about that prior to setting off across the Alps. Instead, the recent past should have told him not to try it.

It has been argued that the Romans never would have allowed Carthaginians to remain dominant in Spain, and would have continued interfering there until Hannibal had had no choice but to fight.[11] Rome's alliance with Saguntum (a locality well south of the Ebro line of 226 B.C.) and the Romans' later ultimatum to Hannibal not to interfere there certainly point in this direction. Since it was only a matter of time, why not make war on their territory and not his? This does seem to be a reasonable projection of Rome's strategic trajectory. Yet at this point Spain was far from Italy, and there were much more pressing problems closer to home. Hannibal could have waited, could have concentrated on further expanding and consolidating in Iberian areas not sensitive to the Romans, a resort to "salami tactics," as it's now sometimes called.[12] But he gave little impression that he ever considered *not* going to war with Rome. An invasion of Italy was the best way of doing it, but that didn't make it ultimately a good idea. So, rather than being guided by a cold assessment of his chances, it seems more likely that his vision was colored or even clouded by an Alexandrian dream of conquest for its own sake and for the great and still growing family grudge against Rome. And these motivations, in turn, led to some questionable choices in friends.

[2]

If Romans harbored a national nightmare, it was the Gauls, their Celtic neighbors. Since the traumatic sacking of their capital in 390, the Gauls had persisted in their sudden spoils-driven incursions into Roman territory, a succession of predatory raids meticulously tallied by Polybius (2.18–21), who seems to have understood their traumatic cumulative effect.

For the Romans, the Gauls had come to symbolize irrationality, violence, and disorder in ways that would have given Freudians, had they had the opportunity to set up shop on the Tiber, a field day. Given the degree of significance they invested in individual military prepotency, it was no trivial matter that Romans obsessed over their short stature in comparison to Gallic warriors.[13] And the Gauls' size was compounded by a notably frightful appearance—lime-washed spiked hair, muscular torsos naked to the waist wielding elongated slashing swords—and demonic battlefield zeal, usually described in the most lurid terms. They rushed at their adversaries "like wild beasts," full of "blind fury," persisting in their attacks "even with arrows and javelins sticking through them."[14]

While these were clearly stereotypes, there is little reason to doubt their basis in fact, or to doubt the head-hunting proclivities of Celtic warriors. The profile was accompanied by recognized and equivalently generic weaknesses—drunkenness, lack of endurance, sensitivity to heat, tendency toward panic, mindless indiscipline—but still adds up to a very frightening specter if it was bearing down on your legion or your homeland. At least that's the way the Romans saw it, an ever-aggressive barbarian menace.

Actually, Rome had turned the tables on the tormentors. Gradually the victims had taken the offense, reprisals had morphed into conquest, and the Gauls had become convinced that, in the words of Polybius (2.21.9), "now the Romans no longer made war on them for the sake of supremacy and sovereignty, but with a view towards their total expulsion and extermination."

The Gauls were part of a broad band of Celtic-speaking tribal cultures stretching from central Europe into northern Italy through the Alps, north into the Low Countries, across France, and then into central and western Spain. The tribes were pre-state chiefdoms basically dependent on agriculture, and they appear to have been dominated by a distinct warrior class comprising both nobles and commoners who also existed as itinerant fighters. As such, these tribes were a floating body of potential mercenaries who could very quickly coalesce into large, if inchoate, force structures of the kind that had traditionally bedeviled the Romans. Militarily they represented a range of skills, with up to a third being noble equestrians, mostly heavy cavalry and some charioteers, and the remainder an undifferentiated mass of pedestrian swordsmen.[15] All were very aggressive in combat, fighting essentially as individuals. The frenzied behavior—screams, wild gesticulations, and war dances—that so appalled the Romans would be recognized by modern anthropologists as rather typical of warrior cultures. Such fighters could be incorporated into the force structures of more advanced societies—the Carthaginians plainly did so during the First Punic War and after, but it remains unclear whether Carthage had been compelled to employ them fighting in their traditional manner or had been able to shape them into specialized units.[16] Arguably, the transition from traditional fighters to specialized units enabled Hannibal to gain a key advantage at Cannae, but for the moment the Celts that most worried the Romans marched along a time-honored warpath.

After the Gauls' attack in 390, serious unrest recommenced in 338 B.C., when the Boii stirred up local tribes and some Transalpine warriors to attack Ariminum (modern Rimini), settled three decades earlier as part of the Roman incursion on behalf of the land-hungry poor, into the fertile plains of northern Italy, which they called

Cisalpine Gaul. Gallic bickering soon blunted this attempt, but two years later continuing problems with the Boii forced Rome to send an army to restore order.[17] The trouble had just begun. In 232, Caius Flaminius, the farmers' friend and Hannibal's eventual victim at Lake Trasimene, pushed through a law as a tribune to parcel out captured Gallic lands to poor citizens in small plots rather than sending them out in concentrated colonies, thereby inviting a deluge of Romans.

Inevitably, the anger of the dispossessed Celts boiled over. In the spring of 225, Boii from around what is now Bologna, Insubres from the area of present-day Milan, and Taurini from the Piedmont were joined by a band of itinerant warriors from the Alps, the Gaesatae, to self-organize into a host seventy thousand strong, which then poured through the Apennine passes and fell upon Etruria, the rich area in the northeast high on Italy's boot. Shades of the devastating attack on Rome in 390—the Gauls were laden with booty and were just three days' march from the panic-struck city—only this time they chose to withdraw in the face of the four legions of consul L. Aemilius Papus that were heading north to intercept them. Unfortunately, the Gauls ran into another double consular army headed by C. Atilius Regulus, hastily recalled from Sardinia. At Telamon, trapped between the two jaws of what was the biggest force the Romans had ever accumulated prior to Cannae, the Gauls were forced to form lines back-to-back and fight for their lives. It was a desperate encounter that saw the severed head of Regulus delivered to one of the Celtic chiefs, but at the end of the day, forty thousand of the invaders lay dead and another ten thousand were taken prisoner by the Romans.[18]

The emergency was over, but Rome was far from finished with the Gauls. The next year both new consuls descended on the Boii with armies and forced their submission. In 224, it was more of the same, with now-consul Flaminius and his colleague Publius Furious both moving into the tribal territories of the Insubres and Cenomani. Here Flaminius won a great victory over a combined force of around forty-thousand Gauls, a victory featuring an on-the-spot tactical innovation that has recently stirred up some scholarly controversy. Being backed up against a river—a bad habit of Flaminius's—his tribunes gave the maniples of the first line the spears of the *triarii,* the idea being to keep the Gauls and their long slashing swords at bay during their initial charge. It worked, and Polybius (2.33.1–6) is clear that the legionaries subsequently finished matters with their short swords. Modern historian Martin Samuels, however, arguing that the Greek historian was confused about the legionary's equipment at this point, uses this passage to indicate that all fought primarily with long thrusting spears, both here and seven years later at Cannae.[19] While Samuels' points about the Roman army are interesting in other respects, this argument is just not convincing, given Polybius's general reliability and knowledge of military detail. We can rest assured the Romans fought with the *gladius* at Cannae, and meanwhile would continue using them to kill Celts.

Thoroughly battered, in 222 the Gauls sued for peace. But the senate spurned their offer and instead sent both consuls with armies to throttle them still again. At Clastidium, one of the consuls, Marcus Claudius Marcellus, single-handedly killed and stripped the armor from the Gallic chief Britomarus, winning the *spolia opima,* immortality of the most Roman sort. His colleague, Cn. Cornelius Scipio, was also gainfully employed, successfully storming the site of modern Milan and the capital of the Insubres. Both were now made men, especially Marcellus, destined to play major roles and to die fighting in the Second Punic War. Yet again the tribes surrendered and were stripped of more land. Rome's response was to push farther north, in 218 planting colonies of six thousand each at Placentia and Cremona on either side of the Po River, still further inflaming Gallic resentment.[20]

This anger would prove to be a magnet for Hannibal, providing a ready source of allies, supplies, and fresh bodies when he and his army spilled off the Alps, depleted and hungry. The potential for an amalgam with the restive tribes of Cisalpine Gaul was a brilliant insight and was the basis for his decision to invade Italy by land from the north. The Gauls were essentially the pot of gold at the end of his long journey.[21] Yet no prize comes without its cost. It has been said that Hannibal's objectives in Italy were limited, but an affiliation with the Gauls could only have served to convince the Romans of the opposite. These were not ordinary foes. The Gauls represented something altogether more frightening and dangerous to the Roman soul, and by joining them, Hannibal took on an onus that would serve to define the coming conflict in the starkest possible terms. So it was that what we refer to as the Second Punic War was frequently called by the Romans "the war against the Carthaginians and the Gauls."[22]

[3]

In the winter of 219, Hannibal arrived in New Carthage, awaited by envoys from Rome who warned him not to interfere in a dispute between their ally Saguntum and local tribes, and also reminded him not to cross the Ebro line of 226. The fact that the Romans had chosen to align themselves with a city well to the south of this line, and then had taken up for the city in a dispute with Carthage, not only echoed the Mamertine episode that had kicked off the First Punic War, but exemplified Rome's characteristic pattern of defensive aggression.

Hannibal must have known what this implied. Most modern historians follow Polybius and Appian in saying that Hannibal thought it necessary to send home for instructions, though he prejudiced the case by presenting the situation as the Romans and Saguntines inciting Carthaginian Spain to revolt.[23] Having apparently received permission to do what he saw fit, Hannibal attacked Saguntum, taking it after a brutal eight-month assault that left the adult population massacred and a good quantity of the copious loot in Carthage as a matter of public relations.

Yet the Roman historian and senior senator at the time, Fabius Pictor, disagreed completely. He argued that Hannibal began the war on his own initiative, and that not a single one of the notables in Carthage approved of his conduct toward Saguntum.[24] If "notables" meant the traditional oligarchs, then Hanno's impassioned speech against the war, cited by Livy (21.10), very probably represented more than a lonely voice in the political wilderness. "Is it your enemy you know not, or yourselves, or the fortunes of both peoples? . . . It is Carthage against which Hannibal is now bringing up his . . . towers; it is the walls of Carthage he is battering with his rams. Saguntum's walls—may my prophecy prove false!—will fall upon our heads."

But the delegation of high-ranking Romans sent to Carthage was demanding as the price of peace the surrender of Hannibal and his senior officers for trial as war criminals, a bribe that was at once infuriating and possibly beyond the Punic capacity to deliver. So when the most senior Roman—Livy (21.18.1) tells us it was Fabius Maximus— eventually announced that in the folds of his toga he held both war and peace and it was up to the Carthaginians to choose, the presiding suffete told him to do so instead. Fabius replied that war fell out, and a shout rang out in response: "We accept it!" From all appearances this was hardly what we might call a measured deliberation. Quite probably it was a decision also lubricated with Barcid silver and success with the popular faction, but the real story was that Carthage had not fully recovered from the first struggle with Rome and was unable and ultimately unwilling to throw its full weight behind a second.

Back in Spain, Hannibal was not sitting on his hands awaiting a decision from Carthage. Instead, he was expecting word from the agents he had sent forward, possibly even before Saguntum's fall, to explore the proposed route into Italy and to make contact with the tribes of Cisalpine Gaul.[25] When the emissaries returned to assure him that the passage over the Alps, while difficult, was possible and that he would be welcomed upon arrival, the invasion was a go.

Meanwhile, he had been using the winter of 219–18 to make all the key decisions, not just planning for the expeditionary force, but seeing to the defense of Spain and even Africa. He was a man very much in charge of events. An early cross-baser—cross-basing being the means by which the Romans later successfully garrisoned their empire— Hannibal sent a force of nearly sixteen thousand Iberians to guard the vulnerable African home front, and brought an equivalent number of reliable Libyans, Numidians, and Liby-Phoenicians to Spain and placed them under brother Hasdrubal to keep watch over Barcid land.[26]

Yet most of his efforts must have been devoted to putting together his land armada, an apparently bloated entity of ninety thousand infantry and twelve thousand cavalry, along with thirty-seven elephants—really a force within a force.[27] This was probably deliberate. Most were likely to have been recently recruited Spaniards— Iberians, Lusitanians, and Celtiberians—raw but potentially good close order horse and foot soldiers; but at the core was the army initially forged by Hamilcar, veteran professionals—wickedly effective Numidian light cavalry and meticulously trained African heavy infantry, the centerpieces in all of Hannibal's future tactical shenanigans. Italy was a long way off, and much as his father had done on the way to Spain, Hannibal it seems meant to use the trek to train and toughen his force into the steely instrument he would need to take on Rome. He must have foreseen that this would be a Darwinian exercise, with many falling by the wayside or off icy cliffs in the Alps, though he may have underestimated the wastage. His African troops in particular were not likely to be tolerant of the cold weather at altitude. Still we can assume from this initial force structure that he believed that most of his veterans would survive the journey and that the newbie Spaniards who remained from the expendable outer layer would arrive as tough as the rest.

Hannibal was already bound to his veterans in a way no prior Carthaginian general could claim; he had not only lived with them and fought with them, he had literally grown up with them. Yet the march to Italy would prove the first great test of his leadership. There were multiple initial challenges, but in the Alps there was a real possibility of total disintegration. He rose to the occasion, but it was a near thing, and he probably completed the journey also transformed, tempered by danger and driven by a new sense of ruthless desperation.

He was not alone, never alone. Relatively little is known about the officers and unit commanders who left with him on the great adventure, but as with many other illustrious captains, they appear to have been a close group of friends and family, and with few exceptions they appear to have stayed with him for the duration.[28] As is appropriate for a "brotherhood of arms," his youngest brother, Mago, acted as his right hand at Trebia and as his virtual co-commander at Cannae. Another Barcid, nephew Hanno—the son of the admiral Bomilcar and Hannibal's sister—though barely an adult, may have led the Numidian cavalry at Cannae. Another Hasdrubal, not the brother Hasdrubal who was left in charge in Spain, was known to have headed the army service corps, and as commander of the Celtic and Spanish cavalry at Cannae, he closed the final escape route on the Romans. Then there was the cheeky critic of Hannibal's strategic sense, the brilliantly opportunistic commander of horse, Maharbal, whom Plutarch calls a Barcid.[29] Polybius (9.24.5–6; 9.25) identifies two other officers, Hannibal Monomachus and Mago the Samnite, as particularly good friends, and certainly as tough customers—the former advising his namesake to teach his men to eat human flesh to get through the Alps, and the latter so notoriously greedy that even Hannibal avoided disputes with him over spoils.

Together this group seems to have formed an inner circle of advisors—a general staff, if such a thing can be applied to a decision-making process about which so little is known. Several others are named—Carthalo, an officer whose light cavalry captured two thousand fugitive Romans after Cannae; Gisgo, who worried about the size of the Roman army before the battle; Adherbal, chief of engineers; Bostar and Bomilcar, apparently aides.[30] The remains of this group are obviously skeletal, an archaeology of bits and pieces, with no individual besides Hannibal even remotely taking shape as a personality. Yet corporately, they formed a cadre brilliantly attuned to their commander's intent, instinctively carrying out his will with a timing that could only have come from complete and mutual trust. Without them Hannibal never would have made it to Italy, and with them, once there, he would win victory after victory.

[4]

He had a narrow window of time to arrive; the Alpine passes close down with snow and ice by mid-November. Conventional wisdom has it that he would have wanted to leave New Carthage in the early spring, but it seems more likely he had to wait until late May or early June. Once he left Barca land, his army would have had to forage, and the harvest would have begun to become available during this time frame, and progressively later as he moved north.[31] This was to be a continuing theme for the entire war. Hannibal's army would move or not move according to the rumbling of its stomach, and as much as anything else, the Romans' understanding and manipulation of this most unrelenting fact of life would save them from defeat. A soldier on the march burns between four and five thousand calories a day, or between two and three pounds of food; for an army of fifty thousand that meant over sixty tons daily, and Hannibal's initial force would have required more than twice that amount, plus forage for thousands of cavalry horses and pack mules—quite literally a tall order.[32] For the initial 280-mile march to the Ebro, there were probably supply dumps, but once they passed this point, Hannibal and friends were on their own. This was their Rubicon.

It was here, Livy reports (21.22.8–9) that the aspiring conqueror dreamed of a ghostly youth sent as a guide. The apparition told Hannibal to follow him and not look back. However, like Lot's wife, the mortal could not resist. He turned to discover an immense serpent amidst thunderclaps tearing up the landscape, and when he inquired what this meant, he was told "that it was the devastation of Italy: that he should continue to advance forward, nor inquire further, but suffer the fates to remain in obscurity." Thus reassured, he headed off into the unknown.

But as he went, he apparently tried to create a buffer zone to the north by pacifying the tribes as far as the Pyrenees, stripping off an occupation force of ten thousand foot soldiers and a thousand horse under a certain Hanno (not his nephew) and also leaving him all the heavy baggage. Upon reaching the base of the Pyrenees, the army was more than half the distance to Italy but was still burdened by a considerable number of unhappy campers. During the ascent through the col de Perthus, an easy pass approximately twenty-six hundred feet high, a group of three thousand Spanish Carpentani mercenaries turned back toward home, apparently sending a thrill of apprehension through the entire army.[33] Hannibal's reaction was unpredictably mild; he not only made no attempt to stop them, but he also gave leave to another seven thousand he observed to be restless. There must have been another twenty thousand infantry and two thousand cavalry whose departure went unrecorded. Like a moon rocket shedding stages, Hannibal seems to have been consciously lightening his army for the tough road ahead. Polybius (3.35.7) tells us that, stripped of its malcontents and impedimenta, the remaining force entered coastal Gaul a much leaner fighting machine of fifty thousand foot soldiers and nine thousand horse.

Blocking the way near Perpignan was a confab of worried and potentially belligerent Gauls, uncertain of just what the appearance of this army of strangers implied. Anxious to avoid an unnecessary fight, Hannibal offered a barrage of gifts and assurances that he was just passing through, which won him a free march all the way to the Rhône. He followed the traditional route of what would become the Via Domitia and what is today the Languedoc coastal motorway, completing around seven hundred miles of the nine-hundred-mile journey and shedding another twelve thousand infantry and one thousand cavalry, possibly leaving them for garrison duty.[34] Here, on the banks of the Rhône, probably sometime past the middle of September, things got a lot more complicated.

Glowering from across the river at the point where he wanted to ford—Polybius (3.42.1) tells us it was about four days' march from the sea—was a concentration of particularly aggressive Celts, the Volcae, whose obvious intent was to dispute his passage. Hannibal's reaction was clever and also characteristic; after spending two days collecting boats and canoes, he sent a strong force of cavalry under his nephew Hanno approximately twenty miles north, to a point near what is today Avignon, where they crossed and headed back down to lie in wait behind the Celtic camp. Smoke-signaled that they were in place, Hannibal ordered his main body to begin the crossing, which drew the Gauls racing from their encampment to stop the foreigners at the riverbank. Instantly Hanno attacked from the rear, leaving the Volcae flabbergasted and fleeing for their lives as the Punic vanguard carved out a beachhead sufficient for the rest of the army to cross in safety. It was a signature Hannibalic move, and the surprise cavalry attack from the rear was destined to seal the doom of many Romans. The strategy also harkened back to a nearly identical flanking maneuver that Alexander had pulled off at the Hydaspes River (modern Jhelum River) a century earlier. The Punic commander's nearly endless bag of tricks was certainly energized by his tactical creativity, but, surrounded as he was by learned Greeks, we can also assume his choices were informed by state-of-the-art military history and perhaps a bit of hero worship.

The next day was a busy one, filled with implications for the future. First off—and this must have been a surprise—he heard that there was a Roman fleet anchored at the mouth of the river, and immediately sent five hundred Numidian cavalry to check out numbers and intent. Next, he assembled his men and introduced to them a delegation from Cisalpine Gaul—one Magilus and several other chieftains—as a way of reassuring the men that a happy reception awaited them on the far side of the Alps. When Hannibal noticed gloom concerning the prospective climb, he asked the men if they thought these Boii "had not crossed the Alps in the air on wings?"[35] Then, as if on cue, once the gathering dissolved, the Numidians raced back into camp. They had gotten much the worst of an engagement with a reconnoitering band of Roman cavalry, who, having discovered the main body of the Punic army, had then turned back to report its presence. Very suddenly and most unexpectedly, the wraps were off Hannibal's invasion.

Another general might have stayed put and readied his army for the inevitable Roman assault, but this Barcid was not easily distracted and seems to have understood that a delay of even a few days could have precluded crossing the Alps that year.[36] He immediately ordered his infantry to start marching north along the river, and sent his cavalry south as a screen.

But if he was in a hurry, he was also a Carthaginian and therefore was not about to leave his elephants on the wrong side of the river. So Polybius (3.46) describes for us the construction of a massive two-hundred-foot-long dirt-covered pachyderm pier and ferry arrangement, onto which the great beasts were lured and on which they were then towed across the river. Most stayed on the ferry, but some panicked and fell into the water, drowning their mahouts but still making it to the other side by using their trunks as snorkels. This proved to be quite a spectacle, but it also represented considerable time and energy devoted to a questionable military asset.

The crossing ended well, though. When the army of Publius Cornelius Scipio (father of Scipio Africanus) and his brother Cnaeus (whom we last saw storming the capital of the Insubres) arrived at the Punic campsite, Hannibal was three days gone and far up the river. Without supplies, there was no way the Romans could chase him. Besides, there was no clear idea of his route or intentions. It would have been like tracking a ghost in the wilderness. This would prove the curse of the team of elder Scipios, good generals but always just slightly out of phase with opportunity—the playthings of fate.

The Romans wanted to fight the war in Spain and Africa, and had it not been for Hannibal's march, this would have been a perfectly reasonable plan—simultaneously striking at the nest of the Barcids and at Carthage's vulnerable home front.[37] Thus, for the year 218, the two consuls, Publius Cornelius Scipio and Tiberius Sempronius Longus, were sent to Iberia and Sicily with the appropriate military and naval assets. Sempronius sailed for Lilybaeum, the jumping-off point to Africa, and set about preparing for the invasion. But Scipio was detained.

Yet again Cisalpine Gaul was in rebellion. This time it was the Boii and Insubres, probably encouraged by rumors of Hannibal's coming, chasing the Roman settlers from the new and unfortified colonies of Cremona and Placentia, blockading them at Mutina (modern Modena), and then taking a senatorial commission prisoner when the Romans attempted to negotiate. To make matters worse, a relief column commanded by the praetor L. Manlius Vulso was twice ambushed and then besieged at Tannetum.[38] Publius Cornelius Scipio, who was in the north preparing to set sail for Spain, was an obvious source of troops to clean up this mess. Under senatorial orders, another praetor, C. Atilius Serranus, sheared off one of his own legions along with five thousand allies and quickly relieved Manlius, but then he kept the force to sit on the situation. This meant Scipio had to levy more forces, which took valuable time.

Finally, after a long delay, Scipio sailed from Pisae (modern Pisa), hugging the coast of Liguria and pulling into Massilia, a staunch Roman ally and a place where he might be updated on the state of play in Spain. Instead he learned, probably to his amazement, that Hannibal was just up the River Rhône. Being a Roman, he immediately sought to engage. But it took time to disembark his army, and having missed the Carthaginians, Scipio made a fateful and strategically prescient decision. Despite the improbable nature of the invasion route, Scipio seems to have understood that Hannibal was going to attempt a transalpine crossing, but neither had Scipio forgotten that the seat of Barcid power remained in Spain. So he split the difference, sending the bulk of his army on to Iberia under his brother, the former consul Cnaeus, while he himself returned to northern Italy to take command of the two legions there to await Hannibal, should he make it across intact.

Hannibal might not have made it, but for catching a lucky break. After four days of marching up the Rhône, the Punic force came to a place of indeterminate location, known in the sources as "the island," inhabited by a prosperous tribe of Gauls in the midst of a leadership dispute between two brothers. The brothers turned to the outsiders to mediate, and Hannibal threw his weight behind the eldest, one Braneus, thereby earning his gratitude, and more important, grain supplies, replacements for worn-out weapons, warm clothing, and boots suitable for high altitude. Braneus even sent experienced guides and a cavalry escort all the way to the foothills of the Alps.[39] Hannibal was not one proverbially dependent upon the kindness of strangers, but as he stared up at this forbidding wall of mountains before him, he may have suspected that the aid of these Gauls could spell the difference between success and failure.

[5]

Of all antiquity's sanguinary events, none has drawn more ink than Hannibal's passage across the Alps.[40] It seems that almost as soon as the Carthaginians stumbled down onto the Lombard plain, quills began hitting the parchment in an endless orgy of speculation that proceeds to this day, most of it concerned with delineating the path Hannibal took.[41] This question will not be settled here, or addressed beyond out-lining a few of the more probable contenders. All that is necessary to know really is that he did it, and this is not only beyond dispute, but it overshadows all else, since this accomplishment set the conditions for one of the most important wars in recorded history. Certainly earlier bands of amorphous Celts had managed the crossing and had then surged down into Italy. But this was the first time a highly organized army attempted such a stunt, an army already far from home base and numbering in the tens of thousands—including cavalry, engineers, and logistical elements, not to mention elephants. The term "stunt" is no misnomer. For as desperate as the circumstances grew, there was a the-atrical aspect to the episode; that is the way the ancients interpreted it and that is probably how Hannibal would have wanted it remembered, eclipsing Alexander's sweep into Asia and recalling the mythical Alpine crossing of Hercules.[42]

The high Alps were inhabited by a thin penumbra of Gauls known as the Allobroges, eking out a meager living as subsistence farmers, supplemented by freebooting, and networked so that word of a large force of flatlanders to be preyed upon would reverberate rapidly from glen to glen. Almost as soon as the Punic columns began ascending the valley leading through the first and lower range of the Alpes du Dauphiné, Hannibal began noticing tribesmen shadowing them from the heights, each day growing more numerous and less concerned with concealing themselves.

Worried, Hannibal sent his scouts (probably companions of Mag-ilus's, since Braneus's guides had returned to "the island"[43]) forward, and soon learned that to reach the pass over the initial range the army would soon have to thread its way through a narrow gorge, where the Allobroges were preparing an ambush. However, he also learned that the Gauls obligingly returned to the comfort of their village at night-fall. The wily Carthaginian therefore unveiled his "keep the campfires burning" trick destined to fool so many Romans. He marched his army to the mouth of the narrow ravine, settled down the main body, and then under the cover of night led a troop of light cavalry unobserved to the heights above where the Allobroges normally congregated.

When the Gauls returned the next day, they found Hannibal loom-ing like a guardian vulture, which deterred them for a while. But then the sight of the Carthaginian column—so slow and vulnerable, often trudging single file on precipitous ledges—proved too tempting and the Allobroges tribesmen came charging down, hurling rocks, rolling boulders, and launching arrows. Pack animals began to bolt and plunge off the cliffs, dragging their handlers to the rocks below. Hannibal hesitated to intervene, wanting to avoid even greater confusion. Finally, realizing he risked losing most of his supplies and transport, he stormed down upon the attackers, killing some and driving off the rest. The situation stabilized, and a morose silence settled over the men as they moved out of the gorge and toward the pass above, followed by the elephants, which had been led carefully across the ledges without loss.[44]

A measure of revenge, though, lay just ahead in the form of the attacking Allobroges' fortified township, now all but abandoned and primed for sacking by the angry Carthaginians. The fate of the remaining inhabitants goes unrecorded, but it cannot have been good, especially after the Punic soldiers found some of their compatriots, foragers who had been recently captured, bound and held as prisoners of an uncertain fate in hovels scattered about the village. The Carthaginians also picked the place clean, gathering enough grain and cattle to last the next three days' march.

Proceeding down the first ridge and across the valley, the army at last came within sight of what the Alps were all about—truly high Alps. Where the peaks of the previous barrier had topped out at around five thousand feet, these loomed as high as thirteen thousand feet, an apparently impenetrable barrier to an army whose Cisalpine Gallic scouts seemed to have lost their way.

Enter a delegation of elders from the local tribes. Bearing olive branches and purporting to be cowed by Hannibal's recent victory over the Allobroges, they offered him provisions and guides to lead him over the mountains. Hannibal may have been skeptical, but he was also probably desperate for supplies and directions; so he went against his instincts, took some hostages, and once again became dependent upon the kindness of strangers. It was a near fatal error.

For ambush, not guidance, was their intent. Over the next two days these Gauls led the Punic force in the general direction of the Italian frontier, but all the while funneled warriors from the network of surrounding villages into a trap calculated to produce maximum lethality. So for the second time Hannibal found himself standing before the entrance of a long, narrow, very deep gorge. Sensing Gallic treachery, he took the precaution of re-forming his column with the pack train in the middle, the elephants and cavalry at the head, and the heavy infantry to the rear. Polybius (3.53.1) says it saved the army from utter destruction. Still, Hannibal stood on the precipice, about to become ensnared in a deadly combination of bad company and bad country. Of the approximately forty thousand men who entered the gorge, only 65 percent would survive the week or so it took to reach the Lombard plain.[45]

Initially the atttacking Gauls were divided into two elements: those stationed along the cliffs above, and a larger group shadowing the Punic column at ground level. The Gauls waited until virtually all of the Carthaginian army had been swallowed up by the defile and then delivered their first thrust against the rear guard, which, turning in unison, checked it. Had the heavy infantry not been in the back, the Gauls might have rolled up the entire force from the rear. Still, the Carthaginians could not prevent a devastating assault from above, as the tribesmen once again began bombarding the column and especially the pack animals with rocks, boulders, spears, and arrows—a hail of projectiles that this time could not be stopped, only endured. The Gauls even managed to establish a blocking force on the narrowest part of the path, effectively cutting the Carthaginian army in half. Still, there was only one way out, and that was forward, so the vanguard pushed ahead.

It was at this point—the first and only during the entire campaign—where the Punic pachyderms truly earned their keep. Doubtless enraged by the barrage of rocks, the elephants were even more intent on exiting the gorge than their compatriots, and they proved considerably more effective at doing so, since the Gauls blocking the exit had never dreamed such beasts existed, and scattered in terror before them. Spilling out of the far end of the defile the forward portion of the Carthaginian force was saved. Hannibal, never slow to grasp an advantage, seems to have led the elephants back to break up the Gauls obstructing the rear of the Punic column, thereby rescuing the remainder of his army, minus the heavy casualties they must have taken.[46] All told, it was far from Hannibal's best battle, and things would soon get a lot worse.

At high altitude, with winter breathing down his neck, a hungry army at his back, and now without guides, Hannibal was plainly disoriented. He had been led into this valley partly because of its gorge and the opportunities afforded for ambush, but also apparently because it ended with one of the highest and most remote of all the southern

Alpine passes. Which brings us to an equivalently bewildering intellec-
tual pass: Which Alpine pass was it?

There are two basic routes Hannibal could have taken. He might
have left the Rhône and followed the Isère River to the Arc and then
passed over the Petit Mount Cenis or possibly the col du Clapier (the
two favored by most scholars).[47] Or he might have passed over the
Savine-Coche,[48] which was close at hand. Alternatively, he could have
turned off the Rhône slightly farther south and passed along the
Drôme and Durance rivers and climbed through the col de la Traver-
sette.[49] All lead to the vicinity of Turin, where we know he emerged. In
the absence of definitive archaeological evidence, of which there is not
a scrap, the truth will remain buried deep in the past, despite a mountain of argumentation, opinion, prejudice, jealousy, and perhaps even
hatred—a perfect example of an academic dispute grown bitter because so little is truly at stake. For our purposes, all we really need to
know is that he and his army suffered horribly but eventually made it
across.

There was no turning back; time was too short. He had to push
ahead as rapidly as possible. Wanting no part of the elephants, the
tribesmen pretty much left the Carthaginians alone afterward, and the
march to the summit proved relatively straightforward, with the vanguard making it by noon of the next day. So, nearly three weeks since
leaving the Rhône and nine days after entering the Alps, they were literally in sight of their goal.

After resting the troops for two nights and waiting for stragglers at a
camp just below the crest, Hannibal rousted his army at daybreak for
the descent into Italy. The top of the pass provided a splendid vista
of the Po valley and the green plains that stretched beyond; so he gathered them here for a pep talk, promising that from this point it was all
downhill—a few battles, and Rome would be theirs.[50]

He was right at least on the first count, but the icy path down was a
great deal steeper than the ascent, and shortly the mountain was shedding Carthaginians and their animals like so many flakes of dandruff.
After several hours of baby steps and the progress of only a few
hundred feet, the column lurched to a halt blocked by a landslide. Hannibal came forward and thought there might be a way around by climb-
ing to a ledge overhead, but the men in the caravan, after making
some headway in the fresh snow, began slipping and plunging off the
thousand-foot cliffs when the tracks of those ahead turned to ice. Real-

izing this would never work, the general ordered his army to settle down for the night and conferred with Adherbal and his engineers.

Ten thousand feet high, his men strewn over a frigid wind-whipped mountainside without food, this might have been literally the end of the road had not the planners had a plan. They were for carving a completely new path along the side of the mountain to replace the part obliterated by the slide, and in the morning Hannibal ordered his Numidians to start excavating.

All went well until they encountered a huge boulder too big to move and impossible to circumvent. Livy (21.37.1–4) tells us the engineers came up with a unique solution. They built a great fire with wood transported from lower altitudes, and when the rock's surface was sufficiently hot, they poured the troops' rations of sour wine over it to create fissures that might be enlarged with iron picks and wedges until the entire mass was broken apart. With this obstacle removed, the remainder of the detour was completed in short order, enabling Punic scouts to find their way to the valley floor in a matter of hours.

Over the next day the engineers widened the entire path sufficiently to allow the beasts of burden and vital cavalry horses—by now certainly near starvation—to pass safely down to the lush vegetation of the foothills and begin grazing their way back to health. The men set about building a base camp and presumably foraging for anything they too could sink their teeth into. Thousands of feet above, the Numidians still toiled, further widening the path for another three days to accommodate thirty-seven very special members of the Carthaginian force, the panzer pachyderms.[51] They made it down, but in such poor shape that it looked as if none would survive. But remarkably, after a few days of grazing, they all regained their strength. Hannibal must have been relieved. After all, every team needs mascots.

On the whole, though, his army was not what it had been, especially in terms of numbers. When roll was taken of the infantry at the base camp, only 40 percent were Spaniards—eight thousand remnants of what must have been the bulk of the force when the journey had begun at New Carthage. On the other hand, fully twelve thousand of the African foot soldiers—the tough core of Hannibal's father's army—had made it.[52] It's also interesting that half of the original cavalry force—now amounting to six thousand—survived, especially since equine attrition is proverbially higher than among humans.[53] Hannibal would need every one of the cavalrymen and would use them to great effect, particularly the Numidians. Still, the entire army now amounted to only twenty-six thousand members of a force that had originally numbered more than a hundred thousand. Many had been left behind or had deserted, but still, the two weeks or so in the mountains had plainly taken a huge toll. With the exception of Scipio Africanus, of all the enemies Hannibal faced over the next sixteen years, none proved more lethal than the Alps. Yet he had escaped their craggy clutches and descended upon Italy with a viable force structure, and once it got some food and some rest, it would prove effective beyond all expectation. His was now a freeze-dried army, hardened by the danger and cold of the mountains and capable of immediate expansion. . . . Just add Gauls.

THE FOX AND THE HEDGEHOG

[1]

Had the ancient Greek poet Archilochus and the modern philosopher Isaiah Berlin been magically transported to northern Italy in November of 218 B.C., they might well have speculated on the strategic prospects. "Hannibal knows many things, but Rome knows one big thing," the Greek might have proposed. To which Berlin might have replied, "Perhaps at the outset. But then the fox could get stuck in a rut, and the hedgehog might learn new tricks." This would have been the Second Punic War epitomized.

It has been called "the first world war in the history of humankind,"[1] a plausible statement at least within the confines of the Mediterranean basin, since the strategic action extended to Sardinia and Sicily, even spilled east into Macedonia, and had to be decided by a two-step process beginning in Spain and then moving to Africa. Yet the conflict is remembered as an Italian war; it was here that the most sustained and vicious combat took place, and the most damage was done—although the nature and longevity of the effects remain controversial. Still, it's a safe bet that most of the suffering occurred in Italy. Adrian Goldsworthy, one of the very best historians covering this era, counts twelve major land engagements taking place between 218 and 202—three times the number of the First Punic War—with more than half being fought on Italian soil.[2] And during the entire conflict, Romans lost only battles that took place on the Italic peninsula. This can be attributed to a single factor . . . Hannibal, the central agent of destruction, their nemesis. Elsewhere, with the exception of the running fights that killed the Scipio brothers, and a few other skirmishes, the Romans were uniformly victorious. Their armies were better, their navy had become utterly dominant, and their commanders were at least as good as the other Carthaginians. The sole exception was the eldest Barcid brother; he was the hand that stirred the Second Punic War. In all respects—causal, tactical, operational, political, even sociological—it was truly Hannibal's war.

But if he held the spotlight throughout, he left the stage a loser. In the end he was smacked down by the central non sequitur of the Western way of war: victory in battle does not necessarily mean victory in war. One triumph simply led to another triumph and another, until he found himself confined to a rut in the toe of Italy and eventually back in Africa. Meanwhile, the Romans fell back on a hedgehog who taught them to avoid being mauled by the fox, while they gradually mastered the fox's tricks and conjured his equal. But first they would writhe and bleed beneath his claws.

[2]

Since Hannibal had lost much of his army in the Alps, his outlook was not likely to have been improved by what he found waiting for him in the Po valley—Gauls grown coy, and Publius Cornelius Scipio . . . again. He would deal with them in turn. The Taurini occupied the area into which the Punic force had descended, and were at the time preoccupied with fighting the neighboring Insubres. Hence, when Hannibal sent emissaries to their principal stronghold—probably at the site of modern Turin—asking for alliance and supplies for his starving troops, they rebuffed him. In no mood to be trifled with, Hannibal promptly laid siege to the place and took it in three days. He then made an example of the inhabitants, executing the men and boys and letting his soldiers loose on the women and food stores—both devoured, no doubt, with alacrity. All the Gauls in the immediate vicinity took the hint and sent representatives with pledges of allegiance, and very soon the Punic ranks began to swell with increments of both native cavalry and infantry.

But if, as Polybius (3.60) tells us, the remaining Celts of the northern plain were also inclined to join him, they were blocked from doing so by the advance of Scipio's legions, moving west from Placentia, even pressing some reluctant Gauls into service as they went. Hannibal for his part had decided his best course was forward, hoping his army would attract Gauls as he proceeded. The lethal contest between fox and hedgehog had begun.

Publius Cornelius Scipio was already in trouble. Although Hannibal was surprised and impressed by how fast the Roman consul had made it back from the Rhône, this was only the same general and not the same army Hannibal had avoided earlier.[3] (That force had been sent to Spain with brother Cnaeus.) After reporting to the senate that the Carthaginians were crossing the Alps, Publius Scipio had been told to proceed to the Po and delay them as best he could, while the other consul, Tiberius Sempronius Longus, and his legions were recalled from Sicily to support Scipio. So, for the second time in his consulship, Scipio was forced to build himself a new army, this time with a combination of raw recruits and the veterans who had been roughly handled by the Gauls under L. Manlius Vulso.[4] But if Scipio had any doubts about his soldiers, he was also a Roman and anxious to engage the Carthaginians before they had time to fully recover from their Alpine journey. Therefore, he marched his army purposefully along the north bank of the Po, crossed its tributary the Ticinus with the Roman equivalent of a pontoon bridge, and moved to within a few miles of where the Punic army was known to be camped.

Meanwhile, Hannibal had been acting vulpine, toying with a few victims, and in the process reminding his troops of just what was at stake.[5] Calling them together he had a number of Allobroges captives brought in. He asked if any were willing to engage in single combat, the prize to the winner being freedom, arms, and a fast horse; and the prize to the loser being freedom from the present misery in the form of death's oblivion. When all volunteered, the winning pair (or pairs, if you believe Livy's version) was chosen by lot and fought to the death, at which point the remaining prisoners congratulated victor and vanquished alike as being far better off than themselves. Hannibal then elaborated on the theme, reminding his men that their situation was exactly that of the Allobroges. They could conquer, or die fighting— both alternatives much preferable to being captured and led away in chains to a life of servitude and misery. Message sent and received— only desperation would trump Rome's determination.

Sensing combat was near, Hannibal recalled Maharbal and the five hundred Numidian horse he had sent out to forage, and gathered virtually all of his cavalry to accompany him in an initial attempt to make contact. Scipio, likely remembering how easily the Numidians had been scattered on the Rhône, was also in a combative mood here at the Ticinus. To reconnoiter he brought with him a smaller force of heavy cavalry, along with a body of pedestrian *velites,* whom, after the Punic force had been spotted by its dust cloud, he sent forward, expecting the *velites* to act as a screen with their javelins. They crumpled instead. For Hannibal, having realized that his cavalry significantly outnumbered the Romans', had placed his heavy Spanish troopers in the center and Numidians behind each wing, in position to envelope, and then he had charged, driving the terrified *velites* back through the advancing Roman horse before they'd had a chance to do any damage with their javelins. When the heavy cavalry of both sides came together, combat took the form of a vicious dismounted mêlée—one characteristic of Roman horsemen but also likely prompted by the run-down condition of the Carthaginians' mounts. Here the Romans easily gave as good as they got, but on either side the Numidians drove around the flanks, first riding down the fleeing *velites* and then turning back upon the rear of the Roman cavalry, causing them to flee.

It was probably around this time that Scipio was seriously wounded and in danger of being captured. Most sources credit the consul's rescue to his seventeen-year-old son, who led a band of horsemen back into the fight to surround and protect his fallen father.[6] This was more than just an inspirational tale of filial loyalty; the young man, also named Publius, would eventually earn the moniker Africanus as Hannibal's conqueror at Zama. But that day was far off, and in the meantime this young Scipio would spend the remainder of his adolescence suffering at the hands of the Carthaginian, and, evidently, learning from him.

The fight itself has been dismissed as little more than a skirmish.[7] Still, it must have been a confidence builder, demonstrating what the Punic force most needed to know—that it could fight successfully in Italy. Even more important, the encounter demonstrated the same thing to the Gauls. It also unveiled what would be Hannibal's most devastating trick—pinning the center and then attacking the rear through double envelopment.[8] Cavalry would prove very important in the upcoming war, and this encounter near the Ticinus River left little doubt whose was better. Not only did Roman horsemen display an unfortunate tendency to fight on foot, but they also showed little ability to work effectively with light troops, who themselves would prove chronically inferior to their Carthaginian counterparts. All these revelations of weakness Hannibal would use to great effect to counter and manipulate Rome's real strength in heavy infantry. So if Ticinus was simply a prelude, it was nevertheless a prophetic one.

Publius Scipio was now in a desperate situation, both personally and with regard to his suspect force structure; yet he was apparently a man who knew his own limitations. Before Hannibal—who expected a major battle in a day or two—knew what had happened, the Romans were gone, crossing to the south bank of the Po on their pontoon bridge and racing east toward the relative safety of Placentia. By the time the Carthaginians reached the bridge, Scipio's engineers had cut its moorings; six hundred stranded Roman troops were captured, but immediate pursuit of the main body was now impossible. Instead, Hannibal marched in the opposite direction, up along the north bank of the Po until he found a place suitable for fording. He left it to Hasdrubal, head of the service corps, to get the army across, while he went ahead to meet with Gallic emissaries, who were now ready to jump aboard the Punic bandwagon with solid offers of soldiers and supplies.[9]

The Carthaginian pursuit of Scipio could now resume, probably picking up Gauls like a rolling snowball as the army proceeded along the south bank of the Po. Two days later Hannibal reached his goal and deployed for combat in front of the Roman camp, apparently set slightly west of the River Trebia, a challenge Scipio declined to accept. This was a signal of Carthaginian dominance that no Gaul was likely to miss, including those currently pressed into Roman service. That night a body of two thousand Gallic infantry and two hundred cavalry massacred and beheaded a few Romans sleeping nearby, then bolted from the camp, going over to Hannibal, whose army was parked a few miles away.

Scipio realized that his position was untenable—if his own Gauls betrayed him, soon all the Gauls would flock to Hannibal. So he prepared his army to slink off under the cover of darkness, a barometer of his sense of urgency being the pain he would inevitably suffer from his wound along the way. Withdrawal in such close proximity to the enemy was inherently dangerous,[10] and upon learning that the Romans were on the march, Hannibal instantly launched the Numidians to ride them down. Fortunately for the Romans, the Numidians were apparently still hungry and stopped to loot the abandoned encampment, a distraction that gave Scipio time to get his army across the River Trebia and heading for higher ground, where he might construct a fortified camp sufficiently strong and well placed to keep the Carthaginians at bay.

Hannibal, at least for the moment, was apparently content to not pursue Scipio and instead play the Gaul magnet, but feeding his army was and would be a continuing preoccupation. Nearby Clastidium, the place where Marcellus had won the *spolia opima* four years earlier, was known to be a major Roman grain storage site. The Carthaginians were about to attack it when the commander, one Dasius, and the allied garrison went over to the Punic side. A number of sources suspect that this was more than simply a matter of good luck.[11] The traitor in charge was a native of Brundisium in the south, where loyalty to Rome was most problematic, and this event may indicate some initial penetration by Hannibal's agents into an area where he would later have his greatest political success. That Dasius's subordinates were most likely Latin allies may have also given Hannibal hope that the alliance might be broken at other points—a chimera, as it turned out. Nevertheless, it is also true that from this point until shortly after Cannae, Hannibal appears to have enjoyed an uncanny awareness of Roman intentions and capabilities. While the armies were in the north, this can partly be explained by Gauls serving on both sides, and later by the flow of deserters. Still, there remains an intelligence advantage that is never adequately resolved by the historical sources. This advantage whispers of a mole or moles with ears close to the top of the otherwise sacrosanct monolith on the Tiber.

Tiberius Sempronius Longus and his consular army were now back in Italy. Livy (21.51.6–7) has them sailing from Sicily to Ariminum (modern Rimini) high on the Adriatic side of the Italian boot, but it would have been dangerously late in the season for such an extended voyage. More probable is Polybius's (3.68.9–14) version of them marching to the same destination along the Via Flaminia, reaching this point in early December. On the way, the historian reports, they passed through Rome, where the consensus was that the skirmish at the Ticinus constituted but a minor setback. Infantry, not cavalry, mattered, and that Sempronius's army—presumably more capable than Scipio's—had to do little more than show up to decide the showdown with the Carthaginians.

So, brimming with confidence, Sempronius reached the River Trebia in mid-December and settled his men down next to Scipio's secure camp. He found his colleague still nursing his wound and generally depressed about the prospects of successfully engaging the Punic army. Scipio argued that the winter months were best spent training what remained of his mostly inexperienced force, while this period of inaction would also cause the mercurial Gauls to begin drifting away from Hannibal. Some have maintained that this reasoning was a later invention designed to protect the Scipionic reputation,[12] but it was also very good advice.

Sempronius would have none of it. He was, after all, a Roman, and one whose consulship's hourglass was quickly running down. Likely his every instinct told him (as Scipio's had earlier) to aggressively seek glory in battle as quickly as possible. Hannibal almost immediately provided the pretext.

Some of the local allied Gauls were apparently two-timing him, hedging their bets and keeping channels open to the Romans. Hannibal knew this was dangerous and unacceptable, and sent out several thousand Celts and Numidians to ravage their territory between the Trebia and the Po. The Gauls in turn appealed to the Romans for help. Sempronius jumped at the opportunity, deploying his own cavalry and about a thousand *velites* to deal with the raiders. They caught the Punic marauders scattered and weighed down with booty, and sent them racing pell-mell to the Carthaginian camp. Realizing what had happened, the Carthaginian commanders of the outposts sent a covering force forward, which in turn chased the Romans back to their encampment. This tit-for-tat action took on a momentum of its own, with both sides feeding reinforcements until all the Roman *velites* and cavalry were engaged and the fighting ebbed and flowed uncontrollably across a wide area. Just as it threatened to escalate into a full-scale battle, Hannibal called a halt. Polybius (3.69.12–13) tells us because the Punic commander knew a "decisive engagement should never be undertaken on any chance pretext and without definite purpose." Yet it is likely that Hannibal called a halt not because the tit-for-tat action had no "definite purpose" but because the halt itself had a purpose of its own. He was, to use the modern idiom, "preparing the battlefield," specifically that portion that lay between the opposing commander's ears.

Sempronius was elated by his apparent success, especially since it had been accomplished by the very parts of the force that had been defeated under Scipio. Despite his colleague's continued warnings against rash action, Sempronius made up his mind to seek a decisive engagement as soon as opportunity knocked—exactly what Hannibal, short on supplies and long on fickle Gauls, wanted. Livy (21.53.7–11) tells us he had been briefed on Sempronius's impulsiveness, and he now set about building a battle around it.

The opposing camps were separated by the River Trebia, a shallow braided watercourse swollen by winter rains. On Hannibal's side beyond the west bank was a broad, flat, treeless plain ideal for cavalry, but it was also the kind of terrain favored by Roman infantry—in other words, the obvious site of battle. Studying the ground to the south, Hannibal discovered a streambed overgrown with vegetation ideal for hiding ambushers. The night before the date he intended to fight, Hannibal secretly sent his brother Mago and a mixed force of two thousand Numidians into this position, with orders to hit the Romans from the rear at the appropriate moment.

At dawn, beneath brooding skies and a cold driving snowfall, the bait was set. Hannibal sent the Numidian cavalry across the river with orders to harass the Roman outposts and lure them and whoever would follow back across the Trebia. Sempronius, playing the human equivalent of Pavlov's dog, responded exactly as expected, sending all four thousand of his cavalry and six thousand *velites* after the Numidians, and ordering his heavy infantry to muster immediately and march out of camp without even having their breakfast. This force, sixteen thousand Romans and twenty thousand allied—basically two consular armies[13]—dutifully waded chest deep across the ice-cold Trebia, marched onto the plain beyond, and deployed for battle in the standard pattern, Romans in the center and allies on the wings—a process likely to have consumed several frigid sleet-laced hours.[14] Hungry, wet, and cold—even for soldiers as tough as Romans, this was not a good way to start a battle.

While the Numidians ran the Roman cavalry and *velites* into exhaustion, Hannibal ordered eight thousand light infantry forward to support them and act as a screen. Only then—after his men had eaten their fill, had armed and rubbed themselves down with oil in front of their campfires—did he lead them out onto the field of battle. He was probably outnumbered, but not decisively so, his army having been swelled by around fourteen thousand Celts.[15] He had a clear advantage in cavalry, both in numbers and quality. His infantry formed a single line, Africans and Spaniards to the right and left, with the Gauls in the center, where their individual size and ferocity might blunt the forward surge of the Roman legionaries, hopefully until the other Punic force components could seize the advantage. The Spanish and Gallic cavalry were placed on the flanks, where they were joined by the Numidian horse, back from harassing the Romans, a body of five thousand on either wing . . . and, it appears, the elephants, probably half-frozen and almost useless. It was time to fight.

The battle opened with the Punic cavalry bearing down on the Roman horsemen, who were now stationed in two groups of two thousand on the flanks of the allied infantry. They didn't stay long; exhausted and outnumbered, they were routed and scattered by a combination of Punic cavalry and a cloud of javelins thrown by the Carthaginian light troops, who had moved back to their own wings. The Punic cavalry and light infantry now began enveloping both ends of the long Roman line, swarming the allied heavy infantry from all directions and beginning to roll it up.

The fight went better for the Romans in the center. The *hastati* and *principes* seemed to have absorbed the initial shock of the individual Gallic swordsmen and were methodically grinding through them, and some of the African units, when Mago and his Numidians emerged from hiding to hit the Roman line in the rear. The Romans' forward momentum slowed as the *triarii* turned to face this threat. The younger Barcid's timing was fortuitous; if the core body of Romans had broken through the Punic forces quickly, they might have had the opportunity to part in the middle and pivot back to support the flagging allied flanks. Instead, Mago managed to throw the entire line into confusion,[16] and soon after, both *alae* and the adjacent Roman units disintegrated into useless human blobs.

Ten thousand legionaries in the middle, though, maintained their formations and finally broke through the Punic line. But with no flanks left to defend and only Carthaginians and the ice-cold Trebia to the rear, they kept marching right off the battlefield and made their way to Placentia and safety. For most of their trapped compatriots, however, death was the only refuge. While there are no casualty figures,[17] most men likely fell prey to Carthaginians, drowning, or simply exposure.

Almost certainly the tempo of battle was progressively determined by hypothermia. As the day wore on, the snow turned to a cold penetrating rain that must have sucked the vitality from all the combatants. At least the Carthaginians had been acclimatized in the Alps; many of their adversaries had been basking in the warmth of Sicily not much more than a month earlier. Livy (21.54.9) refers to the Romans after crossing the Trebia as scarcely able to hold their arms, and growing progressively weaker as the day wore on. Because Hannibal had made sure that the Carthaginians had eaten breakfast and otherwise pre-pared themselves, they must have had a body heat advantage at the be-ginning, but Livy (21.56) makes it clear that they grew increasingly benumbed. At the end, the fighting and even the slaughter must have taken place in stiff-limbed slow motion, with no attempt made to cross the river and take the Roman encampment. Instead, the Carthaginians staggered back to their own camp, and stayed there, cold and passive for the next several days, a period during which many of their pack ani-mals and almost all of the elephants succumbed to exposure.[18] This hy-pothermic lassitude probably saved Scipio and the Romans left to guard the camp; they were able to escape by rafting down the Trebia, and eventually joined the other fugitives at Placentia.

It appears[19] that Sempronius tried to disguise the magnitude of his defeat, sending messengers to Rome to announce that a battle had taken place and that only the storm had deprived him of victory. Quickly his countrymen learned the truth—Hannibal and his army re-mained secure in their camp, virtually all the Gauls had gone over to him, and fragments of two consular armies were scattered in various localities, cut off from supply except by the River Po. The situation was obviously serious, but the first steps taken to shore up Rome's position seem pointed in the wrong direction. The Romans readied a fleet of sixty quinqueremes and reinforced Sardinia and Sicily, as if the main threat would come from Carthage and not Hannibal. Still apparently trying to salvage his reputation, Sempronius, Livy (21.57.3–4) tells us, boldly made his way to Rome to preside over the consular elections. The results there also reflected a sense of emergency, though not nec-essarily good choices. Joining C. Servilius Geminus as consular col-league was Caius Flaminius, the Gauls' archenemy and, because he'd provided them with Gallic land he'd conquered, the Roman farmers' friend. He was definitely a controversial figure, particularly among the wealthier elements of the nobility, but his career was all about pum-meling the Gauls, and he was known to be a man of action. One can al-most hear the conventional wisdom along the Tiber: "Flaminius is just the man to take care of this problem up north." But he had yet to meet Hannibal.

The ancient Greeks had a term, *aristeia,* for a serial display of heroic excellence—a sort of berserker kill-fest in which a central character hacks down any and all who stand in his way—in *The Iliad,* for instance, when Achilles single-handedly routs the Trojan army. The term seems appropriate for Hannibal; such was the magnitude and audacity of his initial series of victories over the Romans. Trebia marked the beginning of the series, and Cannae the climax. But in the first contest he had already revealed the qualities that would make him one of the greatest soldiers who ever lived—his X-ray vision into the minds of his opponents, his trickiness and penchant for surprise, his judicious use of his men, both in their care and feeding and also in how he applied each force component to maximum advantage.[20] (The only significant Carthaginian casualties were the Celts who had been placed in the center to absorb the brunt of the Roman assault—troops of uncertain loyalty, virtually untrained, and easily replaceable at this point.) It was a virtuoso display, but unfortunately for the Romans, Hannibal was far from satisfied.

For in the winter of 218–17 his position and that of his army were far from secure. Food must have been a constant concern. Livy (21.57–8) speaks of several Punic attacks on supply depots near Placentia, and a failed attempt to cross the Apennines to find better foraging. Modern historians[21] often dismiss these accounts as inventions, but these stories certainly speak to a very basic preoccupation in an environment where Gallic agriculture likely did not produce significant surpluses.

This may have been reflected in Hannibal's treatment of his prisoners. The Roman captives, whom he expected to ransom, he fed only enough to keep them alive. The Roman allies in his hands he treated better, and after a time he gathered them together, informing them that his war was against Rome and for the liberty of Italy's people.[22] With this he freed them all without ransom. This is generally seen as the first step in Hannibal's political and information campaign to undermine Rome's alliance structure, and it undoubtedly was. But it is also worth mentioning that it left him with hundreds, perhaps thousands, fewer mouths to feed.

His precarious status and the questionable hospitality of his hosts were further evidenced in the tale Polybius and Livy both tell of Hannibal having to wear various disguises, even different-colored wigs, to avoid assassination at the hands of the locals.[23] The Gauls had not rallied to the Punic standard in order to find their own territory as the seat of war and the kitchen table for what amounted to an occupying army. If Hannibal wanted to keep the Gauls as allies, he had better move south as soon as the weather turned.

[3]

Springtime for Hannibal meant winter for Etruria and Rome.[24] Actually, there were two ways he could have gone. The Apennines form the spine of Italy, dividing it longitudinally. Therefore, he could have marched east toward the Adriatic side and then headed south, where he was likely to find support among those most recently conquered by Rome. This route also would have brought him closer to Carthage. Alternatively, he had the choice of moving down to the passes of the Apennines and heading west into Etruria, leaving open communications with the Po valley and Spain, and also putting himself in a position much more directly threatening to Rome itself. Given his motives and his true base of support in Iberia, he chose the latter.

Knowing their own geography, the Romans hedged their bets. They sent Geminus north along the Via Flaminia (the same route probably taken by Sempronius) to Ariminum, where he could combine his new recruits with Publius Scipio's veterans[25] and cover the eastern corridor down the peninsula. Flaminius had already arrived at this destination, assuming office here and not in Rome, thereby flouting tradition and skipping the religious rituals normally presided over by an incoming consul. To compound matters, he ignored the commissioners sent to recall him. Instead, he added the remnants of Sempronius's force to his own legionaries and moved to Arretium, where he thought he would be in a position to block the Apennine passes leading toward Etruria.[26]

He wasn't. Hannibal gave him the slip crossing at the Porretta pass,[27] and then struck out through the flooded marshes surrounding the River Arno. This was not simply a matter of deception; as usual the Punic commander had a hidden agenda. The march also would serve as a means of toughening the Gauls and weeding out the weak ones. This trek would be a swampy version of the one over the Alps. He lined up his army with the Spaniards and Africans intermingled with the baggage train, the Celts sandwiched in the middle, and Mago and the Numidians to the rear to keep the whole mass moving and the Gauls from turning back. Those who survived slogged continuously for three days and nights. They had to; in this inundated terrain there was no place above water to rest except upon the corpses of the many fallen pack animals. Cavalry horses frequently lost their hoofs. Hannibal, atop the last surviving elephant, contracted a case of ophthalmia so severe that he lost the sight of one eye.[28] All told, it was a bad trip. But when the Carthaginians emerged from the morass somewhere around Faesulae (modern Fiesole), the army was not only clear of the Romans, but also it had rid itself of fair-weather Gauls and begun the process of fully integrating the remaining Gauls into the force structure.

Hannibal's swarm of scouts and spies had been busy. They confirmed that the rich Etrurian plain was ripe for the plucking and that Flaminius, still at Arretium, was a commander every bit as impulsive and belligerent as Sempronius and just as easy to trap. Hannibal decided to lead him on a fool's errand south. And as he traveled he understood exactly how to distract the Roman commander; nothing would infuriate the farmers' friend more than Hannibal's foragers' descending like a plague of locusts onto the villages and fields of Rome's allies. Here in the heart of Italy, Flaminius had only to follow the smoke columns to follow Hannibal, a humiliating circumstance that could be stopped only by bringing Hannibal into action, which Flaminius was determined to do.

Both Polybius and Livy maintain that Flaminius was discouraged by his subordinates, who advised him to await reinforcement from Geminus.[29] He ignored them, and also in typical Flaminius fashion, he overlooked a series of ill omens (here is where the hard-to-pull-up tent standards came into play), and probably did so appropriately, if only because he was a Roman and was predisposed to fight. Besides, Hannibal was on the move; how could his colleague Geminus have been expected to catch up? It also says something that Flaminius's army was joined by a host of irregulars carrying chains for the prisoners they expected to take and enslave after an easy victory. So Flaminius, as always with his ear more attuned to vox populi than to the council of prudence, went forward in hot pursuit.

No more than a day ahead, Hannibal came upon Lake Trasimene and saw opportunity along the route before him—a narrow plain that separated the shoreline from a parallel track of steep hills, the entrance to which was a blind defile. He slowed his army so that late in the day Flaminius would march up and see him entering the gulch, and later

Flaminius's scouts would observe the Punic campgrounds near the far end of the line of hills. The Romans settled down for the night outside the gulch entrance. Hannibal, under the cover of darkness, led his forces back down a parallel path on the other side of the hills and stationed the men high along the hills' reverse slopes, awaiting the arrival of dawn.

The next day—June 21, 217 B.C.[30]—broke with a heavy ground fog hanging over the lake and its environs. It is unclear whether the Romans were already deployed into three parallel columns of *hastati*, *principes*, and *triarii* when they entered the defile, but they may have been, since they were expecting action in the near future. But they had no idea they were walking into what would be remembered as the biggest ambush in history, the only time an entire large army was effectively swallowed and destroyed by such a maneuver.[31]

With amazing self-control the Punic forces waited silently above as the Romans marched along the lakeshore, gradually filling the narrow plain until the Romans made contact with Hannibal's stopper force of Africans and Spaniards, at which point Hannibal gave the signal for all his troops to come charging down the hill. Emerging out of the mist, they hit virtually the entire length of the Roman army simultaneously, completely surprising and quite probably freezing them into terrified passivity. There was no going back, the Carthaginian cavalry had sealed the defile. Livy (22.5–6) tries to make the case that many stood and fought bravely; some may have, but Polybius's (3.84) pathetic description seems more in line with the circumstances.

> Most of them were cut to pieces in marching order, as they were quite unable to protect themselves. . . . Those again who had been shut in between the hillside and the lake perished in a still more pitiable manner. For when they were forced into the lake in a mass, some of them quite lost their wits and trying to swim in their armor were drowned, but the greater number, wading into the lake as far as they could, stood there with only their heads out of the water, and when the cavalry approached them, and death stared them in the face, though lifting up their hands and entreating to be spared in the most piteous terms, they were finally dispatched either by the horsemen or in some cases by begging their comrades to do them this service.

Nor did Flaminius survive the attack. The Gauls who had long suffered at his hands went straight for him, easily recognizable by his splendid accoutrements and also, if you believe Silius Italicus (5.132), because he wore a Gallic scalp on the crest of his helmet. For a while his bodyguards fought the Gauls off, but then an Insubrian horseman, whom Livy names Ducarius, charged through the dense mass and first slew Flaminius's armor bearer, and then, knowing the consul's face, ran him through with a lance.

The killing spree continued for about three hours, a slaughter so intense that neither side was aware that they were fighting in the midst of a major earthquake that had shot across central Italy.[32] According to Fabius Pictor, around fifteen thousand Romans joined their leader that morning in death.[33] Another six thousand Romans, probably near the head of the column, seem to have brushed past those in front of them and headed for the hills. Polybius claims they could not see—possibly due to the fog—what had befallen the rest of the force until they reached higher ground, and by then it was too late to help. More likely they were simply demoralized, which better explains their taking refuge as a body in a local Etrurian village, and their abject surrender to Maharbal and his Spaniards and Numidians a little later. At that point they were added to the other prisoners, now totaling fifteen thousand, all of whom Hannibal assembled after the fighting had ceased. As at Trebia, he slapped the Romans in chains and sent the allies home without ransom, but with the same message that he was all about liberating them from the tyrants on the Tiber. Livy (22.7.2) says some ten thousand men were scattered and eventually made it back to Rome; whether this number included the allies Hannibal let go is impossible to say. One thing was and remains clear, however. In a matter of hours an entire consular army had simply vanished.

If ever a Barca lived up to the family appellation Thunderbolt, it was Hannibal at this moment. But it is unlikely that this brilliantly conceived trap materialized out of thin air. Hannibal would not have soon forgotten the two ambushes he'd suffered in the Alps, and it is plausible that they provided the seeds of his plan at Trasimene—the same scheme of assaulting a force on the march, hiding and then attacking from above, leaving no avenue of retreat, and setting a death trap to the side. Had the Romans made this connection, it might have further mortified them. Here was an adversary who not only learned from his mistakes, but found ways to leverage them to his own advantage. He was dangerous not only on the battlefield, but anywhere in his vicinity.

For Hannibal it was an altogether felicitous encounter—after the Alps, the winter, and the swamp, his troops had been exhausted and probably capable of only a short, sharp action. His own losses were low, around fifteen hundred, most of them Celts, who'd likely seen at least some compensation in the opportunity to kill the hated Flaminius. And Hannibal's good fortune was not at an end. There were scouting reports that the remaining consul, Geminus, had sent a large cavalry force down to support Flaminius and that it was now in the area, presumably unaware of what had happened. So Hannibal sent the enterprising Maharbal and the Numidians to deliver still another unpleasant surprise.

Back in Rome, the city was rife with foreboding. Days passed. Wives and mothers wandered the streets quizzing any and all on the fate of the army. As the frightening gossip clarified, a great crowd formed around the senate house, demanding solid information from the magistrates. Finally, a little before sunset the urban praetor Marcus Pomponius emerged to announce only: "We have been defeated in a great battle." So the rumor mill ground on, with the women who were gathered at the city gates awaiting their men—or at least some word of them—gradually realizing a great many would not be coming home.[34]

Meanwhile, Pomponius kept the senate in constant session from sunrise to sunset, racking their collective brains as to how they might deal with a threat that over the course of seven months—punctuated by Ticinus, Trebia, and now Trasimene—had grown exponentially to the point where it was shaking the foundations of the state. For these disasters were palpably worse than those of the First Punic War, having fallen heavily upon the more prosperous elements, who served in and commanded the legions—not upon the poorer and less politically significant types, who rowed the warships that had been lost in the earlier contest. Existentially, the army was at the center of Rome's conception of itself. Losing in this fashion and leaving an invader free to ravage the Italian countryside was humiliating almost beyond the capacity of words to describe.[35]

Then, after three days of deliberations, news arrived that Gaius Centenius, who'd been sent to help Flaminius with a force of four thousand horse—most of Rome's remaining cavalry—had been surprised and surrounded by Maharbal probably somewhere near Assisi.[36]

Half of the men had been killed immediately, and the rest had surrendered the next day. Still another substantial Roman force had been obliterated. At this moment there was nothing left standing between Hannibal and Rome itself, except an easy hundred-mile march down the Via Flaminia. The situation seemed truly desperate, and the senate fell back on what was the system's last bulwark in the face of disaster. For the first time since 249, when Rome's navy had been wiped out off Sicily, a dictator was appointed.

[4]

He was Quintus Fabius Maximus, the same man Livy believed had told the Carthaginians that he held war or peace in his toga. It may not have been him, but he was the sort who could have said such a thing and been taken seriously. He was fifty-eight years old, had been twice consul and once censor, and was from an ancient clan, one that had already earned the title Maximus—"the greatest." Owner of an impeccable pedigree, he was exactly the type Rome turned to in emergencies. Just the name Fabius sounds august, but actually it relates to what had once been the family business, bean farming. And symbolically, temperamentally, and strategically, he was the Beanman matched against the Thunderbolt. For like the hedgehog, Fabius Maximus understood one big thing—Hannibal's never ending need to feed his army. To win, Rome did not have to defeat him in battle; they had to simply restrict his ability to provision his troops. Once the dictator took to the field, it became apparent that this involved two essential expedients: the removal or destruction of crops and livestock in the path of the Punic force, and the relentless interception and attrition of Carthaginian foraging parties.[37] In the meantime, Fabius would scrupulously avoid a field engagement with Hannibal, electing instead to shadow his every step, but at a safe distance and always taking the high ground to avoid being brought unwillingly into battle.

It is important to realize that the Fabian strategy, from the outset, was seen by Romans not as a magic bean but as a bitter pill. Their entire orientation was offensive; they were acculturated to seek battle; they had been conditioned to believe their military system would triumph over any general, no matter how clever. They were also farmers, whose instincts were to protect, not burn, their fields. Everything

Fabius proposed, while prudent in the face of military genius, went against the Roman grain.[38] A later generation who benefited from his policies would apply to him the title Cunctator ("the Delayer"), and even this was not altogether positive.[39] At the time, his countrymen employed less flattering sobriquets—Verrucosus for the wart that grew above his lip; Ovicula ("Lambykins"); and "Hannibal's *paedagogus*," after the slave who followed Roman schoolboys and carried their books.[40] His countrymen also subverted and resisted his approach, undermining his authority even within the short space of his six-month term of office. It probably felt like the right thing to do, but it was a path that led directly to Cannae.

His term actually began with a focus on what was perceived to be the immediate danger to the city. First he sought to explain Flaminius's defeat in a way the people could understand—that is, Flaminius's failure to perform the appropriate religious rites, and his ignoring obvious omens of the gods' displeasure. Fabius had the senate consult the prophetic Sibylline Books and then charge a praetor with performing the prescribed rites to assuage the gods.

Fabius did have a deputy, Marcus Minucius Rufus, his master of horse. (The dictator himself had to get special permission to serve mounted.[41]) Together they looked to the defenses of the city, and it may be that Minucius was ordered to assemble the *legiones urbanae* by a certain date.[42] It also seems that two additional legions were raised to replace those lost by Flaminius, and that these set out with Fabius up the Tiber valley to meet those of Geminus, who had been ordered to proceed down the Via Flaminia toward Rome. To make it absolutely clear who was in charge, when the consul's army was spotted, a message was sent that Geminus should come into the dictator's presence without lictors and as a private citizen. Rome now had a clear leader and a covering force, but by this time it must have been apparent that Hannibal had gone elsewhere.

Given the quality of his intelligence, the Punic commander may well have been aware that nothing stood between him and Rome after Trasimene; but he also would have known that his army was badly run-down and in no shape to besiege what was one of the most heavily fortified population centers in the Mediterranean world. So instead he headed east, crossing the Apennines again on a ten-day march to the rich Picenum district along the Adriatic coast. During this march, he allowed his men to plunder and abuse the local populations to their hearts' content. They must have been a motley crew at this point, the men exhibiting symptoms of scurvy and the horses afflicted by mange—both the result of vitamin deficiencies.[43] So Hannibal let the soldiers gorge themselves on the fresh produce of the area, and bathed the horses with sour wine until both man and beast gradually regained their health and vitality.

But with Hannibal, R & R seldom meant repose. Polybius (3.87.3) tells us that, while in Picenum, he rearmed his African troops with "select weapons" captured in very large quantities. This process, which the historian says began after Hannibal won the "first battle" with the Romans,[44] raises some interesting questions. Were they being given the *pilum* and *gladius*? If so, this implies their transformation primarily into swordsmen,[45] which seems to be contradicted by Plutarch, who says (Marcellus, 12.2) the Libyans "were not javelineers, but used short spears in hand-to-hand fighting." This description likely eliminates the *pilum* as an add-on. Whether the Africans adopted the short sword is still at issue, but given the short sword's lethality and compactness, the addition remains plausible, at least as a sidearm. It is fairly certain they did not carry long pikes and therefore fight as a phalanx. The only evidence that they did carry long pikes is an apparent mistranslation of the Greek word for "spear."[46]

Livy (22.46.4) does say that the Libyans at Cannae could have been mistaken for Romans, since they were equipped with Romans' captured gear. Probably he is referring to their defensive accoutrements, which is what an observer would have noticed. Since a lot of equipment had been captured, it stands to reason that the Africans, who were Hannibal's key maneuver force, would have gotten the best of it—an oval *scutum* (a shield heavy enough to preclude using the long two-handed pike of the Macedonian phalanx), the best Montefortino helmet, a full set of greaves, and, most important, a ring-mail cuirass rather than simply a *pectorale* heart protector. These articles left them as a group considerably better protected than most of the Romans. They were now true heavy infantry, and this equipment upgrade serves to explain their impact at Cannae; when they closed the trap on the Romans, it could not be pried open.

Before leaving Picenum, Hannibal also belatedly reestablished contact with Carthage, informing the city by seaborne messengers of what had transpired since he'd left Spain. Polybius notes that this is the first time Hannibal had touched the coast since reaching Italy, but still he had left the city without word for more than a year. Had he really wanted or needed instructions from Punic central, it seems he would have made a more concerted effort to contact them earlier. Instead, he waited until he had good news, especially for the Barcid faction at home. And apparently it elicited the responses he wanted—rejoicing and promises to support in every possible way the two campaigns in Spain and Italy. Perhaps as public relations, it worked, but in the case of the latter theater the results proved negligible.[47]

[5]

Refreshed, rearmed, and likely remembering his dream of the serpent tearing up the Italian countryside, Hannibal headed south to begin the next more overtly political phase of his campaign. He applied the sinuous column of his army—in hopes of weaning away his enemy's allies, of provoking further Roman action in their defense, or of simply demonstrating that the Romans could not protect their allies. Advancing down the Adriatic coastal plain into Apulia, foraging as he went, he turned southwest about two thirds of the way down the Italian boot and headed toward Aecae,[48] probably on intelligence that Romans were in the vicinity. He found Fabius Maximus camped nearby with an army of forty thousand—four legions and their allied equivalents—having reached this spot after an extremely cautious journey guided by constant reconnoitering. Hannibal immediately marched up, deployed, and offered battle. But Fabius would have none of it, leaving the Punic commander to withdraw and lecture his troops on the newfound timidity of Romans.[49]

There ensued a cat-and-mouse, or rather a fox-and-hedgehog game—with Hannibal employing all manner of artifice to incite his opponent, and Fabius clinging to his one big thing, avoiding a showdown. The Punic force was like a shark, to survive it had to keep moving, sending out between one half and two thirds of its numbers to forage.[50] To make this more difficult, Fabius had earlier tried to impose a "scorched earth" policy, ordering all those in the Carthaginian path to take shelter in fortified places, but only after destroying all structures and supplies. Given the amount of booty the Carthaginians managed to cart off, this policy was probably honored more in the breach than in the observance, but even partial implementation must have had the effect of dispersing the foragers and leaving them more vulnerable to attack. This was Fabius's opening. Keeping his own men concentrated and fed from local supply dumps, he sent out hunter-killer teams to prey on isolated Carthaginians, and in the process he rebuilt the confidence of what must have been a demoralized and inexperienced force.

Almost from the outset it seems Minucius, Fabius's master of horse, objected to the inevitable rural destruction, calling it craven, and champing at the bit for a more aggressive approach. It must have been hard for any Roman to take, especially since, as Minucius noted, the dictator's habit of camping on high ground created "beautiful theaters for their spectacle of Italy laid waste with fire and sword."[51]

Keeping the pressure on, Hannibal pillaged his way west across the Apennines into Samnium, heading toward Campania and the most fertile agricultural district in Italy, the fabled plain of Capua or *ager Falernus*. On unfamiliar ground, he apparently had some trouble reaching his destination; here is where he crucified one or perhaps several guides when they misunderstood his badly pronounced Latin and took him in the wrong direction.[52] Meanwhile, Fabius, following Hannibal's eventual path down the Volturnus River valley, a day or two's march behind, realized that the steep narrow pass at the valley's head was the only viable entrance and exit from the plain. All he had to do was occupy this defile—which he did with four thousand men, stationing the rest of his army in a camp high on a nearby hill—and he had the Carthaginian trapped. Hannibal could plunder to his heart's content, but the odds were on his returning only to find his path blocked, which is exactly what happened. Laden with loot he would need for the coming months, and faced with the necessity of establishing his winter quarters in a more defensible locality, Hannibal was left to consider his options.

The fox is most unpredictable after dark, and so was the Carthaginian. Appian (Han.14) claims it was here that a desperate Hannibal had his Roman captives slaughtered, but this seems unlikely, since at this point prisoners were still being ransomed and Hannibal needed the money. Besides, he had other beings to sacrifice.

He ordered Hasdrubal, the head of the service corps, to collect a herd of two thousand oxen from the vast throng they had assembled and attach bunches of dry wood to their horns. He rested his troops until around three A.M., and then formed the heavy elements, cavalry, and baggage into a column and began ascending the pass. Meanwhile, he had his herdsmen, accompanied by Numidian skirmishers, light the bundles and drive the animals up toward the ridges on either side of the pass. Maddened by the fire, the beasts raced erratically ahead, drawing the attention of the Romans guarding the pass. They followed in pursuit of what they thought were the torches of the Carthaginian force, only to be greeted by scorched bovines and a hail of Numidian javelins. Fabius also observed the fires and, thinking it a trap, refused to budge from camp. Left unobserved, Hannibal and the main body cleared the now unoccupied pass without incident, sending some Spaniards back to rescue the Numidians on the ridges.[53]

To Roman eyes at least, Fabius was made to look like a coward and an idiot, with Minucius becoming increasingly vocal and contemptuous in his criticism. Hannibal made a feint toward Rome, but the dictator held to his policy with apparent serenity, dogging Hannibal and keeping to the high ground. It was probably around this time, with the Carthaginian force meandering eastward toward Apulia, that the Punic commander sought to heap calumny atop his opponent's already soiled reputation. Informed by deserters that the Carthaginians were passing an estate owned by Fabius, Hannibal had his troops meticulously destroy everything around it, leaving only the dictator's property untouched. When news of this masterful psychological operation reached Rome, it had the intended effect of further undermining the dictator's popularity.[54] Sensitive to appearances, Fabius sent his son Quintus back to the city to sell the farm, the money from which he used to ransom Roman prisoners. Yet the damage had been done. Fabius was recalled, ostensibly to conduct certain religious rites, but more probably to explain his apparently dilatory conduct of the war. He left Minucius with strict instructions not to engage the enemy, but the master of horse had other ideas.

Sometime in the early autumn of 217 the Punic army marched up to a small fortified place called Gerunium, sitting in the midst of a rich Apulian agricultural district. Immediately Hannibal settled on his winter quarters. But when he offered the population terms, they refused him—a serious mistake. His troops made short work of the defenses and slaughtered the survivors.[55] Leaving the fort walls intact and preparing the houses inside to serve as granaries, he set about building a fortified camp for his forces around the outer circumference. Before long he was sending two thirds of the men out in foraging parties scampering about the countryside gathering grain for the months ahead like squirrels with swords.

At least until Minucius and the Romans arrived looking for trouble. Hannibal called back a third of his foragers and marched out against the Romans, sending two thousand Numidians to take a hill between the two armies. The Romans responded by capturing the hill and building their camp on top. Hannibal kept his forces consolidated but after a few days resumed foraging. Minucius went after the marauders, and even began assaulting Hannibal's forward camp—what amounted to Fabian tactics on speed. The normally belligerent Carthaginian seemed uncharacteristically passive; he retreated to Gerunium after considerable losses and was subsequently more circumspect with his raiding for rations.[56] Minucius, it seemed, was the man of the hour.

He certainly was in Rome. News of his success swept through the city. Romans were hungry for a victory—any victory—and this one was apt to have gained in perceived significance as its telling passed from mouth to mouth. Likewise, the repute of Fabius, who had yet to return to the field, suffered by comparison. So much so that one Metilius, the tribune of the plebes (the only office retaining its power subsequent to the appointment of a dictator), passed a law equalizing the master of horse's imperium with that of Fabius. Prominent in recommending this measure, Livy (22.25.18–19) says, was a recent praetor, Caius Terentius Varro. The historian is plainly contemptuous of this politician, portraying him as the lowborn son of a butcher and as an utter demagogue. But Varro's already elevated status and subsequent election to the consulship argue the contrary. It is a safe bet, however, that Varro objected strenuously to Fabius's approach to fighting Hannibal, and that when he gained power, things would be different.

In the interim, however, Minucius and Fabius were left to settle their differences. With the dictator's return to the Apulian front, the question of who would command, now that they were equals, immediately arose. The master of horse initially favored unitary control assumed on alternate days, but Fabius succeeded in convincing his colleague to divide the force, each retaining the equivalent of a consular army. Fabius no doubt argued that the consular army was the most efficient and easily controlled fighting instrument. Minucius promptly took his half and set up a separate camp about a mile distant, possibly at the forward position the Carthaginians had been forced to abandon.[57]

Hannibal had been biding his time, very much aware, by virtue of his superior intelligence, of the rift between the two Roman commanders. He also understood them. He had learned to respect Fabius for his caution, but Minucius could be tricked, and Hannibal had already set him up for a fall. Just as in the first battle, there was now a hill separating Hannibal and Minucius, a hill that Hannibal planned to occupy, banking on Minucius's trying to recapture it in a repeat of his earlier success. Hannibal had also surveyed the surrounding terrain, and although it was treeless, it contained many depressions capable of concealing substantial numbers of troops, the same ploy as at Trebia. On the night before he planned to fight, Hannibal sent out about five hundred horsemen and five thousand light infantry to hide themselves in clumps of several hundred.

At dawn Hannibal took the hill, so that Minucius, lacking a vantage point, had no idea he was not alone as he prepared for battle. Instead, the Roman commander concentrated on getting the Carthaginians off the high ground, first sending his light troops, then his cavalry, and finally the legionaries, all of whom Hannibal thwarted with reinforcements of his own. Next, Hannibal had his cavalry sweep down on the Romans, scattering their horse and sending the *velites* careening helter-skelter back into the main body of legionaries. This maneuver destabilized the maniples sufficiently so that when swarmed by the concealed Carthaginians, the army melted into a crowd.[58] Once more disaster was at hand.

But thanks to Fabius Maximus, it did not materialize. He had apparently anticipated such an outcome and had taken the precaution of marching out of camp and deploying nearby, providing a rallying point for the fleeing troops of Minucius. Having already sprung his trap and felled a considerable number of *velites* and legionaries, Hannibal chose not to press the issue. He had secured his base at Gerunium and would spend the winter there well supplied, resting his army, and probably further integrating its force components, while the Romans were held at bay.

Both Polybius and Livy would have us believe that this incident effectively rehabilitated Fabius and his policies.[59] Livy has Minucius returning to the dictator's camp with his army and once again subordinating himself and his troops in the most abject sort of way. Polybius adds that back in Rome respect for the dictator's cautious approach was miraculously restored. If so, it was short-lived. Sometime in De-

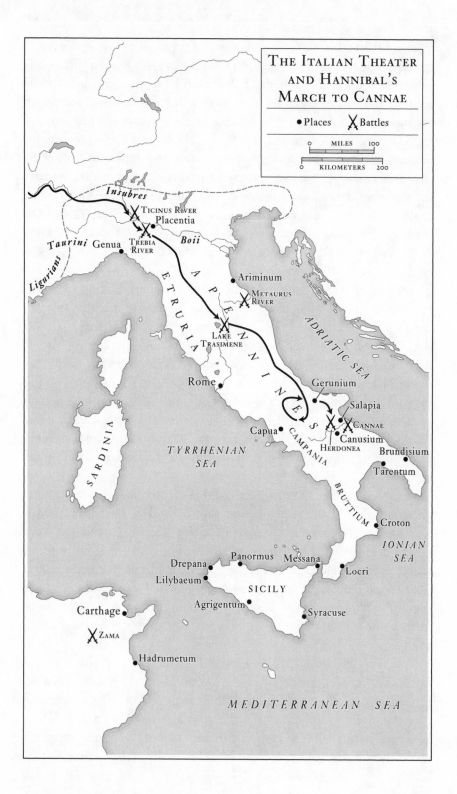

Insubres
TICINUS RIVER
Placentia
Taurini Genua
TREBIA
RIVER
Boii
Ligurians
ETRURIA
A
P
E
N
N
I
N
E
S
Ariminum
METAURUS
RIVER
Lake
TRASIMENE
ADRIATIC SEA
Rome
Gerunium
Salapia
Capua
Canusium
CANNAE
HERDONEA
Brundisium
CAMPANIA
*TYRRHENIAN
SEA*
SARDINIA
BRUTTIUM
Tarentum
Croton
*IONIAN
SEA*
Panormus
Drepana   Messana
Lilybaeum
SICILY   Locri
Agrigentum
Syracuse
Carthage
✗ZAMA
Hadrumetum
MEDITERRANEAN   SEA

cember 217 the terms of Fabius and Minucius came to an end. Power returned to the original consul, Geminus, and to Flaminius's replacement, M. Atilius Regulus, both of whom now took command of the army that was keeping an eye on Hannibal. The consuls were content to stay put, but the next consular elections would bring to the fore men with an agenda entirely different from that of Fabius Maximus.

Hannibal had shown himself to be the most dangerous sort of opponent, but thus far his political success in Italy had been minimal, leaving him without a fixed base and obliged to wander the countryside in search of food. That was where Fabius wanted him, with his troops acting not as soldiers but as vulnerable scroungers. Another year of this might have starved and weakened this cunning invader out of existence.[60] But Romans remained Romans. They retained a huge manpower advantage, and their every instinct beckoned them to battle. Unfortunately, the battle proved to be Cannae, and the hedgehog was left to watch from the sidelines as the fox had his way yet again.

VI

CANNAE

[1]

The winds of change echoed along the Tiber as the year 216 began, and though a skeptic might have heard the winds howling disaster, most Romans seemed confident they were blowing toward a quick and decisive victory.

The strategy seemed sound; pressure would be applied in all the appropriate directions. Marcellus, the reliable and hyperbelligerent *spolia opima* winner, was sent to keep an eye on Sicily, the fleet there having been augmented for a potential invasion of Africa.[1] More on target, in late 217, Publius Scipio, now recovered from his wound, had joined his brother Cnaeus and his two legions in Spain with eight thousand fresh troops and a small fleet. Both Scipios had been given the proconsular imperium to tear up Barca land and rob Hannibal of his base. Nor was Hannibal's Gallic connection overlooked. Twice-consul L. Postumius Albinus was given two legions and dispatched north to break the rebellion in Cisalpine Gaul and seal off any further support from that quarter. But the central objective, the overwhelming priority, was to directly confront Hannibal and crush him beneath the weight of Rome's key advantage, military manpower. Everything points to a corporate decision to stage a great battle and obliterate the invader once and for all. Fabius was out, the bludgeon was in.

Viewed from the comfortable perspective of subsequent events, the reasoning that led to Cannae is easy to dismiss. But it was far from implausible. Arguably, there was a fundamental Hannibal problem: if you didn't beat him, you couldn't get rid of him. On the other hand, if the Punic force were to lose even one significant battle, it was too far from any secure base to survive. Just one Roman triumph, a single day's victorious fighting, would put an end to the invasion.[2] The string of

previous defeats could be convincingly attributed to impulsive commanders, impiety, bad weather, bad luck, bad timing . . . The excuses
were endless. Meanwhile, Romans still had good reason to believe in
their military system—after all, its fundamentals would provide security for nearly another half millennium. They had merely to supersize
it and leave nothing to chance.

Of course they were wrong, and Fabius Maximus had been right.
Lacking a secure base, Hannibal probably could have been attrited out
of existence. But the victory at Cannae would allow him to sink his
claws deep into Italian soil, and then he would prove far harder to up-
root. So the battle proved to be much more than a human tragedy and
a tactical debacle; it was the strategic basis of fifteen more years of
Hannibal, what must have seemed at times like perpetual Hannibal.
About the only things the Romans could salvage from Cannae were
Scipio Africanus and perhaps ten thousand disgraced survivors, and
one day they would avenge themselves and Rome by drawing the
Carthaginian away and then defeating him nearly as badly as he had
defeated them. But that day was still far in the future.

[2]

Deciphering any political environment is difficult, more so an environment twenty-two hundred years old and littered with deceptive contradictions, patronage relationships, and family alliances. Although
modern historical scholarship has clarified the climate of opinion and
motivation to some degree, we will never know exactly what Romans
were thinking in 216. Therefore, while it is possible to say that as the
year began, attitudes had hardened and grown more overtly aggressive,
certain issues remain veiled in obscurity.

For example, Livy (22.33) tells us that a Carthaginian spy, who had
gone unnoticed for two years, was caught right around this time. His
hands were cut off, and then he was let go. In the same breath Livy adds
that twenty-five slaves were crucified for forming a conspiracy in the
campus Martius, the field where Roman troops customarily drilled. The
two events seem related. Why else would they be mentioned together?
Also, from this point Hannibal's intelligence advantage begins to di-
minish, or at least it appears to, on the basis of available narratives. Was
this spy the Punic mole, and were these slaves his spy ring? It can be in-

ferred as such, but not with certainty. It may be that the Romans avoided saying too much about what could have been considered an embarrassment and a vulnerability.

Other deceptions are more apparent. Both Livy and Plutarch would have us believe that the consular elections of that year, which determined the commanders at Cannae, were basically contests between the impulsive "people," whose choice was the lowborn knave and demagogue C. Terentius Varro, and the prudent patriciate, who managed to secure the elevation of the wise and experienced Lucius Aemilius Paullus as a brake on his hotheaded and foolish colleague. The historians even stage a tête-à-tête during which Fabius and Paullus agree that the former's strategy of avoiding battle is the best approach and that the impulsiveness of Varro is virtually as dangerous to Rome as Hannibal.[3] Livy even insinuates that on the day of the battle, Varro issued his orders to fight without bothering to inform Paullus.[4] Polybius, while less hyperbolic in his denunciation of Varro, is nevertheless plainly sympathetic to Paullus and largely absolves him from blame. But all of this becomes more difficult to swallow in light of the fact that after Cannae the apparently incompetent Varro was given a number of other important commissions and even military commands—although this also may have been a means of shifting the blame. Meanwhile, Polybius's exculpatory portrayal of Paullus fades somewhat when it is realized that Paullus was the grandfather of the historian's patron, Scipio Aemilianus.[5]

Modern historians have come to understand that a more likely explanation is that Varro, the first member of his family to rise to the consulship, and largely without illustrious descendants, was tagged by later generations as Cannae's designated scapegoat, while Paullus's reputation was rescued by the later propagandizing of his powerful family.[6] Actually, Varro may have served under Paullus during his first consulship three years before, when they'd been campaigning in Illyria, and both were probably now on the same side of the debate over how to fight Hannibal.[7]

This amalgam of confrontationists was likely built around the powerful families of Aemilii and Cornelii, particularly the Scipionic branch, and included Minucius and Metilius, the tribune who'd worked to elevate Minucius to equality with Fabius Maximus. Probably they were opposed by the Fabii and the older, more conservative members of the senate, who could be assumed to have stood on the side of patience and the gradual attrition of the invader. Yet the policy of patience was plainly in eclipse, perhaps even among some of its adherents. After all, they were every one of them Romans, and the Roman default position was to fight. A measure of this enthusiasm was that as many as a third of the senate joined the army at Cannae, and most of the other senate members had close relatives among the ranks.[8] This showdown with Hannibal was intended to be the *magna mater* of all battles, and an analysis of those selected for magistracies in 216, especially as military tribunes, shows them to be considerably more experienced in military matters than was usually the case.[9] Plainly much of the leadership was ready to stake their future and the future of their respective gene pools on this gigantic roll of the dice.

So were the rest of Rome and Rome's allies. The contemplated instrument of destruction was to be an army roughly twice the size of any previously assembled by the Romans to operate as a unit.[10] Varro and Paullus would each command double armies of four legions plus equivalent allied units, but the whole mass was expected to fight together—eight legions and eight *alae*, in effect a quadruple consular army. Given that a Roman army operated best as a maneuver unit when it was composed of two legions and two *alae*, there was reason to suspect that this monster might prove inherently unwieldy—a lumbering Frankenstein of a force at best, and at worst a paralytic, a quadriplegic consular army. And this raises the question of who actually would be in charge overall. Meanwhile, to compound the effect, each of the legions, and presumably the *alae*, was increased from forty-two hundred to fully five thousand, which added up to a grand total of eighty thousand infantry.[11] As we shall see, quantity had a quality all its own ... but not the one the Romans expected.

The sole area where the force seems somewhat shorthanded was cavalry—six thousand, two thirds of it allied, when the normal legionary and *alae* component might have been expected to yield almost ten thousand.[12] Apparently recent losses, especially those of Centenius, had taken their toll, and this too would prove telling at Cannae.

More specifically, the army that would confront Hannibal had two basic components. The first was the force left to keep an eye on him at Gerunium, an experienced element with a history of heart-stopping ups and downs—mostly the latter. Its core was built around the two legions that Publius Scipio had managed to salvage from the defeat at Trebia, soldiers who earlier had been repeatedly ambushed by Gauls.

The legions had later been taken over by Geminus, then transferred to Fabius Maximus to chase and lose Hannibal, and then they'd nearly been destroyed under Minucius. To make up for casualties and other attrition, they were bound to have been reinforced on multiple occasions, but at least the veterans had served together and under the same officers for a period of years.

The second element was essentially virginal, the Roman portion consisting of four new legions all recruited around the beginning of the year. While these troops as individuals appear to have received the rudiments of military training as part of their upbringing, the process of integrating them into maniples and teaching them to fight as units not only took time—presumably the spring and early summer—but would have resulted in only a thin behavioral veneer of mutual trust and confidence, which, without the experience of actually fighting together, could be ripped away fairly easily in an emergency to reveal a substrate of panic and helplessness.[13] Next to nothing is known about the allied components, but if this was a newly recruited force, it's hard to imagine they were any more tested than the Romans, nor would they have been used to their officers, who were also Romans.

It is not clear when the two forces joined together. Polybius (3.106.3) talks about sending new recruits forward for experience skirmishing, but these recruits appear to be reinforcements for the legions already at Gerunium. Although Livy (22.40.5) maintains that the new legions arrived before Hannibal left winter camp and headed toward Cannae, modern opinion[14] favors a delayed linkup, as late as less than a week before the battle. Given this, it's hard to imagine that the Romans' juggernaut was in any meaningful way integrated; rather, it remained two separate armies that on the day of battle would be cut up and welded together for its moment of truth, tactically a dubious proposition.

Yet it could be argued, and probably was at the time, that the Roman military system made their troop formations inherently interchangeable, and therefore more easily mixed and matched. No doubt the injection of experienced leadership was counted upon as a lubricant. And there was the intangible of morale. The allied forces in particular were furious over Hannibal's rampage across the Italian countryside and were vengefully eager for combat. Meanwhile, the Roman troops seem to have been embarrassed, not daunted, by previous defeats and were now grimly determined to prevail.[15]

To seal the deal, the establishment did something unprecedented.

Livy (2.38.2–5) tells us that once the allied levies arrived, the consuls had the military tribunes formally administer an oath to all the infantry and cavalry that they would depart from their ranks only to secure a weapon, kill an adversary, or save a comrade. Previously, the historian notes, this had been a voluntary pledge among the soldiers themselves; now flight in the face of the enemy was against the law. To some societies and some armies this might have seemed a mere formality, but the Romans were literalists and legalists. And as we shall see, it was this oath that would determine the fate and futures of those who might have thought themselves otherwise lucky to escape the death trap at Cannae.

As a fighting force, the fated quadruple consular army was large and full of Romans, both good things. But it was also full of vulnerabilities. It had a substantial number of light troops, perhaps as many as twenty thousand, but they were of suspect quality. If not the "armed servants" one source calls them,[16] they were clearly not as effective as their Carthaginian equivalents. These soldiers had been scattered like chaff at Ticinus and Trebia . . . though they did seem to stiffen somewhat under Fabius and Minucius. Still, it is probably telling that Rome's staunch ally, old King Hiero of Syracuse, looking for ways to help, thought it wise to donate one thousand light troops of his own, some of them archers (apparently the only archers at Cannae).[17]

The cavalry was probably even weaker; it had already suffered savage losses, and the skills involved are not easily replicated on short notice. The ranks were probably swelled a bit by members of the senate, who were by definition equestrians, yet many would have been old and past their military prime. Besides, the majority of cavalry were allies, and Hannibal's well-advertised leniency toward them could be expected to have an impact on their fighting spirit in a pinch, especially among forces with the greatest ability to get off the battlefield in an emergency.

The obvious strength of the Cannae army was its heavy infantry. Even if it could not be screened effectively by light troops and its flanks protected by cavalry, it was big enough to be relatively immune from harassment, provided it could maneuver and win decisively with some degree of dispatch. Yet this was also a force subject to emotional volatility—its better half, the experienced element, had been defeated more than once by Hannibal, and the other part was a mass of neophytes, with all that that implied. Temperamentally, it was an army likely to overreact—prone both to excessive enthusiasm and passive despair. Judging by his plan and its results, this was exactly what its Barcid nemesis anticipated.

[3]

It is not certain when Hannibal left Gerunium and headed south, but he likely would have waited until the early summer, when the crops were ripening and his troops could forage. Livy concocts a tale of an attempted ambush and then a night escape in the face of the already united Roman army, but Polybius's version that Hannibal marched out past the guarding force of Geminus and Regulus, who were under orders not to engage until Varro and Paullus arrived with the rest of the army, is simpler and more plausible.[18] The historians agree on one point: the Punic force was hungry. Whether on the basis of good luck or good intelligence, Hannibal gravitated to Cannae, around sixty miles south of Gerunium, nearly to the Adriatic coast. Here he captured a grain storage and supply dump in the ruined citadel on the heights of the otherwise abandoned town. His food problem solved, at least temporarily, he made no further effort to move, and this was telling.

Cannae sat at the bottom edge of an immense treeless plain, the largest south of the Po.[19] It was ideal for cavalry operations and large-scale maneuvers, exactly the terrain for magnifying Punic military advantages. By this time Hannibal probably understood that the Romans were intent on a showdown and were putting together a monster of an army for the occasion. So far, his efforts to chip away at the Italian alliance had come to nothing. He needed a really spectacular victory to generate the kind of political impact to begin breaking off Rome's affiliates. This was the perfect time and place to inflict it. Staying here was tantamount to accepting the challenge. He had only to await his opponent's arrival.

But, being Hannibal, he probably kept himself busy preparing the reception. If we accept Polybius's version of the events leading up to the battle, the Punic army may have been alone at Cannae for several weeks.[20] This is a dangerously long time to give any commander to prepare a battlefield, much less a commander with Hannibal's fertile military imagination. By this time he was likely on a first name basis with every rise and depression, every twist in the River Aufidus, every potential campsite, every approach and escape route, every possible advantage he could squeeze out of the surroundings and then blend with a battle plan that seems to have been derived from his cumulative observations of Roman fighting tendencies and the capabilities of his own troops. As always, much remained to be determined by chance and the circumstances of the actual engagement, but it's a safe bet that during this respite Hannibal's mind seldom wandered from the upcoming test.

His plan when it was finally hatched implied a great deal of faith in his army. This faith was not misplaced. The gang of desperadoes that had stumbled off the Alps not much more than a year and a half earlier had been but a scrawny prototype of the force that now awaited the Romans at Cannae. Freeze-dried no more, the men and horses had regained their health, had eaten their fill, and were rested. We know that key elements had been systematically rearmed with the best of the captured equipment, and it is likely that many others had picked up bits and pieces of what had once been Roman weaponry.

Another change had to do with the Gauls. By this time they were much more reliably integrated into the fighting force. They still fought together, to take advantage of their peculiar tactical characteristics, but at Cannae small units of Gauls were interspersed with Spaniards, indicating that their tribal allegiances had been effectively superseded by the command system that controlled the rest of the army.[21] Very likely the process that had begun for the Gauls on the slog through the Arno marshes was now complete. They were now not only fierce and brave individually; they were also disciplined, well trained, and above all reliable at the unit level. And as such they would play a critical role at Cannae.

Psychologically, this was an army that had known nothing but the most decisive sort of success since it had entered Italy. In a life-and-death struggle, confidence is crucial, and the recent past had given these men every reason to believe in their own fighting skills, as well as their commander's ability to drive opponents into positions of utter vulnerability and near helplessness. Many must have already killed Roman soldiers personally and must have also observed them reduced to an abject state, begging for mercy. That was Hannibal's point when he reassured an officer worried about the size of the opposing force at Cannae. ("In all this multitude there is no one who is called Gisgo.") For Carthaginians, more Romans simply meant more Romans to kill.

This was the dark side of a truly professional fighting force, especially one that fought with edged weapons; they were used to killing, inured to it. They would kill without hesitation. It was a terrible advantage that the Carthaginians had and that most of the Romans at Cannae lacked.

Nowhere was this more evident than in the cavalry, probably the most lethal Punic fighting component. As had been true since Trebia, the Spaniards and Gauls rode together as a shock element, although now they were almost certainly better trained and integrated. The Spaniards carried two light throwing spears, a sword, and a round shield, or *caetra*. The Gauls, primarily composed of nobles, were more heavily armed and armored, with chain mail, metal helmets, and a stout thrusting spear. The two groups would have been an impressive one-two combination, with an initial hail of javelins followed by closer, more decisive engagement.[22] This was a force more than capable of taking on anything the Romans had on horseback, and likely predisposed to fight in the same very confrontational way—one entirely different in its ethos from the other face of Punic cavalry.

They were the Numidians, Hannibal's version of killer bees, proverbially swarming their opponent if given even the slightest opening. The Numidians were the closest thing a western Mediterranean battlefield saw to an inner Asian steppe horseman. They lacked only the steppe horseman's deadly composite bow, relying instead on a brace of light javelins and a slashing dirk. Characteristically, Numidians pinned and herded their foes through absolute mastery of their hyper-agile ponies, and then ran the enemy down with ruthless efficiency, able to cut their hamstrings even at a full gallop. Like the steppe horsemen, they were fatally easy to underestimate. Riding bareback and carrying only a light shield for protection, they avoided hand-to-hand combat and were largely incapable of direct confrontation. Polybius (3.72) describes them as "easily scattered and retreated, but afterwards wheeled round and attacked with great daring—these being their peculiar tactics." Yet in the hands of a commander as opportunistic as Maharbal, they could destroy an entire force once it became even slightly demoralized and ready to bolt.

All together, Hannibal's cavalry now numbered around ten thousand, two thirds more than when he'd entered Italy, and more to the point, they were enjoying a five-to-three quantitative edge over the Cannae-bound Romans, whose horsemen were by far inferior in quality also. Looked at another way, the Carthaginian force had one horseman for every four foot soldiers, while the Roman ratio was one to thir-teen, a strong indication that the Punic army was far better adapted to the flat terrain on which the battle almost certainly would be fought. All in all, it constituted a yawning gap, and one that would soon send the Romans stumbling down the initial steps toward tactical ruin.

Numerically, the Carthaginian advantage in cavalry was nearly re-versed with regard to infantry. Polybius and Livy both agree that forty thousand foot soldiers would have been available to Hannibal at Can-nae, a figure modern sources support.[23] But if the infantry were out-numbered two to one, the quality of the Punic soldiers was better, and not just in terms of confidence and prior experience killing Romans. The Carthaginian force was notably less homogenized than its Roman equivalent, and in those various parts were vested a variety of fighting skills tailor-made for a commander with Hannibal's protean military imagination. The ancient sources provide no specific figures for the various contingents, but modern historians have made a number of in-formed estimates that seem basically in agreement.[24]

The approximately eight thousand Punic light troops were probably proportionately even more outnumbered by the Roman *velites* than was the case with their comrades in the other infantry arms, but the relative difference in personal capabilities was equivalently lopsided in the other direction. Basically, Roman skirmishers were men either too young or too poor to take their place in the maniples. The Carthagini-ans were specialists—screening and harassment was their business.[25] Numidian javelin men, perhaps six thousand of the total light troops, proved particularly adept at cooperating with their horse-borne coun-trymen and seem to have intensified the effects of the cavalry's swarm-ing tactics. Though less numerous, the other major component of the Carthaginian light infantry—the Balearic slingers—were, if anything, individually even more lethal. They were both feared and coveted as mercenaries throughout the western Mediterranean. Much overlooked by modern historians, the sling was capable of launching a projectile toward its target at up to 120 miles per hour—fast enough to kill a man at fifty paces.[26] While light troops in general played a secondary role at Cannae, at least until the later stages, one shot delivered by a slinger early in the battle may have played a critical role in compromising the Roman leadership.

Hannibal's close order heavy infantry probably numbered around thirty-two thousand at this point and came in three varieties: Gauls,

Iberians, and Libyans. Despite the heavy infantry's having suffered relatively severe casualties at Trebia and Trasimene, there probably remained around sixteen thousand Gauls, whose shock value and increased reliability we have already considered. There were likely about six thousand Spaniards left at this point, a fraction of the original contingent that had made up the bulk of the army when it had departed New Carthage. In Darwinian terms, we can assume the fittest survived. Nevertheless, Polybius (3.114.4) leads us to believe they wore no armor, but only a purple-bordered linen tunic, and possibly not even a helmet; but since a lot of captured Roman equipment was available, this may not be entirely accurate. Tactically, these Iberians were most interesting because they fought like Romans, first throwing a heavy javelin not fundamentally different from a *pilum*, and then weighing in with either a straight or a curved short sword and a large oval shield. Interspersed with Gallic units, they could be construed as having had a stabilizing effect on the critical center at Cannae, allowing the more impulsive Gauls to rush forward, hack away for a while, and then fall back, leaving the Spaniards to fight the pursuing Romans on their own terms.

Finally, there were the Libyans, presumed to be Hannibal's best-drilled and most elite maneuver element, since they were the first to receive Roman equipment and because they formed the jaws of the trap that snapped shut on the Romans at Cannae.[27] Thus far he had used them scrupulously and in ways they would take few casualties, so of the twelve thousand who had come down off the Alps, probably around ten thousand remained. But if these African spear-fighters formed the teeth of the Punic force structure, the other elements were the claws and muscle and sinew of this beast of battle. Hannibal's genius as a commander was his ability to devise and execute a plan that used all the parts in concert to swallow and digest a much larger prey.

[4]

We pick up the Roman juggernaut where we left it at the beginning of Chapter II, slouching toward Cannae, proceeding with the utmost caution. The Romans may have found the flat coastal terrain reassuring, since it gave Hannibal nothing to hide behind should he try to stage an ambush. No doubt they sent the cavalry out to reconnoiter just in case.

According to Polybius's version, the two halves of the great army probably joined up on the road in late July, with Geminus (Regulus, the other proconsul, seems to have been sent back to Rome because of advanced age, to be replaced by Minucius) having followed Hannibal south at a respectful distance, and Varro and Paullus intercepting Geminus near Arpi, roughly two days' march north of Cannae. With the army combined, there were eighty-six thousand mouths to feed. So it made sense to keep the contingents separate for as long as possible. The hunger of the army would also place time constraints on the commanders to seek decisive combat once they got within striking distance of Hannibal. Ironically, it seems perhaps the dinner tables had turned; though Livy (22.40.7–8) would have us believe that as battle approached, Hannibal was also running out of food. If true, and not merely the historian's way of saying Fabius had been right all along,[28] both sides needed a fight quickly.

The Romans had no trouble locating Hannibal, since he was hardly hiding, and they set up camp initially approximately six miles to the east on the broad plain that runs down to the Adriatic. There ensued an elephantine pas de deux, as the two armies warily closed the distance while at the same time trying to gain some tactical and psychological advantage.

The Romans, however, were literally of two minds, since Varro and Paullus followed the tradition of alternating command daily when consuls operated together—just what Fabius had refused to do the year before, which had thus enabled him to save Minucius. Because of the curtain of blame later cast over Varro, it is hard to separate actual disagreement between the two consuls from aspersions dumped on Varro retrospectively. If it is conceded that both consuls wanted to fight, and most modern historians do concede this, the evidence such as it is points to Paullus as the more cautious of the two, particularly worried about being caught on the flat ground ideal for Carthaginian cavalry.

The vicinity of the anticipated field of battle was dominated by high ground to the southeast, where the abandoned town of Cannae and Hannibal's first camp were located, and bisected by the River Aufidus, a shallow, narrow watercourse running in a northeasterly direction toward the sea. The terrain to the northwest, over and beyond the left bank of the river, was broad and flat. The area between the right bank and the highlands toward Cannae, while still level, was more broken and constricted. Hannibal almost certainly preferred the left bank but could and would fight on the right side; both Roman consuls wanted to avoid the left side and stage the battle in the most confined area possible. The days preceding August 2, 216, were an extended test of wills that saw Hannibal unsuccessfully harass the Romans with light troops as Varro initially approached. Then Hannibal moved his camp to the left bank and formally offered battle on this side, first to Varro and then to Paullus, only to be refused. Finally, Hannibal sent Numidians after the Romans' water bearers, and this gesture provoked the Romans into action, albeit on the right side of the Aufidus.[29] Meanwhile, the Romans had moved too close to withdraw safely, and so they split their army into two camps, leaving two thirds on the left side of the river and the remainder in a smaller enclave on the right bank. The stage was set.

The Roman battle plan at Cannae can be summarized in three words: "pack the middle." Because this approach would play into Hannibal's own scheme and lead to a great disaster, it is easy to dismiss the plan as nonsensical. It wasn't. Rather, it had a clear purpose, to maximize the Roman numerical advantage in infantry while minimizing the obvious Carthaginian superiority in cavalry. It was also based on past experience. At Trebia, ten thousand legionaries had finally managed to hack their way through the center of the Punic line, and had they been able to do it sooner, they could have split and pivoted to crush the Carthaginians attacking on each flank. Even amidst the surprise and demoralization of Trasimene the impetus of around six thousand Romans had carried them through the Carthaginian stopper force, only to be captured later. We can assume that Varro and Paullus and those advising them were confident in the ability of their troops to puncture the heart of the Punic line, and were intent on doing this as rapidly as possible. Geometrically this called for a narrow, thick formation, exactly the configuration on the day of the battle described by Polybius (3.113.3), "placing the maniples closer together than was formerly the usage and making the depth of each many times exceed its front."

Breaking though in this manner was decidedly not a matter of simple momentum, like some gigantic rugby scrum pushing inexorably forward. Romans fought primarily with short swords, so the cutting edge was by definition the first line of combatants. True, *pila* could be launched from several rows back, but any soldier behind around line eight would probably have hit a fellow Roman up front.

The real arguments for this type of human geometry had to do with order, endurance, and psychology. Long narrow columns are easier to keep together, and, they therefore move faster and more cohesively on the battlefield.[30] The many lines to the rear also insured an almost inexhaustible supply of fresh fighters to take the place of the fallen and exhausted, a kind of conveyor belt of shark's teeth. Finally, a great many of the Roman participants at Cannae lacked combat experience; the middle of such a formation was a safe, psychologically reassuring place for them. One source equates this to the human instinct to herd together for mutual comfort, but without considering that this was actually prey behavior.[31] The thickened manipular order could be expected to have massive combat endurance, which would make the formation almost impossible to defeat by frontal attack, and would thereby allow the unit to move steadily forward. But what would happen if it faced the unexpected, was hit from an unanticipated direction? At this point herding behavior might become just that, dissolving the maniples into a crowd compressed to the point of mass helplessness. The legions would lose the ability to replace frontline fighters through now nonexistent gaps between units. It was a prospect not pleasant to contemplate, and one we can be pretty sure the Romans failed to consider.

Hannibal may have. Just how much he knew of the Romans' plans prior to battle is impossible to say. Though Livy (22.41.5–6) maintains that "all the circumstances of his enemies were as familiar to him as his own," whether Hannibal understood beforehand the degree to which the Romans would pack the middle remains open to question. Yet his experience fighting them would have warned him of their will and of their ability to break through in the center, and the likelihood of their trying it again. Also, given his knowledge of Greek military practice, he was doubtless familiar with the Athenian tactics at Marathon in 490, when the Greeks withheld their center and crushed the Persians with their wings.[32] As the day of battle approached, all of this must have been taking root in Hannibal's fertile brain as he roughed out the framework of an even more lethal trap. As we shall see, the final details would await the contingencies of the battlefield, but the basic plan of using the Romans' own greatest strength against them was inherent in Hannibal's deployments and therefore had to have been plotted in advance.

Though there is a tradition of viewing Hannibal as simply being up to his usual tricks—hidden attackers and fake surrenders[33]—the key deception at Cannae was far more subtle. In essence, the trap was hidden in plain sight, something that even today does not seem to be fully understood. Basically he planned to string a line of combined Gauls and Spaniards between two very deep columns of Libyans positioned on either flank, so that viewed from above the formation would look like a backward block letter *C*. The idea was that as the legionaries rushed forward, the Gauls and Spaniards would give way in a measured fashion (this was critical), leading the Romans farther and farther in between the two columns of Libyans, who would then be in a position to stage a devastating simultaneous attack inward from either flank, stopping the Romans dead in their tracks and leaving them all but surrounded.

Maps of the battle, which are invariably drawn from a bird's-eye perspective, make the net results clear enough, but also reveal the central deception in a way that leaves open the question: "Why would anyone be dumb enough to walk into such an obvious trap?" But from ground level it would have been far from obvious.

The analogy of American football is helpful. This very intricate game can be enjoyed and understood by the public precisely because it is viewed from on high; the deception is designed to be seen at ground level, and from this perspective deceptions are profoundly confusing, requiring all manner of coaching, cues, and experience so that players are not fooled on every play. As the Romans approached the Carthaginian line, all they would have seen was a continuous line of men, with no way of knowing the varying depth at either side. As the Romans pushed forward, their attention would have been focused straight ahead and toward the center, where they were making the greatest progress. When the Punic flanks attacked, most of the Romans would not have realized it was even happening. They would have known only that their body of men had strangely come to a halt. By this time it would have been too late. They were as good as dead.

Assuming that Hannibal did not have direct knowledge of the Romans' plans and simply had to anticipate what they might do, the Carthaginian's plan faced several worrisome contingencies. Expecting his adversaries to pack the middle implied they would deploy on a fairly narrow front, not much wider than his own. Should the Romans march onto the battlefield in a more normal formation, their advantage in numbers would leave the Carthaginian line seriously outflanked on both sides, affording a perspective that would not only betray the depth

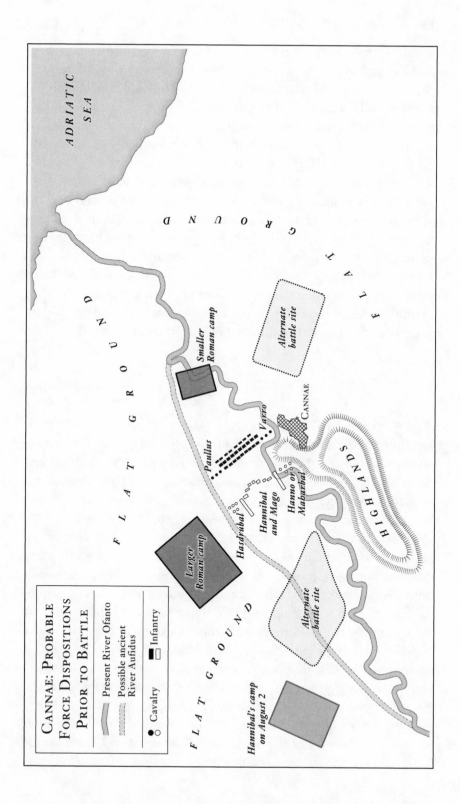

CANNAE: PROBABLE
FORCE DISPOSITIONS
PRIOR TO BATTLE

Present River Ofanto
Possible ancient
River Aufidus
● ○ Cavalry
■ □ Infantry

ADRIATIC
SEA

FLAT GROUND

FLAT GROUND

FLAT GROUND

FLAT GROUND

HIGHLANDS

Smaller
Roman camp

Larger
Roman camp

Hannibal's camp
on August 2

Alternate
battle site

Alternate
battle site

Paullus

Hasdrubal

Hannibal and Mago

Hanno or
Maharbal

CANNAE

VARRO

of the Libyan columns, but also would force the Carthaginians to abandon the ambuscade by pivoting outward to make up the difference. Also, the Roman and allied cavalry could not be ceded the initiative; if they were allowed to sweep around to either side of the Carthaginians, the jaws of the trap would be revealed and their commanders could be warned before it was too late. None of this happened; instead the Romans played into Hannibal's hands as if choreographed; but such schemes are always vulnerable to the unexpected and this could account for the shadow of what is possible to interpret as Plan B in the sources—Appian's (Han. 20) story of Hannibal concealing some cavalry and light troops in ravines on a hill (presumably the bluffs leading up to Cannae[34]) with orders to attack the enemy rear as at Trebia, and Livy's (22.48) tale of 500 Numidians staging a fake capitulation, being conducted behind enemy lines, and later producing hidden swords and assaulting from this quarter. Neither is taken very seriously by modern historians; but they were hardly out of character for a fox full of tricks.

[5]

As the sun rose on Tuesday, the second day in August, the scarlet tunic signifying battle could be seen displayed above the tent of Terentius Varro, whose turn it was to command the Cannae army. Polybius says Varro's men were eager for the fight, were at a near fever pitch of anticipation from the waiting.[35] Orders would have been distributed to the tribunes in the night. The tribunes then would have assembled the men and cavalry in time to march out of camp just after dawn, cross the river, and join the troops in the smaller encampment on the right bank. All were now present, with the exception of ten thousand (probably a legion and an *ala*) left to guard the main camp and stage an assault on the Punic encampment during the battle. It is likely that the men guarding the main camp were the bulk of those fated to survive the day and become the living ghosts of Cannae.[36] Those less fortunate, around seventy-six thousand men, would move into the customary formation—*velites* out front; *triplex acies*, compacted in the middle; and cavalry on the flanks—all awaiting the Carthaginians and destiny.

But exactly where were they? The short answer is that we will never know the precise site of the battle for sure; but that said, the issue has stirred up enough controversy over the years to make it worth considering. Geographically, there are basically two reference points—the location of Cannae itself and the River Aufidus, now called Ofanto. There are also two reliable historical artifacts: we know from Polybius that the battle was fought on the same side of the river as the smaller Roman camp, and the Roman line faced roughly south, with its right flank anchored by the river.[37] It also makes sense that the Romans would have wanted their left flank resting against the highlands on which Cannae was perched, the idea being to make it impossible for Hannibal's cavalry to sweep around either side to envelop them. The problem is that the distance between the bluffs and the modern Ofanto is far too narrow to accommodate anything like the size of the Roman army, no matter how compacted.

This led a number of respected scholars to propose that the battle was actually fought on the left side of the river,[38] or on a broad plain to the east of Cannae.[39] But the problem with the first view is that it clearly contradicts Polybius, who seldom made this sort of mistake; the drawback to the second is that the flat area to the east is easily wide enough to give Hannibal's cavalry complete freedom, which raises the question of why Varro would have bothered crossing the river to fight there. Yet all of these interpretations assume that the course of today's Ofanto is identical to that of the Aufidus, likely a bad bet, given the passage of twenty-two hundred years. This assumption is questioned by modern historians Peter Connolly and Adrian Goldsworthy.[40] Their ingenious alternative is that the ancient river ran considerably to the north as it passed Cannae, leaving flats of about 1.3 miles, wide enough to fit the Roman order of battle as it was assembled that day. This hypothesis remains open to conjecture, but this alternative location seems to be the most plausible for what would shortly become the most prolific killing ground in the history of Western warfare.

If this was indeed the point of deployment for the Romans, it must have inspired great confidence. The inexperienced citizen and allied cavalry, stationed at the extreme ends of the line, right and left respectively, had been relieved of any offensive responsibilities; the cavalry had simply to guard the flanks while the infantry did its work.

Similarly, the numerous but qualitatively inferior *velites* that were spread out in front of the army had no particular mission once the force was deployed, and they could conveniently retreat between the maniples if pressed.

Meanwhile, the reinforced *triplex acies* seemed unstoppable, and if anything slowed it down, it was at least impenetrable. It must have appeared to Varro and Paullus that they had finally positioned their forces in a way that even Hannibal could not bend to his own advantage.

Now it was his turn to do just that. Hannibal apparently sent the Balearic slingers and Numidian foot soldiers across the river at about the same time the Romans crossed, but the mission does not seem to have been to interfere with enemy deployments so much as to set up a perimeter behind which the Punic cavalry and heavy infantry could line up.[41] When this was done and he was certain the Romans were ready to fight, Hannibal followed. We can conjecture that the cavalry crossed the river first to reinforce the screeners. Next the Gallic and Spanish infantry joined them, lining up in the center, followed by the two bodies of Libyans, who took their place on either side but remained in columns to form the backward block letter C. By this time the horsemen would have split apart and moved to the flanks, the Spanish and Gallic heavy cavalry on the left facing their Roman equivalents, and the Numidians on the right matched against the allied mounted elements.

As orderly and purposeful as these pre-battle rituals seem in print, the real thing must have provided, even before the fighting started, plenty of distractions and cause for disorientation. At this point the field must have been a jumble of cacophony—horns blaring, drums pounding, swords beating on shields, shouts and war cries reverberating back and forth, to and fro—all the sounds that men muster as they steel themselves to face death and intimidate those they hope will be their victims. Also, more than 125,000 men and in excess of 15,000 horses tramping about in a confined area must have kicked up huge quantities of dust, and it appears that Hannibal's familiarity with the environment now dovetailed with his desire that the Romans not accurately perceive the true nature of his infantry formation. He had apparently observed earlier that a southeasterly wind, the Vulturnus, gusted with increasing force during the morning, and could be counted on to whip up the dust and blow it into the Romans' faces, a vexation apparently confirmed by a fragment from the near-contemporary poet Ennius.[42]

Finally, and probably most important, this was August in southern Italy; we can count on it having been hot, and it was bound to get hotter as the day progressed. Most of the Roman heavy infantry and at

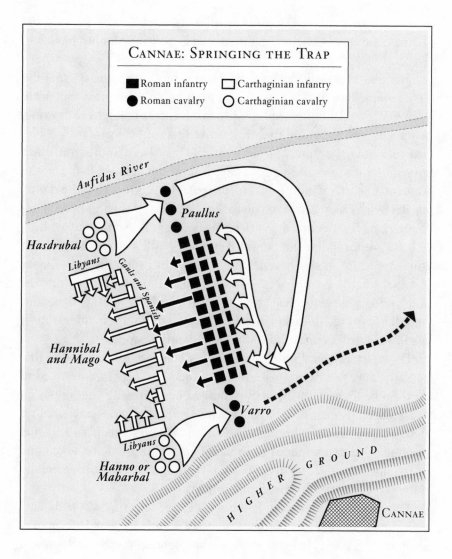

CANNAE: SPRINGING THE TRAP

■ Roman infantry   □ Carthaginian infantry
● Roman cavalry   ○ Carthaginian cavalry

Aufidus River

Hasdrubal

Paullus

Libyans

Gauls and Spanish

Hannibal
and Mago

Varro

Libyans

Hanno or
Maharbal

HIGHER GROUND

CANNAE

least the rearmed Libyans would be burdened with between fifty and eighty pounds of arms and armor (see Chapter II, section 5) as they fought for their lives throughout the day. If Trebia had been orchestrated by hypothermia, Cannae was destined to be an inferno where untold thousands were likely to be felled by heat exhaustion, and access to drinking water may well have allowed the Carthaginians to persist in their butchery during the last and most murderous phases of battle.

So it was as they began to fight. The ancient sources agree that the light troops were first to engage, and from Polybius we hear they were evenly matched, neither side gaining an advantage before withdrawing, as was customary, behind their respective lines of heavy infantry.[43] If it had been otherwise, presumably we would have heard more from other sources. So it seems the *velites'* numerical preponderance had won the Romans at least a standoff—an auspicious start, considering the multiple drubbings they had taken on earlier occasions. Still, the Punic auxiliaries may have inflicted a very significant casualty at the outset. Livy (22.49.1) reports that the consul Aemilius Paullus, who was with the Roman citizen cavalry, was dealt a severe head wound from a slinger just as the battle commenced—an injury bad enough to leave him unable to ride a horse and bad enough to force his bodyguard to dismount in order to protect him. Polybius does not mention this incident, but it is still suggestive, considering what was about to happen.

The first decisive Punic move came when the Spanish and Gallic cavalry under Hasdrubal—leader of the service corps and destined to perform brilliantly on this day—charged headlong into the opposing horse on the Romans' right flank. With their adversaries anchored on the river and outnumbering the Romans by more than two to one (around sixty-five hundred to twenty-four hundred), there were none of the normal wheeling maneuvers. Instead the Carthaginians seemed intent on going right through the Romans.

The combat that ensued, Polybius (3.115.3) tells us, "was truly barbaric." In large part this was because it was mostly on foot. Roman cavalrymen had a decided proclivity toward fighting on the ground, and many of these troopers must have been inexperienced and new to their mounts.[44] But they also may have chosen to dismount because of Paullus's wound. Plutarch maintains that when the consul was forced from his horse and his attendants got off theirs to protect him, the cavalry assumed a general order had been given and so also dismounted—a development that supposedly caused Hannibal to comment: "This is more to my wish than if they had been handed over to me in fetters."[45] While it is unlikely the Punic commander actually observed the cavalry getting off their horses, the act nonetheless proved fatal to most of the outnumbered Romans, who were basically annihilated. This is also where many of the Roman senators and others of the equestrian class would have gathered to fight, and ended up making their last stand. It is not clear if Paullus died here—he and his staff may have escaped to join the rest of the army—but Livy's version makes it seem that this was his end. So at a point when the battle had barely begun, it seems logical that the republic had already been dealt a grievous blow. And it would only get worse. Rather than chase down the last of the survivors who managed to get back on their horses and flee, Hasdrubal reeled in his men from the pursuit, then rested and re-formed them to inflict further mayhem on another part of the battlefield.

Meanwhile, the heavy infantry engagement had begun and had already taken shape, literally, in an unexpected way. As the line of Gallic and Spanish infantry advanced (one source estimates the formation was roughly 840 men wide and 26 deep[46]), it bowed outward to form a crescent. While some maintain this was natural for a line of men moving forward,[47] others believe it was a last-minute decision on Hannibal's part.[48] Whichever it was, this convex formation had an immediate and beneficial effect for the Carthaginian side. For as the Roman *hastati* charged and reached *pila*-throwing distance, the shape of the line left only a narrow group in the Punic center vulnerable to this potentially devastating missile barrage, and may have led many legionaries to waste their shots while still out of range.[49]

The same thing would have happened as the sides closed for swordplay. Initially at least, the Roman manipular order and their own training would have more or less automatically kept their line straight, and so only the center group of Spaniards and Gauls would have been engaged. The key to Punic success turned on the interior line retreating slowly and in a controlled manner. This was why Hannibal and his brother Mago (presumably joined by other officers and Celtic nobles) stationed themselves here, immediately behind the front, to better manage the action and encourage these most critical of fighters. And the initial geometry of battle served exactly its purpose by committing only a relatively few combatants, and by keeping the huge Roman force at bay until the legionaries in the middle managed to push those at the Carthaginian center back.

As we imagine clusters of bare-chested Gauls flailing their broadswords, interspersed with Spaniards fighting from a crouch behind their shields, all seeking to fend off the surging Romans—themselves bashing forward with their *scuta,* seeking an opening for their *gladii*—we should not forget that this sort of combat, essentially a series of individual duels, was both physically and emotionally exhausting. It could not be sustained for more than a few minutes. Once the Punic line failed to collapse immediately, these spasms of violence had to be followed by rest periods when both sides drew back to catch their collective breath for a few minutes. War cries and insults might have been hurled back and forth, followed by *pila* and other projectiles picked up or passed forward, and then close combat would have been reinitiated. Over time the lulls would have grown longer and the mêlées shorter.[50]

This interrupted rhythm of violence also was to the Carthaginians' advantage, allowing them to regroup, regenerate, and fall steadily backward in relatively good order. Seeing this, the Romans naturally pushed ahead with increased confidence and growing excitement, focused on their objective of breaking through at the center as quickly as possible. As this happened, the retreating Punic line began to assume an increasingly concave shape, and a critical juncture was reached. Polybius (3.115.6) reports that the Gallic and Spanish infantry in the middle were forced into such a rapid retreat that the Punic line started to break up. As the Roman tide surged forward, it cast caution and training aside and followed the line of least resistance, crowding inward toward the center. The intervals separating the three lines of the *triplex acies,* and the spacing between maniples, disappeared, and its general organization started to disintegrate. Collectively, the legionaries thought they could see victory just ahead, but it was a mirage; instead, as-yet-unnoticed defeat stared them down from either side in the form of two serried blocks of Libyan heavy infantry, the jaws to the Carthaginian trap.

The moment of Hannibal's killer epiphany had arrived. The order went out, and man by man the Africans on both the left and right sides pivoted inward, dressed their ranks, and in unison fell upon the Roman flanks, most likely the location of the least-experienced citizen and allied troops.[51] There was little the Romans could do in response besides turning as individuals to face the threat; as units, their formations were too compressed and disorganized to maneuver effectively. They were reduced to a crowd of loners trying to fight off a coordinated engine of destruction. Meanwhile, the emotional shock waves rippled inward, spreading paralysis throughout the Roman ranks and halting the forward momentum of the entire army. Their fate was all but sealed.

That took place in another quarter. Terentius Varro, the overall Roman commander, was with the allied cavalry numbering around thirty-six hundred on the left wing, doing not a lot in the face of a roughly equal number of Numidian horse under either Hannibal's nephew Hanno (Polybius 3.114) or the resourceful Maharbal (Livy, 22.46.7). The Numidians skirted and swarmed their adversaries as best they could,[52] but were probably thwarted by the Cannae bluffs anchoring the Romans' position creating the kind of standoff the Romans had wanted on their flanks, a standoff likely satisfactory to Varro. It was around this time, Livy maintains, that the Numidians supposedly staged their fake surrender. But even if this did occur, the Roman consul, who would have had little idea of what had taken place on his opposite flank, was shortly in for an even more unpleasant surprise.

Hasdrubal, fresh from obliterating the Roman horse on the other side of the combat zone, led his reconstituted force of Gallic and Spanish heavy cavalry across the battlefield behind the deployed lines of legionaries, and was soon bearing down on the allied horse with a force that was nearly twice the size. But even before the Carthaginians could bring the charge home, their intended victims evaporated in a panicked stampede, apparently sweeping Varro and his attendants along in their wake. The Numidians, devastating in pursuit, took out after them, killing or capturing all but three hundred of the allies, though Varro escaped to nearby Venusia with seventy of his bodyguards.[53] With Paullus very possibly killed on the right, and Varro removed from the left, Hasdrubal may have already shorn the quadruple consular army of both its consuls.

Yet the focus of his appetite for destruction remained unerring. Rather than rising to the bait of the chase, yet again the Punic commander re-formed his cavalry and instead headed toward the rear of the Roman infantry, quite apparently intent on closing their last avenue of escape. Here, Polybius tells us (3.116.8), Hasdrubal delivered multiple charges at different points, seemingly with devastating effect.

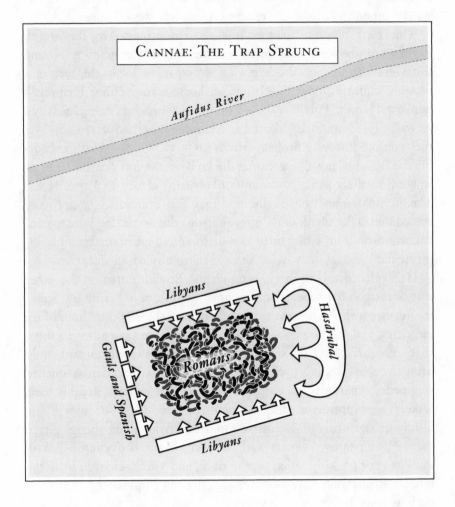

CANNAE: THE TRAP SPRUNG

Aufidus River

Libyans

Gauls and Spanish

Romans

Hasdrubal

Libyans

On first glance this seems puzzling, since the *triarii* in the rear should
have been well equipped to turn and resist, lining up on one knee with
their shields resting against their shoulders and their long spears protruding to form a barrier that horses would not charge. But instead of a
solid wall of *triarii*, it is far more likely the Roman rear was cluttered
with a soft mass of up to twenty thousand *velites*, who had withdrawn
behind the maniples shortly after the battle had begun.[54] Most of them
were probably adolescents, were very lightly protected, and were lacking room to throw their javelins, and with no avenue of escape, they
were virtually the perfect prey for heavy cavalry. Terrified by the
horses and the slaughter of their comrades, they would have recoiled
inward, exposing their backs and hamstrings to spear thrusts and sword
slashes while they pressed desperately against an ever more compacted
and undifferentiated human mass.

The same crowding into helplessness must have been taking place
on the flanks, as the Libyans on either side continued to press home
their attack, an ever-tightening human vise. Meanwhile, the nearly
routed Gauls and Spaniards, no longer pursued by the Romans at the
forward edge of battle, would have been given time to regroup and turn
the tide in their favor. A terrible dynamic was taking place. Assailed
from all sides, beyond the control of its officers, with those on the outer
edges having no place to go but inward, the Roman army, by pressing
itself into paralysis, was becoming if not the instrument of its own destruction then at least complicit in the process.

Somewhere between sixty-five thousand and seventy thousand Romans and allies—depending upon how many had already fallen—were
now surrounded. Tactically the battle was over, but the killing had just
begun. There was no alternative. The army was still too large and full
of fight to be taken prisoner; besides, with its leadership immobilized in
the press, it had no real means of surrender. The only choice was its effective extermination, a task the Carthaginians accomplished through
systematic butchery almost until the sun set on this terrible day.

Not only does the process beggar description, but exploring the details of the massacre might seem to serve little purpose beyond pander-
ing to some bloodlust with a kind of pornography of violence. Yet war
is truly terrible, and to turn our eyes away from its results is in itself an
act of cowardice. Hannibal's great victory, his tactical masterpiece
celebrated through the ages, produced, in the end, little more than
corpses. But this is probably better illustrated by recounting the subse-

quent course of events than by moralizing over it now. Nevertheless, there is a more prosaic but still historically valid reason for prying into the details of this exercise in mass homicide. As one source put it, "What remains unclear is how encircled troops, with nowhere to run, could be slaughtered in such a one-sided fashion."[55] We live in an age when killing is cheap, virtually automated; that was far from the case at Cannae. Other than those who succumbed to the heat, each of the men who died had to be individually punctured, slashed, or battered into oblivion. One modern source estimates that in order for the necessary killing to be accomplished in the eight hours that Appian (Han. 25) estimated the fighting lasted, over one hundred men had to be dispatched every minute.[56] Yet even this astonishing figure underestimates the swiftness and profusion of the slaughter, since the estimate assumes that the killing took place at a regular rate throughout the day and not in a great spasm toward the end, as actually happened. In essence, so many victims, so little time, and that doesn't even attempt to reflect on the ruthlessness and horror of it all.

Nevertheless, logic tells us that the liquidation of the Roman army at Cannae, if it is possible to reconstruct at all, must have been a matter of mechanics and motivation. We can start here. Among the ancient sources, only Polybius (3.116.10–11) has left us something approaching a plausible description of what must have been the most horrific several hours in all of Western military history: "The Romans, as long as they could turn and present a face on every side to the enemy, held out, but as the outer ranks continued to fall, and the rest were gradually huddled in and surrounded, they finally were all killed where they stood." In other words, they were finished off from the outside in, peeled like an onion. This makes sense, at least basically, but there were likely to have been other lethal dynamics at work.

Hannibal's skirmishers—the Numidian foot soldiers and Balearic slingers—having earlier withdrawn to safety behind his main line, must have been intact and available. It's hard to imagine that he wouldn't have had them let loose a hail of javelins, stones, and even expended *pila* onto the stationary mass, a deadly barrage that could hardly have missed in such a target-rich environment, nor avoid inflicting serious injury on Romans who were either too crowded or too exhausted to raise their heavy shields for protection.[57]

Meanwhile, the infantry of Libyans, Gauls, and Spaniards would have continued with their grim work at the circumference. One modern source in an otherwise believable reconstruction of the carnage describes victims "dispatched with frenzied blows, usually to the head."[58] This seems to miss the mindset implied in the quantity and rapidity of the butchery. Hannibal's soldiers were practiced killers; very likely most had adopted the cooler, utilitarian approach of the predator, having drawn on our emotional heritage as hunters of the most prodigious and ruthless sort. Moreover, they would have known how to kill quickly and efficiently. If the victim's back were turned, then a spear or sword thrust to the kidneys would have been so painful as to instantly paralyze, and would have killed within seconds through massive internal bleeding. Or if the victim were facing forward, an equivalent stab to the lower abdomen would have produced the same results almost as fast. Yet such a death stroke—or even more so, multiple death strokes rapidly delivered—implies a certain acceptance, or at least passivity, on the part of the recipient.

This is something the ancient sources—all of them Romans or Roman sympathizers—deny. They would have posterity believe Cannae was, in the words of Polybius (3.117.1–2), "a battle in which both the victors and vanquished displayed conspicuous bravery," a battle in which the Romans fought stubbornly to the bitter end.[59] Given what has been learned through modern combat studies, this does not seem likely. Even among elite units, when sufficient casualties have been suffered, the whole group slides into a state of apathy and depression more extreme than is encountered in almost any other kind of human experience. "Unable to flee and unable to overcome the dangers through a brief burst of fighting, posturing, or submission," writes military psychologist Lieutenant Colonel Dave Grossman, "the bodies of modern soldiers quickly exhaust their capacity to energize and they slide into a state of profound physical and emotional exhaustion of such a magnitude and dimension that it appears to be almost impossible to communicate it to those who have not experienced it."[60] Were Romans tougher and more stoic than modern combatants? Perhaps, but as far as we know, the mental makeup of the ancients was similar to our own. How else would so many of their recorded deeds make sense to us? It seems, then, that the reason why it was possible to kill so many so fast is that most of the victims faced death without resistance. Would this paralyzing combat fatigue have afflicted everyone, and to the same degree? Probably not. Anecdotal evidence indicates that some would have gone down fighting no matter what the circumstances. But the circumstances were really bad, well beyond the limits of most.

If it is possible to conceive of hell on earth, this human abattoir at Cannae must have been the equal of any hell that history in all its perversity has managed to concoct. Thousands upon thousands packed together, unable to move, beset by the cries of those in extremis, many of them dressed in now useless chain suits and cooking-pot helmets beneath the broiling sun, without prospect of water, only death offering any relief whatsoever. As time passed, more and more men would have fainted from the heat, slid to the ground, and been trampled beneath the feet of their comrades, their bodies and discarded shields tripping still others who would then have fallen similarly to their deaths. At the outer edges especially, but also in the interior, where javelins rained, the ground would have grown slick with Roman blood, which would have brought down still others. As at Lake Trasimene the hopeless would have begged their fellows to finish them—presuming there was room for even a short sword thrust—or simply would have done the deed themselves. The stink of death and all the bodily functions that accompany it must have come to pervade the atmosphere and compound the wretchedness of those condemned to take their last breaths there. There was no place worse.

Here and there it is possible to catch a glimpse, even if it's only a statistic, of a shadow of an actual person caught in the grip of this misery. We know that of the forty-eight military tribunes at Cannae, twenty-nine did not survive. Most would have died in this central killing field, since it was their job to lead the legions. Both quaestors, Lucius Atilius and L. Furius Bibaculus, were likely here also, as were Geminus and Minucius—all of them dead.[61] If Paullus had not been killed earlier on the wing, as Livy suggests, then he too met his end here—according to Polybius (3.116.15), "in the thick of the fight." This brings to mind the fate of Paullus's son-in-law.

Nineteen-year-old Publius Cornelius Scipio was young for a military tribune, but he had already seen a lot. He had saved his father's life at Ticinus and had likely been part of the disaster at Trebia, and perhaps even at Trasimene. At Cannae we know he was attached to the Second Legion, and, given his social standing and his relationship to Paullus, it doesn't seem likely that the young Scipio was with the ten thousand left to guard the camp.[62] So probably he found himself caught in the dwindling remains of the Roman infantry, once again ensnared by Hannibal's trickery. It must have been a learning experience, but perhaps a futile one in the face of almost certain death. Yet, contrary to all expectations, he would survive and elude capture, as did thousands of others also apparently hopelessly trapped.[63] Here again this seems to have been a matter of mechanics.

Body buildup had to have become the central problem of the Carthaginian executioners, piles of dead obstructing them from getting at more Romans, not to mention all that slippery blood. A point of diminishing returns must have been reached and a new approach required. Logically this would have suggested a change of venue, a shift in the killing field to less cluttered terrain. The controlled release of clumps of legionaries away from the main mass would have effectively served this end. These Romans could then be run down and killed (or taken prisoner). But this also would have opened a window of opportunity for the Romans, who might have organized into wedges capable of defending themselves until they could reach either of the two camps and some sanctuary, however temporary.[64] Many never could have made it, especially if they got separated. But chance, this opening, and the inevitably growing exhaustion of their Carthaginian tormentors would have collaborated to sweep away from this disaster the core of a class of survivors who would live to fight another day. Young Scipio, it seems, was one of them.

Finally the killing must have trailed off. Polybius maintains that Hannibal rounded up approximately two thousand Romans who had climbed up and hid in the ruins of Cannae, and also captured both Roman camps immediately after the battle.[65] While Hannibal may have captured the refugees in the ruins, it doesn't seem likely that his troops were in any shape to overwhelm a fortified area, no matter how dispirited the inmates. Sleep was probably the only item on their agenda.

If this makes sense, then Livy's story (22.50.4–12) of what went on in the two Roman camps that night appears believable. Most of the men seem to have been in shock. But those in the larger enclave, having avoided the main disaster and having participated in only a brief failed attempt on Hannibal's camp, were probably in better shape. These men were still organized and were being led by their officers, who undoubtedly were aware that their present position was untenable. They sent a runner to the smaller camp and ordered them to break out and join

forces, so that both elements could slip away under the cover of darkness and make for Canusium, a walled town about twenty-five miles to
the southwest. The message fell on deaf ears, until one of the surviving
military tribunes, P. Sempronius Tuditanus, made an impassioned
speech and got six hundred (Frontinus says it was only sixty-two) men
to follow him out to join the others. Not everybody from the big camp
was willing to leave. But Livy indicates that some four thousand legionaries and two hundred cavalry in this group arrived safely at Canusium, where they were eventually joined by several thousand other
survivors; meanwhile, another forty-five hundred found their way to
Venusia, where Varro had taken refuge. All of these men were destined
to be reorganized and branded with the stigmatic title *legiones Cannenses,*
the living ghosts of this terrible battle.[66]

How terrible? Dawn of the next day revealed approximately 45,500
legionaries and twenty-seven hundred cavalrymen strewn about a
space not much larger than a single square mile.[67] As the Carthaginians
set about despoiling the bodies and searching for their own among the
dead and half dead, even they were shocked by their handiwork. Livy,
the ancient cinematographer, leaves us a scene as surreal as any other
in military history:

> Here and there amidst the slain there started up a gory figure whose
> wounds had begun to throb with the chill of dawn, and was cut down
> by his enemies; some were discovered lying there alive, with thighs
> and tendons slashed, baring their necks and throats and bidding their
> conquerors drain the remnant of their blood. Others were found
> with their heads buried in holes dug in the ground. They had appar-
> ently made these pits for themselves, and heaping the dirt over their
> faces shut off their breath. But what most drew the attention of all
> beholders was a Numidian who was dragged out alive from under a
> dead Roman, but with a mutilated nose and ears; for the Roman, un-
> able to hold a weapon in his hands, had expired in a frenzy of rage,
> while rending the other with his teeth.[68]

If this does not give pause, it is possible to resort to statistics. By way
of approximation we can consider each Roman weighed 130 pounds—
they were lighter than modern men. Then there would have been well
in excess of six million pounds of human meat left to rot in the August

sun—the true fruits of Hannibal's tactical masterpiece, at least for an air force of vultures.

The fate of the others remaining at Cannae was not much better, particularly if they were Roman citizens. According to Livy's timetable, Hannibal, after allowing his troops much of the day for looting, next made short work of the two camps, gathering up nearly thirteen thousand prisoners. When these men were added to those taken from the ruins on the hill and to those taken from the battlefield, the total was slightly more than nineteen thousand captives.[69] Many of the Romans would end up as slaves in Greece and Crete, still there more than two decades later—another of Cannae's many legacies.

Hannibal too was left to wrestle with the outcome of Cannae. The fight had cost him between fifty-five hundred and eight thousand men, but at least half of these had probably been Celts, and the army was basically intact.[70] Meanwhile, his men had recovered gold rings numbering in the hundreds, some taken from captives but most pried from the lifeless fingers of senators and equestrians.[71] In a single day Hannibal had decimated a substantial proportion of Rome's leadership, a blow that some might well have considered mortal. Maharbal, Hannibal's brilliantly opportunistic cavalry commander, was apparently one who thought so. Livy tells us (22.51.1–4) that sometime after the battle, amidst the congratulations of the Barcid's henchmen, Maharbal warned that no time was to be lost, and held out instead the prospect of dining in the enemy capital within five days. "Follow me: I will go first with the cavalry, that the Romans may know that you are there, before they know you are coming!" It was the most audacious of proposals. March on Rome! Finish it now! When Hannibal hedged and refused to make an immediate decision, Maharbal's reply was equally impulsive: "So the gods haven't given everything to one man; you know how to win a victory, Hannibal, but you don't know how to use one."

Assuming the incident actually took place[72]—it was very much characteristic of both men: Maharbal seizing the main chance, and Hannibal the gambler growing cautious in the face of overwhelming good luck—it strikes at the heart of Punic prospects and is therefore hotly debated. On balance, scholarly opinion seems to support Hannibal for not trying it. Some argue that he was short on pack animals and the logistical support needed to move his army 250 miles to Rome with the necessary alacrity.[73] (This argument seems odd, given the journey from Spain and the Carthaginians' tromp through the swamp.) Other scholars maintain that even if he had gotten to Rome, he couldn't have done much productive,[74] and he lacked siege equipment.[75] (He could have built some.) Still others are of the opinion that Hannibal was better off trying to break the Roman alliance, win on a solid base of support, and then negotiate.[76] (We shall see how that worked out.) In fact there were many good reasons for not marching on Rome, and only one good reason for going.

Unlike the scholars, Field Marshal Bernard Montgomery, a soldier, thought Maharbal was right.[77] Maharbal seems to have understood that when a more powerful adversary is down, it has to be dispatched. Rome still had huge manpower reserves; there was no such thing as a peace party; this was a state that bargained only with the defeated. Hannibal's single chance of winning the larger war was to begin marching his army toward Rome. Even if it had taken him a month to get there, the tension in the city would have only built with reports of his coming. And ultimately his appearance outside the walls might have broken the spirit to resist, or might have led to Rome's sending an ill-prepared force out to another catastrophic defeat and ultimate capitulation. Or not. In the end it still would have been a long shot. But it was his only shot. Instead, Hannibal chose another route, and the war became only a matter of time.

[6]

Still, if Rome was not about to collapse, there were certainly cracks ... and not just in the façade. At Canusium it seems things almost reached the point of falling apart. The survivors were treated kindly by the locals, especially a wealthy woman named Busa, who gave them food and fresh clothing. Among the survivors were four military tribunes (for some reason Tuditanus is not mentioned): Lucius Bibulus; Quintus, the son of the former dictator Fabius Maximus; Appius Claudius; and Publius Scipio, who, despite being the youngest of the group, emerged as its dominant personality in what was shortly to become a crisis situation.

The episode began when a reliable source informed them that within the group of survivors, a cabal of young nobles led by M. Caecilius Metellus and P. Furius Philus, whose father had shared the consulship with Flaminius in 224, were ready to give up on Rome, abandon Italy, and become mercenaries abroad. When the other tribunes agreed to form a council to discuss this stupefying piece of intelligence, Scipio would have none of it, demanding immediate action. Leading a few followers, he burst in on the conspirators with drawn sword and took them into custody, but not before demanding on pain of death that they swear an oath of allegiance to the state.[78]

The nascent mutiny put down, Scipio and Appius learned of Varro's presence in Venusia and sent him a message asking if the consul wanted them to deliver their forces to him or wanted them to remain in Canusium. Varro promptly marched his own troops over to them. This may be significant.

Besides the obvious motive of concentrating forces, the reasons for Varro's decision and the later treatment of the *legiones Cannenses* could be connected. Had the conspiracy gone beyond the young nobles and extended to the troops, making it necessary for Varro to reach Canusium quickly, in order to stabilize the situation? Or alternatively, did the errant consul rescue his own reputation at the men's expense, by giving the appearance of restoring order where there had not necessarily been disorder? It's impossible to know. What is known is that Varro, having exited the battlefield at a full gallop, was later remarkably well treated by his countrymen, while the *Cannenses,* who left under rather more duress, were effectively banished. Rank certainly has its privileges, but the contradictions here are hard to ignore or explain.

Back in Rome the city's population was on the ragged edge of panic, "expecting Hannibal every moment to appear," Polybius (3.118) tells us shortly before he effectively signs off, the remainder of his description of the war surviving only in fragments. For better or worse Livy becomes our primary oracle, framing subsequent events with a dramatist's eye.

Accordingly, Rome's streets are described as echoing the wailing of lamenting women, because the initial reports indicated that the Cannae army had been crushed and there were no survivors. The senate met to take measure of the situation, with Fabius Maximus arguing for gathering more intelligence, sending the women indoors, and preventing anyone from leaving the city. It was only after a letter arrived from Varro verifying the disaster—but adding that he was with ten thousand survivors at Canusium and that Hannibal was still at Cannae not doing much of anything—that the cloud of terror began to dissipate and enough traction was gained for the senate to begin serious planning. What emerged was a characteristic combination of superstition, practicality, and adamantine stubbornness.

Existentially, beating back the dread and propitiating the gods called for extraordinary—what we would call barbaric—measures. Perhaps conveniently, two of the vestal virgins were found not to be so. One of the two women comitted suicide before she could be buried alive with the other, while the seducer was beaten to death by the *pontifex maximus,* the chief priest. Meanwhile, the priest's colleagues were consulting the Sibylline Books for other goddess-calming measures, and found the answer in more live interments—this time two couples, Greek and Celtic, male and female. And if human sacrifice did not prove sufficient, the city fathers thought to send fellow senator and historian Fabius Pictor to Greece to consult the Delphic oracle for more ideas on atonement. In a further attempt to restore emotional equilibrium, the senate officially limited mourning to thirty days, but the senate still had to call off the annual festival to the goddess of the harvest, Ceres, since the rituals required married women who weren't in mourning, and few were available.[79] Rome did regain its composure, but these steps, plainly meant to be viewed as extreme, reflect the degree to which the news of Cannae had shaken the inhabitants.

Yet beneath the veil of ritualistic excess, the senate remained clearheaded, making the leadership and personnel decisions necessary to deal with the immediate crisis and to restore Rome's capacity to defend itself. Almost immediately the stalwart Marcellus, apparently no longer in Sicily, was sent to Canusium, where he would reorganize the *Cannenses* and put them back in fighting shape, while Varro was sent specific instructions to return home, possibly to nominate a dictator.[80] (Upon arrival he would be greeted rapturously "for not having despaired of the Republic." Acidly, Livy reminds us that a Carthaginian arriving back in Carthage under similar circumstances would have been punished with the utmost rigor—that is, he would have been crucified.[81]) The man chosen as dictator was very experienced—M. Junius Pera, a former consul and censor, with the highly capable Tiberius Sempronius Gracchus acting as master of horse. Together they set about rebuilding Rome's force structure.

In time there would be a huge manpower pool available, but in just two years Hannibal had killed at least a hundred thousand of Rome's soldiers, and the recruiters on the Tiber behaved as if they were more than a little shorthanded. Just one thousand new cavalry could be raised, a number reflecting Hannibal's prodigious attrition of the equestrians. To levy more foot soldiers for two new *legiones urbanae*, the draft age was lowered and boys of seventeen or even younger were called up, along with reinforcements from the Latin allies.[82] Yet more telling was the enlistment of six thousand criminals and debtors, who had to be equipped with the Gallic arms taken by Flaminius for his triumph in 223. Finally, and most significant, the city's slaves of fighting age were promised freedom upon discharge if they were willing to join the war effort, a call that was answered by eight thousand of them, who were subsequently known as *volones*, or volunteers. Their owners were compensated with state funds, the cost of which, Livy (22.57.11–12) notes ominously, exceeded the amount that would have been required to ransom the prisoners held by Hannibal.

Back in Apulia, the Carthaginian was in an avuncular mood. As he had after Trebia and Trasimene, he let the allies he held go free, yet again professing his goodwill. He then turned to the Roman captives and sought to explain himself, which was something new. He was not pursuing a war to the death with Rome, he explained; he was fighting "for honor and empire." Just as his Carthaginian predecessors had yielded to the success of Roman arms, now it was time for Rome to accept defeat in the face of his own skill and good fortune.[83] It was a speech that might have been given by Pyrrhus or any other Hellenistic monarch, a perfectly reasonable speech. The rules of war as he saw them dictated that, after such a string of beatings, the vanquished, presuming they were in their right minds, admit defeat. That was the way the "great game" of the Mediterranean basin was played; it was time Rome got used to it. He was prepared to be generous. The captives were to be ransomed for a reasonable price; ten of their own number would be sent to Rome to work out the details. Carthalo, a Carthaginian cavalry officer, would accompany them to present Punic peace terms. It's impossible to know if Hannibal really expected his initiative to work, but it seems unlikely that he anticipated the reception that the delegation actually got.

As the group approached the city, the senate had the dictator, Pera, send a lictor to meet them and inform Carthalo that he would not be received and that he had to leave Roman territory by nightfall. So much for a negotiated peace. There was some sympathy for the captives, but not enough. In the speech the leader of the prisoners gave to the senate, Livy (22.59) has him argue that ransoming their number would be cheaper than purchasing the previously mentioned volunteer slaves, and comparing themselves favorably with those who took refuge at Venusia and Canusium, "men who left their swords on the field and fled."

These pleas fell on deaf ears, especially those of T. Manlius Torquatus. He delivered a savage rebuttal. Although he did concede that the troops at Canusium were better judges of courage and cowardice than the captives, he revealed little regard for either group. The negligence of the captives was twofold: first, "they fled to the camp when it was their duty to stand firm and fight," and second, they surrendered the camp.[84] It was left unsaid but still implied that all those who had left the battlefield, captives and escapees alike, had violated the oath administered before the battle never to break rank except in the pursuit of duty.

The point, for the moment at least, was that the captives were not to be ransomed. The senate even went so far as to forbid their families to raise money privately to free them. This plainly went against precedent; just the year before, Fabius had paid prisoners' ransoms with the proceeds from the farm Hannibal had left untouched. The Roman leadership wanted to send a message not just to its own soldiers, but to Hannibal, to shock him with the degree of their determination.[85] Whatever he might think, in their eyes this was a fight to the finish.

When the delegation reluctantly returned with the bad news, Hannibal's mood—though not necessarily his strategy—hardened. Appian (Han.28) maintains that Hannibal had those of senatorial rank fight as gladiators for the amusement of the Africans; some were slaughtered; the rest were sold into slavery. The last, at least, we know was true. Polybius in a fragment (6.58.13) reports that Hannibal lost his joy over the victory at Cannae; he now knew he was in for a long fight.

But as hardheaded and hard-hearted as was the image presented along the Tiber, the Roman leadership still had to work within its means. After Cannae much of southern Italy was leaning toward Hannibal, and Rome needed a presence to fend off the momentum toward the Punic side. The new *legiones urbanae* and the scratch force of slaves and criminals were not yet trained. The only trained men were the *Cannenses.*

We next hear of Marcellus in the autumn of 216, first at Casilinum, then at Nola, parrying Hannibal's thrusts at the latter town with his army of survivors. Livy conflates what was probably a series of desultory skirmishes into a tactical victory featuring a surprise sortie out of the city gates, but even he questions the number of losses inflicted on the Punic force.[86] It was not much in the way of revenge. Still, the *Cannenses*, now divided into two legions, showed themselves to be once again an effective fighting force and one ready to take the field against its nemesis. If nothing else, the men had amply demonstrated their loyalty to the state. Yet they were not forgiven, even in the face of further disaster.

As the terrible year 216 came to an end, Rome settled down for a change of leadership. But no sooner had L. Postumius Albinus—who had been sent in the spring to Cisalpine Gaul with two legions plus allies to break the rebellious Celts—been elected in absentia to his third consulship than news filtered into the city that he and his entire army had been ambushed and annihilated. To add insult to injury, the victorious Boii beheaded the fallen consul-elect, hollowed out his skull, and subsequently used it as a drinking cup. But more to the point, Rome was down another twenty-five thousand troops.[87] It did not matter; by December of 216, the new *legiones urbanae* were ready and were given to Marcellus.

No longer needed, the *Cannenses* would now get what they deserved, at least in the eyes of the senate. Taxes had been doubled so that all soldiers could be paid in cash immediately, except for those who'd fought at Cannae. They got nothing.[88] But this was secondary compared to being shipped to Sicily. Here they would stay until 204, removed from their families and their livelihood, effectively banished. It was a terrible punishment, inflicted upon them because they were seen as having broken an oath never before required, which had made them, technically at least, deserters.[89] Rome had lost a great battle and needed a scapegoat. Rather than blame the strategists and commanders who had planned it, the powers that be turned on the survivors. The logic, the same as for decimation (*"pour encourager les autres"*), might have made sense at the time. But these ghosts of Cannae would live to haunt the republic. For one day, legionaries would look to their generals and not Rome for a future, and that perspective would spell civil war and absolute rule. This more than anything else was the battle's legacy.

VII

AFTERSHOCKS

[1]

It didn't take long for the seismic reverberations from Cannae to start tilting the playing field in Hannibal's direction . . . or so it seemed. Almost immediately a number of the nearby Apulian communities—Aecae, Arpi, Herdonea, and Salapia—threw in with the Barcid, and as he moved west into the hill country of Rome's old enemies the Samnites, most of them went over to him also.[1] Grabbing momentum by the horns, he split his force for the first time, ordering his brother Mago south to pick up as much support as he could muster among the Oscans, Lucanians, Bruttians, and the Greeks in cities on the coast. Mago would then continue his journey alone back to Carthage, where he would deliver Cannae's good tidings and press for reinforcements, which he could then lead back to Italy. Mago would return to Italy, but not before becoming sidetracked for upward of a decade, and without ever reuniting with his elder sibling.

Hannibal, meanwhile, soldiered west into fertile Campania for the second time, looking for more new friends. His first target, the seaport of Neapolis (modern Naples), rebuffed him, but there was something far better in the offing—Capua, the second city in the Roman confederation and a place notorious for its wealth and luxury, symbolized by its perfume market, the fabled Seplasia. But Capua was far more than a fleshpot; its leadership class was deeply intertwined with Rome's through marriage and economic ties. It was a vital and valued Roman ally.[2] Yet, despite every inhabitant holding Roman citizenship, the lower classes since the Battle of Trasimene had been restive and increasingly inclined toward secession. In the wake of Cannae and Hannibal's approach, the pressure in this direction increased dramatically, until the only thing holding back the flood was the hesitance of the local nobility.

In particular, three hundred young cavalrymen from the city's best families were serving alongside the Romans in Sicily, a position that would leave them hostages if Capua changed sides. Their parents, amidst the political turmoil, managed to have a delegation sent to the surviving consul, Terentius Varro, for an assessment of the military prospects. Seen through Livy's eyes (23.5.4–15) Varro proved no better diplomat than general. "Legions, cavalry, arms, standards, horses and men, money, and supplies have vanished either in the battle or in the loss of two camps the next day. And so you, Campanians, have not to help us in war, but almost to undertake it in our stead." In other words, you're on your own.

But not for long. The Capuans' next move was to send the same delegation to Hannibal. Needless to say, he was entirely more accommodating, agreeing that in return for their allegiance the Capuans would continue to rule themselves, would be under no obligation to supply him with soldiers, and were to be given three hundred Roman prisoners to exchange for their horsemen in Sicily (an unlikely prospect, as we have seen).[3] To seal the deal Hannibal sent the Capuans a defensive garrison, and then entered the city in triumph, telling their senate that Capua would soon be "the capital of all Italy."[4] Intoxicated by the moment, his new allies responded by burning their remaining bridges to the Tiber, arresting the Romans in the city and shutting them up in a bathhouse, where they suffocated. Capuans would live to regret their enthusiasm, but in the shadow of Cannae the alliance must have seemed an obvious recognition of a new political reality. The Campanian city would take its place at the head of a realigned southern Italy, and Hannibal had a cornerstone upon which to begin constructing a stable edifice of control. Even more alluring, at least for the moment, he had a destination.

The Carthaginian army's winter sojourn in Capua is the stuff of ancient legend. As French archaeologist and historian Serge Lancel explains, those three proverbial symbols of dissipation in classical antiquity—wine, women, and warm water—(not to mention soap and perfume) turned Hannibal's fine-tuned instrument of destruction into a bunch of skulking hedonists, at least according to Livy in his famous passage on their epic sleepover.[5] He even has Marcellus, no slouch as a luxury lover, let on that "Capua was Hannibal's Cannae."[6]

None of this should be taken literally. For one thing, only a small portion of the army could have been quartered there without fatally alienating the population. Besides, this was a force destined to fight successfully in Italy for more than a decade longer.[7]

Yet Livy's point should not be dismissed. Every alliance comes with a price tag. By succumbing to the allure of having stable friendships— bases, a steady source of supplies, political allegiance—Hannibal took on the burden of protecting them. It would prove a heavy load for a military vagabond. Life on the road had been hard and uncertain, but it had afforded Hannibal the strategic advantage of being able to show up anywhere, a maddening possibility if you were Rome. With assets to defend, he was now tied down—cut off, for instance, from the Gauls far to the north and their supplies of fresh king-size fighters.

Not only was the fox forced to guard the henhouse, but the hens themselves had considerable strategic limitations, having been politically contaminated by their former hegemon. As mentioned earlier, Rome's system of treaties tied allies directly to it and not to one another. Removing this dependency left no common bond, no basis for larger amalgams, and this condition was only compounded by the fierce internal factionalism of the south, especially among the Greeks.[8]

With this came an equivalent reluctance to contribute troops, especially for duty outside of home territory. This left Hannibal reliant on his own field army to fend off a succession of Roman forces drawn from their own very deep manpower base. Over time some numbers of Italians were successfully integrated into the Punic force structure, but the structure's core remained Libyan, Numidian, Spanish, and Gallic. As the Carthaginian traveling force was gradually eroded by casualties, by the need for garrison troops, and eventually even by age, what Hannibal needed was reinforcements.

That was to have been Mago's job, the point of his triumphant return to Carthage. To set the stage, Hannibal's youngest brother ordered that the baskets full of golden rings pried off the fingers of senators and equestrians at Cannae be poured out in the vestibule of the meeting hall of the elders. Addressing the elders, he spoke glowingly of victories achieved, consuls humiliated, casualties inflicted, captives held, allies won over, of Italy in revolt, and above all, as victory grew near, he spoke of aiding Hannibal with all the resources at the state's disposal— more troops, but also money for pay, and food for the soldiers who had already served so well in Carthage's name.[9]

The speech evidently went over well; it's hard to be pessimistic in the face of such good news. Nevertheless, Hanno, by now undoubtedly aged, and still apparently at the head of the anti-Barcid faction, found reason for doubt. He wondered aloud why, if Hannibal had killed so many Romans, he needed more soldiers. Why, if he had accumulated so much booty, did he need more money and provisions? Why, if Italy was in revolt, had no Latins come over to the Carthaginian side? Still more pointedly, Hanno asked Mago if the Romans had sent any ambassadors to treat for peace. When Hanno received no satisfactory answers, he concluded, "We have on our hands, then, a war as entire as we had on the day Hannibal crossed into Italy."[10]

Still, if not exactly a voice in the wilderness, Hanno was plainly in the minority. Most were apparently inclined to believe that at least moderate exertions could bring the war to a speedy conclusion. The elders voted for a small force of four thousand Numidians to be sent to Hannibal, along with more money and that Punic panacea, forty elephants. Yet Livy (23.14.1) points out that these resources were raised in a dilatory fashion. Nor would Mago be joining them. Instead, he was sent to Spain to recruit a larger force, but by the time he was ready to depart for Italy, the situation in Iberia had deteriorated and he was needed there to fight. Meanwhile, sometime in the summer of 214 the admiral Bomilcar finally delivered the Numidians and elephants at Locri on the coast of Bruttium.[11] It was to be the only time during the entire war that the city of Carthage would send Hannibal reinforcements in Italy. The elders showed entirely more interest in Spain, Sardinia, and especially Sicily.

This did not amount to a ringing endorsement for Hannibal's great adventure. Most modern authorities seem to see this lack of enthusiasm as largely a matter of circumstance and not reticence. Still, the reluctance of Hanno appears to represent more than just Hanno. We have already seen that Carthage had been badly hurt by the First Punic War and the subsequent revolt of Hamilcar's mercenaries. Many of Carthage's citizens must have recognized that in terms of demographics Carthage was no match for Rome, especially in a land war. No matter how impressive Hannibal's initial successes might have seemed, some in the Carthaginian power structure—particularly the remaining old ones who had seen Rome's staying power in the first war—would have continued to view Hannibal's invasion as reckless and futile. These men seem to have convinced the others to pursue the war by concentrating on areas outside of Italy, particularly those of traditional Carthaginian interest. In Spain the motives of the Barcids and the

skeptics at home coincided, less so in Sicily and Sardinia. But ultimately, Hannibal was left high and dry in Italy, and was finally forced to
look only to his two brothers for reinforcement. And that would cost
both their lives.

[2]

Back in Rome it remains an open question whether any of this was fully
understood. What must have been overwhelmingly clear was that
Rome's strategy of trying to end the invasion with one knockout blow
had not worked. Never again would the Romans leverage their massive
manpower resources into one huge host. Armies would be raised (and
frequently lost), but in the future, bets were to be hedged. It followed
that, after Cannae, pitched battles became less frequent, and were
fought less to destroy the adversary's maneuver units than to defend or
threaten population centers, now the key pieces on the field of play.
Rome had an advantage here, because Hannibal could not allow himself the luxury of becoming stationary for a long siege. Raids and skirmishes became the most typical form of combat, in part because most
of the campaigning transpired along the rugged spine of central Italy,
the Apennines, terrain where it was nearly impossible to force a set-
piece battle on an unwilling foe.[12]

All of this calls to mind the strategy of Fabius Maximus, and in the
shadow of Cannae, Romans had little alternative. The consular elections of 215 marked the beginning of a three-year period when Fabius,
his son, and his family ("Beanmen" all) dominated politics. Their strategy of delay was given free rein, and one, not coincidentally, when
Hannibal's Thunderbolt accomplished relatively little.[13]

Yet the approach had changed, had altered with circumstances,
amounting to Fabian II. Fabian I had simply consisted of dogging
Hannibal—avoiding battle while seeking to starve him by weakening
his foragers. The updated version was more positional. Battle was still
avoided and foragers attacked, but more attention was paid to geography and local politics. After Cannae and the defection of Capua, a military front was developed along the line of the Volturnus River and
extended across Italy through northern Apulia between Luceria and
Arpi; if at all possible Hannibal would not be allowed to stray farther
north. Within this band Fabius attempted to reinstitute his "scorched

earth" policy, threatening to pillage the area himself if this was not done.[14] This was likely to have been more bluster than substance with regard to those who remained loyal, but Fabius and the Romans were deadly serious with regard to the less steadfast.

Defectors would be punished. Siege craft among the Romans had not reached the level of technical sophistication it was to achieve later, but Hannibal had to be wary of trying to relieve an invested ally, since the process was inherently casualty producing, and his manpower was precious. Besides, it could leave him pinned down and tactically vulnerable. His problem would only grow worse if more than two targets were under assault simultaneously and he was faced with the prospect of splitting his force. So the manpower-rich Romans had an inherent edge in this form of warfare. Targeted allies who strayed learned to their regret that Hannibal could not protect them, while the terrible price they paid kept the others in line. On the other hand, Fabius remained careful not to give confederates reason to revolt by pressing them too hard for men and money, or by overreacting to rumors of contemplated desertion.[15]

Nevertheless, the scale of operations maintained by the Romans was truly immense. Even in 215 they were able to field fourteen legions.[16] Adrian Goldsworthy estimates that in the ten years following Cannae, more than twenty legions were regularly in the field (a high of twenty-three legions was reached in 211 and 207), supported by an equivalent number of allied troops.[17] Some legions may have been undermanned and used for garrison duty, but the sheer numbers give pause. Using a conservative pre-Cannae figure of forty-five-hundred troops for each legion and each *alae*, this amounts to on the order of 180,000 troops raised year in and year out. This is an extraordinarily large figure for a preindustrial military, and does not even consider the manpower requirements of the Roman navy, which remained substantial throughout.

Plainly, this sort of war was expensive, and even if the study of ancient economics remains murky, it is apparent that after Cannae the primitive Roman financial system was showing signs of massive strain. As we saw at the end of the last chapter, in order to pay the soldiers (though not the *Cannenses*), the tax on Roman citizens, the *tributum*, had to be doubled in 215. This statistic, however, must be balanced against the chronic devaluation of the Roman currency. In 217 the bronze as— the basic coin, if you can call it that—weighed one Roman pound;

three years later it was one sixth as heavy. This devaluation prompted
the creation of a new medium of exchange based on the silver denarius, which itself had to be devalued before the war was over.[18] Exactly
how this economic ax cleaved Roman society is hard to say. Military
contractors surely did well, and also, because there were monetized
property qualifications for service in the Roman army, currency devaluation would have broadened the draft pool. But somebody had to pay
the bills, and as the fighting dragged on, reconquered defectors were
obvious targets. Marcellus's epic fleecing of Syracuse and Fabius's en-
slavement and sale of much of Tarentum's population provided the ar-
chetypes. Fabian II meant war truly on a societal scale.

The updated Fabian strategy also called for better leadership. The
time for amateurish generals had passed, as had single-year commands
for truly competent ones. In the face of Hannibal, quick leadership
turnover had to be sacrificed, even if it meant electing the same men to
the consulship over and over, and extending the imperium indefinitely
to efficient proconsuls and propraetors.[19] This extended imperium had
already been in place for the Scipio brothers in far-off Spain, but now
it took hold in Italy. In particular, a group of men in their fifties and six-
ties, who'd reached their maturity during the First Punic War, came to
dominate the Second, particularly after Cannae. In addition to Fabius
Maximus himself, there was Marcellus and Quintus Fulvius Flaccus,
all of whom held the consulship at least four times, which was unprecedented. On a slightly less elevated tier were Tiberius Sempronius
Gracchus (twice consul, once master of horse), Marcus Livius Salinator (twice consul), and Gaius Claudius Nero. Not all of these men sub-
scribed to the Fabian style of warfare—Marcellus and Nero were
exceedingly aggressive—but all were excellent soldiers and capable of
working together. Hannibal's days of picking off prima donnas were
not quite over, but for the most part he now had to face Team Roma, a
grim and determined bunch.

[3]

Cannae's reverberations shot out from Italy's coasts in all directions.
Hannibal's war had already been trans-Mediterranean, given the Barcid power base in Spain and Carthage's complicity, but now the roster
of contestants broadened in the wake of Rome's perceived vulnerabil-

ity. In the rollicking world of Hellenistic geopolitics, piling on was a frequent handmaiden of defeat, emblematic of the system's very cynicism and, in its meddling with Rome, myopia.

There were few more enthusiastic practitioners of piling on than the young king of Macedon, Philip V, a perennial kibitzer in the affairs of Greece, and any other place he thought he saw an opportunity for self-aggrandizement. According to Polybius (5.101.6–8), ever since Philip had heard of the debacle at Trasimene, he had been eying Rome's protectorate on the east coast of the Adriatic. The protectorate had been established in 229 to thwart the Illyrian pirates, and was a continuing thorn in the side of Macedon's monarchs, who resented the presence of outsiders but were afraid to do anything about it. Now with word of Cannae, Philip's horizons broadened, his fear of the Romans evaporated, and the possibility of an alliance with Rome's apparent subjugator loomed large.

Philip's diplomacy may have been adroit, but it was hardly discreet. According to Livy, the delegation he sent to Hannibal was captured twice by the Romans.[20] On the first occasion they were let go, having given the excuse that they were actually on their way to negotiate an alliance with the senate. The second time, they were caught red-handed with Carthaginian officers and a text of the treaty, which was delivered to the Roman archives, where Polybius found and preserved it.[21]

An odd combination of Greek and Old Testament–like diplo-speak, the treaty mentions as signatories not only Hannibal but Carthaginian elders Mago, Myrkan, and Barmocar. The presence of these names has been sometimes seen as indicating that the metropolis and not the Barcid was in charge, even in Italy.[22] But if this was the case, why didn't Philip send the delegation to Carthage rather than to Hannibal to seal the alliance? If nothing else, Hellenistic monarchs had an eagle eye for who held the initiative. And in that regard this was a document typical of the "great game" mentality, promising very little up front beyond bland assurances of mutual support, and getting specific only about transfers of Greek properties to the Macedonians once the war was won. Most significant, the treaty foresaw the continued existence of Rome, even in defeat. While Livy's (23.33.10–12) far less convincing rendition of the treaty envisions a Macedonian invasion of Italy, probably Hannibal looked upon the whole thing as a potentially useful way of distracting the Romans, another problem for them to cope with that would drain their strength. The treaty—Polybius's version at least—is worth considering, since it is about as close to a first-person look at the motivation of Rome's enemies as we have left. What emerges is more calculating than deadly serious. The Romans, for their part, were utterly committed to the war, and they would neither forgive nor forget this alliance of convenience.

As it turned out, the Romans easily handled the extra burden of the First Macedonian War, which mainly played out in raids and quick sieges. The Romans engineered it so that Greek mostly fought Greek, and Rome seldom had to commit more than a legion of their own troops, supported by elements of their ample fleet.[23] For his part Philip badly underestimated the Romans' ability to practice divide-and-rule politics among the fractious Hellenes.

Critical in this success was Marcus Valerius Laevinus, who during his propraetorship beginning in 215 set the conditions of victory—parrying Philip, keeping him on the defensive, and distracting him from any contemplated linkup with Hannibal in Italy. In 211, Laevinus concluded a treaty with Macedon's recent adversaries the Aetolian League, having convinced them that Rome was winning the war with Carthage. There commenced a series of joint raids against Philip and his friends that kept him and his army racing from threat to new threat to yet another threat.[24]

But after Laevinus left for home to assume a well-deserved consulship, Philip and his friends staged a comeback. In 207, Philip led a massive raid into the Aetolian League's territory, while Philip's allies in the Achaean League smashed the Spartans at Mantinea—yet another decisive drubbing, on perhaps the most famous battlefield in ancient Greece.[25] Reeling, the Aetolians had had enough, and, like any sensible Hellenistic player would do, they cut their losses by making a separate peace with Philip. The Romans were not pleased with their former ally, but neither were the Romans about to give up. They threw an additional ten thousand infantry, one thousand horse, and thirty-five quinqueremes back into Illyria.[26]

In the face of the resulting stalemate, representatives from the Epirote League (Pyrrhus's former home base) interceded and managed to negotiate an end to the hostilities, the Peace of Phoinike in 205. Philip got to keep most of what he had grabbed, and unlike other treaties with the Romans, this one was negotiated between equals. Philip probably thought he had won.

But the Romans had always fought with an eye to Hannibal, making sure he derived absolutely no benefit from what they must have considered a most unholy alliance with Philip V. For Philip, the alliance with Hannibal had been Hellenistic business as usual; for Romans a stab in the back, which would be avenged virtually as soon as they finally disposed of their Barcid tormentor. For mainland Greeks—Macedonians and all the rest—this Cannae-inspired treaty with Hannibal was a disaster of the first order, marking the beginning of the end of their independence. Once drawn into the Greeks' affairs, the Romans would not leave them alone.

[4]

Already in Rome's sway, the Greeks of Sicily proved no more sagacious in Cannae's aftermath, allowing themselves, through their own vicious factionalism, to be drawn into a conflict that much more clearly pitted Rome against Carthage rather than against Hannibal. For their part, the Carthaginians waged a kind of parallel struggle that complemented Hannibal's, one oriented toward areas of traditional interest, and fought with the same on-again, off-again military inefficacy characteristic of Carthage's overseas imperial adventures in the past.

This was most evident in Sicily but was also paralleled in 215 by an abortive effort to snatch back Sardinia, whose seizure by the Romans in 240 during the revolt of Hamilcar Barca's former mercenaries had so embittered Carthaginians. Believing the place was ripe for revolt, Carthage sent a fleet under Hasdrubal the Bald, who was delayed long enough by bad weather that the Romans were able to reinforce Sardinia with a legion under hard-core T. Manlius Torquatus, who was last heard from in the senate denouncing the Romans taken prisoner at Cannae.[27] When Hasdrubal finally came ashore, Torquatus made short work of the operation, hammering Hasdrubal's landing force, capturing him, and stamping out the nascent rebellion. Even the retreating Carthaginian fleet was roughly handled by a naval squadron under Fabius Maximus's nephew lurking off the African coast. It was the last Punic move in this direction.[28] The effort in Sicily was to be much more sustained, if ultimately no more successful.

The battle in Sicily began and essentially ended in Syracuse, which controlled a band of territory basically running the length of the island's east coast, the rest of Sicily being administered by Rome as a result of its victory in the First Punic War. Syracuse's longtime ruler, Hiero, was a trusted Roman ally, but he was also old—at least in his seventies and quite probably in failing health. Hiero's eldest son, Gelon, his head turned by Cannae, was on the brink of denouncing Syracuse's alliance with Rome, when he suddenly disappeared under mysterious circumstances. Hiero didn't survive much longer. His heir, Gelon's feckless fifteen-year-old son named Hieronymus, following his father's inclination, and under the influence of his entourage, sent a delegation to Hannibal so that an agreement could be roughed out. The wily Barcid also sent back two scheming Carthaginian brothers of Syracusan descent who had served in his army in Spain and Italy— Hippocrates and Epicydes. If there was ever a poison pill, it was these two, who sowed dissent from the moment they arrived in Sicily.

Smelling defection, the praetor Appius Claudius—last seen at Canusium as one of the surviving tribunes who backed the young Publius Scipio against the cabal of defeatists—had his suspicions confirmed when the ambassadors he sent to renew the alliance were asked mockingly by Hieronymus "How had they fared at the battle of Cannae?"[29] The new treaty would be confirmed in Carthage, but plainly it was already a done deal. Not that it mattered for Hieronymus or the entire royal family; they were quickly murdered in a spasm of blood-curdling political violence that left the interlopers Hippocrates and Epicydes vying for predominance with a ragtag force of mercenaries and fully two thousand Roman deserters.

Realizing the situation was deteriorating fast, the senate in 214 sent Marcellus, currently serving his second consulship, to Sicily, where he joined forces with Appius Claudius. When Hippocrates and Epicydes moved their band to the nearby city of Leontini, Marcellus followed them and stormed the place, taking it on the first assault. Unfortunately, while the consul busied himself with the traditional punishment for deserters—the Roman men were stripped naked, flogged, and then beheaded—the two Syracusan brothers escaped. On their way back to Syracuse, they met up with a pro-Roman relief column, whom they won over by convincing them that Marcellus was actually butchering Leontini's citizenry.[30] This group the brothers then led back to Syracuse, where, after a short struggle, they managed to kill their rivals and assume control, putting the city firmly in the ranks of Rome's enemies.

"Hannibal had certainly picked his men well," writes one modern historian[31] of the brothers and their brilliant manipulation of the political chaos within the walls of Syracuse. But Marcellus's actions during the Leontini episode, actions which gave Hippocrates and Epicydes the opening they needed, could be inferred to have been as much motivated by the desire to punish Roman deserters as the desire to get his hands on Hippocrates and Epicydes, and around the political situation in general. Marcellus certainly did not intend it, but letting Syracuse slip through his fingers was a heavy price to pay for punishing some apostates—though two thousand is a very substantial number.

Deserters are not much dwelled upon by patriotic historians such as Livy. But the question looms: Could more than a few of these deserters actually have been members of the *legiones Cannenses*, exiled to Sicily, shunted to the side without a combat role, angry and disgusted at their treatment? It certainly seems possible, and could account for the continuing senatorial bitterness toward these ghosts of Cannae.[32] But it does not seem likely; more probably the deserters were garrison troops gone native. For while he was in Sicily Marcellus seemed favorably disposed toward troops he had already commanded in Italy. Later, when the *Cannenses* petitioned Marcellus to be removed from the sidelines and included in the operations against Syracuse, he immediately wrote the senate requesting permission to use them. The wording of the reply, which Livy quotes, is interesting:

> The senate saw no reason why the interests of the republic should be entrusted to the hands of soldiers who had deserted their comrades, in battle, at Cannae. If Marcus Marcellus, the proconsul, thought otherwise, that he should act as he deemed consistent with the good of the state and his own conscience, with this proviso, however, that none of these men should be exempt from service, or be decorated for valor, or be brought back to Italy, so long as the enemy should be in the land of Italy.[33]

The indications are that Marcellus had every need for the *Cannenses*, for the siege of Syracuse proved a gigantic enterprise. It appears that Marcellus and Appius waited until the spring of 213 to begin operations. In the meantime they gathered resources and modified their equipment for what was to be one of the few attempts in any of the three Punic wars to take a strongly fortified place by direct assault.[34] And it failed utterly.

Syracuse was vast compared to most ancient cities, and the Roman generals were perfectly aware of the strength of its encircling walls, girding it both inland and along the coast and the harbor district, the products of a succession of paranoid tyrants with penchants for public works. What the Roman generals hadn't counted on was the ancient equivalent of a rocket scientist organizing the city's defense . . . none other than Archimedes, one of the greatest mathematicians who ever lived and, unfortunately for the Romans, a weapons designer of rare creativity. So, when the attackers began their assault—Appius on the landward side and Marcellus along the harbor district or Achradina— they found a physics instructor, or at least his mechanisms, lying in wait for them.

Marcellus had modified some of his quinqueremes into siege craft, lashing them together and mounting on their bows scaling ladders that could be raised by pulleys and then lowered against the walls—a kind of thematic variation on the First Punic War's "crow" boarding bridges, which the Romans now called *sambucae,* for their resemblance to harps. In this case the harps played only sour notes, as chronicled in a fragment by Polybius, himself an expert on siege craft and an obvious fan of Archimedes.[35]

As Marcellus's *sambucae* approached supported by sixty quinqueremes filled with assault troops, the Romans found themselves barraged by a hail of projectiles launched from a succession of catapults carefully calibrated to cover all ranges. Forced to attack at night, it only got worse as they drew closer and were raked incessantly by "small scorpions"[36] (probably crossbows) shot from narrow loopholes cut in the fortifications. When the attackers finally got the *sambucae* into place and their extensions deployed, great beams pivoted out from the walls and dropped stones and lead weights to shatter the ladders. These beams also released clawlike devices to catch the prows of the ships themselves, which were then ratcheted upward until they were nearly vertical. Then the ships were suddenly released, which caused them to capsize and sink. All told, it was a debacle that left Marcellus joking ruefully at his helplessness in the face of Archimedes, and left his troops prone to panic if they saw so much as a plank or a rope projecting from a wall.[37] Appius did no better with his landward component, being subject to much the same treatment. They were not about to give up, but from now on they would rely on blockade and eventually subterfuge.

Enter the Carthaginians. Specifically, a large force sent over from Africa under Himilco (twenty-five thousand foot soldiers, three thousand horse, and twelve elephants) landed on the south coast of the island and quickly took Agrigentum, an important base in the First Punic War that had been lost to the Romans after a long siege. Marcellus, too late to prevent the fall of Agrigentum, did intercept a column of approximately ten thousand Syracusans led by Hippocrates that had broken the Roman blockade and was on its way to join the Carthaginians. Although most of the infantry was killed or captured, Hippocrates and around five hundred cavalry managed to reach Himilco, who then advanced to a river just south of Syracuse. Worried, Marcellus had already fallen back on Roman lines when a force of fifty-five Punic quinqueremes commanded by Bomilcar sailed into the Syracuse harbor, making it look like the Roman blockade would soon be broken.[38]

But as usual the Carthaginians dithered. Himilco and Hippocrates, rather than pressing the issue at Syracuse, wandered off—first failing to intercept a reinforcing Roman legion that was marching from the northwest coast, where it had landed, and later concentrated on sowing rebellion inland. Bomilcar, worried about his fighting strength, retreated to Africa.[39]

Marcellus, uncertain in the spring of 212 whether to pursue Himilco, finally resolved to tighten the noose around Syracuse. Since Marcellus's troops had already been augmented by one legion, it seems likely that he began employing the *Cannenses* at this point, for he would need troops, because he had a plan to get into the city. The plan was based on two vital bits of intelligence: the Romans had learned that one part of the wall was lower than previously thought, and the Syracusans, who were in the midst of celebrating a three-day festival to the goddess Artemis, had been given lavish quantities of wine by Epicydes to compensate for a general lack of food. Drinking on an empty stomach being what it was and is, Marcellus and most of his army managed to break in on the last night of the blowout and seize nearly the entire city—with the exception of the Achradina and a nearby citadel—before the stupefied population realized what had happened.[40]

Himilco and Hippocrates raced back, intent on relieving the situation, but fate intervened in the form of a virulently infectious disease that swept through their encampment, killing both of them and most of their soldiers. The infection spared Marcellus's and Appius's forces, whose tightly organized camps and sanitary procedures may have saved them.[41]

Yet when it came to Sicily, the Carthaginians were proverbially persistent. Back in Africa, Bomilcar, who had been running the blockade and bringing in at least some food to what remained of Punic Syracuse, convinced the leadership to send him back with a massive relief force—130 warships and 700 transports stuffed with supplies. Fleet in hand, Bomilcar crossed quickly from Carthage but then hesitated to round Cape Pachynus just south of Syracuse, apparently held up by unfavorable winds. Afraid that Bomilcar would return home, Epicydes sailed out and convinced him to risk a naval engagement. Marcellus—outnumbered and with no naval combat experience to speak of, but forever belligerent—ventured forth, willing to fight the Carthaginians.

For a few days the fleets lay at anchor on either side of the cape. Finally, Bomilcar came out and appeared ready to pass beyond the promontory—one modern historian calls it "perhaps, the supreme moment of the war."[42] But Livy reports (25.27.12) that when the Carthaginian admiral saw "the Roman ships bearing down on him, terrified by something unforeseen, he made sail for open water, and, after sending messengers to Heraclea to command the transports to return to Africa . . . headed for Tarentum."

Epicydes quickly fled to Agrigentum, as Syracuse was now beyond hope of relief. Resistance continued for a while, in large part motivated by the Roman deserters, who knew what would happen to them if captured, but the betrayal of a key citadel and the surrender of the Achradina marked the end of what remains one of the most famous sieges in world history. Marcellus was inclined to be merciful but, being a Roman, let his men pillage the city. He also had given orders that Archimedes be spared, but a legionary cut the old man down, the story being that he had refused to be drawn away from his calculations.[43] Property rights were given the same regard as academic freedom by the rampaging Romans, who picked the place clean—so clean that the haul brought home by Marcellus for his ovation was said to have kick-started the city's passion for Greek art![44]

The plight of the *Cannenses* continued. Later, when he was back in Italy serving his third consulship, Marcellus would upbraid the senate for not allowing him, in return for his many services to the state, to redeem Cannae's survivors. Yet the senate remained unmoved and had

already sent the remnants of the army defeated at the First Battle of
Herdonea to join the *Cannenses* in exile, both groups to suffer the additional indignity of not being allowed to set up their winter camp within
ten miles of any town.[45]

Nonetheless, it appears that it was largely these troops, this band of
military pariahs, who were expected to put down the remaining
Carthaginian resistance in Sicily, which sputtered anew after the fall of
Syracuse. The resistance was now focused on Agrigentum under Himilco's replacement, Hanno; the ever-resilient Epicydes; and a new-
comer, sent over by Hannibal from Italy, named Muttines, a Libyan
cavalry commander of considerable skill and energy. Leading a force
of Numidians, Muttines raised sufficient havoc to force Marcellus, who
had yet to return to Rome, inland to confront the threat. Near the
Himera River, Muttines waged several successful skirmishes against
Marcellus's outposts, but then was drawn away to deal with a mutiny. In
his absence, Epicydes and Hanno—the latter apparently particularly
envious of his colleague's success and disdainful of Muttines's lack of
pure Carthaginian blood—decided to give battle and were crushed,
losing thousands of troops and eight elephants. Marcellus might have
followed up his victory and put an end to the conflict, but since he was
a Roman, the lure of high office apparently caused him to leave Sicily
in late 211 to stand for consul.[46]

The *Cannenses* were left to hold down the fort—in their eyes more
probably left holding the bag—and without their general, the situation
deteriorated. For back in Africa, still clinging to the vision of a
Carthaginian Sicily, the leadership anted up one more time, sending
eight thousand infantry and three thousand Numidian horsemen.[47]
Muttines used them ruthlessly to ravage the countryside, a matter of
no little importance, since rural Sicily was a massive producer of grain,
and since Rome, with Hannibal loose in Italy, needed all the food it
could get. Roman troop morale was low, and without adequate defense,
towns began to defect to the Carthaginian side. The situation was in
limbo, sufficiently serious that the senate was ready to send Marcellus
back to Sicily. But Sicilians in Rome, mortified by Marcellus's prior lust
for loot, protested so vociferously that he was persuaded to exchange
commands with Marcus Valerius Laevinus, whose steady hand we saw
holding Philip V in check.[48]

Laevinus proved equally effective in Sicily, perhaps more so since
luck was on his side. After settling some disorder in Syracuse, he went

straight for Agrigentum, where he found the enemy in disarray and, in the case of Muttines, positively mutinous. Hanno, still jealous and contemptuous of Muttines's origins, had replaced him and given his own son command of the Numidians. Outraged, the Libyan was ready to deal, so when Laevinus and his army marched up to the city wall, the gate swung open and legionaries poured in. Hanno and the everlasting Epicydes slipped out another portal and made it to Africa, but their forces were liquidated, the city fathers were beheaded, and the population was sold into slavery. The rest of Sicily quickly got the message.

The war here was over. Rome was firmly in charge. Carthage had proved exceedingly persistent in its attempts to regain a foothold on the island, especially when compared to the lack of support for Hannibal in Italy, but the Carthaginians' time here was at an end. So was any pretense of Sicilian Greek independence. The Greeks had squandered their independence here, as they would elsewhere. Sicily would become a breadbasket for Rome, Laevinus being careful to reestablish agriculture before departing the island in triumph. Muttines too prospered. Granted Roman citizenship and taking the name of his patron, Laevinus, he would command troops twenty years later in the war against Antiochus. There was even an inscription at Delphi to him and his four sons—Publius, Caius, Marcus, Quintus . . . Romans through and through.[49] The *legiones Cannenses*, on the other hand, got nothing. They remained on the island for another six years, as invisible as ghosts, figuratively sitting on their shields, waiting for a break.

[5]

Spain was critical and always had been. For it was not only Hannibal's launching pad, but his familial base of support since his father had turned it into Barca land. Carthaginian and even Phoenician presence had long preceded them, however, having been drawn to Spain's precious metals. These factors would now leave the authorities in Africa more inclined to send reinforcements here than directly to Hannibal in Italy. Money and habit—these seemed to matter most to the elders back home; so the Barcids and the authorities in Carthage were to be united in their determination to hold on to Spain.

Romans may have missed some of the subtleties of this condominium; but they certainly understood from the beginning that the source of their Hannibal problem was Spain. And they recognized the importance of neutralizing it lest it reinforce him.[50] Hence, as the Second Punic War opened, they launched the older Publius Scipio and his brother Cnaeus along with two legions in this direction. When the two brothers chanced upon but missed Hannibal at the Rhône, Publius had Cnaeus and most of the army continue on to Iberia, while he backtracked to Italy to await the invaders. Late in 217, recovered from the wound he'd gotten for his troubles at the Ticinus, Publius was sent west again with eight thousand fresh troops to join his brother. This was just the beginning of a long and frustrating conflict. But Rome would never give up on Spain, even if it took two generations of Scipios to strip the area of Punic influence.

The Iberian Peninsula was a tricky place on which to operate, a country where large armies starved and small armies got beaten, Henry IV of France would later comment.[51] At this point it was inhabited by three separate groups—Lusitanians in the west, Iberians in the south, and Celtiberians inland to the north—all of them tribal. But loyalties among these groups were far weaker than among the Gauls, the essential allegiance here being to locality, generally small fortified villages, effectively atomizing the power structure. Raiding was continuous, and amalgams formed around chieftains perceived to be dominant, but loyalty did not generally extend much beyond success or failure in the last battle. This was important, because in this campaign both Carthaginians and Romans would depend heavily on indigenous mercenaries, and each side would be victimized when their force structure melted away with disastrous suddenness.[52]

Nevertheless, even before his brother's arrival, Cnaeus Scipio campaigned effectively. After establishing a rear base at the Greek city of Emporion, he sailed along the coast of what is now Catalonia, landing at several points and easily winning over the locals, until he ran into the force Hannibal had left with the commander Hanno shortly before he crossed the Pyrenees. They met in battle at a place known as Cissa, where Cnaeus routed the Carthaginians, and captured Hanno, all the baggage that Hannibal had entrusted to him, and one Indibilis, a powerful local chieftain whose shifting loyalties would come to epitomize the treacherous political terrain upon which the war here would be waged. For the moment, however, it was clear sailing for the Romans all the way down to the Ebro River.

Hasdrubal, the Barca brother who'd been left in Spain to mind the family enterprise, raced northward with a limited number of troops when he heard of Hanno's misfortune. catching and destroying some isolated elements from Cnaeus's fleet, but then withdrew to New Carthage rather than risk an engagement with the main Roman force.[53] Held to the standard set by most Carthaginian captains, the middle Barcid sibling was competent enough; yet he also proved a kind of pale shadow of his elder brother, attempting a number of the same feats and almost always falling short. But he certainly had staying power, and never ceased trying to further Hannibal's interests, until it cost him his head a decade later.

Meanwhile, in the spring of 217, Hasdrubal traveled north again with a much larger force—a fleet of forty war galleys led by a commander named Hamilcar, and an army directly under himself. They worked their way along the coast until they reached the Ebro. But to no avail. When Cnaeus heard they were nearby, he went straight for them with his own fleet, fortified by warships from Rome's ally Massilia, and made short work of the ensuing sea battle. After losing two ships and having the oars and marines sheared off four others, the Carthaginians fled ashore, banking on the protection of their army, but the Romans, full of confidence, rowed right after them and towed away nineteen of the beached ships with no apparent Punic intervention.[54] After this maritime humiliation, the Carthaginians would not again contest Rome's command of the waters off the Spanish coast. Livy even has Hasdrubal retreating all the way to Lusitania (modern Portugal) and the Atlantic, and being defeated several more times by tribes at the instigation of Cnaeus,[55] but more likely the Roman rested on his laurels and awaited the arrival of his brother.

Publius Scipio reached Spain in the grim shadow of Rome's defeat at Trasimene, and both brothers were given the proconsular imperium to take the offensive and at all costs keep the Carthaginians here off balance and unable to gather the men and resources to reinforce Hannibal.[56] For nearly six years they did just that—according to the sources, at least—outwitting and outfighting their adversaries, piling success upon success. Unfortunately, their successes were all based on the quicksand of Spanish tribal politics and were ultimately confounded by Carthage's increasing determination to build up its own forces in Spain.

To accomplish their purpose the Scipio brothers worked out a strategy not altogether different from the one pursued triumphantly by their successor, Scipio Africanus—not necessarily making Spain Roman, just not Carthaginian, and sealing it off from Italy. To do so they had to hold the Ebro and the approaches to the Pyrenees and then extend control along the coastal road southwest toward the fertile valley of the Baetis River (modern Guadalquivir) and the seat of Punic power.[57] Along the way to Saguntum, the town where Hannibal had started the war, the Scipio brothers received an unexpected boon when a Spanish chieftain named Abilyx persuaded the Carthaginian commander here to turn his hostages over to him, and then Abilyx treacherously turned them over to the Romans, who won the allegiance of the locals by returning them to their homes. Or so the story went, as recounted at some length by Polybius (3.98–9) as indicative of the sagacity and magnanimity of the Scipios compared to the Carthaginians, but really illustrating just how quickly the tables could turn on either side in this complex environment.

Meanwhile, Hasdrubal Barca had been endeavoring to put his house's house in order. After suppressing a tribal rebellion, in 216 he received, along with a small contingent of reinforcements, orders from Carthage to join his brother in Italy. Acting every bit a Barcid, he replied that if the elders were really serious about such an invasion and wanted to keep control of Spain in his absence, they had better send him a more substantial force, which they promptly did under Himilco. Duly fortified, Hasdrubal set out with his relief expedition along the coast road moving toward the Ebro, probably in early 215.[58]

This was exactly what the Scipio brothers had been sent to prevent, and in the wake of Cannae, it was imperative that they make a stand. They concentrated their forces just south of the river near the town of Ibera. The battle that ensued has been compared to Cannae, or more properly to Cannae gone wrong. It appears that Hasdrubal used the same type of alignment as his brother, with a strong force of Africans and local Carthaginians on either wing flanking a middle consisting of unenthusiastic Spaniards. The Spanish center could not hold. The Romans broke through in the middle, but despite being attacked from both sides, they were able to pivot outward and wrench apart the jaws of the trap.[59] What followed was near annihilation, capped by the Scipios' taking the Carthaginian camp and the expeditionary baggage train. Hasdrubal escaped with a few retainers, but Ibera had pushed him back to square one, and the dream of reinforcing his brother faded into the distance.

As recorded by Livy, the next four years down to 211 were filled
with Scipionic victories that seem exaggerated or don't make much
sense because they put the brothers too far south, especially since it appears that the brothers didn't manage to finally recover Saguntum (less
than a hundred miles down from Ibera) until 212.[60] More likely, with
their supply of legionaries diminished by time and battle, the Scipio
brothers spent the years treading water, content with their primary
mission of blocking a Barcid reunion in Italy, while Rome devoted
most of its energy and troops to the fighting in Campania and Sicily. In
211, with these campaigns winding down, the Scipios felt confident
enough to strike out toward the heart of Punic power in and around the
Baetis valley and along the southern coast. Unfortunately, their hopes
were vested not in Roman reinforcements from home but in twenty
thousand Celtiberians they had recently hired.[61]

Meanwhile, their adversaries were considerably enhanced, reconstituted through Carthaginian cash, the ready supply of Spanish swords
for hire, and significant additions of Africans, particularly Numidian
horsemen. Not only had Hasdrubal managed to rebuild his own army,
but in the wake of Ibera, he was joined by his younger brother Mago
and the force of thirteen thousand Mago had originally recruited for
Italy,[62] and by a third element under another Hasdrubal, this one the
son of Gisgo. Now there were three armies facing the Scipio brothers
where there had been only one.

As the campaign kicked off, the forces of Mago and Hasdrubal
Gisgo were operating together about five days' march from the Romans, while Hasdrubal Barca's army was closer, at a place called Amtorgis. It was the Scipios' intention to hit both elements simultaneously,
lest Mago and Hasdrubal Gisgo, hearing of an initial Carthaginian defeat at Amtorgis, escape into the wilderness to wage prolonged guerilla
warfare. This meant that the Scipios had to split their forces. Publius
took two thirds of the Roman and Italian allied troops and headed off
toward Mago and Hasdrubal Gisgo, leaving Cnaeus with the remaining
regulars plus the Celtiberians to deal with Hasdrubal Barca. It was a
fatal mistake.

Hasdrubal Barca, raised in this environment, knew that Celtiberians
who'd been bought once could be bought twice, and immediately entered into secret negotiations with their leaders. Before Cnaeus realized what was happening, money had talked and the Celtiberians had

walked, leaving Cnaeus abandoned, vastly outnumbered, and with little choice but to head for the hills, the Carthaginians in hot pursuit.[63]

By this time, brother Publius was already dead. As his column had
approached Mago and Hasdrubal Gisgo, it had been harassed relentlessly by Numidian cavalry, brilliantly led by a young African prince,
Masinissa. This prince was destined to play a major role in the eventual
collapse of Carthage, but at this point he was a Punic retainer and was
doing his job with ruthless efficiency. To make matters worse, Publius
had found out that the Carthaginians were about to be joined by
seventy-five hundred more tribesmen under the same Indibilis whom
we last heard of as a captive and presumed thrall of Cnaeus after the
battle of Cissa. Desperate to recapture the initiative, Publius Scipio
had ducked out of camp at midnight—leaving only a small garrison—
and headed toward Indibilis, found him, and engaged in a running fight.
But then Masinissa and the Numidians, whom Publius had thought
he'd slipped by, had appeared on his flanks, followed shortly by the
forces of Mago and Hasdrubal Gisgo. Soon enough Publius, in the
thick of the fighting, had been fatally skewered by a lance, and upon
hearing the news, his troops had broken, only to be run down and
slaughtered by Masinissa's horsemen.[64]

Cnaeus fared no better. Now the victorious Carthaginian commanders raced to unite with Hasdrubal Barca, bringing with them
Masinissa and the lethal Numidians. Attempting a getaway, Cnaeus
and his troops quietly broke camp and staged a night march, but before
the sun set, the Numidians were upon them. Forced to fight on the
move, the Romans' pace slowed, and with the main Punic element not
far behind, Cnaeus led his men to a marginally defensible position on a
barren rocky hilltop. The Romans were surrounded by an overwhelming force, had no timber available, and were unable to dig a trench, so
they took refuge in a circle behind their baggage and packsaddles. It
was a scene reminiscent of Little Bighorn, Cnaeus's Last Stand, though
a few survivors did somehow manage to escape and reach the small
garrison Publius had left in his camp.[65]

An equestrian who had served with Cnaeus named L. Marcius Septimus managed to reconstitute what was left of the Scipio brothers' legionaries. With these men, Marcius was able to hold some ground
north of the Ebro, but Livy's recounting of a series of his victories over
Carthaginian forces does not seem plausible.[66] There were just not

enough legionaries left alive in Spain at this point to do much more than cling to a foothold. Still, Marcius plainly had some success. The men took the unusual step of electing him their commander, and he reported his exploits back to the senate, referring to himself as propraetor—apparently annoying this very traditional body. So in the late fall of 211 they sent out between ten thousand and twelve thousand infantry and around one thousand horse under C. Claudius Nero, the highly aggressive and innovative leader, who assumed overall command.[67]

Characteristically, the Carthaginians seem to have lost momentum. They failed to make a concerted effort to expel the Romans, apparently dispersing instead to reassert control over their traditional Iberian territories. This gave Nero an opening to fall upon Hasdrubal Barca, trapping him when he foolishly camped in a defile called the Black Stones. Ensnared, and perhaps aware of Hannibal's escape from Fabius Maximus in the canyon of the Volturnus, Hasdrubal promised to leave Spain with his army and return to Africa if Nero would let him go, but then he kept postponing negotiations while filtering his troops out at night, ultimately making his own getaway in the morning mist.[68] It was a vanishing act worthy of Bugs Bunny. But Nero was no Elmer Fudd; four years later he would trap Hasdrubal once again, and this time there would be no escape.

For now, however, Nero apparently had other items on his agenda, and he returned to Rome at the end of the year. Yet Spain was too important to leave in limbo. Barcid power was still intact, and with it the most plausible and dangerous source for Hannibal's reinforcement. The seven-year project of the Scipio brothers was unfulfilled, and their deaths remained unavenged. All of these things Rome would soon address with one gigantic leap of faith; they would send to Spain both a dutiful son and destiny's child—another Scipio, the one who later would be called Africanus.

[6]

The epicenter of the war, of course, stayed in Italy, and the fighting there, in and around Campania between the years 212 and 210, would in large part dictate the outcome. It was at this point, both geographically and temporally, that the power of Rome and the relentless logic

of Fabian II would finally and irrevocably take hold. Hannibal would
not leave the Italian peninsula for another seven years, but the impos-
sibility of his enterprise would be revealed here in Campania, as would
his subsequent confinement in the south. What made history's conclusion so decisive was that even though Hannibal continued to operate
brilliantly at the tactical and operational level—he remained virtually
as tricky and lethal as ever—his strategy failed. His was a supreme
overreach in the face of overwhelming power.

The application of Fabian II had almost immediately inflicted pain
on those who had strayed from Rome's embrace, for Hannibal could
not be everywhere at once, and in his absence were likely to be Roman
forces burning fields and threatening population centers. In one telling
passage Livy has some of the battered Samnites tell Hannibal that their
suffering made it seem that the Romans and not Hannibal had won the
battle of Cannae, to which he could only reply that he would "over-
shadow the memory even of Cannae by a greater and more brilliant
victory."[69] In other words, his only answer to their plight was to inflict
tactical defeats on the Romans when and if they were willing to fight.
This he would do, but in the end it would not make much difference.

By 212 the Roman vise was tightening around central Italy about a
third of the way up the boot, with several separate forces abroad. The
focus was on Campania and the principal turncoat city Capua. Two
consular armies—one under Appius Claudius, who now had reached
the highest magistracy, and the other commanded by his colleague
Quintus Fulvius Flaccus—were devastating the countryside and defeating Punic efforts at food relief.[70] The hungry Capuans sent an ur-
gent appeal to Hannibal for support. Hannibal was at Tarentum, a great
prize, most of which he had just taken through a ruse. To stop the rural
depredations, he dispatched a force of two thousand cavalry to Capua,
but by this time the consuls had moved to blockade Capua itself. This
drew Hannibal and the rest of his army, intent now on another "brilliant victory."

But he was unable to force a decisive engagement, and the two consuls moved away from the city in different directions, knowing he
could follow only one and that the other could return. Hannibal decided to pursue Appius Claudius, but the Roman commander outfoxed
the fox, leading him in circles, and both Roman armies ended up back
at the distressed city, this time for good. Soon they were joined by a
third army under Claudius Nero (not yet dispatched to Spain), and to-

gether their six legions set about constructing an encircling inner wall, a ditch, and an outer wall, a traitor's noose around what had been Hannibal's most prized spoil of Cannae. Strategically, the Romans had won hands down.

There was more to the story. Roman armies kept disappearing. Livy, our sole source, records much of this, but ever the patriot, he may have put the best face on it. Most mysterious was the demise of the force of slaves (*volones*) that had been hastily organized after Cannae and subsequently employed to good effect by the able T. Sempronius Gracchus. Then abruptly the historian reports the death of Gracchus at the hands of treacherous Lucanians and the sudden dispersal of his army, causing one modern source to wonder if Livy was masking a defeat.[71]

Next there was the odd tale of a senior centurion, M. Centenius Paenula, who had talked the senate into giving him an army of eight thousand Romans and allies (later supplemented by an equivalent number of local volunteers) on the grounds that he was intimately familiar with Lucanian territory and could succeed where other commanders had not. Unfortunately, according to Livy, Hannibal chanced upon Paenula having abandoned the chase after Appius Claudius, and annihilated the force—though the Romans were characterized as having fought bravely until their centurion was killed and they scattered. More probably, Hannibal knew exactly what he was doing, saw a chance to pick off an isolated Roman force, and slaughtered them with his usual efficiency, killing fifteen thousand out of the original sixteen thousand.[72]

But Hannibal was not through. Before the year 212 was out, he returned to Apulia rather than Capua, and, like a fox on the move, began stalking another plump Roman prey. The praetor Cnaeus Fulvius Flaccus, brother of the consul, was there with an army of eighteen thousand, twisting arms and dragging a number of defector towns back into the Roman fold. According to Livy (25.20.6–7), success had eroded the caution of both Flaccus and his men, always a bad idea when Hannibal was in the neighborhood. In the vicinity of the town of Herdonea, the Carthaginian set his trap. Hiding three thousand light troops in the surrounding farms and woods and cutting off the avenues of flight with cavalry, he offered battle at dawn, and when the Romans accepted, Hannibal gobbled them up. Following the Terentius Varro precedent, Flaccus fled the field immediately with two hundred horsemen, but of those remaining, barely two thousand escaped with their lives. They apparently scattered in all directions since their camp had also been taken.[73] This was Hannibal's most decisive win since Cannae, and a drubbing Romans very apparently found humiliating. Unlike Varro, who was congratulated for not having given up on the republic, Flaccus was tried by the senate for high treason and barely escaped with his life.[74] However, the same fate as the *legiones Cannenses* was accorded to the survivors of Herdonea, indefinite banishment to Sicily.[75]

As if this were not bad enough, two years later, in 210, another Fulvius (proconsul Cnaeus Fulvius Centumalus) was caught and defeated by Hannibal, again at Herdonea. The Romans lost their camp and a consular army (two legions—the 5th and 6th—and two *alae*), as many as thirteen thousand men. This Fulvius would not be tried, since he fell in the field along with eleven military tribunes, but yet again the survivors were exiled to Sicily for the duration to join the ghosts of Cannae.[76]

Quite plainly, at the operational and tactical levels of war Hannibal and his army had lost none of their edge, but that edge was nearly irrelevant strategically. Rome persevered and would persist in replacing armies lost; meanwhile, Rome's relentless grasp would continue to narrow Hannibal's playing field and circumscribe his future.

Symbolically and actually, all of this was epitomized by the wretched fate of Capua. The year 211 found the Romans fully committed to the siege under Appius Claudius and Quintus Fulvius Flaccus (both now proconsuls), with about half of the legions that were stationed in Italy participating.[77] A vast logistical structure had been emplaced to support them, and the surrounding territory had also been stripped of foodstuffs, while inside the city the population grew hungrier as the triple line of circumvallation was pushed to completion. For a while the Campanian horsemen were able to sally out with some success, but then a centurion named Quintus Naevius came up with the idea of using picked *velites* who would ride in tandem with the Roman cavalry and then support them on foot when they came upon a Capuan horseman. This plan effectively shut down the last remaining morale builder.[78] The Capuans were sealed off.

Realizing that the city would inevitably fall unless he did something, Hannibal marched up from Bruttium with only a picked force without baggage, looking to fight the Romans in the field. But the Romans refused to budge from behind their lines. Thwarted, Hannibal decided on a direct assault and coordinated with the Capuans, who were to attack from the inside while he sought to break through from the outside. The Capuans were quickly turned aside, but a cohort of Hannibal's Spaniards led by three elephants broke through the Roman lines and threatened Flaccus's camp. But then the Romans, rallied by the same Naevius, threw the Spaniards back, and the Carthaginians retreated with a considerable loss of precious troops.[79] Worse perhaps for those inside the city, there was no way that Hannibal could stay, since the Romans, following the relentless logic of Fabius Maximus, had already removed virtually everything edible from the countryside.

But if the republican hedgehog knew the value of his "scorched earth" policy, the Punic fox was never without a plan B. Hannibal decided to march on Rome. At this point Polybius briefly reenters the picture in a fragment and there are some discrepancies with Livy over which route Hannibal took, whether he was followed, and what transpired when he arrived.[80] What remains clear is that Hannibal was waging psychological warfare, endeavoring to use his own terrifying image along the Tiber to induce the Romans to release their stranglehold around Capua and rush to the relief of their own capital. The days of Roman impulsiveness, credulously falling for Hannibal's tricks, were largely over. Both historians agree that there was panic abroad within the city but not among the leadership. They called his bluff; the grip around Capua was not to be relaxed. Money also spoke. Livy tells us that the very land adjacent to Rome on which Hannibal was camped was sold at this time without a diminution in price; very apparently the purchaser considered the Barcid little more than a squatter.[81]

Shortly before he retreated back to Bruttium, abandoning project Capua, Hannibal was heard to say that he had twice missed capturing Rome—once because he had lacked the will, the other because he had lacked the opportunity.[82] He was right on both counts. Had he listened to Maharbal after Cannae, he might have overawed the distraught Romans. Now he had no chance.

As Polybius (9.26.2–6) explains, after Capua's fall it became clear to all that Hannibal could not watch over widespread allies; nor could he afford to subdivide his army and scatter garrisons among them, due to his numerical inferiority. Instead, he was obliged to abandon still more newly acquired friends in order to consolidate his forces and holdings in what would become a slowly diminishing domain in the south. The war was far from over, but its outcome in Italy was all but decided.

As for the Capuans, their fate would instruct the others. Without hope they threw themselves upon the mercy of the Romans, frequently an oxymoron. Those city fathers who had not had the good sense to commit suicide were beaten with rods and beheaded; the rest of the population was sold into slavery—war paying for war, and fools paying with their lives.

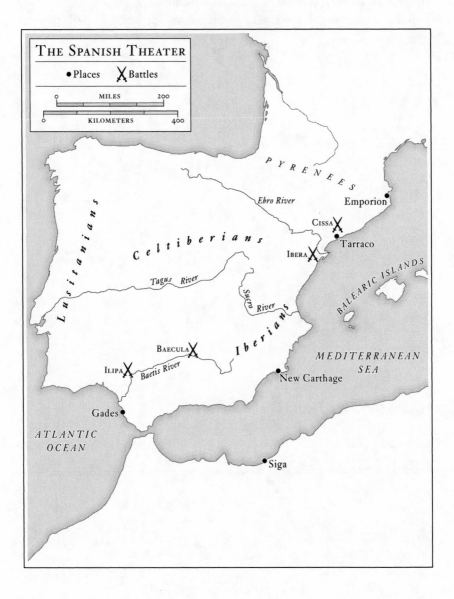

THE SPANISH THEATER

● Places ✗ Battles

MILES 200

KILOMETERS 400

PYRENEES

Ebro River

Emporion

Cissa ✗

Tarraco

Celtiberians

Ibera ✗

Lusitanians

Tagus River

Sucro River

Iberians

MEDITERRANEAN
SEA

BALEARIC ISLANDS

Baecula ✗

Ilipa ✗

Baetis River

New Carthage

Gades ●

ATLANTIC
OCEAN

Siga ●

VIII

THE AVENGERS

[1]

Young Publius, son and nephew of the Scipio brothers recently martyred in Spain, was barely twenty-five when he was invested with the proconsular imperium to venture to Iberia as supreme Roman commander. It was without precedent in the republic's constitutional history.[1] Too young to have held either the consulship or praetorship, he was elevated through a special election of the Comitia Centuriata rather than being appointed by the senate, which was the norm. Even considering the deceptive nature of Roman politics, this was all pretty odd.

Some modern historians find the roots of the assignment in factional and familial squabbles over war policy, and just how much emphasis to put on the Spanish theater,[2] but Livy (26.18.5–6) provides a simpler explanation that makes a lot of sense—nobody of consequence much wanted the posting. Conventional wisdom found the real glory in Italy and in the prospect of getting rid of Hannibal. This was likely why the grim and gifted Caius Claudius Nero headed back to Italy after only a short, if successful, Iberian interlude.

Still, even if Spain was a dirty job, strategic considerations demanded that somebody had to do it, and making young Scipio that somebody was an attractive if unorthodox solution. The very name Scipio was a known quantity in Iberia, not only among the legionaries remaining there, but also among those tribes who might still be inclined to take the Roman part in the struggle. Then there was the poetic justice of sending a highly motivated young Scipio to avenge other dead Scipios. But most compelling perhaps was the nature of this particular Scipio.

It is pretty apparent that the young man destined to become

Africanus was already an impressive figure. Livy himself, who could look back on a succession of late republican demagogues, found Scipio even at this stage astonishingly preoccupied with his own public persona. This was a young man who did little to discourage rumors that his very birth was the result of a congress between his mother and a rather large serpent, that he reached decisions within sacred confines presumably in consultation with Jupiter himself, and that he acted on the basis of divinely inspired dreams.[3] Potent stuff for the very superstitious Romans, but this image also required the personal gravitas to pull it off without looking ridiculous.

This he had—the ancient equivalent of "the right stuff." As was the case with Hannibal, the obvious comparison was between the young Publius Scipio and Alexander, the Mediterranean basin's beacon of imperial ambition. Livy was frank to admit it—the same youth, good looks, cultural literacy, and penchant toward Pan-Hellenism, an ornate façade beneath which beat the heart of a born soldier—decisive, opportunistic, and ruthless. Of course, Alexander really was a Greek, seemed convinced of his divinity, and was probably crazy; Scipio was a Roman and, as far as we can tell, entirely more down to earth.

In this regard Polybius helps to complete the picture. He declared that if his readers looked beneath the glamour and good fortune, they would find a calculating spirit grounded in careful preparation and attention to detail, a person whose supposed magnanimity masked a shrewd and even cynical eye for the main chance.[4] Scipio was a young man capable of the most brutal sort of retribution; yet when it suited his purposes, he would befriend the very Numidian prince, Masinissa, who was so instrumental in the deaths of his father and uncle.

And it was this sort of pragmatism that enabled him to reshape the Roman *triplex acies* from a serried battering ram into a dynamic battlefield instrument capable of attacking and winning from several directions. This spark of creative genius would prove to be what Rome ultimately needed in a commander to defeat Hannibal.

But it came at a price. From beginning to end Scipio's career betrayed a restlessness with the norms and constraints imposed by Roman politics and senatorial domination. When confronted, he inevitably— if grudgingly—acceded, but in establishing this pattern he set a precedent of personal ambition that led eventually to Caesar and the collapse of the republic. So, it seems that in order to save the state from

Hannibal it was necessary to generate the very type of individual who would ultimately destroy it. This was the true Barcid curse upon Rome.

For the moment, however, Scipio was exactly the commanding presence the situation demanded, particularly in Spain, where he acted with extraordinary self-assurance and sagacity from the moment he arrived in the summer of 210 with approximately eleven thousand fresh troops.[5] At Tarraco (modern Tarragona), on safe ground north of the Ebro, he called together local tribal leaders and gave them an enthusiastic pep talk. Then he continued touring the areas under Roman control, congratulating the troops for holding on, and singling out the commander they had elected, L. Marcius Septimus, for special praise, thereby cementing the troops' loyalty.

The legionaries having settled down into their winter quarters, Scipio began reorganizing them, blending his reinforcements with the various elements remaining from his father's and uncle's armies. He was intent on forging them into a homogenous whole, now numbering around twenty-eight thousand infantry and three thousand cavalry.[6] Meanwhile, he was incubating an amazingly audacious scheme for the coming campaigning season. We have a good idea what he was thinking, since Polybius bases his account on a letter detailing the plan Scipio wrote once the war was over.[7] Even before arriving in Spain, Scipio understood that his relatives' defeats had resulted from splitting their forces, and from the treachery of the Celtiberians they had hired. Yet by this time he had learned that the Carthaginians were on similarly shaky ground with the tribes to the south, and that they too had divided their forces—Mago was somewhere beyond the Strait of Gibraltar, Hasdrubal Gisgo was far west in Lusitania, and Hasdrubal Barca was around the headwaters of the Tagus River in the vicinity of today's Toledo. All of them being more than ten days' march from Barca central, the vital city of New Carthage.[8] This was to be Scipio's target of opportunity.

The scheme he hatched was virtually a mirror of its architect—breathtakingly daring. Yet hedged by meticulous planning and good intelligence. While still in winter quarters, he not only obtained a plan of the city, but had been told by some fishermen that it might be approached from several angles through a shallow lagoon that could be forded at low tide. This was critical, since Scipio had also learned that the city was guarded only by approximately one thousand troops, who could not be everywhere at once. His window of opportunity was a narrow one, defined by the ten or so days it would take for the scattered Carthaginian forces to converge on the city. Polybius tells us that Scipio also understood that in the case of failure he could evacuate his men by ship, since Romans controlled the seas, and if he succeeded, the Romans already would be behind New Carthage's fortifications.[9] His bets were covered.

Just in case, before he crossed the Ebro and headed south in the spring of 209, Scipio left three thousand foot soldiers and five hundred horse with an experienced subordinate to keep an eye on the Tarraco locals, and he told only Gaius Laelius, his boyhood friend and career right-hand man, of his plans. The arrival of Scipio and his army came as an unwelcome surprise to the New Carthaginians, who reacted with an uncharacteristic and ultimately unwise verve for defending the place. Two thousand of them joined the commander—yet another Mago—and his mercenaries with the intent of meeting the Romans outside the city walls. For his part Scipio had gathered the troops and given them the usual exhortations (i.e., "the first one over the wall gets the gold crown"), but with a characteristically Scipionic twist. He told them that the entire plan had been given to him in a dream by the god Neptune, whose help they could all count on.[10]

The operation might as well have been scripted by divine intervention. The eagerest locals initially sallied out and fought bravely, until they were overwhelmed by Roman reinforcements, thereby culling the most audacious of the defenders as they retreated through the city gates. Still, the locals rallied and were able to throw back the first Roman assault with scaling ladders, and probably took heart that they could hold out until relieved by one of the scattered Carthaginian field forces.

But they hadn't counted on Scipio's determination . . . or his guile. Rather than allowing the normal several days of rest after a failed attack, Scipio waited only until late in the afternoon before throwing his force again at the portion of the wall where the main gate was located; but not before leading a picked contingent around to the other side of the fortifications, the side bordered by the lagoon. Just as the onslaught in front was cresting, the ocean tide turned and began emptying the shallows, giving the legionaries here every reason to believe Neptune himself was busy with his trident, literally bailing them out. The Romans waded across with their ladders and easily mounted the wall there, which was now drained of defenders, who had moved off to meet the primary attack. Racing along the top to the main gate, the Romans forced it open just as their comrades in front gained a foothold on the battlements.[11] After that it was a deluge of mayhem, with Scipio ordering his troops to kill anything that moved, before beginning the more methodical pillaging.[12]

But Scipio was far too practical to simply let his legionaries gorge themselves on a prize this valuable. Rather than merely shatter what was the Barcid piggy bank, the central emporium/treasury/arsenal of the entire enterprise, he would make it work for himself and Rome. The next day he assembled the ten thousand surviving inhabitants and told them of his plans for them. Full citizens were sent home free; artisans were made slaves of the Roman state, to pursue their trades in public workshops on the promise of eventual freedom; and the rest, presumably slaves, Scipio used to man the eighteen ships captured in the harbor and to supplement his own crews.[13] Mago the commander, two members of Carthage's council of elders, and fifteen other captive Carthaginian legislators would be packed on a quinquereme and sent to Rome, along with Laelius and the good news of Scipio's victory.[14]

Finally, Scipio turned to the Spanish tribal people who had been held hostage within the city, more than three hundred individuals. Besides giving them gifts, he urged them to write to their relatives at home informing them of their safety and of Scipio's willingness to repatriate them should their tribes side with Rome. When a Spanish noblewoman begged that the female hostages be treated "with more proper consideration than the Carthaginians had done," he first missed her meaning, and then assured her he would look after them "as if they were his own sisters and children." Around this time, his soldiers tried to present Scipio, who was known to like women, with a young girl of surpassing beauty, but instead of bedding her, he delivered her back to her father or her local lover, depending whether you believe Polybius or Livy.[15] Whoever it was, this was exactly the sort of gesture that won over a population, and epitomized Scipio's sagacity and self-control.

The sudden descent on New Carthage, carried out under the noses of three enemy field armies, proved a master stroke. In a single blow Scipio transformed the entire cast of the war in Spain. New Carthage had been the powerhouse of the Barcid Iberian empire, the repository for three decades of looting and confiscations, and their own personal military-industrial complex. Now all this gold and silver and industriousness was Roman. Given this setback to the Barcid family power and prestige, it is also possible to hypothesize a parallel shift among Carthaginians, with the subsequent financing and direction of the war in Spain sliding more toward metropolitan Carthage and relative new-comer Hasdrubal Gisgo, and away from the Barcid brothers in Spain, Mago and Hasdrubal. Whatever the case, it was completely apparent that the initiative now lay with Publius Scipio.

Nor was he about to let it go. He turned New Carthage into a hive of activity, constantly exercising his navy and rigorously training his troops in repeated five-day cycles that combined long marches with sword and javelin practice and weapons maintenance.[16] He also may have begun instituting the new infantry tactics he would spring on the Carthaginians the following year.[17] Meanwhile, under skilled foremen and his own supervision, he set the rest of the population to work in what Polybius (10.20.6–7) called "a workshop of war," with "everyone busily engaged upon the preparations of weapons." Yet he was still fac-ing three hostile armies. Putting his own force in the best possible con-dition addressed the purely military dimension of the problem, but this was Spain, and adroit diplomacy with the tribes might prove equally corrosive to his enemies.

So as the winter of 209–8 approached, he returned to Tarraco, where he called together deputies of Rome's native allies, both old and new. It proved the beginning of an avalanche of tribal defections from the Carthaginians, sweeping along, not unexpectedly, the ever pliable Indibilis, who made a career of switching sides.[18]

Watching group after group slip out of his camp with the intent of joining the Romans, Hasdrubal Barca decided to make a fight of it with Scipio before his army entirely melted away. If he won, he would have the time and security to plot his next move. If bested, he was prepared to give up on Spain, head across the Alps with the survivors, fill up on Gallic mercenaries, and then join Hannibal.[19]

For his part, Scipio not only was ready to rumble, but was ready specifically to fight Hasdrubal, who was closest, before the other two Carthaginian armies could converge on him. He even drew the crews from the fleet into his legions, in an effort to ensure he would not be outnumbered. He left Tarraco in the spring of 208 and, as he moved south, linked up with Indibilis and his contingent, finally locating the Carthaginians at a place called Baecula (the modern town of Bailén).

Upon hearing of Scipio's approach, Hasdrubal moved to a very strong defensive position on a flat-topped hill protected by steep banks in the front and on the sides, and by a river to the rear. Some have argued that this position indicated that Hasdrubal didn't really want a fight, but it seems more likely he was hoping Scipio might hesitate long enough for Mago or Hasdrubal Gisgo to arrive. Or perhaps he was hoping to lure the Roman commander into a problematic uphill slog, which was exactly what happened.[20]

Scipio waited two days, perhaps hoping the Carthaginians would come down off their hill, but then, worried about the imminent arrival of the other Punic armies, Scipio resolved to attack. The choice was hardly as rash as it might seem. The force structure he wielded was a far different instrument from the traditional three-line bulldozer militia of even the recent Roman past. Scipio had raised the training to a much higher level, one sufficient for major components to break apart and maneuver truly as independent units, but still in a coordinated fashion.[21]

The Romans began the attack with a direct assault in the center by the *velites*, whose enthusiasm and apparent training set the conditions for success. The velites *worked* their way up the hill under a barrage of missiles, gained a foothold at the top, and then routed the Punic covering force. This initial move seems to have surprised Hasdrubal, who began to form up his heavy troops near the ridgeline.

It was too late. Scipio had already divided his own heavy forces, leading one half himself and giving the other to Laelius, and set them off on a flanking maneuver on either side of the hill. They raced to the top, deployed from column into line, and then executed a pincer movement against the Carthaginian formation before it was fully formed. It was a rout, but in an almost melodramatic turn of events (think Professor Moriarty, or Dr. Fu-Manchu, or Ming the Merciless slipping through the righteous clutches of Flash Gordon), Hasdrubal managed to exit stage left with his treasure chest, his elephants, and a goodly portion of his heavy troops, heading off toward Italy with the hope of joining his elder brother.

The Barcid's latest disappearing act caused Scipio biographer H. H. Scullard to label Baecula a tactical victory but a strategic defeat.[22] In one sense this is certainly true. It was the singular achievement of Scipio's father and uncle to have prevented Hannibal's reinforcement from Spain at a truly parlous time for the state, but they had also ended up dead because of tactical miscues in the face of superior forces. Had

Scipio taken off after Hasdrubal, he might have eventually found himself sandwiched between this retreating force and the forces of Mago and Hasdrubal Gisgo. Besides, the situation in Italy was now far more to Rome's advantage than it had been earlier, when Hannibal had truly been on the loose. Meanwhile, even with the middle Barcid brother gone, Scipio was still outnumbered in Spain and had to be careful.

So he set himself up in the security of the captured Punic camp atop the hill and set about reinforcing his position. First he disposed of his battle prisoners, sending the Spaniards home without ransom, and ordering the Africans to be sold as slaves.[23] (Livy tells us that during this process the quaestor came across a particularly handsome youth, who claimed to be of royal Numidian blood. He was sent to Scipio, who discovered him to be the nephew of Masinissa, who had helped run down his father and uncle. Another might have exacted familial revenge, but Scipio, looking to the future, had the boy sent back to his uncle under armed guard.[24]) Next, Scipio presided over a procession of nearby tribal leaders ready to pay their obeisance to Rome, paving the way for further incursions toward the valley of the Baetis River and the remaining Punic strongholds. The Spaniards, including the shifty Indibilis, could barely contain their enthusiasm, saluting Scipio as "king." The prudent Scipio replied that while he appreciated the sentiment, such a title was bound to set teeth on edge in Rome, so he suggested instead "imperator," a title that had already been bestowed upon him by his troops. In fact this was the first chronicled example of such a title being given to a victorious Roman general. It would not be the last.[25]

[2]

Back in Italy, Marcellus was looking to crown his storied career by at last getting rid of the Punic incubus. Plutarch (Marcellus, 28) reports, "No man ever had such a passion for anything as he had for fighting a decisive battle with Hannibal. This was his dream at night, his one subject for deliberation with friends and colleagues, his one appeal to the gods."

Upon returning to Rome after Sicily, Marcellus was notably more aggressive than the other Roman commander, an approach that was bound to put him somewhat at odds with Fabian II and its namesake. Yet the differences between Marcellus and Fabius should not be exaggerated; for the time being both continued to operate within the context of the overall plan—Fabius acting as Rome's shield and Marcellus as its sword.[26]

The year 209 proved to be a watershed for this partnership and also for the Roman confederation, which after nearly a decade of war was showing signs of fraying, and not just at the edges. Apparently, many of the survivors of the Second Battle of Herdonea the year before, those subsequently exiled to join the ghosts of Cannae indefinitely on Sicily, had been Latin.[27] Now twelve of the thirty Latin colonies announced to the Roman consuls that they could no longer furnish their quota of fighting men or the money to support them. They were bitter and tapped out. Manpower was at the heart of the Roman military advantage, and Latins were at the heart of the alliance—the next best thing to being a full citizen—so this was a significant warning. Wisely, the senate did nothing beyond refusing to talk to the Latin colonies' envoys—a Roman version of the "silent treatment"[28]—but the signal did not go unnoticed. Progress, real progress, had to be made soon.

One key was to recapture Tarentum, the rich Greek port city on the inner side of Italy's heel and, besides Capua, Hannibal's most prized acquisition since Cannae. The plan was for Fabius Maximus to besiege the place by land and sea, but to do this safely it was necessary to keep Hannibal off his back. This was where Marcellus came in.

Before he realized what was intended for Tarentum, Hannibal moved up into Apulia as far as Canusium, where he tried to stir up the inhabitants against Rome. But instead he was intercepted by Marcellus with a large army, including the 18th and 20th legions, and Caius Claudius Nero commanding one of the *alae,* Marcellus having been ordered out of winter quarters with the object of picking a fight with Hannibal.[29]

After some initial maneuvering, this is exactly what he did. If we are to believe Livy, who may have made the episode sound more decisive than it actually was, the first day ended with the Romans being pushed ingloriously off the battlefield. But Marcellus's après-combat harangue so humiliated the legionaries, that after a night of rest and contemplation they retook the field determined to prevail. Then, at a key point the Romans managed to stampede Hannibal's elephants—always the weak link—back into the Punic lines and drive the Carthaginians into their camp.[30] Suspiciously, however, when Hannibal characteristically slipped away under the cover of darkness, Livy tells us Marcellus had too many wounded to follow. Whatever the actual tactical outcome, the Roman commander had certainly stood up to Hannibal, as he had done on several occasions previously, and in doing so he had accomplished the strategic purpose of the operation.

For back in Tarentum, Fabius Maximus had succeeded, through a plot with a Bruttian member of the Punic garrison, in gaining entry into the city. Once inside, the Roman troops ran wild, slaughtering Carthaginians, Tarentines, and even some of the Bruttians indiscriminately. Hannibal raced to the scene, marching day and night, but by the time he arrived, it was too late. He then concocted an elaborate plot to draw Fabius into combat, one that Fabius might have fallen for, had it not been for bad auspices.[31] Instead the Delayer stayed to concentrate on looting the place, recovering immense quantities of gold and silver and selling some thirty thousand Tarentines into slavery. This was the windfall Rome needed to recoup its public finances, and it was a fleecing so exorbitant that Livy tried to defend Fabius on the grounds that, unlike Marcellus at Syracuse, Fabius at least left some of the statues.[32]

Meanwhile, as the year drew to a close, Marcellus, "Rome's sword," returned home to face critics who charged that after Canusium he had spent too much time licking his wounds. These critics even threatened to take away his imperium. Marcellus not only blunted this effort, but managed to get himself elected to his fifth consulship. The politics and factions behind this maneuvering remain obscure,[33] but the overall message seems clear: Marcellus and his consular colleague, T. Quinctius Crispinus, were expected to behave even more aggressively. Rome once again was looking beyond the strategy of Fabius Maximus and contemplating outright victory over Hannibal.[34]

After some preliminaries, the year 208 found the two consuls and their armies joined in Apulia near Venusia, determined to fight the first full-scale confrontation with Hannibal since Cannae. The Carthaginian commander was stationed a few miles off, and the ground separating the opposing forces was dominated by a large heavily wooded hill. Such an eminence was a likely site for a secure camp, but instead Hannibal, ever the trickster, saw grounds for an ambush. He seeded the hill with concealed Numidians lying in wait. Obligingly, Marcellus and Crispinus decided to take a small mounted force to reconnoiter the place. There is some disagreement between Livy's version and Polybius's fragment regarding the details of the event, but the outcome was perfectly clear. Marcellus was run through and died on the spot, and Crispinus was mortally wounded, though he escaped.[35]

Hannibal gave Marcellus an elaborate funeral, but then used his signet ring to try to get a band of deserters disguised as Romans into Salapia, the place where Hannibal had earlier enjoyed the company of a local prostitute. Crispinus managed to foil this plot before he died by warning the neighboring communities not to trust any message supposedly sent by his colleague. Still, it was pretty obvious that the Punic fox had lost little of his edge and remained full of schemes. It was equally clear that Marcellus, whom Polybius cruelly labeled as having acted "not so much like a general as like a simpleton,"[36] had not been up to beating him. Modern historian J. F. Lazenby considers Marcellus a kind of archetype of conventional Roman generals, "brave, hard and competent," admirable qualities but, when faced with a military genius, plainly not enough.[37] Against a force so protean, Rome would have to fight fire with fire.

[3]

For the moment things were looking grim, even desperate, along the Tiber. And it was not just a matter of restive Latins; there were ominous reports of unrest in Etruria (Tuscany today), the rich area in the northeast. For reasons beyond historical comprehension, Terentius Varro had been again invested with the imperium and sent to Etruria to bring some hostages back to Rome. Upon his return, he delivered such an alarmist report that he was given a legion and ordered to return. This marked the start of Etrurian troubles that would only grow worse with the arrival of a new Barcid menace.[38]

Hasdrubal Barca was on the move, and his progress had been monitored with increasing alarm along the Tiber. Envoys from Rome's friend Massilia reported that Hasdrubal had crossed into coastal Gaul, and later Rome's own agents sent back word that the Carthaginian intended to traverse the Alps in the spring of 207. Next, the praetor L. Porcius Licinus dispatched news that the Barcid was again mobile, having recruited eight thousand of the northern tribesmen known as Ligurians. Finally, and most shocking, the Romans learned that Hasdrubal had been given a friendly reception by the Alpine Gauls, had slid through the mountains more easily and directly than his brother, and was now in Italy laying siege to Placentia earlier than anyone had thought possible.[39]

These trip reports were potentially devastating psychologically. The Romans had waged war on their own territory at great cost in casualties and devastation for upward of a decade, and although Hannibal had been effectively cornered in the south, he obviously remained capable of flummoxing even their most experienced commanders. Now the Romans were faced with a second Gaul-fortified Barcid visitation from out of the Alpine mists, one potentially even more disastrous, should Hasdrubal manage to join forces with his diabolical brother, a true nightmare scenario. ("Not even the first invasion caused as much terror and confusion in Italy," reported the ever hyperbolic Silius Italicus. "Men said that here was a second Hannibal, . . . and the two generals, gorged with Italian blood . . . were doubling their strength; the enemy would come in headlong haste to Rome.")[40]

Fortunately, those in charge saw through the situation and acted accordingly. In fact, Rome was now battle-hardened, far stronger, and more militarily capable than when Hannibal had first entered Italy. For the year 207, fully twenty-three legions were to be fielded. This was the greatest number in the war and was equaled only in 211 during the relentless siege of Capua. But after Rome lost two consuls simultaneously to Hannibal, the perception must have been that the senate needed to make sure the right men now assumed command. The obvious choice for consul was the very dynamic and experienced C. Claudius Nero. He had been among the conquerors of Capua, had nearly put an end to Hasdrubal in Spain, and had been with Marcellus at Canusium when, at the very least, they had kept Hannibal away from Tarentum.[41] Yet his very boldness left a sense of unease and sparked a desire by the leadership to balance him with a more prudent soul as colleague.

Marcus Livius Salinator was hardly a conventional choice. After sharing the consulship in 219 with Lucius Aemilius Paullus and successfully fighting the Illyrian War, Salinator had been convicted for mishandling the booty and had withdrawn in disgrace to his estates for more than a decade, letting his hair and beard grow long, and wearing only shabby clothing. Still, his leadership skills and cool head were not forgotten, and in 209, Marcellus and Laevinus convinced him to return to the senate, where he said very little and remained his unkempt self, at least until the censors forced him to cut his hair and put on a clean toga. Further complicating matters, Salinator and Nero, perhaps for temperamental reasons, were notorious enemies. But the perceived emergency was pressing, and under the auspices of Fabius Maximus the senate reconciled these two strong personalities—fire and ice— and they formed a notably effective consular team.[42]

Yet, the object of all this attention, Hasdrubal Barca, was once again proving himself to be no Hannibal, not even close. Instead of exploiting his sudden arrival and striking immediately into the heart of Italy, Hasdrubal dawdled around Placentia, which Hannibal himself had judged too well defended to take, apparently to impress the Gauls he wanted to recruit, only belatedly giving up its siege and heading down the peninsula.[43] Hasdrubal had a choice of going either west or east of the Apennine mountain spine. On the west, Varro was waiting in unsettled Etruria, and on the east, the capable praetor Licinus was athwart the Adriatic coastal route, with Salinator waiting in Rome, poised to join either one, depending on which way the Barcid turned. Hasdrubal went toward the Adriatic, with Licinus retreating and harassing him all the way, as Salinator raced north to join forces.[44] And even worse for the Barcid, his own plea for reinforcements would bring still more Romans down on his head.

After he left Placentia, Hasdrubal dispatched a letter to Hannibal saying he would meet him "in Umbria." The letter was carried by a party of six horsemen—two Numidians and four Gauls. This was a shot in the dark—sending a bunch of foreign-looking, and presumably not Latin-speaking, horsemen off through a country crawling with enemies and expecting them to find Hannibal, who was always a moving target during campaigning season. It has been suggested that the letter was intended for capture and was meant to mislead the Romans as to Hasdrubal's projected route,[45] but it appears that Hasdrubal was already being closely monitored by Licinus, and if by chance the letter had gotten through, wouldn't it have confused Hannibal? ("Meet me in Umbria" was hardly specific.)

As it happened, the horsemen made it almost the entire length of the peninsula, arrived at Metapontum (near the arch of the boot) only to find Hannibal gone, and were soon captured by foragers near Tarentum. They brought them for interrogation to Nero. The Roman had been dogging Hannibal back and forth through Bruttium and Apulia in a confusing series of actions that had left the two armies camped in close proximity again near Canusium. Once the predictably rough treatment of the prisoners revealed the truth, Nero decided to stage a vanishing act of his own. He took seven thousand picked troops—six thousand foot soldiers and one thousand horse—from his much larger force and slipped them out of camp under the cover of night, leaving the Carthaginians none the wiser.[46]

Quite plainly the days of Hannibal the omniscient were over; it was now the Romans who held the intelligence advantage and were capable of strategic maneuvers under the cloak of secrecy.[47] Until they were well away from camp, Nero's men were under the impression they were going to stage a raid on a nearby town. Then he told them the truth; they were heading north to join Salinator.

Messengers fanned out ahead along the 250-mile route requesting provisions as the troops raced north with nothing but their weapons. Livy (27.45) paints a scene of patriotic enthusiasm, with throngs gathered by the side of the road competing with one another to give the soldiers what they needed, and cheering them as they passed. Back in Rome, however, word of the consul's bold move provoked more anxiety; the voice of the street fretting over Nero's leaving a hollow army camped in front of the dreaded Hannibal, and remembering the events in Spain, when Hasdrubal had eluded Nero, leaving him "baffled like a little child."[48] Polybius, who was not inclined to exaggerate, agrees, stating in a fragment, "Rome had never been in such a state of excitement and dismay, awaiting the results."[49]

The future was in good hands. As Nero neared the combined camps of Salinator and the praetor Licinus at Sena Gallica, he dispatched couriers to ask how the forces should best link up, and was advised to enter secretly by night. The newcomers would be housed in the existing tents, to minimize their footprint and avoid betraying their presence to Hasdrubal, who was just five hundred yards away.[50] All went well, and on the following day Salinator and Licinus held a council of war with Nero. Assuming Nero's men needed rest after their long forced march, Salinator and Licinus suggested postponing a confrontation for several days. Nero objected in no uncertain terms, arguing that delay would only squander the advantage he had gained by his bold move and heighten the danger down south, since it was only a matter of time before Hannibal discovered he was gone and sprang into action. Nero was right, and the others saw it immediately. An order went out for the combined army to move out on the double and begin deploying for battle.[51]

Hasdrubal stood ready to accept the challenge, lining up his army in front of their camp. But then as he rode forward with his bodyguards, the Barcid smelled—if not a rat, then at least road-hardened Romans, noticing some particularly battered shields, some unusually stringy horses, and a general swelling of the legions facing him. He had his trumpeters sound an immediate retreat and sent out scouts to survey the Romans more carefully. The scouts reported that the encampment itself looked normal, yet the bugles had sounded just once in the prae-tor's camp but twice in Salinator's. Instantly Hasdrubal realized he was facing both consuls, and his mind turned in a fearful direction.[52] What bothered him was not so much the apparent reinforcement of the Roman legions here; uppermost, it seems, was the haunting thought that the second consul's presence meant that Hannibal had suffered a crushing defeat and that Hasdrubal's assistance had come too late. This at least would best explain his decision to retreat.

He sought refuge under the cover of night and ordered his men to silently collect their baggage and head back toward the Metaurus River, around twelve miles to the northwest, in hopes of finding a ford and safety. Then, being no Hannibal, he lost control of the situa-tion. His guides, unwatched, absconded, and his troops, many of them Gauls, tended to fall out and go to sleep. When the caravan finally blundered into the Metaurus, Hasdrubal told them to follow the bank, but it grew steeper and more circuitous and provided neither a place to cross nor much progress away from the pursuing Romans.[53]

First Nero rode up leading the cavalry, then Licinus followed with the *velites*, both of them harassing the Carthaginians to a standstill. At this point Hasdrubal saw his best chance in establishing a camp on a steep hill by the bank of the river. But shortly after he began work, Sali-nator marched up with the heavy troops in full battle array, ready to deploy. Now Hasdrubal had no choice but to fight.

According to Ovid[54] and the Roman calendar, the day was June 22, 207 B.C. As usual the exact location of the climactic battle remains un-known, with at least six sites south of the river having been proposed,[55] but at least we have a fragment from Polybius (11.1–3.6) describing the action, which can act as a check on Livy. There are some differences between the two historians' accounts, but in the main they can be reconciled.

Hasdrubal seems to have anchored his line on the steep hill with the partially constructed camp, leaving his least reliable troops—the Gauls—there, since it was the easiest point to defend. In the center, if we are to believe Livy,[56] Hasdrubal placed the Ligurians he had recruited on the way to the Alps. For the moment they were fronted by a screen of ten elephants. Finally, on his right were his most trusted troops, those he had brought with him from Spain; this was his attack force, and as the fighting developed, the elephants would be shifted in front of them with the aim of compounding their momentum.[57] That was the hope at least.

For their part the Romans lined up with Salinator on the left facing the Spaniards, Licinus in the center, and Nero on the right looking at an uphill battle against the Gauls. As the action opened, Nero found he could make no progress, not because the Gauls were fighting so hard, but simply because the terrain made advancing nearly impossible. Using his head and his force structure for something besides a battering ram, Nero cut loose the rear ranks of his part of the line and marched them over to the extreme left, setting up for a devastating flank attack on the Punic right.

Here Salinator was engaged in a furious struggle with the troops from Spain, the elephants as usual sowing confusion as they trampled both sides with panicked impartiality. Nero soon broke the stalemate, leaving the Spaniards in a death grip, front and rear, to be cut to pieces. Most were killed at this point, along with six of the elephants; the remaining four elephants wandered off to be recovered later. Meanwhile, the Romans had rolled up the rest of the Carthaginian line and had reached the campsite, where, Polybius reports, they butchered many of the Gauls, whom they found drunk and asleep.[58] As for Hasdrubal, Livy and Polybius agree that once he saw that all was lost, he made no effort to escape but died bravely in the midst of the fighting.[59]

Nero, the architect of the victory, made sure Hasdrubal's corpse was recovered and that he, Nero, had a full measure of revenge for being given the slip back in Spain. Like Scipio, Nero had plainly been working with his troops and upgrading their tactical capabilities, giving them the capacity to radically shift objectives and exploit opportunities as the situation developed on the battlefield. His secretive advance to the Metaurus stands as one of the most dramatic and successful strategic maneuvers of the entire war. The maneuver was capped off by his leaving the night following the battle and driving his weary legionaries back to their camp near Canusium in six days—almost fifty miles a day, one of the greatest marches in history.[60] But as good a general as Nero was, Hannibal remained in Italy through his consulship and beyond. Earlier, Nero had had roughly the same opportunity as Publius Scipio to deal decisively with the Barcid power base in Spain, and he had made very little of it. Twenty-two hundred years is a long way back for definitive personnel judgments, but the facts speak for themselves. Getting rid of Hannibal was a job for somebody else.

Back in Rome, however, getting rid of Hasdrubal was enough . . . at least for now. Polybius reports that when the news first arrived, the anxious inhabitants refused to believe it, and it was only after more messengers repeated the good tidings that relief and joy swept over the city. All the holy places were decorated and the temples were set to bursting with offerings. Livy would have us believe that "Cannae was avenged" with the death of the Carthaginian general and fifty-six thousand of his troops.[61] But the magnitude of the Roman victory was likely more modest, Polybius's estimate of around ten thousand total Punic casualties, including Gauls, probably being closer to the mark. Except perhaps at its very core, Hasdrubal's army had in no way been qualitatively the equal of Hannibal's. Rather, the circumstances of its recruitment indicate it was more akin to the typical Carthaginian rent-a-force, essentially a disposable asset.

Still, the Romans were happy. At summer's end the generals were brought to Rome. Salinator (who was technically in charge) was given the first triumph of the entire war, and Nero, riding behind him, got an ovation.[62] There was reason to celebrate. After almost twelve years of fighting, Rome had at last won decisively on Italian soil. Polybius concludes that "It seemed to everyone that Hannibal, whom they formerly so much dreaded, was not now even in Italy."[63]

He still was, but the results from the Metaurus filled him with foreboding. As is so often the case in family matters, among the principals he was the last to know, and it could not have come in a more awful manner. The grim Nero had the carefully preserved head of Hasdrubal delivered to an outpost of Hannibal's camp in Canusium, along with two captured Africans to tell him what had happened. Upon hearing the news, Hannibal immediately decamped to Bruttium down in the

very toe of Italy, where he stayed. It was said that, staring at his
brother's dead features, Hannibal declared that he saw the fate of
Carthage.[64] He might have been looking at his own reflection. For he,
more than anybody else, was responsible for the city's doom.

[4]

With the departure of Hasdrubal Barca, the effort to keep Spain Punic
seems to have shifted still more to those representing metropolitan
Carthage, though not necessarily with any more success. To fill the
void, Hanno, a new general, was sent over from Africa with reinforcements and money to hire recruits in Celtiberia, where he joined Mago,
the remaining Barca brother in Spain.[65] Scipio, whose spadework with
the Spanish tribes was paying off, knew all about this effort and was determined to nip it in the bud. He sent the propraetor M. Iunius Silanus
with a flying column after them. Guided by Celtiberian deserters, the
Romans arrived without warning, found the enemy split into two
camps, and ended up routing first the largely untrained Spaniards and
then the Carthaginians who'd come to their support. Hanno was captured, but Mago managed to escape with all of his cavalry and around
two thousand veteran infantry. He eventually found refuge with Hasdrubal Gisgo at Gades (modern Cádiz), Hasdrubal having been basically chased there by Scipio after dispersing his army.[66] So 207 ended
in Spain not much better than it had in Italy for the Punic cause.

Yet Hasdrubal Gisgo, now pretty plainly the generalissimo in Spain,
was far from finished. He still had a base at Gades, plenty of money for
mercenaries, and the persistence of a true Carthaginian. By the following spring he and Mago had managed to reassemble the scattered
Spaniards and hire still more to put together a force that, if you believe
Polybius,[67] numbered seventy thousand foot soldiers, four thousand
horse, and thirty-two elephants—all intended for a decisive blow
against Scipio. Whereas he had refused battle the year before, now
Hasdrubal Gisgo crossed the Baetis River, marched to the vicinity of a
town called Ilipa (around eight miles north of modern Seville), and sat
down on high ground backing an open plain—a clear sign he wanted a
fight.[68]

Scipio arrived similarly predisposed, but probably significantly outnumbered. His force consisted of a basic consular army of two legions

and two *alae*, plus an equivalent number of local warriors recently raised from Spanish tribal allies, for a total of around forty-five thousand infantry and three thousand cavalry. As he was setting up camp on the opposite side of the field, Scipio received an unambiguous indication that the Carthaginians meant business: Mago and Masinissa swept toward the legionaries in a coordinated cavalry attack. But the two quickly discovered that this was one hard Roman to catch off guard. Behind a nearby hill Scipio had already concealed an equivalent number of his cavalry, who then galloped out to hit the Punic horsemen in the flank, eventually chasing them back to their lines in considerable disorder.[69]

And Scipio was hardly through messing with Carthaginian minds. The next several days were repetitious but inconclusive—some desultory skirmishing among the cavalry and light troops, along with the heavy infantry deploying but never advancing to within fighting range. The Punic forces took the field first, lining up with their best troops— the Libyans at the center, flanked by the Spaniards on either side and the cavalry and elephants at the wings. The Romans would then follow in a roughly similar manner—legionaries at the center, the *alae* on their flanks, and their own Spanish troops to the outside, with cavalry covering each end.

Having gotten the Carthaginians used to this routine, Scipio set about wrong-footing them, ordering his men to eat an early breakfast and to march out of camp at dawn, and just to make sure his wake-up call was not missed, he sent his cavalry and *velites* right up to the enemy camp to let loose a wave of javelins.[70]

Hasdrubal Gisgo reacted reflexively, ordering his own cavalry and skirmishers out to meet the Romans, and his infantry to take the field in the same order and formation as usual—all before anybody had a chance to get breakfast, the same trick Hannibal had pulled on Tiberius Sempronius Longus at the River Trebia. And there would be more, a Scipionic bait and switch. Once out on the field, Hasdrubal realized that the Romans were now lined up with the Spaniards in the middle and the two legions and *alae* flanking them on either side, facing his weakest troops. Yet if he tried to redeploy, he ran the risk of Scipio's attacking in the midst of the maneuver and creating havoc; so he waited . . . and waited.[71]

For Scipio was in no hurry. He let hunger and the heat of the day have their exhausting way with the Punic troops of the line, while his cavalry and *velites* continued sporadic skirmishing with their Numidian opposites. Hours probably passed before he sounded the retreat and opened the files to let them pass through, and subsequently stationed them on each wing.[72]

At this point the real maneuvering began. Scipio ordered his whole line to start moving forward until they closed to approximately five hundred paces, at which point he had the Spaniards continue to march forward slowly, thereby pinning the Africans. Meanwhile, he broke each of his wings off to operate separately, taking command of the right and leaving the left under Silanus and Marcius, the commander the troops themselves had earlier elected. There followed a complicated evolution, which Polybius describes in highly technical language open to multiple interpretations.[73] The choreography seems to have consisted of everybody taking a quarter turn to the right or left in order to form two columns (led by the *velites* and cavalry, and followed by the *triplex acies*). The commanders then wheeled the columns around and marched toward each Carthaginian flank until, right under the noses of the enemy, they wheeled again, repeated the quarter turn, and re-formed the three-tiered battle line. Since a column of men can move much faster than the same number of men in a line, Scipio managed to very quickly put his cavalry and *velites* on each Punic flank and allow his legionaries to get at Hasdrubal's Spaniards, while leaving his own Spaniards unengaged.[74] The Carthaginians watched it all happen, beguiled, doing nothing until it was too late.

Modern sources agree that such a move (whatever it exactly constituted) was not only extremely dangerous in such close proximity to the enemy, but testified to the extraordinary training and discipline of the legionaries involved. Ilipa was plainly a step beyond Baecula and far in advance of Varro's force at Cannae. By first manipulating the formal rituals by which battles were begun, and then through precise and daring maneuvering, Scipio had overcome a significant numerical disadvantage and had put his force in a position to crush their adversaries. It was a feat worthy of Hannibal himself.[75]

The Roman horsemen and skirmishers made a point of going after the Carthaginian elephants, panicking them under a cloud of javelins and sowing confusion as the elephants ran amok.[76] The Spaniards on the Punic wings put up a surprisingly stout resistance, but outflanked by the *velites* and cavalry and assaulted ahead by the legionary meat grinder, they slowly began to give ground. Meanwhile, the Africans in the middle remained unengaged, unable to force the fight with the Spaniards facing them, or come to the aid of the wings without fatally disrupting the stability of the formation. Their only option it seems was to follow the step-by-step retreat.[77] Hasdrubal did what he could to encourage them, but then the Roman pressure caused the Spaniards on the wings to collapse, and everybody seems to have cut and run. The Carthaginian forces appear to have reformed their ranks at the base of the hill backing the battlefield, but the Romans drove them to their camp, which the Romans were about to storm when a sudden and particularly violent cloudburst put an end to the fighting.[78]

Most of Hasdrubal's force remained intact, but its spirit was broken. Spanish desertions the next day convinced him that it was hopeless to stay put and try to defend the camp, so he slipped away that night with the remainder of his army. To make it to Gades and safety, he would have had to cross the Baetis, but Scipio with the aid of local guides beat him to the fords. Blocked, Hasdrubal turned in flight toward the Atlantic coast but was quickly brought to bay by Scipio's cavalry and skirmishers. Once the legionaries arrived, Livy says it was less a battle than "a butchering as of cattle."[79] Hasdrubal escaped with barely six thousand of his men to a nearby hill, which by its very steepness allowed them to defend themselves.

Still, surrounded and without means of supply, their situation was hopeless, the Romans maintaining a blockade apparently aimed at demoralizing rather than annihilating the survivors. Soon enough, Hasdrubal Gisgo fled to Gades, but not before arranging for ships to evacuate him back to Africa. Masinissa also escaped, but only after talking over his options in secret with Silanus, whom Scipio had left in charge while he returned to Tarraco. Mago was the last of the principals to come down off the mountain. He would join Hasdrubal Gisgo briefly in Gades before the latter withdrew; the last of the Barcids in Spain, Mago was also the last to give up the fight there. Abandoned by their leaders, the rest of the army simply evaporated, which allowed Silanus to join Scipio and announce that the war here was over.[80] This was premature, but major Carthaginian resistance in Spain was at an end.

Scipio was already concerned with a canvas broader than Iberia—broader, it soon became evident, than that of his colleagues in Italy. For he understood that once Barcid power was broken in Spain, the key to getting rid of Hannibal was the vulnerability of Carthaginian home turf. As war opened in 218, the senate had had every intention of invading Africa, but then Hannibal had brought the fight to them instead, and twelve years later they were still distracted. Not Scipio. The summer of 206 found him already working both sides of the African pressure point—not simply the Numidian prince Masinissa, but also his archenemy, Syphax.

Two rival Numidian kingdoms, both of them unstable, occupied central North Africa at this point. Massaesylia, the larger of the two, lay to the west; the other, Massylia, was much smaller and was sandwiched between its near-namesake and Carthaginian territory to the east.[81] Both were dominated and manipulated by Punic power but were also restive and rebellious. Earlier the Carthaginians had used Masinissa's father, Gala, the Massylian king, to drive Syphax, ruler of the Massaesylians, from power.[82] Now, however, Gala was dead and his throne was in dispute, while Syphax was back firmly in charge and was anxious to expand his power. Seeking to take advantage of the situation, Scipio first sent his alter ego, Laelius, to convince Syphax to ally himself with Rome, but when the king proved evasive, Scipio sailed over from New Carthage himself.

As Scipio's two quinqueremes approached the harbor of Siga, Syphax's western capital, Scipio found to his horror that none other than Hasdrubal Gisgo, on his way back to Carthage with seven smaller but more nimble triremes, had just made landfall and was now in a position to even the score after the shutout at Ilipa. Making the best of a bad situation, Scipio raced into port before Hasdrubal had time to weigh anchor, and once in port, neither man was willing to offend the king by coming to blows in his very harbor.[83]

So in an unlikely turn of events, and at Syphax's insistence, Scipio would dine with his most recent mortal enemy, sharing the same couch, and trading pleasantries. Hasdrubal left deeply impressed, not only finding Scipio even more charming than he was lethal on the battlefield, but also concluding that Syphax, if left to his own devices, would soon be under the spell of the general and in the Roman camp. Scipio thought so too, and sailed away assuming he had a new ally. But Hasdrubal had a daughter; history would know her as Sophonisba (the Punic name was Cafonbaal), just one of a string of North African spellbinders from Elissa to Cleopatra, and she would soon have Syphax wrapped around her little finger.

Back in Spain, Scipio apparently wanted to use the rest of 206 to tie up loose ends so he could return to Rome and stand for the consul-ship.[84] But he got more than he bargained for. The Iberian Peninsula re-mained a fractious place, and ejecting Punic power and making the peninsula Roman proved to be two very different things.

Initially, Scipio and his lieutenants—Marcius in particular—divided up to conduct a series of punitive expeditions against tribes and localities that had withheld their allegiance. Although these expe-ditions were generally successful, the resistance proved unexpectedly bitter. (The fighters in a place called Astapa, for instance, slaughtered their own women and children before waging a suicidal sortie.[85] This should have been a hint; the Romans in fact were poised atop a vol-cano.)

The first eruption ensued shortly, when Scipio fell ill and rumors began to circulate that he was near death. Not surprisingly, Indibilis was among the first responders, rallying numerous Iberian and Celt-iberian warriors and staging a broad-based rebellion.

Worse still, the news of Scipio's illness rebounded back on his army. Eight thousand troops garrisoning a town called Sucro, complaining that they hadn't been paid and had been left to stand idle, mutinied, de-manding either to be led into battle or sent home and discharged. This mutiny was both dangerous and symptomatic. The exciting and prof-itable days of campaigning against booty-laden Carthaginians were plainly near an end in Spain; the future was anti-insurgency with its combination of boredom and terror. Thus far, deployment in Spain had proved to be a one-way ticket, with some of Scipio's troops having been on station for upward of a decade.[86] So the promise of a long and in-conclusive counterinsurgency campaign had implications far beyond the Sucro mutineers. These implications may be reflected in Livy's (28.24.13) apparently phony naming of the chief conspirators, Caius Albius (White) and Caius Atrius (Black), the former being from Cales, one of the Latin towns that had refused to supply men in 209, in part because of interminable overseas service.[87]

At any rate, Scipio, now recovered, reacted rapidly and decisively. He surrounded the mutinous elements with a larger body of his forces, gave them a long and embittered speech, and then, while the loyal troops pounded their swords against their shields, had thirty-five of the ringleaders brought before them naked and in chains to be beaten and then beheaded. Last, he had each of the remaining mutineers take an individual oath of allegiance before he paid them all and promised that their transgressions would be forgotten.

This constituted a dramatic turn of leadership, to which both Livy and Polybius devote considerable space,[88] but it was also pretty plainly a stopgap measure. Nevertheless, Scipio's actions united the army sufficiently to enable him to conduct a swift and successful campaign against Indibilis, who characteristically escaped, eventually to be killed in still another rebellion after Scipio was gone. Rome was destined to be mired in more than a generation of continuous internecine warfare here, and the final conquest of northwest Spain did not come before the time of Augustus Caesar. But for Scipio, that was somebody else's problem; he was destined to be remembered as Africanus, not Hispaniensis. He had come to Spain to get rid of Barcid power, not to make the place Roman; now he was interested in getting rid of Hannibal.

Still, before leaving, there remained the matter of Mago Barca holed up at Gades, and also Masinissa, who was with him. Quiet negotiations with the African prince had continued intermittently, and like Syphax, he desired a personal meeting with the Roman general before entering into a compact. Scipio agreed to a secret rendezvous, thinking it important enough to journey all the way from Tarraco to a remote location in the Baetis valley. Masinissa, telling Mago that the horses were wasting away in the confined quarters of Gades, which was on a small island, asked and received permission to cross over and stage some raids inland. Instead, Masinissa headed for the Romans.

If you believe Livy (28.35), who is our only source for the meeting, it was virtually love at first sight. Not a word was said about Masinissa's role in the death of Scipio's father and uncle, nor about Scipio's budding relationship with the Numidian prince's mortal enemy, Syphax. Instead, Masinissa testified that his long-held desire to serve Rome, though perhaps thwarted in Spain, would come to fruition in Africa. Should Scipio be sent to Africa and Masinissa inherit his father's vacant throne, then Masinissa was "confident the hours of Carthage will be numbered." Scipio, who knew a good cavalry commander when he saw one, was delighted. It was the beginning of an enduring friendship between Masinissa and this Scipio, and Scipio's grandson, even; for the Numidian was destined to live for a very long time. It was also the beginning of the end for Carthage; for the city never had an enemy more persistent than Masinissa. Meanwhile, as the two departed from their initial tryst, Masinissa received permission to raid the territory of some of Rome's local allies—lest Mago suspect something was amiss.

The youngest Barcid brother was busy with schemes of his own. Discouraged by Scipio's quelling of the mutiny and his defeat of Indibilis's rebellion, Mago had just about given up hope of success in Spain and was planning a return to Africa, when he received money and orders from Carthage to take his fleet to Italy instead, recruit an army of Gauls and Ligurians and then try to join Hannibal.[89] Being a Barcid, however, he had an alternative agenda, a surprise raid on New Carthage, a mirror image of Scipio's own, aimed at regaining the family military-industrial complex and turning the Iberian tables on the Romans. Before Mago left, however, he shook down Gades, wringing all the money he could from the inhabitants, which proved a mistake. The foray on New Carthage went badly—the New Carthaginians had been forewarned and were no longer Barcid friendly—and upon returning to Gades, Mago discovered that the gates were barred against him. More than insulted, he invited the city fathers to confer, and promptly crucified them.[90] He then sailed for Ibiza to begin staging his own invasion of Italy, his departure marking the termination of Barcid and Punic power in Spain. Scipio could go home.

[5]

The conquering hero returned to Rome in late 206 with a fleet of ten ships crammed with, among other spoils of war, 14,342 pounds of silver and a great quantity of other coins destined for Rome's flagging treasury.[91] He met the senate on the *campus Martius* and, within the sacred confines of the temple of the war goddess Bellona, gave them a rundown of his achievements in Spain. He reminded them that he had faced down four enemy commanders (two Hasdrubals, Hanno, and Mago) and four Carthaginian armies, and that upon his leaving not a single Punic soldier remained in Spain. He added that although a triumph had never before been awarded to a victorious commander who had not held the appropriate magistracy, perhaps, considering his service to the state, he might be the first exception. They turned him down cold.

Still, he got its equivalent from the crowds that gathered in the streets of Rome to catch a glimpse of the man of the hour, Publius

Cornelius Scipio. Livy (28.35.6–7) describes him during this period as being in the "bloom of youth," with long flowing hair and virtually oozing virility. If it had been possible for there to be a rock star in ancient Rome, then he would have been it . . . and just as incongruous to some of the dour members of the senatorial establishment.

But not to the people. His house just behind the forum was virtually under siege. He was similarly surrounded at the Temple of Jupiter as he sacrificed a hundred oxen—a hecatomb he had promised his patron deity while still in Spain. At the Comitia Centuriata, presided over by outgoing consul and family friend L. Veturius Philo, he was elected consul virtually by acclamation, with most of the other magistracies going to political allies, including his consular colleague P. Licinius Crassus, perhaps the richest man in Rome, and *pontifex maximus* since 212. More good news for Scipio: the senate had decided that the consular provinces for 205 would be Bruttium at the toe of the peninsula, where Hannibal was, and Sicily; but since Crassus as chief priest could not leave Italian soil, this meant that Scipio would get the island, which was the natural staging ground for an invasion of Africa. It was it seemed a fait accompli, wired by the Cornelii and those others who believed in truly taking the offensive and giving it to Rome's rising star.

The plan would not go down smoothly. The opposition in the senate would object with a churlishness that reminds us that politics in Rome were always personal and that ambition in the service of the state was still, and very nakedly so, ambition—a corrosive force that would one day tear apart the republic. This sulfuric climate is captured by Livy in two speeches purportedly given by the principals, which, unlike pre-battle harangues, may well reflect what was actually said.

The first speech was given, appropriately enough, by the great Delayer, Fabius Maximus. He opened by arguing that the African strategy was not settled and that Scipio insulted the senate by maintaining it was. Dissembling that he was too old to be jealous, he asked the young general's pardon "if I do not rate even your glory above the welfare of Rome." "Hannibal is formidable still," Fabius said, and it was Scipio's duty to confront him in Italy, since the state could not afford two separate armies, one for Africa and one on home soil. Fabius remembered Regulus's ill-fated African expedition during the First Punic War, and also raised the specter of Mago's sailing to Italy and attempting to join his brother. "My opinion is that Publius Cornelius was elected consul for the republic and for us, not for himself and his personal ends, and that the armies were enlisted for the defense of the city and Italy, not that consuls in the arrogant manner of tyrants may transport them to whatever lands they choose." This concluding statement encapsulated all that the old guard found dangerous about this charismatic new-comer.[92] For, as French historian Serge Lancel notes, in a dim way Fabius sensed the rise of a new class of rulers inclined to appeal to the people, and also to the army, since it is likely the senate had heard of the "imperatorial"—if not "imperial salutation"—the general had been given by his troops in Spain.[93]

Fabius's suspicions would not be assuaged by Scipio, who chose to argue his case on its merits alone. Rather than Regulus, he urged the senators to remember that Agathocles of Syracuse, besieged at home by Carthaginians, had successfully diverted the hostilities by invading Africa. But why bother with old stories, he added, when there was no better illustration of taking the offensive than Hannibal himself? Yet the Barcid had far less hope of Rome's allies joining his cause than Rome did of splitting off Carthage's oppressed dependencies. The enemy had no citizen soldiers, Scipio reminded the senate, but relied on mercenaries "as fickle as the wind." As far as the central issue, Scipio assured the senate he was not ducking it: "Yes, Fabius, I shall have the antagonist you give me, Hannibal himself. . . . I shall draw him after me. I shall force him to fight on his native ground, and the prize of victory will be Carthage, not a handful of dilapidated Bruttian forts. . . . It is Africa's turn to be devastated by fire and sword."[94]

Stirring words, vengeful words, but Livy tells us the senatorial reaction was only lukewarm, since rumor had it that if Scipio failed to get his colleagues' approval for the invasion, he intended to bring the plan before the people. Technically legal, this was absolutely without precedent—the Roman political equivalent of dirty pool—exactly the sort of tactic that would eventually tear the republic apart.[95] Another old guardsman, Quintus Fulvius Flaccus, four times consul and one of the principal conquerors of Capua, took up the interrogation, asking Scipio point-blank if he was ready to accept the senate's decision in the matter, only to receive the ambiguous reply that "he would do what was in the interest of the state."

This was plainly unacceptable. But after a day of cooling off and maneuvering, a compromise was reached. Scipio agreed to accept the senate's decision, but probably with the assurance that he had the votes to give him Sicily as his province and permission to cross to Africa if he thought it was "to the advantage of the state."[96]

Yet there was a very significant proviso. As far as the senate was concerned, an invasion was one thing, an army to conduct it was another. Apparently acting on Fabius's claim that Rome could not afford separate forces for home and Africa, Scipio was denied permission to levy troops in Italy. He could only call for volunteers and aid in the form of ships and supplies from the allies. Some historians think this tradition is either false or exaggerated, but both Livy and Appian affirm it.[97] Since his Spanish army had mutinied, it is logical to assume that Scipio viewed those troops as a spent entity, and troops who had returned to Italy after long service were not likely to be subject to further conscription. He did manage to gather seven thousand volunteers, though this was clearly not enough. Still, he must have known that there were potentially useful legionaries still in Sicily, soldiers who, despite all manner of neglect and abuse, had remained loyal. For he had served with them at Cannae.

IX

RESURRECTING THE GHOSTS

[1]

Scipio was in no hurry. In all probability he did not even arrive in Sicily until the late spring of 205, and would not push off to Africa for another year.

There certainly would have been pressure to make his move sooner. Up north, Mago Barca had already crossed over to Liguria with an army and would soon stir up sufficient trouble that the authorities in Carthage would send him reinforcements and Rome would bolster their blocking force in Etruria with more troops and the reliable M. Livius Salinator. However, this probably didn't satisfy nervous souls along the Tiber.[1] Meanwhile, in North Africa, Masinissa, in the midst of fighting and losing a civil war with Syphax over his father's kingdom, grumbled about the delay in the Roman invasion. Yet Scipio's only concession was to send his trusted wingman, Laelius, off on a raid of the African coast, which provided nothing more tangible than a spate of panic in Carthage, some booty, and contact with Masinissa, who met him with a few horsemen and many complaints.

Scipio's consulship lasted only a year, as did technically his African imperium. Still, Scipio seems to have understood that his support was sufficient to extend his imperium indefinitely (though not without controversy, as we shall see). The New Carthage raid in Spain had removed all doubt that he could move quickly if the situation demanded it. However, he did not move swiftly against Africa. It seems he had his own internal clock, in this case paced by the need to lay his plans carefully, to ensure logistical support for what promised to be a vast operation, and above all to build a winning army out of what amounted to scraps.

Livy (29.1.1–11) opens his description of Scipio's sojourn in Sicily with an anecdote that may or may not be apocryphal but certainly exemplifies Scipio's ingenuity in putting together a fighting force.[2] Upon arriving with his volunteers, who apparently were just in the process of being divided into centuries, he withheld three hundred of the most strapping young men, who were neither armed nor assigned to units, and were probably pretty puzzled. He then conscripted an equivalent number of Sicilian horsemen, all of them from the local nobility and none too willing to serve on what was likely to be a long and dangerous expedition. When a nobleman, appropriately coaxed, expressed his reservations, Scipio posed an alternative: house, feed, train, mount, and arm one of the unassigned youths; a proposition all of the remaining Sicilians jumped at, thereby creating an enthusiastic nucleus for his cavalry out of a recalcitrant pack, what amounted to something out of nothing. True or untrue, Scipio was about to attempt something comparable on a much larger scale.

Upon inspecting the troops stationed in Sicily he had inherited, Livy tells us, Scipio selected the men with the longest service records, particularly those who had served under Marcellus and who were skilled in siege and assault operations.[3] Plainly, Livy was referring to the *legiones Cannenses*—now called the 5th and 6th legions, made up of the survivors of Cannae and the two battles of Herdonea. Scipio did not have any reservations about their record, for he understood, Livy adds, that "the defeat at Cannae had not been due to their cowardice, and that there were no other equally experienced soldiers in the Roman army."[4]

Yet at this point the military disaster was eleven years in the past, and many would have reached the age of marginal military utility; hence Scipio inspected the men individually, replacing those he thought unfit with the volunteers he had brought from Italy. This process generated two exceptionally large legions, which Livy sizes at sixty-two hundred foot soldiers and three hundred horse apiece— a figure that is open to debate by modern historians but that probably reflected the general's innovative approach and the danger he faced.[5] It also left him with units that would have been to some degree heterogeneous, and certainly unacquainted with his tactical innovations. In all probability, then, he began training them early, and this process consumed much of the time it took to get ready for the invasion.[6]

Livy also adds that upon selecting the veterans "he then billeted his troops in various towns," which was significant, since earlier the

Cannenses—when they'd been joined by the survivors of the First Battle of Herdonea—had been burdened by the senate with the additional indignity of not being allowed to winter in any settled area.[7] In countermanding this prohibition, Scipio not only thumbed his nose at the establishment along the Tiber, but demonstrated yet again his keen understanding of how to build loyalty. Livy describes the *Cannenses* ready to depart for Africa as "sure under Scipio and no other general, they would be able . . . to put an end to their ignominious condition."[8] For these men understood what they would be up against with Hannibal—had already been served a bitter draft of his trickery—and therefore must have seen Scipio and his new model for fighting as their vehicle to revenge and rehabilitation.[9] Unexpectedly, though, they would have the opportunity of returning the favor, of saving their commander from disgrace, long before they had the chance to confront their Carthaginian tormentor.

It all began with a target of opportunity. Late in 205 a group of prisoners in Scipio's camp, a group from Locri—deep in Bruttium on Italy's toe and one of the last cities loyal to Hannibal—offered to betray its citadel to the Romans. Scipio jumped at the opportunity, sending a force of three thousand from nearby Rhegium under two military tribunes, with one Quintus Pleminius acting as legate and overall commander. After some complications, Locri was taken, with the physical abuse and looting proceeding in a particularly brutal fashion, including even the plunder of the famous shrine of Persephone. But that was just the beginning. The Roman garrison formed two rival gangs, one loyal to the tribunes and the other to Pleminius, and began openly fighting over booty. As a result, Pleminius had the tribunes flogged—highly unusual for men of their rank—and was in turn beaten nearly to death by the other side.[10]

When Scipio got wind of the situation, he hopped a galley to the mainland and sought to slap a tourniquet on what at this point was merely a distraction, acquitting Pleminius and having the tribunes arrested. He'd made a bad choice. After the general returned to Sicily, Pleminius had both tribunes tortured and then executed, and did the same thing to the Locrian nobles who had complained to Scipio in the first place.[11]

Word of these outrages reached the senate in early 204, and Scipio's enemies, led by Fabius Maximus, leapt at the chance to exploit the situation. Compounding matters, the senate had been primed by a string of scandalous rumors pertaining to Scipio's conduct, the source being the quaestor in Sicily, Marcus Porcius Cato, destined to become Scipio's lifelong enemy. Cato is known to history as a stern embodiment of austere Roman virtues and as an inveterate hater of things Greek, and of Carthage and Carthaginians. According to Cato, Scipio had been cavorting in Syracuse like a Hellenistic dandy—dressed in effete cloaks and sandals, spending way too much time in the gym, and lavishing money on his soldiers, who were using it to wallow in corrupting activities.[12]

In his denunciation of Scipio, Fabius fastened onto this last aspect. Reminding his colleagues of the mutiny in Spain, which he maintained had cost Rome more troops than had been killed in battle, Fabius argued that Scipio "was born for the corruption of military discipline" and therefore should be relieved of his command forthwith. Pleminius and the situation in Locri were bad enough, but claiming the discipline of the entire expeditionary force had been undermined by indulgence, when that force was largely made up of suspect *Cannenses,* would not be overlooked.[13] Scipio's ally Metellus did what he could in the way of damage limitation, but in the end the senate took a very senatorial tack, sending a commission of ten to Sicily to judge Scipio's culpability and, more to the point, to examine the readiness of his forces. Ready or not, now was the time for the ghosts to step into the limelight.

They did not disappoint. After settling matters in Locri, the commissioners crossed over to Syracuse, where Scipio had assembled his entire army and fleet in a state of readiness sufficient to conduct an immediate amphibious operation. The commission was then treated to a rigorous series of maneuvers, not simply parades but actual tactical evolutions and even a mock sea battle in the harbor. After a further inspection of war materiel, the commissioners were convinced that if Scipio and his army could not defeat Carthage, then nobody could. They left in a mood more reflective of victory than simply of good preparations—a view they impressed upon the senate, which promptly authorized the invasion at the earliest opportunity using whatever troops in Sicily the general desired.[14] The *Cannenses* had vindicated their commander and were at least partway down the road to redemption.

Probably sometime in the late spring of 204[15] the invasion force assembled at Lilybaeum on the western tip of Sicily approximately 140 miles across open water from Carthage. Livy's (29.25.1–2) estimates of the force's size range widely from around twelve thousand men up to thirty-five thousand, so it's impossible to say with any precision how big the army really was. But two legions of six thousand, plus two *alae* of equal size, along with cavalry numbering around 2400—basically a pumped-up consular army totaling approximately 26,400—is a ballpark figure. With considerable ceremony—suitable sacrifices, speechifying, and throngs of spectators lining the harbor—the army, along with forty-five days' worth of food and water, were stuffed into four hundred transports guarded by only forty war galleys. (Scipio may have been short of oarsmen. Besides, the Carthaginian navy had not proved much of a threat.) Then the fleet headed out to sea in the general direction of Africa.

Without navigational equipment, such a voyage was always something of a leap of faith, but after a foggy night, land was sighted early the next day. Scipio's pilot declared the spot to be the Promontory of Mercury (modern Cape Bon). But rather than head for what Livy says was his original destination—the Emporia, a rich area far to the south[16]—Scipio allowed the wind to take him forty miles west to the "Cape of the Beautiful One" (modern Cape Farina), where he landed. This put him in the vicinity of the city of Utica and about twenty-five miles north of Carthage, which lay at the base of the semicircular Gulf of Tunis bounded by the two capes. It was a good location, close enough to throw a scare into the Carthaginians but far enough off to allow the Romans some breathing room to get unpacked. It worked.

The sight of the Romans, who set up camp on some nearby hills, panicked the entire countryside, sending a stream of inhabitants and their livestock back toward the safety of fortified places, particularly Carthage. Livy tells us that a thrill of dread spread through the city, which spent a night without sleep and prepared for an immediate siege.[17] The next morning a force of five hundred cavalry under Hanno, a young nobleman, was sent up the coast to reconnoiter and if possible disrupt the Romans before they could fully establish themselves.

They arrived too late. Scipio had already posted cavalry pickets, who easily repelled the Carthaginians, killing a good many in the ensuing pursuit, including Hanno himself. Meanwhile, Roman marauders were already abroad gathering up who and what had not managed to flee.

This was a substantial haul, including eight thousand captives, which the savvy Scipio promptly shipped back to Sicily as the first fruits of war paying for war.

More good news for the Romans appeared shortly in the form of Masinissa, who arrived, Livy says, with either two thousand or two hundred horsemen. It was probably the latter, since the Numidian prince was basically on the lam from Syphax, but Scipio understood that when it came to Masinissa, numbers meant nothing; he was a veritable "army of one."

Back in Carthage, plans to resist were plainly in disarray. Hasdrubal Gisgo, the city's most experienced available soldier, had been sent elsewhere. He'd belatedly been charged with putting together an army, and was camped about twenty-five miles inland with his hastily formed force, waiting to be joined by Syphax's Numidians before attempting to engage the Romans.[18] In his absence, the Carthaginians almost reflexively threw together another cavalry force under yet another Hanno—this force composed of a core of Punic nobility and apparently just about any local tribesman who could ride a horse and was available for hire—for a total of around four thousand men.[19]

It was summer, and when Scipio heard the cavalry were quartered in a town rather than camped out in the countryside, he marked them as a bunch of potential victims and planned accordingly. Masinissa would act as the bait, riding up to the gates of the place—Livy calls it Salaeca, about fifteen miles from the Roman position—to draw the Punic riders out with his small detachment. Masinissa would then gradually lure them into a chase, which would end with the main body of Scipio's cavalry advancing under the cover of hills to cut them off. As it turned out, the enemy was so sluggish that Masinissa had to ride up to the place repeatedly before they would even come out, and he spent additional time in mock resistance and retreat before they took up the pursuit toward the line of hills where the Romans were hiding. But in the end the Punic riders went for it and were surrounded by the Romans and Masinissa's men for their troubles, losing Hanno plus nearly a thousand men in the initial engagement, and another two thousand in the ensuing thirty-mile chase, two hundred of the Punic nobles being among the victims.[20] Another bad day for Carthage.

It would be hard to maintain that the city reacted promptly or well to the crisis. They must have known it was coming; many Carthaginians remained in Sicily, and Lilybaeum was reputedly swarming with spies.[21] Nevertheless, there seems to have been no attempt by the Carthaginian navy to intercept the Roman armada or contest its landing, nor, Livy tells us, had an army of any strength been prepared in advance.[22]

This is hard to explain, and the explaining is not made easier by history having been written by friends of Rome. Carthage's fortifications were formidable—Scipio would not even attempt a siege—so it is possible to argue this as a source of negligence and overconfidence. But the invasions of Agathocles and Regulus had already shown just how vulnerable the surrounding areas were, and how much of a danger this vulnerability was to the entire city. Nor does Carthage's presumed overconfidence explain the obvious terror of the city's population once Scipio arrived. Arguably the Carthaginians were never very good at war, only persistent, and this could help account for their lack of planning.

A lack of support for this particular war would have been more telling. The political environment within Carthage during the Second Punic War is impossible to reconstruct, but we know from the statements of Hanno the Great that there was opposition to the conflict. Also, a Punic peace delegation would later lay the blame for the war at the feet of Hannibal and his faction. Whether true, partially true, or not true at all, the Romans were not about to accept such excuses from Carthage. Like the proverbial accomplice to the crime, perpetrators or not, the Carthaginians were now caught in the clutches of blame and would suffer the penalty for their weakness.

[2]

But they were far from finished. Winter found Scipio cut off from his supply base in Sicily and camped around his beached fleet on a barren promontory (*castra Cornelia*) about two miles east of Utica, which he had earlier tried and failed to take. Parked in front of him about seven miles away in two separate encampments were the armies of Syphax and Hasdrubal Gisgo, which both Polybius (who is back in another fragment) and Livy maintain totaled eighty thousand infantry and thirteen thousand cavalry—numbers most modern sources reject as too large to feed in the winter, but still probably exceeding those of the Romans.[23]

Other commanders might have been depressed; Scipio took to scheming. First, Scipio plotted to win over Syphax, whom he hoped might be weaned from the Carthaginians once he had tired of Sophonisba, Hasdrubal Gisgo's daughter, to whom he was now wed.[24] But the spell she had cast over the Massaesylian king proved stronger than merely the pleasures of the flesh; so the Roman commander began playing a deeper and, as it turned out, more infernal game.

He deceitfully accepted Syphax's good offices in negotiating a peace treaty. Then he sent centurions disguised as servants in his delegations to the enemy camps, and the centurions accordingly scouted the camps' configuration. The Numidians, Scipio's spies reported back, were housed in huts made of nothing more than reeds, while the Carthaginians' were not much better, being put together with branches and available pieces of wood. Like the first two of the Three Little Pigs, they were fatally vulnerable. The talks intensified, framed around the basic principle of mutual withdrawals—the Carthaginians from Italy and the Romans from Africa—and Scipio's agents continued piling up details on the camps, especially the entrances.[25] Scipio even made it look as though any military plans he had were related to renewing the siege of Utica. For their part, the Numidians and Carthaginians increasingly let their guard down around their camps as the negotiations seemed to mature.[26] Finally, and tellingly in terms of Punic motivation, Syphax was able to send a message that the Carthaginians had accepted terms. Scipio played for time and set about preparing for his real intention—a night attack on the two camps.

It was a barn burner of an operation. Scipio divided his force in halves, and marched them over a carefully surveyed route, timing it so they reached their targets around midnight. The first group, under Laelius and Masinissa, hit the Numidian encampment first, breaking in and torching the reed huts so that within minutes the whole place was engulfed in flames. Many of the men were incinerated in their beds, others were trampled at the gates, and those who managed to get out were cut down by waiting Romans. For the horribly burned, death must have been a form of mercy.[27]

When the Carthaginians saw the conflagration in the other camp, a number concluded it was an accident and rushed out unarmed to help the Numidians—only to fall prey to the other half of Scipio's legionaries, already lurking in the shadows. The Romans then forced their way into the Carthaginian camp and set fire to the place, which burned just as furiously and with the same deadly consequences. Both Hasdrubal and Syphax managed to escape, the former with around four hundred horse and two thousand foot soldiers, but we can be sure that fire and sword took a terrible toll on those who remained. Livy puts the dead at forty thousand, but this is based on his exaggerated estimation of the size of the force.[28] Polybius provides no numbers, but does say of the attack that "it exceed[ed] in horror all previous events." But then, putting aside the morality of broiling thousands of human beings in their sleep, Polybius adds, "of all the brilliant exploits performed by Scipio this seems to me the most splendid and most adventurous."[29] It certainly was a trick worthy of the master; if nothing else, it demonstrated that he was ready for Hannibal.

Back in Carthage, news of the disaster was greeted with dismay and dejection. Many citizens, including a number of notables, had been killed, and there was a general fear that Scipio would immediately lay siege to the city. When the suffetes called the council of elders into session, three positions emerged. There were those who wanted to treat for peace with Scipio immediately (probably a nonstarter, given the results of recent negotiations). The second position was held by those who were for recalling Hannibal to "save his country." (This could be interpreted as an intermediate position, since it would not only help Carthage defend itself, but might also mollify Rome by removing him and presumably Mago from Italy.) And then there were those who wanted to rebuild the army and continue the war. (Livy tells us that Hasdrubal Gisgo, who was back in the city, plus the whole of the Barcid faction, combined to push this proposition, which "showed a Roman steadfastness."[30] Hasdrubal retained overall command and took to recruiting Carthaginians, whose enthusiasm probably increased when Scipio failed to show up but instead seemed intent on taking Utica. Meanwhile, envoys were sent to Syphax, who was inland at a place called Abba, to encourage him to stay the course.

But another Carthaginian already had the Massaesylian king well in hand, stiffening, this time, his resolve. Sophonisba had delivered such a passionate plea not to desert her father and the city of her birth that Syphax was now fully in tune with the Punic program and was busy arming every Numidian peasant he could round up.[31] Almost simultaneously further good tidings arrived in the form of four thousand newly enlisted Celtiberian mercenaries, whose presence was something of a trenchant commentary on Scipio's lack of thoroughness in

subduing Spain.[32] Syphax soon marched with these forces to join Hasdrubal's, so that within thirty days (late April to early May 203) there
gathered an army of around thirty thousand at a place known as "Great
Plains"—likely the modern Souk el Kremis.[33]

When Scipio heard of this concentration—good intelligence was
another advantage of having Masinissa on your side—he reacted immediately. Leaving his fleet and part of his army to maintain the impression that the siege of Utica continued as his primary objective, he
headed inland with the remainder of his force—all the cavalry and
perhaps most of his infantry, though he may have brought along only
the *legiones Cannenses,* since allied contingents are not specifically mentioned.[34] Traveling light, they arrived at the Great Plains after a march
of five days.

Scipio's objective was clear, to nip this new threat in the bud—to engage posthaste what was obviously an inexperienced and disjointed
force, and obliterate it. This should have been equally apparent to his
adversaries. The Romans were deep inland, far from their base of supply, without visible means of support. The Punic strategy should have
been avoidance, harassment, and then, when Scipio was forced to withdraw, attrition.[35] Instead, within four days they allowed themselves to
be drawn into a set-piece battle. The outcome was never in doubt.

Hasdrubal Gisgo placed his best troops, the Celtiberians, in the center, with the Carthaginian infantry (those salvaged from the camp fire,
plus new recruits) flanked by the Punic cavalry on the right, and
Syphax's Numidians—infantry, then cavalry—positioned on the left.
The Romans lined up their own legionaries in the center—possibly but
not necessarily covered on each side by an *ala*—with the Italian cavalry
occupying the right wing and Masinissa's Numidian horse on the extreme left.

According to both Polybius and Livy the battle was over almost as
soon as it began, the first charge of each of Scipio's cavalry wings scattering the Carthaginians and Syphax's troops, horse and foot soldiers
alike.[36] It has been argued that Scipio's cavalry, which would have numbered fewer than four thousand, was simply not numerous enough to
break up such a large body of men (around twenty-six thousand) and
that there must have been an intervening infantry engagement.[37] Nevertheless, Livy is pretty clear that both the Carthaginian and Numidian components of the Punic force were largely untrained and that it
was Scipio's cavalry specifically that drove them from the field,[38] so this

intermediate stage may not have been necessary. At any rate, nobody disputes the result—the Celtiberians were left very much alone.

Even if it was only the *legiones Cannenses* facing them, the Celtiberi-ans would have been decisively outnumbered. However, they had no choice but to fight. Africa was alien territory if they ran, and they could expect no mercy from Scipio if they surrendered, since he undoubt-edly remembered it was Celtiberian desertions that had led to the death of his father and uncle, not to mention their joining the Punic cause after he had supposedly pacified Spain.

The Celtiberians would have been roughly equal in number to the two legions' worth of *hastati* facing them.[39] But rather than feeding the remaining elements of the *triplex acies* directly ahead, Scipio resorted to his now-characteristic maneuver, turning the *principes* and *triarii* into columns and marching them right and left out from behind the front line to attack the Celtiberians on the flanks. Pinned by the forces ahead, and beset on each side, the Spaniards met death obstinately. In the end, Livy tells us, the butchery lasted longer than the fighting.[40] The ghosts of Cannae, on the other hand, were very much alive, and, having ex-acted a measure of revenge for their commander, they were plainly ready for more.

Yet, the sacrifice of the Celtiberians, by keeping the Romans preoc-cupied until nightfall, had allowed the escape of Hasdrubal Gisgo, who eventually made it back to Carthage with some survivors and Syphax, who headed inland with his cavalry. Determined to retain the initiative, Scipio called a war council the next day and explained his plan. He would keep the main body of the army and work his way back from the Great Plains toward the coast, plundering and sowing rebellion among Carthage's subject communities as he went, while he sent Laelius and Masinissa with the cavalry and *velites* after Syphax.

Both Polybius (14.9.6–11) and Livy (20.9.3–9) provide similar but in-ternally contradictory descriptions of Carthage's reaction to the defeat. On the one hand, they say the news was greeted with utter panic and loss of confidence; but then go on to describe the citizenry's deter-mined preparation for a siege, plans for manning and equipping the fleet for a naval offensive against Scipio's armada gathered around Utica, and the recall of Hannibal as the only general capable of de-fending the city. As always, we can catch only glimpses of the true na-ture of Punic politics. One possible explanation for Carthage's apparently contradictory reactions is that the intermediate position of the three courses cited above was now dominant. Livy states clearly that "peace was seldom mentioned," and it is also probable that the Barcid faction (not to mention the general himself) did not want Hannibal (and presumably Mago) brought back, since it was tantamount to admitting that their great scheme had failed. In the interim, the Punic mainstream seems to have fallen back on the city's traditional naval shield of war galleys as a way out of their troubles.

It was certainly an audacious scheme, with the fleet and the delegation to Hannibal being launched simultaneously the day after the resolution passed. Scipio, now less than thirteen miles away, having just taken over the abandoned town of Tunis, observed the launch with horror. For he understood that the descent of the Carthaginian flotilla would come as an utter surprise to the Romans at Utica. He also understood that his warships, burdened with all manner of siege equipment, were in no condition to maneuver in a naval engagement.[41] The offensive would have worked had not the Punic battle squadron, which likely was manned mostly by inexperienced oarsmen, dawdled, taking most of the day to arrive and then anchoring for the night before forming up to attack at dawn.[42]

This gave Scipio at least some time to prepare, and as usual he responded ingeniously to what could have been a very bad situation. Rather than have his warships protect his transports, he did the reverse. Polybius tells us just before his narrative breaks off that Scipio abandoned any idea of advancing into battle, drew the ships together near shore, and girded the whole mass with three or four layers of merchant vessels, lashed together with their masts and yards to form a wooden coat of armor.[43]

The next morning the Punic force waited in vain for the Romans to come out, only belatedly moving in to attack Scipio's transport-encrusted force. What followed bore no resemblance to a sea fight, Livy says, but instead "looked like ships attacking walls," since the transports' much greater freeboard enabled the thousand or so picked fighters Scipio had stationed on board to cast their ample supply of javelins directly down at the low-slung Punic galleys, effectively stymieing the attack.[44] It was only when the Carthaginians began using grappling hooks that they achieved a measure of success. They managed to haul away sixty transports, which were greeted back home with more joy than the episode deserved—a small ray of sun shining through an unmitigated series of setbacks. Meanwhile, Scipio's fleet was saved, and he would soon receive news from the hinterlands that would send Carthage reeling to the brink of surrender.

After a fifteen-day march Laelius and Masinissa were in the heart of Numidia, reaching first the eastern kingdom of Massylia, where the natives joyfully accepted the young prince as their ruler. But there was still the matter of Syphax, who had withdrawn to the home territory of Massaesylia and was again busy reconstituting his army. Yet again he managed to cobble together a force basically as large as its predecessors, but with each iteration the quality had dropped, now to the point where the army consisted of little more than the rawest of recruits.[45] Nonetheless, he brought them forward to confront the advancing Romans in what turned out to be a ragged cavalry engagement, which was eventually decided when the *velites* stabilized their line to the point where Syphax's men refused to advance and instead began to flee. Either to shame them or out of desperation, the king charged the Romans, whereupon his horse was wounded and he was captured—and was now very much a sinner in the hands of an angry Masinissa.

But also a shrewd one. Masinissa told Laelius that if he would let him ride ahead with Syphax to Cirta, the eastern capital of the Massaesylians, the psychological impact might cause a complete collapse. It did. Upon arriving, Masinissa arranged a conclave with the city fathers, who remained adamant until he dragged Syphax before them in chains, at which point they opened the gates.

Once inside, Masinissa headed for the palace. Here Livy turns cinematic, staging one of the more romantic, though not necessarily implausible,[46] confrontations in all of historical literature. For at the threshold, "in the full flower of her youthful beauty" and with the mind of a true temptress, was Sophonisba. She clasped Masinissa's knees, congratulated him on having better luck than Syphax, and told him she had really only one request: "choose my fate as your heart may prompt you, but whatever you do, even if it means my death, don't surrender me to the arrogant and brutal whim of any Roman. . . . What a woman of Carthage—what the daughter of Hasdrubal—has to fear from a Roman is all too clear." As she spoke, Livy adds perhaps unnecessarily, "her words were now more nearly those of a charmer than of a suppliant."[47]

Masinissa was a goner—probably after the first sentence—and upon further reflection, doubtless from within a cloud of lust, a solution came to mind—marriage . . . marriage so fast that it would become a fait accompli.[48] ("That's no Punic subverter of Rome's allies; that's my wife!")

Predictably, the Romans didn't buy it. When Laelius arrived at the palace, he was ready to drag her out of her marriage bed and send her back immediately to Scipio with Syphax and the other prisoners. Masinissa prevailed upon him to leave her in Cirta while the two of them conducted mopping-up operations. This would give Scipio more time to decide what to do with this veritable man magnet.

Sophonisba's future was probably a foregone conclusion, but Syphax may have sealed her fate. When Syphax was delivered back to *castra Cornelia,* Scipio asked his former guest-friend what had possessed him to refuse that amity and instead wage war. It's not surprising that Syphax fell back on the femme fatale defense. Sophonisba was the venom in his blood, the avenging Fury, who with her plying words and caresses had addled his mind. He then turned the knife by adding that his sole consolation was that this monster of treachery was now his worst enemy's wife.[49]

When Laelius and Masinissa returned from the hinterlands, Scipio took the latter aside and, recalling his own forbearance in the face of the beauteous captive back in New Carthage, made it clear that political expediency demanded that the young man give up his new wife, either as a prisoner or . . . He left the alternative unsaid. Masinissa extemporized and had a slave bring Sophonisba a cup of poison as his means of delivering her from the Romans. She drank without flinching, remarking that if this was the best he could do in the way of a wedding present, she would accept it, but she also instructed the slave to tell her wannabe widower that she would have died a better death had she not married him in the first place.[50]

So perished Sophonisba, still another in a long line of aristocratic Punic suicides. Yet she likely had done more in bed to keep her city safe than Hannibal had accomplished on the battlefield. Nor is this meant as a backhanded compliment. Because of her, Syphax had given Scipio far more trouble than he'd bargained for, and a marriage alliance with Masinissa had held out the promise of neutralizing an adversary who would later prove highly instrumental in the city's ultimate destruction. The match had probably been doomed from the beginning, and she paid for it with her life. But it is hard to deny she died a hero's death.

Back in Carthage, this sort of resolve was fast becoming a diminishing quantity. The narratives of both Polybius and Livy make it pretty clear that Carthaginian resistance had become increasingly dependent on Numidian support, and news of Syphax's capture had tilted the political balance, at least in the council of elders, in the direction of the anti-Barcid proprietors of the vast inland food factory, who were sick of seeing their properties ravaged by Romans and now wanted peace.[51]

Sometime in late 203 the inner council of thirty key elders was dispatched to Scipio's camp to negotiate an end to the war. As Livy tells it, the elders' inclination was immediately betrayed by their prostrating themselves.[52] Essentially, they begged Rome for mercy, blaming Hannibal and the Barcid party as the instigators of the war. This was plainly self-serving, but it was also likely to have been true.

As it happened, Scipio was ready to deal. He could see the strength of Carthage's fortifications, and understood that an unacceptably protracted and costly siege was the only option if he wanted to continue fighting.[53] He was also well aware of Rome's war-weariness and desire to end this terrible conflict. Finally, he must have been aware that there were those back home who wanted his command, so victory on his watch must have had its attractions.

The terms he offered were not unreasonable but were certainly calculated to remove Carthage permanently as a military competitor with Rome. According to Livy, Scipio proposed that the Punic side hand over all war prisoners, deserters, and runaway slaves; withdraw the armies of both Hannibal and Mago; cease interfering in Spain; evacuate all the islands between Italy and Africa; supply large quantities of grain to feed his army and animals; and surrender all but twenty of their warships.[54] As far as a war indemnity, the historian tells us that his sources differed, some saying five thousand talents, others five thousand pounds of silver, and still others double pay for Scipio's troops.[55] Appian also adds several clauses that, if true, make the terms considerably harsher (e.g., forbidding Carthaginians from hiring mercenaries, restricting their territory to the so-called "Phoenician trenches"—an area inland roughly between the east coast of modern Tunisia and its border with Algeria—and giving Masinissa dominion over his home kingdom and all he could take of Syphax's).[56] Finally, Scipio gave the Carthaginians three days to accept, whereupon a truce would take hold while they sent envoys to Rome for final negotiations. The council of elders agreed, and envoys were dispatched, but Livy maintains it was all a ruse to give Hannibal time to return to Africa.[57] This is debatable.

[3]

In Italy the war actually seemed to be winding down. Laelius's arrival in Rome with Syphax and a number of other important prisoners was greeted with joy, and the senate promptly ratified Scipio's crowning of Masinissa as king in Numidia.

Shortly after, the delegation from Carthage arrived and was greeted outside the walls by the senate sitting in the temple of Bellona. We have only Livy's version (30.22 ff) of what transpired here, and according to him the Carthaginians did little to make their case, trying to shift the blame for the war on Hannibal, just as they had before. Hannibal, they maintained, had crossed the Ebro and the Alps on his own initiative and had made war on Saguntum and then Rome without sanction from Carthage. Further, since their government had never broken the treaty that had ended the First Punic War, they asked that it be reinstated! This was cheeky, to say the least—just another example of characteristic Carthaginian trickery, if you believe Livy, who concludes that the Punic suit for peace was rejected.

But Livy's recounting is far from credible, and seems designed to remove any suspicion that later, when the hostilities resumed, Rome would be violating a legal treaty. Whereas Appian (*The Punic Wars*, 31–2) maintains that the authorities on the Tiber left it entirely to Scipio to negotiate peace, Polybius (15.1.3) very clearly states that the senate and the people ratified the treaty. Moreover, Dio Cassius (frag. 17.74) provides further insight by adding that the senate would not treat with the Carthaginians until Hannibal and Mago evacuated Italy, but once this had been done, the senate agreed to peace according to the terms Scipio had arranged. Pretty clearly there was a treaty; it was drawn along the lines originally negotiated in Africa, and it was broken by events that transpired after the Punic armies were ordered to withdraw from Italy. Which brings us back to the Barcid boys.

Up north, for most of the nearly two years after he landed near Genoa in 205, Mago did little beyond recruiting Gauls and Ligurians. Finally, in the summer of 203 he felt strong enough to make his move, and advanced toward Milan, where he accepted battle with four Roman legions, under proconsul Marcus Cornelius Cethegus.[58] While Livy's description (30.18) has been questioned, it is clear that the Punic side was losing.[59] Then Mago was badly wounded by a javelin in the thigh while trying to rally his troops, who, seeing him carried from the field, lost all resolve and bolted, turning a fighting retreat into a rout. But most seem to have made it back to camp, and Mago, despite injury, and ever the Barcid, managed to slip them away in the dead of night and reach the coast with the force largely intact.

Here he met up with the delegation from Carthage summoning him to return to Africa and telling him that his brother was being given a similar order. Neither he nor his army was in any condition to object. Rumor had it that his Ligurian allies were changing sides, and at the very least a sea voyage would be easier on his hurt leg than constant jolting along the road.[60] So, probably sometime in the autumn of 203, he packed up his force and set sail. He didn't make it past Sardinia before the wound killed him, but most of his troops seem to have reached Africa alive and in some sort of fighting condition. But there would be only one Barcid brother left to lead them.

Around the same time, the Carthaginian envoys reached Hannibal in Bruttium at Croton, a Greek town known for its beautiful women. He had settled into a kind of gentlemanly semi-retirement, at one point summering on the grounds of the famous temple of Hera, which he had been sorely tempted to plunder until the goddess had come to him in a dream and threatened to take his good eye if he tried it.[61] He greeted the summons home with anything but enthusiasm. "Gnashing his teeth and groaning," Livy reports (30.201ff), "and scarcely keeping back the tears, he listened to the words of the emissaries.... 'I am being recalled by men who, in forbidding the sending of reinforcements and money, were long ago trying to drag me back. The conqueror of Hannibal is therefore not the Roman people ... but the Carthaginian council of elders.... And over this inglorious return of mine it will not be Publius Scipio who wildly exults, so much as Hanno, who, unable to do so by any other means, has ruined our family by the downfall of Carthage.'"

There could be no clearer statement of the divergent political agendas of the Barcids and the commercial classes of the metropolis. Hannibal's statement was a virtual admission that the conflict in Italy was a familial enterprise—truly Hannibal's fight—and that he did not appreciate being drawn away to save Carthage from the fight's consequences. But he had been boxed in if not defeated by Rome's armies; he had no future in Italy. So, nearly two years after Scipio had first landed in

Africa, Hannibal began packing up his army to "defend" home turf.[62] For he had become, in the words of modern historian Dexter Hoyos, "a Punic Micawber hoping something would turn up."[63] Once, Hannibal had dominated events; now the reverse was true.

Before he left, however, he had a bronze tablet carved that recounted his exploits, and he had it placed in Hera's temple. This was the tablet Polybius had seen and used to record the size of the force Hannibal had brought to Italy. The text has been lost, but we know it was in-scribed not just in Punic but in Greek, the international language of the day, which implies that the tablet was carved less in the spirit of a general on a mission than in the spirit of a Hellenistic hegemon anx-ious to advertise his exploits.[64] Appian reports that during Hannibal's sixteen years in Italy, he destroyed four hundred towns and killed three hundred thousand of Italy's men in battle—perhaps figures derived from Hannibal's list of accomplishments.[65] If so, this list would have been very much in character, for he left little in his wake besides de-struction. Aboard ship, Livy tells us, "he repeatedly looked back upon the shores of Italy and, accusing gods and men, called down a curse upon himself . . . because he had not led his soldiers, bloodstained from the victory of Cannae, straight to Rome."[66] If Maharbal was within earshot, he would have been sorely tempted, but wise not to add, "I told you so."

[4]

The truce held during the winter months despite Hannibal's return, but then in the spring of 202 it collapsed.[67] A Roman convoy of two hundred transports escorted by thirty war galleys was struck by adverse winds as it approached the African coast. The warships managed to row to their intended landfall, but the purely sail-driven merchant vessels were scattered, with many being blown into the bay directly over-looked by Carthage. Seeing the ships abandoned by their crews and knowing they were filled with grain, the Carthaginian people started something like a food riot, and the council of elders felt compelled to send Hasdrubal Gisgo out with fifty ships to salvage the tempting prizes. The vessels were towed back to the city and their contents were added to Carthage's flagging grain supplies. To make matters worse, the three representatives Scipio sent to protest this confiscation apparently had to be rescued from a mob. (Appian says by Hanno the Great.[68]) The representatives were then dismissed without an answer by the assembly of the people and were attacked by ships from Hasdrubal's fleet near Utica, which forced their vessel to be beached. For Scipio this was the last straw; the war was on again.[69]

Why did the Punic side break the armistice? Had the peace negotiations really been just a stalling tactic to provide Hannibal time to return, as Livy maintains? If that was the case, why had the negotiations been necessary in the first place? The Carthaginians had already been secure behind their walls and could have waited. Now they were plainly hungry, so the armistice does not seem to have given them any better access to food. In fact, the original terms of the truce could be interpreted to imply that the Carthaginians had some obligation to supply Scipio's army.

Polybius (15.2.2–3) wants us to believe that it was Hannibal's arrival that had caused a political shift in the city, and there were now few who any longer wanted to adhere to the treaty, placing their trust instead in the Barcid's military skills. But if it was that simple, how are we to interpret Hannibal's choice of landing points, not nearby, placing himself as a shield between Carthage and the Romans, but at Hadrumetum (modern Sousse), nearly 150 miles down the coast to the southeast.[70] It should not be forgotten that our sources are all pro-Roman. We will never know exactly what went on inside Carthage at this critical juncture, but a case can be made that there had always been a sincere desire for peace but in a climate of hunger and desperation, events—possibly orchestrated by Hasdrubal Gisgo and his faction—simply got out of hand. In any case, Carthage made a bad mistake.

Scipio now went after the countryside with a vengeance, sacking town after town in the interior—refusing offers of surrender and then enslaving the towns' populations.[71] Hannibal did nothing. When a delegation from Carthage, overwrought by the devastation, begged him to march on the enemy immediately, he told them to mind their own business, he would decide when the time was right.[72] This hardly looks like Punic solidarity.

Nevertheless, Hannibal did move soon, marching to a place five days southwest of Carthage known as Zama. There were at least three, maybe four, Zamas in ancient Tunisia, so this Zama's exact location eludes us.[73] The impetus for Hannibal's move in this direction seems to have been all about cavalry—actually, a shortage of cavalry, and on both sides. Appian reports that before leaving Italy, Hannibal had been forced to slaughter four thousand of his horses for lack of transports.[74] To make up for the shortfall, he had contacted a relative of Syphax named Tychaeus, who now brought him two thousand horsemen and also brought Syphax's son Vermina, whom Hannibal may have hoped had been going to join him inland with still more horsemen.[75] But most critically, Hannibal wanted to keep Masinissa away from Scipio.

While Scipio was ravaging Carthaginian territory, the young prince was busy consolidating control over his own kingdom and as much of Syphax's as he could gobble. Realizing a showdown was imminent, Scipio sent Masinissa a series of messages telling the prince to join him, and Scipio began moving to shorten the distance between them, eventually ending up in the vicinity of Zama. It was this juncture that Hannibal wanted to prevent.

Anxious to know if Masinissa and his Numidians were already at Zama, the Barcid sent out spies to reconnoiter the Roman camp, three of whom were captured. Rather than put them to the sword, Scipio gave them a guided tour, knowing they would see no Numidians, but also knowing that Masinissa was set to arrive the next day with six thousand foot soldiers and four thousand horse.[76] After hearing from his spies and then witnessing Masinissa's arrival the next day, Hannibal was so struck by the cleverness of the ruse that he conceived an urge to get to know the young Roman general, and sent a herald to arrange a meeting.

That the conference actually took place few modern historians doubt. But what was said is another thing entirely, since Polybius and Livy—both of whom provide elaborate dialogues[77]—agree that the meeting was attended solely by the principals and their interpreters, which makes it highly unlikely that anything of the actual conversation was preserved.

Supposedly they made a stab at negotiating peace terms, but in reality Scipio and Hannibal each must have realized that this was but a prelude to a sanguinary showdown. And on these grounds it is safe to say each valued the meeting as a means of sizing up the other as an opponent. Scipio cannot have forgotten an adolescence spent suffering at the other interlocutor's hands—Ticinus, Trebia, and above all Cannae, when Hannibal's tricks had nearly put an end to his young life, had killed his father-in-law, Lucius Aemilius Paullus, and had brought nearly fifteen years of shame down on the men with whom he now planned to even the score.

Hannibal must have known something of Scipio's biography, perhaps enough to have wished that he had killed the Roman when he had had the chance. Now Hannibal might well have wondered if he was facing his nemesis. He was forty-six years old, at a time when men aged fast. He had lived a hard life, knowing nothing but war since youth. The wily mind of the fox remained unimpaired, but the body must have been tired, no longer the "Thunderbolt" it had once been. Hannibal had always beaten the Romans, or at least slipped from their grasp. But it could well have crossed his mind that this time the opponent and the circumstances were different. Though he was technically in his own country, he was far from support or shelter; if he lost, he was finished.

Back in their camps the respective armies must have been equivalently aware of the stakes and aware that combat, probably decisive combat, loomed. The Roman and Italian infantry contingent was relatively small—around twenty-three thousand (plus six thousand of Masinissa's Numidians), compared to Hannibal's thirty-six thousand to forty-six thousand. In cavalry, though, with the addition of the Numidians, the Roman and Italian force outnumbered its Punic equivalent perhaps about six thousand to four thousand.[78] Although there must have been substitutes and other volunteers, the heart of the Roman force, its soul, was made up of survivors of Cannae and the two battles of Herdonea—all of them prior victims of Hannibal and his veterans. They must have understood that they were about to face these enemies one last time, that in all probability they would either die here at Zama still in disgrace or find redemption at last.

They were in no sense losers; they could look back on a record of fighting well in Sicily, and now in Africa, where they had known nothing but victory. They also must have understood that their previous misfortunes had largely been due to the mistakes of their commanders and the unyielding stereotypical nature of their tactics. Now they had Publius Scipio, who not only had shown them how to exploit battlefield opportunities, but possessed the guile and ruthlessness to truly match wits with their Punic tormentor. Scipio must have been a god to them, by now the repository of all their faith. Still, as they restlessly awaited the final outcome—sharpening their weapons, polishing their armor, and searching for the forgetfulness of sleep—doubts surely remained.

For most had reached—as had so many others on this battlefield—
middle age and had long since shed the optimism of youth. Things did
not have to turn out well; fate might not after all commute their sentence to live as ghosts.

Certainly not if Hannibal had anything to say about it. But he was
plainly operating under some unaccustomed constraints. Not only was
he short on cavalry, his favorite arm for unhinging adversaries, but his
camp contained really three armies, not one. First there were around
twelve thousand Ligurians, Gauls, Balearic Islanders, and Moors, the
remnants of Mago's mercenary force that had continued on to Africa
after he'd died of his wound.[79] Next came a contingent of Libyans and
Carthaginian citizens, probably consisting of survivors of the Great
Plains and those recently recruited by the ever resilient Hasdrubal
Gisgo. (Livy claims a "legion of Macedonians" was also among them,
but most contemporary sources reject this.[80]) Finally, there were Hannibal's own veterans, a force whose makeup constituted a virtual biography of their commander—Africans, Numidians, and Spaniards who
had marched with him out of New Carthage and crossed the Alps;
Gauls who had joined up in the Po valley; and numerous Bruttians
from his later days in the south of Italy—a grizzled force of some of
the most experienced soldiers in history. Through thick and thin they
had remained steadfastly loyal, and he in turn had led them so cleverly
and carefully that they had never yet tasted significant defeat. But they
were now part of a composite force, two components of which were
strangers not only to themselves and Hannibal, but to each other. Hannibal's army was even more mismatched than the great Frankenstein of
an army the Romans had cobbled together to fight at Cannae.[81]

Since there had been no time to fuse these elements into a whole,
Hannibal would seek to fight them as three separate forces—plausible-
sounding but basically a gimmick. There was also a camp full of elephants, more than eighty of them[82]—so many that it suggests that the
bulk had been recently rounded up from the bush and were half-wild.
In retrospect, the only thing on the ancient battlefield more dangerously unpredictable than a well-trained elephant was an ill-trained
elephant. Yet Hannibal at Zama was all about making the best of the
cards dealt to him, creating the illusion of strength, and employing
tricks to cover his weaknesses. Unfortunately for him, his opponent
held a better hand and was not easily fooled.

At dawn the morning after their conference, both commanders

marched their forces out of camp intent on battle. Hannibal placed his elephants out front, apparently hoping for a devastating charge. Next he lined up what had been Mago's force, and in back of them he placed the Carthaginians and Libyans. Finally, several hundred yards to the rear, as a reserve and safeguard against what he probably knew was Scipio's proclivity for flanking attacks, he deployed his own veterans.[83] On his wings he placed his cavalry, Carthaginians on the right and Numidians to the left.

For his part, Scipio had Masinissa's riders covering his right, and the Italian horse under Laelius on the left, with his infantry deployed in the *triplex acies*—*hastati, principes,* and then *triarii*—but not in the normal checkerboard pattern. Instead the maniples were placed directly in back of one another, with corridors between the different units which would be filled with *velites*.[84] Of all the elements of Scipio's army, these light troops may have been the most improved since Cannae. Scipio's experience in Spain with irregulars and these *velites'* own exploits in taking down Syphax both indicate that these were now hardened veterans, capable of slinging missiles on equal terms with anybody that Hannibal had available at Zama, without—this was critical—panicking in the face of his elephants.

The action opened with pachyderm pandemonium. Once the harangues were over (Polybius's version [15.11.11], for what it's worth, has Hannibal reminding his veterans that they were facing some of the "wretched remnants" of the legions they had smashed at Cannae), bugles sounded from all sides, freaking the elephants and causing them to attack prematurely. Those on the left veered off and stampeded back into the Punic Numidian cavalry. Seeing his opening, Masinissa charged and quickly chased them off the battlefield. The beasts in the middle did hit the Roman infantry formations, but chose to follow the *velites,* who were enraging them with javelin fire, up the corridors, out the back, and also off the battlefield. It was much the same story with the behemoths on the right. They did swerve toward the Italian horse, but when greeted with a hail of javelins, they reversed field and crashed into the Carthaginian cavalry, prompting Laelius to charge in hot pursuit of this retreating wing.

The battle had barely begun and Hannibal was without cavalry, but then again so were the Romans, which raises an interesting possibility. It has been suggested that it was a trick, that Hannibal, knowing he was weaker in this arm, had ordered his riders to give ground and draw their equivalents off the field.[85] The plan may have been complicated by pachyderm panic, but the effect was the same. . . . It was now Hannibal's infantry against Scipio's, and crunch time for his ghosts.

The foot soldiers on both sides moved forward, with the exception of Hannibal's veterans, who stayed put. As the two sides closed, the Romans commenced banging their shields with *pila,* and let out a collective war whoop that eclipsed the discordant Babel of cries from the multiethnic Punic force.[86] Nevertheless, Mago's mercenaries fought bravely and aggressively, wounding many Romans among the *hastati.* But the legionaries were undeterred and moved relentlessly forward, driving their opponents back, Livy notes, with characteristic *scutum* punches.[87] As the Punic front tired and looked to support in back of them, the Carthaginians and Libyans initially hesitated, untrained as they were to fight as a coordinated whole. And when Mago's mercenaries eventually broke, fighting appears to have erupted between the two Punic groups, as the Carthaginians refused to let the refugees retreat through their ranks, perhaps on Hannibal's orders, or, as one later historian sarcastically suggests, unconsciously emulating war elephants by turning on their own.[88]

Once confronted by Romans, though, the Punic troops of the second line fought with what Polybius calls "frantic and extraordinary courage," throwing the *hastati* into confusion and checking their forward momentum.[89] At this point the officers of the *principes* began feeding their legionaries into the fight, which got the line moving again and ultimately broke the Carthaginians, Libyans, and the remaining mercenaries, all of whom began to flee, with the Romans in hot pursuit.

But rather than break ranks, the veterans to the rear, on Hannibal's orders, leveled their spears as the Punic fugitives approached, a sure sign they were not going to let them through. Those who were not cut down veered to either side of the Punic line, where they began to congregate and re-form.

A critical moment had arrived. The space between the two forces was now covered with dead and dying men, the ground made slippery by their blood.[90] On the Roman side the *hastati* were in complete disorder from the chase, and the maniples of *principes* were probably somewhat disheveled from their short fight. Only the *triarii* were fully ready to confront the much more numerous Carthaginian veterans, lined up in perfect battle array. It may well have crossed Scipio's mind that he had been tricked by the master into committing too many units too soon, just another Roman commander led cluelessly into the abattoir. His horns sounded the retreat, and he set about attempting one of the most difficult of military maneuvers, reconstituting his formations in the midst of a battle. The ghosts were up to the task, reversing their field, reconnecting with their centurions, re-forming their maniples, and lining up again, this time along a single front, *hastati* in the center and the *principes* and *triarii* on either flank.

For as long as it took, they were dangerously vulnerable. Yet Hannibal with his fresh veterans in perfect order simply watched as the Romans scurried about, brought their wounded to the rear, and above all rested. Opportunity beckoned, and the supreme opportunist marked time. Maybe he was worried about keeping good order while attacking across the corpse-strewn battlefield. Perhaps he was wary of one of Scipio's flanking maneuvers. Whatever the reason, he waited and let the Romans come to him. It would be his undoing.

If fate were a dramatist, there could not have been a better place for an intermission. The issue had been reduced to a fight of soldiers, not generals. The supreme rematch was at hand; after fourteen long years, the ghosts of Cannae would meet their vanquishers again in mortal combat. When they were ready, the Romans marched directly at the Carthaginians and the fight began. As far as we know there were no military sleights of hand, no feints, no hidden reserves, no centers extended or withheld. It was to be a straight-up clash between two supremely experienced hosts of murderously inclined experts with sharp instruments. Polybius (15.14.6) reports, "As they were nearly equal in numbers as well as in spirit and bravery, and were equally well armed, the contest was for long doubtful, the men falling where they stood out of determination."

But then when it seemed perhaps both forces would wear each other away into nothing, the tiebreaker arrived in the form of Laelius and Masinissa back from the chase. The combined Roman cavalry hit the Punic formation in the rear, and the slaughter was on. Most were killed in formation; those who bolted were run down by the horsemen, as the ground was flat and there was nowhere to go. Before it was over, twenty thousand Punic soldiers were killed—with most of the rest captured—at a cost of fifteen hundred Romans.[91] But numbers barely tell the story of Zama. The ghosts of Cannae had achieved a revenge probably unmatched in all of military history. Perhaps the most victorious army in human memory essentially lay dead at their feet, and

Hannibal, one of the greatest captains of all time, had hesitated and lost just about everything. He fled with just a few horsemen back to Hadrumetum. He would live almost two decades longer, occupying a place in Rome's nightmares and a place on the fringes of high politics, but in reality it was now his turn to play the ghost.

[5]

The Second Punic War was over. Its instigator knew it. A military oxymoron—Hannibal without an army—he returned to Carthage thirty-six years after he had left on the summons of the council of elders, warily, no doubt, given that so many failed Punic commanders had ended up on the cross. But his reception was polite, and he stated frankly that there was no hope unless Carthage sued for peace.

Later, when an elder named Gisgo (the same Gisgo who had marveled at the size of the Roman army at Cannae?) objected to Scipio's preliminary demands, Hannibal knocked him off the rostrum and argued passionately that it was inconceivable that any citizen of Carthage did "not bless his stars that, now that he was at the mercy of the Romans, he has obtained such lenient terms."[92] Or so the terms seemed.

The final peace treaty was deceptively mild, largely along the lines of Scipio's original armistice agreement. Carthage would continue to be self-governed following its own laws and customs, and would retain all prewar possessions in Africa. It would surrender its entire navy save ten triremes, and all its elephants, promising to train no more (arguably a benefit for Carthage). The war indemnity was raised to ten thousand talents, to be paid in annual installments over fifty years. This was a huge amount in the ancient world, equating to 572,000 pounds of silver worth more than $120,000,000 at today's prices.[93]

More onerous—sinister even—was the Carthaginians' designation as "friends and allies" of Rome, the same terminology used to subordinate dependencies in Italy, a designation that prohibited Carthage from going to war with anyone unless it had the Roman senate's permission. Appian even maintains they were specifically forbidden to wage war against Masinissa, an inveterate enemy.[94] This proved to be a demon protocol, a pretext for future intervention by Rome, and ultimately the city's doom.[95] But the Carthaginians would try to make the best of it, and for a while it seemed that the new relationship was actually to their advantage.

But beneath a cloak of legalism, Rome, and in particular conservative elements in the senate, remained traumatized by the events of the war and would pursue a course that must be interpreted as deeply vindictive toward those deemed responsible. This agenda of retribution would dominate Roman foreign policy in the opening decades of the second century and more subtly far beyond.

Given their distinctive fear-scape, it was utterly in character for Romans to remember the Second Punic War as "the war against the Carthaginians and Gauls." Now that the Barcid menace had been removed, it was the turn of the Celtic tribes inhabiting the Po basin to suffer the wrath of those along the Tiber. The assault was relentless; during the decade after the year 200, more legions and consuls were sent to Cisalpine Gaul than to anywhere else.[96] Pincered by Roman forces moving both east and west from the coasts, the results were inevitable. The Boii in particular were singled out for a pounding, and by 191 they had been crushed, with half their lands expropriated. The other local tribes—Insubres and Cenomani—were treated better but with the understanding that, at last, they were now Rome's subordinates. Nor had the Romans forgotten that the region's other inhabitants, the Ligurians, had lined up with Mago Barca when he'd arrived in their vicinity. Though it took longer because of mountainous terrain, by 155 they too had been steamrolled.[97]

Philip V of Macedon, whose alliance with Hannibal after Cannae had probably sealed his fate, was also marked for a payback. Philip would protest that he had done nothing to transgress the Peace of Phoinike, and the Roman people were plainly tired—Livy (31.6.3) claims that a motion for war was initially rejected by the Comitia Centuriata—but the senate was implacable and in the end had its way.

Ironically, or perhaps not so ironically, included in Rome's military instrument of retribution was a substantial contingent from the *legiones Cannenses*. They were supposedly volunteers, but after a year, two thousand of them mutinied, bitterly maintaining that from Africa they had been transported back to Sicily and then put on ships to Macedonia contrary to their wishes.[98] The consul P. Villius Tappulus persuaded them to remain under arms, and they were still serving two years later in 197, when under the thirty-year-old Titus Quinctius Flaminius they blundered into Philip's army in the fog-enshrouded hills of

Cynoscephalae. The armies seemed well matched, until an unnamed tribune, availing himself of the flexibility Scipio had engineered into his ghosts, peeled off twenty maniples and led them around to the flank and rear of the heretofore successful Macedonian right.[99] Unable to turn to meet the Romans with their long pikes, the Macedonian phalangites were hacked to pieces by a buzz saw of Roman short swords.

His army destroyed, Philip accepted peace terms very much like those that had been imposed on Carthage. Now he too was no longer permitted to wage war outside home territory without Rome's blessing.[100] In linking himself to Hannibal after Cannae, Philip had only been playing according to the rules of the Mediterranean basin's "great game," but now he learned that Rome played for keeps.

The war's end also meant that the *Cannenses* could get some rest. Although the two victorious legions remained in place, the military threat had passed, and presumably the oldest veterans could be shipped back to Italy relatively quickly.[101] Then, two years after he had proclaimed "the freedom of the Greeks" at the Isthmian Games of 196, Flaminius, still in the process of arranging the new order, discovered as many as twelve hundred of the original Cannae prisoners in Greece. After the long-ago senatorial refusal to ransom them, Hannibal had sold the prisoners to Achaean owners, and they were now bought back and finally repatriated.[102] Six years later, another substantial number of enslaved *Cannenses* would be found in Crete and sent home, fully twenty-eight years after the battle had occurred.[103]

Meanwhile, at the insistence of Scipio the senate instructed the *praetor urbanus* to appoint a commission of ten to allocate some public lands in Samnium and Apulia for Africanus's soldiers, at the rate of two *jugera* (about 1.3 acres) per year served in Spain or Africa. But this equation apparently did not account for the ghosts' time in Sicily.[104] If this was rehabilitation, it was not exactly generous, given the pain and humiliation these troops had endured before acquitting themselves so heroically at Zama, and then at Cynoscephalae. But at least the republic had taken some responsibility for their long-suffering soldiers and had not left it to the initiative of their commander, as would occur so frequently late in the republican era, with disastrous consequences for the stability of the state. In any age, countries that fight a lot of wars are well advised to take good care of their veterans.

But just as the requital for the *Cannenses* seems grudging, so too did the "freedom of the Greeks" prove to be less than it had appeared.

Even though Rome did eventually withdraw all forces from the Hellenic mainland, Greece's implied status as a protectorate made it practically inevitable that Rome would intervene in order to prevent domination by any other element—from within or without. This relationship would ultimately draw the Greeks inescapably into Rome's imperial orbit. For the moment, though, the question was simply whether "freedom of the Greeks" extended to Hellenes living in Asia Minor, and more particularly in Thrace, the European province next to Macedonia. Thrace was now being claimed by Antiochus, the Seleucid basileus and Hellenistic player of the first order. Things might have been worked out between him and the Romans, but in 195, as Hellenistic players were wont to do, he hired a military consultant. Regrettably, the consultant was Hannibal, and from this point Antiochus became a marked man along the Tiber.

Back in Carthage, Hannibal had morphed temporarily into a politician, having been elected suffete in 196 by apparently leveraging a renascent Barcid faction with a program of popular reforms frankly aimed at the commercial oligarchy. It was not surprising that he made enemies, some of whom went to Rome, where they found a ready audience—though not with Scipio Africanus—for their accusations. Over Scipio's objections, the senate decided to send three of their number to Carthage, really to indict Hannibal before the council of elders, but under the guise of settling a dispute between Carthage and Masinissa. Hannibal wasn't fooled; he discreetly left town and made his way to a castle on the coast, where a boat waited to take him to Tyre. It was the beginning of a hegira that would last until his death. But the first sojourn was with Antiochus, and it would not prove an auspicious one for either man.[105]

Had Antiochus really meant to turn his "cold war"[106] with Rome into a winner-take-all contest for dominance of the Mediterranean basin, then the choice of Hannibal as strategist would have been brilliant. The Barcid knew exactly what was necessary for such an effort—an alliance with Philip of Macedon, an invasion of Italy, and if possible persuading Carthage to recommence hostilities.[107] But Antiochus's horizons were limited, and besides, he never trusted Hannibal (despite the latter relating to him the oath he'd taken as a child against Rome) nor took his advice seriously . . . the worst of both worlds—guilt by association without any of its benefits. So in temporizing—always a mistake against the Romans—Antiochus ended up having his army de-

stroyed at Magnesia in 189, the culmination of a campaign orchestrated by Scipio Africanus. For their troubles, the Romans charged him
a fifteen-thousand-talent war indemnity, half again more than they had
charged the Carthaginians, and kicked him entirely out of Asia Minor.

Hannibal continued his wandering, eventually ending up in Bithynia along the shores of today's Sea of Marmara at the court of King
Prusias, who employed him as a city planner, certainly one of his more
constructive roles.[108] Prusias also took advantage of the Carthaginian's
destructive talents. For Prusias was involved in a territorial dispute
with Eumenes of Pergamum, which escalated into open warfare in 186.
Since both were "friends of the Roman people," the senate delayed its
intervention until 183. In the interim, Hannibal took a turn as Prusias's
admiral, reportedly catapulting pots full of poisonous snakes onto
Eumenes's ships, and nearly capturing the king by sending him a message, seeing which ship accepted it, and then going after the royal vessel.[109] Eumenes, "the oriental Masinissa," sent his brother to complain
to the Romans about Prusias's conduct in general, and specifically that
Prusias had used reinforcements sent by Philip of Macedon and also,
presumably, had used the services of Hannibal.

The senate dispatched Flaminius, who was good with Greeks, to
provide what the Romans probably thought of as adult supervision.
Whether it was Flaminius who demanded Hannibal's head, or Prusias
who offered it to propitiate the Roman, is hard to tell. However, the
Barcid, even at sixty-three, was alert enough to attempt an escape
through an underground passage. Unfortunately, he ran into a detachment of the king's guards and, realizing the game was over, took poison,
remarking, "Let us now put an end to the great anxiety of the Romans,
who have thought it too long and hard a task to wait for the death of a
hated old man."[110]

So passed Hannibal into history and legend; nobody was better at
winning battles, but not wars, which is what counts. He died much as he
had lived, as a paladin and warlord whose natural environment was the
ever shifting stage of Hellenistic personality-based power politics.
Rome was emblematic of something much more robust, and that was
why he had lost and the Romans could subsequently take over the
Mediterranean basin so suddenly. Meanwhile, a case can be made that
historians writing from the perspective of the modern monolithic
nation-state have too closely equated Hannibal's acts and those of his
clan with the economic and political vector of Carthage. Certainly he

was never an entirely independent actor; nor was Carthage an innocent bystander to the Second Punic War. But the pro-Roman sources, if read skeptically, seem to point to the Barcids as instigators and the city as just sort of tagging along. For Carthage too stood for something else, and that was making money.

Poor Carthage—if you can say that about a place that burned its young alive. But if you are willing to overlook this unfortunate custom, the city certainly did seem to mend its ways after the Second Punic War. Most fundamentally it seems to have accepted a subordinate position to Rome, to have taken the term "friend and ally" seriously. Setting aside war and imperial ambition, Carthaginians turned to doing what they did best—not only recovering their former prosperity but growing ever wealthier. After only ten years, they offered to pay off their entire war indemnity, which was supposed to have stretched across five decades, a proposal the Romans huffily rejected.[111] Around the same time, envoys from the senate requested very large quantities of grain, including five hundred thousand bushels of barley destined for the army. The Punic side offered it gratis, but the senate insisted on paying.

Factions continued in Carthaginian politics, but no element appears to have been hostile to Rome, and there is no indication that the city was anything but a loyal ally after 201.[112] But they were foolish to flaunt their wealth in the face of the authorities on the Tiber, not so much because it provoked jealousy, but because the Romans were not equipped to understand it and were programmed to think of it in terms of a military threat.

It is obviously impossible to say anything definitive about what ordinary Romans thought of Carthage and Carthaginians. The most revealing literary evidence is probably Plautus's *Poenulus* (*"The Carthaginian"*). The leading character is a Punic merchant named—no surprise here—Hanno who exhibits some negative stereotypes (rings in his ears, a fondness for whores, pretending not to understand Latin when he really does). But Hanno is clearly a comic figure, and not a villain designed to draw upon the Roman audiences' hatred of Carthage when the play was enacted around 190 B.C.[113] Still, this was just one play, and Hannibal had killed a lot of Romans.

Among Rome's leadership class there was certainly still hostility toward Carthage, and although the Africans did have their defenders in the senate (Scipio Nasica, Africanus's cousin, was one), increasingly the tide turned toward the archconservative Marcus Porcius Cato. In 153 he visited the city as part of a delegation sent to arbitrate a dispute between Carthage and Masinissa, and he returned deeply shaken by the obvious prosperity of the place. To a Roman, especially given Carthage's penchant for hiring mercenaries, prosperity meant danger, and he took to ending each of his speeches with "Carthage must be destroyed." At one point he let some fresh figs drop from his toga, maintaining that they had been picked in Carthage just three days earlier and implying that a war fleet could reach Rome just as quickly. Like Freud's fabled cigar, sometimes a fig is just a fig, but apparently not to a Roman. Appian[114] maintains that from the moment Cato's delegation returned, the senate was resolved upon going to war and was simply waiting for a pretext.

Masinissa, by now nearly ninety but still able to ride a horse and lead men into battle, provided the needed cover through his constant encroachments of Punic territory. In 150 when the Carthaginians decided to fight without asking Roman permission and raised an army— an army they promptly lost in the fight—the senate pounced.

First, three hundred youthful hostages were demanded and given. Then the Carthaginians were ordered to disarm, which they did. Finally, the population was told to vacate the city, at which point they chose resistance. The struggle was desperate, lasting until 146, when the city finally fell in a sea of flames. The surviving population was enslaved, and Carthage as a society and a state was history—a true victim of genocide. When the city fell, Polybius was with the Roman commander Scipio Aemilianus—the grandson of Lucius Aemilius Paullus (who fell at Cannae) and the adopted grandson of Scipio Africanus— and saw him weep and recite lines from *The Iliad* on the fall of Troy as he watched the city burn.[115] They may have been crocodile tears.

And what of Rome? How had the experience of the Second Punic War, arguably catalyzed by the defeat at Cannae, affected the Romans' subsequent path through history? In 1965 the then-prestigious historian Arnold Toynbee published a massive two-volume study, *Hannibal's Legacy.* Toynbee argued not only that the Punic invasion had done such grievous harm to southern Italy that it still had not recovered after two thousand years, but also that the invasion had engendered pernicious social forces, such as the replacement of peasant farmers by slave-based commercial agriculture (latifundia), that would persist to the end of ancient civilization.[116] In part due to Toynbee's reputation having declined precipitously, and also because of the grandiosity of claiming damage lasting two millennia, his thesis has been subjected to the most severe sort of criticism, resulting in a tendency to minimize the impact of the Barcid's depredations.[117] Victor Davis Hanson, for example, points out just how hard it is to inflict damage on agricultural assets, particularly crops, by military action.[118] It has also been noted that Rome was already becoming a slave society as far back as the fourth century B.C., and latifundia were in existence well before Hannibal ever set foot in Italy.[119]

Still, the most recent scholarship has moved toward bridging the gap and conceding that Toynbee had a point. Hannibal's army was in the southern corner of Italy for thirteen years, during which time the area was subjected to the most intense sort of raiding. Land may have been hard to destroy, but farm populations could be terrorized, killed, and driven to shelter elsewhere.[120] When farmers and discharged soldiers returned, many lacked the resources to restore their holdings, so they headed for the cities instead. This in turn accelerated the formation of large estates by the wealthy, who had the money to staff them with slaves made plentiful by Rome's martial successes.

And what of those soldiers, epitomized by the ghosts of Cannae, whose long service kept them away from home and family and spelled financial ruin? These men had not much to return to, argues historian Adrian Goldsworthy, and if the senate refused to take care of them in a meaningful and sustained way, then they would naturally look to their commanders for a future, and become in the process more loyal to generals than to the institutions of the republic.[121] The wars in the East would prove very profitable, and would provide the commanders with not only the largesse to take care of their soldiers, but also the wealth to spend on public entertainment, such as the gladiatorial combats that were becoming wildly popular. This not only intensified the nearly mindless competition for office among the *nobiles*, but it helped add the concept of celebrity into the already heady military brew.

Here again the impact of Hannibal cannot be overlooked. His defeat of three plebeian consuls in succession—Sempronius Longus, Flaminius, and Varro—had made it clear that amateur generals would not do and that long-term commanders were a necessity, thereby upsetting the dogma that rulers were interchangeable.[122] Still, better captains, even combined with the strategic approach of Fabius Maximus, had been only good enough to keep the Barcid at bay, not get rid of

him. Various stalwarts—Marcellus, T. Sempronius Gracchus, Q. Fulvius Flaccus, C. Claudius Nero, and even Fabius himself—had crossed
swords with the Punic incubus, but none had proved his master. Finally,
necessity had invented Scipio, a commander whose charisma and re-
sourcefulness had been the match of Hannibal's, and that had done the
trick. Yet this situation also introduced the archetype of Caesar and
Pompey into Roman politics. If you were a republican, that proved a
poison pill. In the end, then, we are thrown back to the point made earlier about Silius Italicus's appearing to argue that in the very act of
fighting Hannibal, Rome put itself on the road to civil war by coming
to rely on charismatic generals for survival. If this is the case, then
Hannibal had the last laugh.

EPILOGUE:
THE SHADOW OF CANNAE

[1]

At no point would Cannae disappear from military history, but its memory, especially its modern memory, has taken on a momentum of its own, accelerating the battle to the level of legend, and glorifying Hannibal as its mastermind. Arguably though this has proceeded in the face of one inevitability—all decisive battles produce losers as well as winners, both victims and victors. Two-edged swords, they cut both ways. Hence, those who proclaim Cannae the most studied and emulated of combat encounters[1] might have done better to consider that at least some of this energy may have been devoted to avoiding another Cannae, not repeating it.

This seems at least marginally true of the immediate historical context. Since neither Hannibal nor Carthage had much of a future, the memory of Cannae and its perpetuation fell to the losers. To Polybius (a Greek with Roman sympathies) and Livy, the battle was a disaster blamed more on the fecklessness and inexperience of C. Terentius Varro than on the cleverness of Hannibal. As for the rest of the historians—Plutarch, Caesar, Tacitus, Suetonius, Sallust, and Vegetius—the lack of any analysis or even specific mention of the battle among any of them probably indicates a proclivity to overlook what was by all accounting a miserable episode for Rome. In other words, Cannae, to the degree that it was considered at all by subsequent Romans, was memorialized as a warning, not as an opportunity.

As the Dark Ages settled over what had been the empire in the west, and Roman military thought here flickered out, Byzantium alone remained concerned with a systematic approach to warfare. Not only was the establishment in Constantinople extremely interested in military leverage since their forces were frequently outnumbered, but martial practice was compiled and recorded in a series of texts that directly addressed the problems and opportunities of commanders. Under the circumstances, the exploits of Hannibal, and in particular the battle of Cannae, might logically be expected to have been remembered in a favorable light. But for the most part these tactical manuals (e.g., *Praecepta militaria* of Emperor Nikephoros II Phokas, or the published portions of the *Taktika* of Nikephoros Ouranos) remain just that, down-to-earth nuts-and-bolts guides to organizing, equipping, and deploying fighting units in the most efficacious fashion. The most interesting of these, however, the *Strategikon,* attributed to the soldier-emperor Maurice, does come tantalizingly close to recommending a Cannae-like approach . . . "Do not mass all your troops in front, and even if the enemy is superior in numbers, direct your operations against his rear or his flanks."[2] Yet the battle is not specifically mentioned, and Hannibal is referred to only twice in unrelated anecdotes. Quite probably the author and others in Constantinople had access to the relevant sources and were aware of Cannae, but the battle does not seem to have been a preoccupation.

It's not surprising, given the individualized and spontaneous nature of medieval combat, that Cannae appears to play little if any role in shaping European warfare during this period. Neither Hannibal nor the battle are mentioned in the age's primary military epics—*Beowulf, La Chanson de Roland,* the Icelandic Sagas, or *El Cid*—although the subject of the latter epic, Rodrigo Díaz de Vivar, did reportedly order that Greek and Roman books on military themes be read to his troops before battle for entertainment and inspiration. Another possible acknowledgment of Hannibal and Cannae involved the Battle of Granson in 1476, when Charles the Rash, of Burgundy, tried to withdraw his center in the face of a determined advance by Swiss phalangites, in order to open the Swiss to attacks on both flanks. However, not only did the Burgundians panic and flee, but we have only historian Charles Oman's word that the appropriately surnamed Charles had the inclination, erudition, and guile to use Cannae as his model.[3] Upon reflection, it seems unlikely.

Classical texts rediscovered during the Renaissance do appear to have a martial component, with a number of military theorists having been influenced by ancient sources. Nevertheless, the specific impact of Cannae is hard to pin down. Leonardo da Vinci, for instance, makes no reference to either Hannibal or the battle in his *Notebooks.* Machiavelli does mention Cannae three times[4] in his *Discourses on Livy*, but only in passing, as a defeat that nearly led to Rome's demise. He blames the defeat on the rashness of Varro, and refers not unapprovingly to the exile of the *legiones Cannenses*. In *The Prince*, Machiavelli praises Hannibal for having brought a multiethnic army to a foreign land and avoided desertions,[5] but then he castigates Hannibal in *The Art of War* for "trifling away his time at Capua, after he had routed the Romans at the battle of Cannae."[6] Tactically, Machiavelli's only relevant observation is that Hannibal was smart to keep the wind and the sun at his back on that fateful day in Apulia.[7] If Cannae informed other Renaissance men, it is not readily apparent.

[2]

An apparent conversion occurred at the very end of the sixteenth century in the Netherlands when two members of the dominant Nassau family, Count William Lodewijk and his cousin Maurice, prince of Orange, hit upon the principle of volley fire through reference to ancient texts. Specifically, they drew inspiration from the interchangeable formations of the Roman *triplex acies*, as described in the *Tactica* of Aelian, as the basis of "countermarching" (troops retreating between ranks after discharging their weapon, and then moving forward upon reloading).[8]

As the two men painstakingly perfected these maneuvers and taught their troops how to use them, William Lodewijk continued to immerse himself in classical literature, particularly Polybius, and in the process fastened on Cannae. In the spring of 1595, William sent his cousin a brief discourse on the battle, suggesting an order of battle that would cast Dutch troops as triumphant Carthaginians and their enemies the Spaniards as the victimized Romans.[9]

What appeared plausible in theory took another five years to apply—at the battle of Nieuwpoort—and produced ambiguous results that testify to the complicated nature of the Cannae template. After various vicissitudes the Dutch did achieve a victory of sorts—forcing the Spaniards to retreat with heavy casualties, but leaving themselves in a strategically vulnerable position . . . hardly a Cannae. In fact, firefighting based on volleying and methodical reloading, a model that was destined to dominate European warfare for most of the next two centuries, was not well suited to produce Cannae-like results, since it was based more on attrition than impetuousness, more on cautious deployment than on decisive tactical maneuvering. This left the battle largely overlooked during the military enlightenment, and as late as the writing of Carl von Clausewitz, who does not mention it.[10] Even at the outset, reservations appear to have overtaken William Lodewijk, who in 1607 advised Maurice, as he prepared for a new campaign, not to seek a Cannae, but avoid falling prey to one![11]

[3]

The modern military image of Cannae as what one modern critic[12] termed "a Platonic ideal of victory" appears to have originated with the obsession of one man, Count Alfred von Schlieffen, chief of the Prussian general staff from 1891 to 1905. Schlieffen's preoccupation with the battle turned on several factors. One was Germany's strategic position, caught between two potential adversaries, Russia and France, which made a fast decisive victory over one or the other highly desirable. The second factor was the example provided by his predecessor on the general staff, Helmuth von Moltke, who in 1870 at Sedan surrounded the French and captured Emperor Napoléon III through a double envelopment, making a German victory in the Franco-Prussian War nearly inevitable. Finally, all of this was informed by Schlieffen's reading of ancient history, specifically the first volume of Hans Delbrück's *History of the Art of War,* with its extensive description of Cannae. Metaphorically at least, a bulb switched on above Schlieffen's head, and suddenly Cannae seemed to beam light on everything.

While this revelation could have taken place as early as 1901, it seems more likely that it came as late as 1909, well after the general's retirement. This is important because until recently it has been assumed that Hannibal's victory was the inspiration behind the so-called Schlieffen plan, which was supposedly the strategic basis for Germany's attack through Belgium and into France during the early stages of World War I. Not only has the very existence of the Schlieffen plan as a comprehensive scheme of battle been questioned,[13] but it is apparent that the chief of staff's recommendations for a war against France from 1901 to 1905 were based on a concentration of force against one flank of the enemy, an approach that simply did not fit Cannae's footprint, despite subsequent efforts to shoe-horn the plan into this context.[14]

This is not to argue that Schlieffen was not Cannae-obsessed or that he did not come to measure much of recent military history against what he called this "perfect battle of annihilation"; it is simply a question of timing. Schlieffen's collected works including his Cannae studies were published in 1913, the year of his death. However, they do not appear to have been very influential until after the end of World War I, when they became a touchstone for those who argued that the German Army had lost the first battle of the Marne (and thus the war) because they had failed to keep faith with Schlieffen's commandments—in the process conflating Cannae and the general's actual advice.[15] This set the tone for a subsequent generation of German military thinkers, a key segment of whom followed Schlieffen "like Thurber's owl" and dreamed of future Cannaes made all the more plausible by the advent of armored vehicles.[16]

Schlieffen's Cannae studies were also influential in military circles outside of Germany during the interwar years. In 1931, for instance, they were translated into English and published by the U.S. Army Command and General Staff College at Fort Leavenworth, availing a new cadre of American officers the opportunity to consider the possibilities.

Hence, World War II would feature a cavalcade of Cannae-savvy military luminaries, a number of whom, especially among the Germans, were looking to inflict such a fate on their adversaries. Heinz Guderian conceptualized his tanks as motorized equivalents of Hasdrubal's cavalry sweeping around the enemy to seal their fate.[17] Similarly, in 1941, while in the process of chasing the British army in the direction of Tobruk, Erwin Rommel noted in his diary that "a new Cannae is being prepared."[18]

Even in the face of disaster, the Germans stuck to the theme; thus Erhard Raus, commander of the 6th Panzer Division near Stalingrad, less than three months before his army's surrender, dubbed a successful day's fighting around an obscure village "the Cannae of Pakhlebin."[19] Seven months later, in July 1943, the German assault on the Kursk salient was intended to achieve a gigantic Cannae—only to result in a disastrous attrition of their attacking armored vehicles on both flanks by the well-prepared defensive-minded Russians. The German Army having been bled white by the dream of Schlieffen's "perfect battle of annihilation," Kursk marked the last time the Wehrmacht was able to mount offensive operations on the Eastern Front. Defeat beckoned.

Yet the Germans were not alone in responding to Cannae's siren song. While the British were more cautious, American commanders were offensive-minded and therefore open to Hannibalic feats of arms. In particular, Dwight Eisenhower had nurtured a lifelong dream of emulating the Carthaginian general's envelopment of the Romans.[20] And for the initial Allied invasion of Germany, Eisenhower envisioned a huge Cannae-like maneuver, employing a double envelopment of the Ruhr.[21] George Patton, the most audacious of the major American commanders in Europe, was also a student of military history and very much aware of Hannibal's feat. Yet his outlook was hardly predictable, and reflects the contingent nature of even so decisive a victory. Writing in 1939, Patton notes: "There is an old saw to the effect that: 'To have a Cannae you must have a Varro' . . . in order to win a great victory you must have a dumb enemy commander. From what we know at the moment, the Poles qualified . . ."[22]

World War II ended and was replaced by inconclusive combat in Korea, the standoff of the cold war, and amorphous insurgency in Vietnam; yet the American dream of Cannae lived on, apparently nurtured primarily by forays into ancient military history at U.S. service academies. So it was that after the 1991 Gulf War, victorious General Norman Schwarzkopf was able to proclaim that he had "learned many things from the Battle of Cannae which I applied to Desert Storm."[23] In fact, the general's famous "left hook in the desert" more resembled the opening German moves in World War I, but no public-relations-conscious war hero was likely to announce that he had prepared another Schlieffen plan, so Cannae it was.

The future remains ambiguous. Given the predominance of anti-terrorism and anti-insurgency, the possibility of maneuver warfare seems, for the moment, distant. Also, given the sophistication of modern intelligence, surveillance, and reconnaissance assets, the kind of deception necessary to produce truly Hannibalic results may prove very difficult to achieve. But as long as men dream of killing other groups of men in very large numbers, we can rest assured, Cannae will not be forgotten.

ACKNOWLEDGMENTS

My books always begin with me far away and a friend from the past making contact. In this case it was Rob Cowley emailing me in Buenos Aires with the news that he was organizing a series on important battles for Random House, and asking me if I was interested in submitting a proposal on Cannae. Soon enough I was buried in the Second Punic War and wondering if the original email had been such a good thing. But now that it's over there is no question it was. So thanks, Rob.

Thanks also for giving me the opportunity to get to know Jonathan Jao, my editor. Good advice given well is a rare commodity, but it's vital in publishing, especially now. So thanks for your steady hand with my "ghosts."

Thanks to my colleagues at the Naval Postgraduate School: Michael Freeman, who read the emerging manuscript chapter by chapter and didn't seem to fall asleep; John Arquilla, who first pointed me to the fate of Cannae's survivors; and also Hy Rothstein who helped me learn to pronounce Cannae.

Since I belong to a family of writers, all outpourings get filtered through the gene pool. Thanks especially to wife, Benjie, son-in-law Nick Taylor, and brother-in-law Jack MacKinnon for careful reads and excellent suggestions.

Finally, thanks to my agent Carl Brandt, who has kept my erratic writing path more or less on track for upwards of two decades.

NOTES

CHAPTER I: TRACES OF WAR

1. John Prevas, *Hannibal Crosses the Alps: The Invasion of Italy and the Punic Wars* (Cambridge, Mass.: Da Capo Press, 1998), pp. 73–74, believes that enough physical evidence of the march existed to personally inspect the route Hannibal took. Similarly, Patrick Hunt of the Stanford Alpine Archaeology Project believes that, unlike Livy, Polybius appears to have known the geography of where Hannibal crossed.
2. Gregory Daly, *Cannae: The Experience of Battle in the Second Punic War* (London: Routledge, 2002), pp. 203–4.
3. Mary Beard, cited by Jane Kramer, "Israel, Palestine, and a Tenure Battle," *The New Yorker,* April 14, 2008, p. 50.
4. The inscription first cited in F. Ribbezo, *Il Carroctodel Sud,* S. ii, vol. 4.2, February 1951.
5. Adrian Goldsworthy, *The Punic Wars* (London: Cassell & Co, 2000), p. 11.
6. Serge Lancel, *Hannibal,* transl. Antonia Nevill (Oxford, UK: Blackwell, 1998), p. 29; John Rich, "The Origins of the Second Punic War," in *The Second Punic War: A Reappraisal* (London: Institute of Classical Studies, 1996), pp. 4, 32.
7. Cited in H. H. Scullard, *Scipio Africanus: Soldier and Politician* (London: Thames and Hudson, 1970), p. 14.
8. Martin Samuels, "The Reality of Cannae," *Militargeschichtliche Mitteilungen,* vol. 47 (1990), pp. 8–9.
9. Hans Delbrück, *History of the Art of War,* vol. 1, *Warfare in Antiquity* (Lincoln: University of Nebraska Press, 1990), p. 311.
10. J. F. Lazenby, *Hannibal's War: A Military History of the Second Punic War* (Norman: University of Oklahoma Press, 1998)
11. Daniel Mendelsohn, "What Was Herodotus Trying to Tell Us?" *The New Yorker,* April 28, 2008, p. 72.
12. P. G. Walsh, *Livy: His Historical Aims and Methods* (Cambridge: Cambridge University Press, 1961), pp. 110 ff., 138ff., and ix.
13. Daly, *Cannae,* p. 24.
14. Delbrück, *Warfare in Antiquity,* pp. 328–31.
15. D. T. McGuire, "History Compressed: The Roman Names of Silius' 'Cannae Episode,'" *Latomus,* vol. 54, no. 1 (1995), p. 118.
16. J. F. Lazenby, *The First Punic War: A Military History* (Stanford, Calif.: Stanford University Press, 1996), p. 1.
17. Dating the origins of war will always be dependent upon the exact definition applied

to war. Still, the proliferation of walled towns and other signs of warfare in the general region of the Neolithic Middle East around 5500 B.C. provide as good a reference point as is presently available for the first appearance of what would become more or less continuous organized violence. Robert L. O'Connell, *Ride of the Second Horseman: The Birth and Death of War* (New York: Oxford University Press, 1995), pp. 73–4.

18. Glynn L. Isaac, "Traces of Pleistocene Hunters: An East African Example," in R. B. Lee and I. DeVore, eds., *Man the Hunter* (Chicago: Aldine Publishing, 1968), p. 259; L.S.B. Leakey, "The Predatory Transition from Ape to Man," *International Anthropological and Linguistic Review*, vol. 1, no. 4 (1953), pp. 201–13.

19. Dating these devices is difficult since they all are organic and degradable; however, it makes sense to place their origins around the time of *Homo sapiens'* so-called great leap forward, around fifty thousand years ago.

20. W. H. McNeill, *The Pursuit of Power: Technology, Armed Force, and Society Since A.D. 1000* (Chicago: University of Chicago Press, 1982), p. 131; see also W. H. McNeill, *Keeping Together in Time: Dance and Drill in Human History* (Cambridge: Harvard University Press, 1995).

21. M. N. Cohen, *The Food Crisis in Prehistory: Overpopulation and the Origins of Agriculture* (New Haven: Yale University Press, 1977), pp. 93, 116.

22. S. J. Mithen, *Thoughtful Foragers: A Study of Prehistoric Decision Making* (Cambridge: Cambridge University Press, 1990), chs. 7–8.

23. Edward O. Wilson, *Sociobiology: The New Synthesis* (Cambridge: Harvard University Press, 1975), pp. 242–3.

24. I. Eibl-Eibesfeldt, *Human Ethology* (New York: Aldine De Gruyter: 1989), p. 405; Dave Grossman, *On Killing: The Psychological Cost of Learning to Kill in War and Society* (Boston: Little, Brown and Company, 1995), p. xxix.

25. For a summary discussion of these characteristics, see O'Connell, *Ride of the Second Horseman*, pp. 36–7.

26. The Stele of the Vultures from Telloh, Early Dynastic III, is presently located in the Louvre in Paris.

27. "Gilgamesh and Agga," in J. B. Pritchard, ed., *Ancient Near Eastern Texts: Relating to the Old Testament* (Princeton, N.J.: Princeton University Press, 1950), lines 1–40.

28. "Sargon of Agade," in Pritchard, ed., *Ancient Near Eastern Texts*, pp. v–vi, 5–52, 268.

29. M. A. Edey, *The Sea Traders* (Alexandria, Va.: Time-Life Books, 1974), p. 61.

30. D. Harden, *The Phoenicians* (London: Penguin, 1980), plate 51.

31. P. Bartoloni, "Ships and Navigation," in M. Andreose, ed., *The Phoenicians* (New York: Abbeville Press, 1988), pp. 72–4.

32. S. P. Oakley, "Single Combat in the Roman Republic," *The Classical Quarterly*, no. 35 (1985), p. 402.

33. See, for example, *The Iliad* 8.174; 11.286; 13.5; 15.509–10.

34. *The Iliad*, 2.385–87.

35. Livy 1.43. "Servian" after the semi-mythical Servius Tullius. For all references to Livy, I have used Loeb Classical Library series (Cambridge: Harvard University Press.

36. Goldsworthy, *The Punic Wars*, p. 44, makes this point about the wars between Rome and Carthage, but with rare exceptions, such as fights over key mountain passes and other choke points, the observation seems true of the whole strategic environment.

37. Agathocles of Syracuse's victorious troops, after they had defeated the Carthaginians in 310 B.C., found thousands of pairs of handcuffs in the enemy's camp. Serge Lancel, *Carthage: A History*, transl. Antonia Nevill (Oxford, UK: Blackwell, 1995), p. 278; see also Goldsworthy, *The Punic Wars*, p. 186.

38. The Melian Dialogue. Thucydides, *History of the Peloponnesian War* (5.84–116).

39. H. H. Scullard, *A History of the Roman World: 753 to 146 BC* (London: Routledge, 2006), p. 142.

CHAPTER II: ROME

1. Adrian Goldsworthy, *The Roman Army at War: 100 BC–AD 200* (Oxford, UK: Clarendon Press, 1996), p. 127.
2. Daly, *Cannae,* p. 29; Lancel, *Hannibal,* p. 104; Lazenby, *Hannibal's War,* pp. 75–6.
3. Lazenby, *Hannibal's War,* pp. 3–4, 75.
4. Daly, *Cannae,* p. 57.
5. Lazenby (*Hannibal's War,* p. 17) states that this was the major difference between Rome and Carthage, which was a nation of traders. This is basically a correct statement but one in need of amplification.
6. Arnold J. Toynbee, *Hannibal's Legacy: The Hannibalic War's Effects on Roman Life* (London: Oxford University Press, 1965), vol. 2, chs. 1, 2, and 6.
7. M. I. Finley, *Ancient Slavery and Modern Ideology* (New York: Viking Press, 1980), p. 81; Tim Cornell, "Hannibal's Legacy: The Effects of the Hannibalic War on Italy," in Cornell, Rankov, and Sabin, eds., *The Second Punic War: A Reappraisal,* p. 98.
8. Cumulative estimates of ancient numbers are always difficult, but such figures seem reasonable in light of the fact that in 211 the population of Capua, the second-largest city in Italy, was enslaved and two years later the Romans sold thirty thousand Tarentines.
9. Goldsworthy, *The Punic Wars,* pp. 257–8.
10. Ibid.
11. H. H. Scullard, *A History of the Roman World: 753 to 146 BC,* fourth edition (London: Routledge, 1980), chs. 3, 5; pp. 128–9.
12. See for example Livy 21.63.2ff, in which he states that Flaminius was hated by the nobility, or 22.25.19 when he disparagingly calls Varro the son of a butcher.
13. Scullard, *Scipio Africanus,* p. 162.
14. Adrian Goldsworthy, *Cannae* (London: Cassell, 2004), p. 63; Goldsworthy, *The Punic Wars,* pp. 42–3.
15. Lazenby, *Hannibal's War,* p. 4.
16. Scullard, *A History of the Roman World,* p. 127.
17. William V. Harris, *War and Imperialism in Republican Rome: 327–70 B.C.* (Oxford, UK: Clarendon Press, 1979), chs. 1 and 2; John Rich, "The Origins of the Second Punic War," in Cornell, Rankov, and Sabin, eds., *The Second Punic War: A Reappraisal,* pp. 18–9.
18. Daly, *Cannae,* p. 57.
19. Goldsworthy, *The Punic Wars,* p. 40.
20. Scullard, *A History of the Roman World,* p. 80.
21. E. S. Staveley, *Historia,* vol. 5 (1956), p. 101ff.
22. Theodore A. Dodge, *Hannibal: A History of the Art of War Among the Carthaginians and Romans down to the Battle of Pydna, 168 BC, with a Detailed Account of the Second Punic War* (London: Greenhill Books, 1994), p. 42.
23. Goldsworthy, *The Punic Wars,* p. 45.
24. See for example Scullard, *A History of the Roman World,* pp. 365–6.
25. Grossman, *On Killing,* pp. 120–3.
26. James Grout, "Gladiators," *Encyclopaedia Romana* (penelope.uchicago.edu/~grout /encyclopaedia_romana/gladiators/gladiators.html).
27. J. E. Lendon, *Soldiers and Ghosts: A History of Battle in Classical Antiquity* (New Haven: Yale University Press, 2005), p. 176.
28. Scullard, *A History of the Roman World,* pp. 146–9.
29. B. W. Jones, "Rome's Relationship with Carthage: A Study of Aggression," *The Classical Bulletin,* vol. 9 (1972), p. 28.
30. Goldsworthy, *The Roman Army at War,* p. 109.
31. E. Badian, *Foreign Clientelae (264–70 B.C.)* (Oxford, UK: Clarendon Press, 1958), pp. 6–7, 154.
32. Scullard, *A History of the Roman World,* p. 363.

33. Goldsworthy, *Cannae*, pp. 49–50.
34. Goldsworthy, *The Punic Wars*, p. 45.
35. Samuels, "The Reality of Cannae," pp. 11, 23–4.
36. Oakley, "Single Combat in the Roman Republic," p. 403.
37. Lendon, *Soldiers and Ghosts*, p. 177–8.
38. Sallust, *Bellum Catilinae* (51.38); op. cit. Alexander Zhmodikov, "The Roman Heavy Infantrymen in Battle," *Historia*, vol. 49, no. 1 (2000), pp. 72–4.
39. Duncan Head, *Armies of the Macedonian and Punic Wars: 359 to 146 BC* (Goring-by-Sea, UK: Wargames Research Group, 1982), p. 157.
40. M. C. Bishop and J. C. Coulston, *Roman Military Equipment* (London: Batsford, 1993), p. 50.
41. Goldsworthy, *The Punic Wars*, p. 47.
42. Livy 31.34.4–6 describes graphically the nature of such wounds inflicted during the Second Macedonian War: "When they had seen bodies chopped to pieces by the Spanish sword, arms torn away, shoulders and all, or heads separated from bodies . . . or vitals laid open . . . they realized in a general panic with what weapons, and what men they had to fight."
43. Flavius Vegetius Renatus, "The Military Institutions of the Romans," in *The Roots of Strategy* (Harrisburg, Penn., 1940), pp. 85–6 (1.12).
44. See Goldsworthy, *Cannae*, pp. 135–7.
45. Peter Connolly, *Greece and Rome at War* (revised ed.) (London: Greenhill Books, 1998), p. 131; Bishop and Coulston, *Roman Military Equipment*, pp. 58–9.
46. Daly, *Cannae*, p. 68; Polybius (6.23.13).
47. Daly, *Cannae*, pp. 64–70.
48. Philip Sabin, "The Mechanics of Battle in the Second Punic War," in Cornell, Rankov, and Sabin, eds., *The Second Punic War: A Reappraisal*, p. 74.
49. Samuels, "The Reality of Cannae," p. 15.
50. Delbrück, *Warfare in Antiquity*, pp. 274–5.
51. Carl von Clausewitz put it at twenty minutes, while J.F.C. Fuller reduced it to fifteen. Goldsworthy, *The Roman Army at War*, p. 224.
52. F. E. Adcock, *The Roman Art of War Under the Republic* (Cambridge: Harvard University Press, 1940), pp. 8–12; Goldsworthy, *The Punic Wars*, pp. 53–4.
53. See for example Daly, *Cannae*, p. 62, fig. 2.
54. Goldsworthy, *The Punic Wars*, pp. 51–2.
55. Ibid., p. 49; Daly, *Cannae*, p. 78. Polybius in particular has nothing to say on this matter.
56. Emilio Gabba, *Republican Rome, the Army, and the Allies*, transl. P. J. Cuff (Berkeley: University of California Press, 1976), pp. 5–6; Samuels, "The Reality of Cannae," p. 12; Lawrence Keppie, *The Making of the Roman Army: From Republic to Empire* (London: Batsford, 1998), p. 33.
57. Daly, *Cannae*, p. 73; Goldsworthy, *The Punic Wars*, pp. 48.
58. Livy, 22.37.7–9.
59. Samuels, "The Reality of Cannae," p. 13.
60. Goldsworthy, *The Punic Wars*, p. 48.
61. Goldsworthy, *The Roman Army at War*, p. 125.
62. Goldsworthy, *Cannae*, p. 49.
63. Ann Hyland, *Equus: The Horse in the Roman World* (New Haven: Yale University Press, 1990), pp. 88–9.
64. Dodge, *Hannibal*, pp. 63–4.
65. Goldsworthy, *The Roman Army at War*, p. 110.
66. See Polybius 6, 27–35; Edward Luttwak, *The Grand Strategy of the Roman Empire: From the First Century A.D. to the Third* (Baltimore, Md.: Johns Hopkins University Press, 1976), p. 55.
67. Goldsworthy, *The Roman Army at War*, p. 113.
68. Ibid., p. 112.

69. Polybius 6.35.4; Daly, *Cannae*, pp. 133–4.
70. This reconstruction largely taken from Goldsworthy, *Cannae*, p. 82; Goldsworthy, *The Punic Wars*, pp. 56–7; Samuels, "The Reality of Cannae," p. 15. See also Polybius, 3.72, 113, 6.31; Livy 34.46, 44.36.

CHAPTER III: CARTHAGE

1. Daly, *Cannae*, p. 132.
2. F. N. Pryce, in H. H. Scullard, *A History of the Roman World: 753 to 146 BC*, fourth edition (London: Routledge, 1980), pp. 163–4.
3. Gilbert and Colette Charles-Picard, *Daily Life in Carthage at the Time of Hannibal*, transl. A. E. Foster (New York: Macmillan, 1961), pp. 154–5.
4. Lancel, *Carthage*, p. 111.
5. Ibid., p. 205.
6. Goldsworthy, *The Punic Wars*, p. 27.
7. Lancel, *Carthage*, p. 43.
8. C. R. Whittaker, "Carthaginian Imperialism in the Fifth and Fourth Centuries," in P.D.A. Garnsey and C. R. Whittaker, eds. *Imperialism in the Ancient World: The Cambridge University Research Seminar in Ancient History* (Cambridge: Cambridge University Press, 1978), p. 59.
9. Charles-Picard, *Daily Life in Carthage*, p. 60.
10. Whittaker, "Carthaginian Imperialism in the Fifth and Fourth Centuries," p. 68.
11. See for example Charles-Picard, pp. 83–4; B. D. Hoyos, "Hannibal's War: Illusions and Ironies," *Ancient History*, vol. 19 (1989), p. 88; see B. D. Hoyos, "Barcid Proconsuls and Punic Politics, 237–218 BC," *Rheinisches Museum für Philologie*, vol. 137 (1994), pp. 265–6 for a summary of the second line of argumentation.
12. Goldsworthy, *The Punic Wars*, p. 29.
13. Charles-Picard, *Daily Life in Carthage*, pp. 111, 116; Hoyos, "Barcid Proconsuls and Punic Politics," p. 267.
14. Ricardo first articulated comparative advantage in his book *On the Principles of Political Economy and Taxation*, in AD 1817.
15. Lancel, *Carthage*, pp. 404–6.
16. Ibid., p. 140. The mendacious Cato may have picked the fig from his own trees.
17. See Appian, *Libyca*, 95, for a description.
18. Scullard, *Scipio Africanus*, p. 117.
19. Diodorus Siculus, 14.77.3.
20. Whittaker, "Carthaginian Imperialism in the Fifth and Fourth Centuries," pp. 89–90.
21. Lazenby, *The First Punic War*, p. 25. There is evidence that Liby-Phoenicians were liable for military service abroad, but this does not seem to have generally been true across the empire.
22. For a differing interpretation of the relationships see Lazenby, *The First Punic War*, p. 21; Lancel, *Carthage*, p. 116; and Goldsworthy, *The Punic Wars*, p. 30.
23. Colette and Gilbert Charles-Picard, *Vie et Mort de Carthage* (Paris: Hachette, 1970), p. 307.
24. Polybius, 1.82.12.
25. B. H. Warmington, *Carthage* (New York: Praeger, 1960), p. 124, estimates that the total population including slaves, women, and children was probably never higher than four hundred thousand. On this basis, it seems reasonable that somewhat more than one in four would be capable of military service.
26. Polybius 1.75.1–2.
27. Samuels, "The Reality of Cannae," p. 20.
28. Daly, *Cannae*, p. 125.
29. Lancel, *Hannibal*, pp. 176–7; Charles-Picard, *Daily Life in Carthage*, p. 98.
30. Head, *Armies of the Macedonian and Punic Wars*, p. 49.

31. Lazenby, *The First Punic War,* p. 27.
32. Modern sources are somewhat divided on the subject, but in the absence of more evidence, many assume citizens and allied Liby-Phoenicians rowed in the fleet. See for example B. D. Hoyos, "Hannibal: What Kind of Genius," *Greece and Rome,* vol. 30, no. 2 (October 1983), p. 172; Goldsworthy, *The Punic Wars,* pp. 31–2.
33. Goldsworthy, *The Punic Wars,* pp. 31–2.
34. Rankov, "The Second Punic War at Sea," in Cornell, Rankov, and Sabin, eds. *The Second Punic War: A Reappraisal,* p. 50.
35. Livy, 30.43.12–13.
36. Plutarch, *Pyrrhus,* 24.
37. Lazenby, *The First Punic War,* p. 35.
38. See for example Harris, *War and Imperialism in Republican Rome,* p. 182ff.
39. Lancel, *Hannibal,* pp. 4–5; Lancel, *Carthage,* p. 365.
40. Polybius, 1.20.1–2.
41. Lazenby, *The First Punic War,* pp. 71–2.
42. Ibid, p. 81.
43. Cape Bon is the modern terminology.
44. Lazenby, *The First Punic War,* p. 110.
45. Diodorus, 23.4.1; Polybius, 1.17.4–6; Diodorus, 23.8.1; Polybius, 1.38.1–5; 1.44.1–2.
46. Tenney Frank, *Cambridge Ancient History,* vol. 7 (Cambridge: Cambridge University Press, 1928), p. 685.
47. Lazenby, *The First Punic War,* p. 114.
48. Appian, *History of Rome: Book 6: The Wars in Spain,* 4; Lazenby, *The First Punic War,* p. 144.
49. Since Hannibal was nine when his father brought him to Spain in 237, it seems likely that he was born around the time his father left for Sicily.
50. Hoyos, "Hannibal's War: Illusions and Ironies," p. 87.
51. Polybius, 1.56.3.
52. Ibid., 1.59.7.
53. Lancel, *Hannibal,* p. 10; C. Nepos, *Hamilcar,* 1.5.
54. Lazenby (*The First Punic War,* p. 164) is quite typical when he says: "We have no census-returns from Carthage, of course, . . . but . . . their losses cannot have been high."
55. Hoyos, "Hannibal's War: Illusions and Ironies," p. 88.
56. Appian, *The Wars in Spain,* 4.
57. Hoyos, "Barcid Proconsuls and Punic Politics," pp. 250–1.
58. Goldsworthy, *The Punic Wars,* pp. 135–6.
59. Polybius, 1.72.3.
60. Appian, *The Wars in Spain,* 4.
61. Nepos, *Hamilcar,* (3.5–8).
62. Hoyos, "Barcid Proconsuls and Punic Politics," p. 251.
63. Polybius, 3.11.5–7; Livy, 35.19.
64. Prevas, *Hannibal Crosses the Alps,* p. 41; Dodge, *Hannibal,* pp. 145–6.
65. Hoyos, "Barcid Proconsuls and Punic Politics," p. 274.
66. Lancel, *Carthage,* p. 379; Lancel, *Hannibal,* p. 36.
67. Lancel, *Carthage,* p. 378.
68. Lancel, *Hannibal,* pp. 40–1.
69. Scullard, *A History of the Roman World,* pp. 196–7.

CHAPTER IV: HANNIBAL'S WAY

1. See for example Goldsworthy, *The Punic Wars,* pp. 157–8.
2. Plutarch, "Fabius Maximus," 6.3; Appian, *Hannibalic War,* 14; 28.
3. Pliny the Elder, *Naturalis Historia,* 3. 103.

4. B. D. Hoyos, "Maharbal's Bon Mot: Authenticity and Survival," *The Classical Quarterly,* New Series, vol. 50, no. 2 (2000), pp. 610–14.
5. Plutarch, *Fabius,* 15.2–3; Livy, 27.16.10.
6. Livy (21.3–4) even cites a tradition that has Hannibal, after his father's death, repatriated to Carthage, only to have Hasdrubal urgently request that he return to Spain.
7. Lazenby, *Hannibal's War,* p. 256. The five occasions were at Lake Trasimene, at Cannae, the destruction of Marcus Centenius's force, the first battle at Herdonea, and the second battle at Herdonea.
8. Goldsworthy, *The Punic Wars,* p. 62.
9. Livy, 25.11.16.
10. Lazenby, *Hannibal's War,* p. 257.
11. Ibid., p. 27; Hoyos, "Hannibal's War: Illusions and Ironies," p. 89; Daly, *Cannae,* p. 10.
12. Abram N. Shulsky, *Deterrence Theory and Chinese Behavior* (Santa Monica, Calif.: Rand Corporation, 2000), p. 30.
13. Louis Rawlings, "Celts, Spaniards, and Samnites: Warriors in a Soldier's War," in Cornell, Rankov, and Sabin, eds., *The Second Punic War: A Reappraisal,* p. 84; Oakley, "Single Combat in the Roman Republic," p. 407.
14. Head, *Armies of the Macedonian and Punic Wars,* p. 57; see for example Dionysius of Halicarnassus, *Roman Antiquities,* 14.
15. Head, *Armies of the Macedonian and Punic Wars,* p. 37.
16. Rawlings, "Celts, Spaniards, and Samnites: Warriors in a Soldier's War," p. 83.
17. Goldsworthy, *The Punic Wars,* p. 139; Jones, "Rome's Relationship with Carthage: A Study in Aggression," p. 28.
18. Polybius, 2.28.10; 2.31.1.
19. Samuels, "The Reality of Cannae," pp. 11, 18.
20. Goldsworthy, *The Punic Wars,* p. 140.
21. Delbrück, *Warfare in Antiquity,* p. 352.
22. Lancel, *Carthage,* p. 384.
23. Polybius, 3.15.7–8; Appian, *The Wars in Spain,* 10.
24. Polybius, 3.8.6–7.
25. Prevas, *Hannibal Crosses the Alps,* pp. 57–8; Goldsworthy, *The Punic Wars,* p. 155; Rich, "The Origins of the Second Punic War," p. 18.
26. Polybius 3.33.17–18.
27. Polybius 3.35.1; Appian, *Hannibalic War,* 1.4.
28. Samuels, "The Reality of Cannae," p. 20; Daly, *Cannae,* pp. 127–8.
29. Plutarch, *Fabius Maximus,* 17.1.
30. Dodge, *Hannibal,* p. 241.
31. Lazenby, *Hannibal's War,* p. 33.
32. Prevas, *Hannibal Crosses the Alps,* p. 85; see also Goldsworthy, *The Roman Arm,* Appendix: Logistics.
33. Prevas, *Hannibal Crosses the Alps,* p. 84; Livy 21.23.4.
34. Polybius, 3.60.5; Lazenby, *Hannibal's War,* p. 34.
35. Livy, 21.30.8.
36. Delbrück, *Warfare in Antiquity,* p. 355.
37. Lazenby, *Hannibal's War,* p. 50.
38. Polybius, 3.40.2–13; Livy, 21.25.10–14; Goldsworthy, *The Punic Wars,* p. 151.
39. Polybius, 3.49; Livy, 21.31.8.
40. Lancel, *Hannibal,* p. 71.
41. Lancel (Ibid.) notes that at the end of the nineteenth century a French scholar counted more than three hundred books and articles on the crossing, and Lancel opines that today a second lifetime would be necessary to cover the entire literature that now exists about the crossing.
42. Ibid.; Goldsworthy, *The Punic Wars,* p. 166.
43. Polybius, 3.50.3–6.

44. Livy, 21.33; Prevas, *Hannibal Crosses the Alps,* p. 114.

45. Hoyos, "Hannibal's War: Illusions and Ironies," p. 90; Prevas, *Hannibal Crosses the Alps,* pp. 127, 151.

46. Prevas, *Hannibal Crosses the Alps,* pp. 129–30; Dodge, *Hannibal,* p. 217.

47. Roger Dion, *"La voie heracleenne et l'itineraire transalpine d'Hannibal,"* in *Melanges a A Grenier* (coll. "Latomus," LVIII) (Brussels: 1962), p. 538; Werner Huss, *Geschichte der Karthager* (*Handbuch der Altertumswissenschaft* series, vol. 3, no. 8) (Munich: Beck, 1985), p. 305.

48. Eduard Meyer, *"Noch einmals Hannibals Alpenubergang,"* Museum Helveticum, vol. 21 (1964), pp. 90–101.

49. Prevas, *Hannibal Crosses the Alps,* p. 172.

50. Livy, 21.35.8–10.

51. Polybius, 3.55; Prevas, *Hannibal Crosses the Alps,* p. 150.

52. Polybius, 3.56.4.

53. Goldsworthy, *The Punic Wars,* p. 168.

CHAPTER V: THE FOX AND THE HEDGEHOG

1. Lancel, *Hannibal,* p. 133.

2. Goldsworthy, *The Punic Wars,* p. 311.

3. Polybius, 3.61.1–6.

4. Livy, 21.39.3.

5. Livy (21.42) and Polybius (3.62–3) have similarly elaborate versions of the same story, apparently believing it emblematic of Hannibal's character and mindset.

6. Livy (21.46.7) is the main source for this vignette, although Polybius (10.3.3–7) mentions it. Livy is also honest enough to note that Coelius Antipater gives credit for the rescue to a Ligurian slave. Nevertheless, Scullard (*Scipio Africanus,* p. 29) argues that Coelius's version was probably a later invention designed to discredit Africanus.

7. Lazenby, *Hannibal's War,* p. 53.

8. Ibid.; Daly, *Cannae,* p. 42.

9. Polybius, 3.66; Livy, 21.47.

10. Goldsworthy, *The Punic Wars,* p. 172.

11. Charles-Picard, *Vie et Mort de Carthage,* p. 239; Lancel, *Hannibal,* p. 84; Goldsworthy, *The Punic Wars,* p. 174.

12. See Goldsworthy, *The Punic Wars,* pp. 175–6, for an examination of this line of reasoning.

13. Polybius, 3.72.11–13. Livy, 21.55.4, says the Romans numbered eighteen thousand, but Lazenby, *Hannibal's War,* p. 56, considers this mistaken.

14. Goldsworthy, *The Punic Wars,* p. 178.

15. Lazenby, *Hannibal's War,* p. 56.

16. Polybius, 3.74.1.

17. Goldsworthy, *The Punic Wars,* p. 180.

18. Livy, 21.56; Polybius, 3.74.11.

19. Polybius, 3.75.1.

20. Lazenby, *Hannibal's War,* p. 58.

21. Goldsworthy, *The Punic Wars,* p. 181; Lazenby, *Hannibal's War,* pp. 59–60.

22. Polybius, 3.77.3–7.

23. Ibid., 3.78.1–4; Livy, 22.1.3–4.

24. With apologies to Mel Brooks.

25. Appian, *Hannibalic War,* 8.

26. Livy, 21.63.1; Goldsworthy, *The Punic Wars,* pp. 183–4.

27. Lazenby, *Hannibal's War,* p. 61.

28. Polybius, 3.78–79; Livy, 22.2.10–11.

29. Polybius, 3.82; Livy, 22.3.8–9.
30. Ovid (*Fasti*, 6.767–8) says the battle took place on June 21. The site of the battle is subject to some dispute. Those interested in the various arguments should see Lazenby, *Hannibal's War*, pp. 62–3; Connolly, *Greece and Rome*, pp. 172–5; and J. Kromayer and G. Veith, *Antike Schlachtfelder in Italien und Afrika* (Berlin: Weidmann, 1912), pp. 148–93. However, it seems that the whole basis for any certainty is undermined by the likelihood that the lake's level and shore must have shifted significantly over the course of twenty-two hundred years.
31. Dodge, *Hannibal*, p. 299.
32. Livy, 22.5.8.
33. Goldsworthy (*The Punic Wars*, p. 189) attributes this figure to Fabius Pictor.
34. This passage of Livy's (22.7. 6–14) is particularly vivid and illustrates the historian's almost cinematic qualities.
35. Goldsworthy, *Cannae*, pp. 59–60.
36. F. W. Walbank, *A Historical Commentary on Polybius*, vol. 1 (Oxford, UK: Clarendon Press, 1957), pp. 410–11.
37. John F. Shean, "Hannibal's Mules: The Logistical Limitations of Hannibal's Army and the Battle of Cannae," *Historia*, vol. 45, no. 2 (1996), p. 181.
38. Goldsworthy, *The Punic Wars*, p. 195.
39. Lancel, *Hannibal*, p. 101.
40. Plutarch, Fabius Maximus, 1; Goldsworthy, *Cannae*, p. 39.
41. Plutarch, Fabius Maximus, 4.
42. Lazenby, *Hannibal's War*, p. 68; Livy, 22.11.3–4.
43. Polybius, 3.87.1–3; Goldsworthy, *The Punic Wars*.
44. Polybius, 18.28.9.
45. Daly, *Cannae*, pp. 89–90, takes this position.
46. Head, *Armies of the Macedonian and Punic Wars*, p. 144. Polybius uses the term *"long-chophoroi,"* which is sometimes translated as "pikemen," but it is clear from his use of such troops as skirmishers that he does not mean they were used in a phalanx, nor that they carried pikes.
47. Polybius, 3.87.4–5.
48. Ibid., 3.88.9.
49. Livy, 22.12.4–5.
50. Dodge, *Hannibal*, p. 317; Shean, "Hannibal's Mules," p. 181.
51. Plutarch, Fabius Maximus, 5.
52. Livy (22.13.5–8) says that was only one guide, but Plutarch (Fabius Maximus, 6.3) maintains it was a number of guides.
53. Polybius, 3.93–94.5; Livy, 22.16–17.
54. Livy, 22.23.4–5.
55. Polybius, 3.100.4.
56. Ibid., 101–102.
57. Lazenby, *Hannibal's War*, p. 72.
58. Polybius, 3.104–5; Livy, 22.28.
59. Polybius, 3.105; Livy, 22.29–30.
60. Shean, "Hannibal's Mules," p. 183.

CHAPTER VI: CANNAE

1. Livy, 22.35.37.
2. Goldsworthy, *Cannae*, p. 74.
3. Livy, 22.39–40.4; Plutarch, Fabius Maximus, 14.
4. Ibid., 22.45.
5. Goldsworthy, *Cannae*, p. 60.
6. Goldsworthy, *The Punic Wars*, p. 199.

7. Lazenby, *Hannibal's War*, p. 74.
8. Goldsworthy, *Cannae*, p. 67.
9. Ibid.
10. The force that defeated the Gauls at Telamon was of a similar size, but this had been the accidental result of two double consular armies trapping a large body of Gallic troops between them.
11. Polybius, 3.107.9–15.
12. Daly, *Cannae*, p. 27.
13. Samuels ("The Reality of Cannae," p. 12) argues that there is little sign of any formal Roman military training beyond experience. This seems extreme. It is true that the evidence is fairly shallow, but there do seem to have been well-established procedures. When, for instance, Scipio Africanus established a training program for his troops at New Carthage (Polybius, 10.20.1–4), it seemed far too well organized to have been simply extemporized.
14. See for example Lazenby, *Hannibal's War*, p. 77; Goldsworthy, *The Punic Wars*, pp. 200–1.
15. Goldsworthy, *The Punic Wars*, p. 200; Goldsworthy, *Cannae*, p. 67.
16. Samuels, "The Reality of Cannae," p. 12.
17. Livy, 22.37.7–9.
18. Livy, 22.41–43; Polybius, 3.107.1–7.
19. Dodge, *Hannibal*, pp. 348–50.
20. Goldsworthy, *Cannae*, p. 75.
21. Ibid., p. 57.
22. Samuels, "The Reality of Cannae," pp. 18–19.
23. Polybius, 3.114.5; Livy, 22.46.6; Lazenby, *Hannibal's War*, p. 81; Goldsworthy, *The Punic Wars*, p. 207. However, Daly (*Cannae*, p. 29) adds that this figure does look "suspiciously like an estimate."
24. Lazenby (*Hannibal's War*, p. 81) estimates around 28,600 line infantry, with 11,400 skirmishers, while Goldsworthy (*The Punic Wars*, p. 207) and Parker (*Cannae*, p. 32) assign around 32,000 to the heavy infantry and 8000 to skirmishers.
25. Delbrück, *Warfare in Antiquity*, p. 326.
26. Foster Grunfeld, "The Unsung Sling," *MHA: The Quarterly Journal of Military History*, vol. 9, no. 1 (Autumn 1996).
27. Samuels, "The Reality of Cannae," pp. 19–20.
28. Appian, Han. 17, also states that Hannibal was short on supplies; Paul Erdkamp, "Polybius, Livy and the 'Fabian Strategy,' " *Ancient Society*, vol. 23 (1992), pp. 127–47.
29. Polybius, 3.110–112; Lazenby, *Hannibal's War*, p. 78.
30. Delbrück, *Warfare in Antiquity*, p. 315.
31. Goldsworthy, *Cannae*, p. 101.
32. Dodge, *Hannibal*, p. 396.
33. See Appian, Han. 22; Livy, 22.48.
34. Edward Fry, "The Field of Cannae," *The English Historical Review*, vol. 12, no. 48 (1897), p. 751, for the geography of the battlefield.
35. Polybius, 3.112.
36. Polybius, 3.117.8; Daly (*Cannae*, p. 29) discusses the disposition of those left behind and agrees with Polybius that the great majority would have been left in the main camp, since the smaller camp would be behind the Roman line and therefore need no more than a token garrison.
37. Polybius, 3.113.2–3.
38. K. Lehmann, *Klio*, vol. 15 (1917), p. 162; Delbrück, *Warfare in Antiquity*, pp. 324–5.
39. J. Kromayer and G. Veith, *Antike Schlachtfelder*, vol. 3, no. 1 (1903–31), pp. 278–388; Lazenby, *Hannibal's War*, pp. 77–9.
40. Connolly, *Greece and Rome at War*, p. 184; Goldsworthy, *Cannae*.

41. Polybius, 3.113; Livy, 22.46.1.

42. Appian, Han. 20; Ennius, Fragment, 282; Livy (22.46.9) also refers to the dust problem.

43. Appian, Han. 21; Livy, 22.47.1; Polybius, 3.115.1.

44. Martin Samuels's characterization of the Roman cavalry ("The Reality of Cannae," p. 13) as being more like "an English public school outing, rather than a military unit," is probably appropriate, considering the losses it had recently taken.

45. Plutarch, Fabius Maximus, 16. Livy (22.47.1–5) roughly follows this version also.

46. Daly, *Cannae,* p. 165.

47. Delbrück, *Warfare in Antiquity,* p. 316.

48. Goldsworthy, *Cannae,* pp. 111–12.

49. Daly, *Cannae,* pp. 185-6.

50. Adrian Goldsworthy's insights (*Cannae,* pp. 127–39) into the nature of this kind of combat are very persuasive. See also Zhmodikov, "The Roman Heavy Infantrymen in Battle," p. 71.

51. Lazenby, *Hannibal,* p. 83.

52. Polybius, 3.116.5–6.

53. Polybius, 3.117.2

54. Daly, *Cannae,* pp. 195–6.

55. Sabin, "The Mechanics of Battle in the Second Punic War," p. 76.

56. Victor Davis Hanson, "Cannae," in Robert Cowley, ed., *Experience of War* (New York: Norton, 1992), p. 42.

57. Daly, *Cannae,* pp. 196–8.

58. Goldsworthy, *Cannae,* p. 153.

59. Polybius, 3.117.1–2; see also Appian, Han. 24.

60. Grossman, *On Killing,* p. 71.

61. Goldsworthy, *Cannae,* p. 155.

62. R. J. Ridley, "Was Scipio Africanus at Cannae?" *Latomus,* vol. 34 (1975), p. 161.

63. Lazenby (*Hannibal's War,* p. 84) reaches this number using a variety of Livy's figures from 22.49–54.

64. Daly, *Cannae,* p. 198.

65. Polybius, 3.117.7–11.

66. Goldsworthy, *Cannae,* p. 159; Frontinus, Stratagems, 4.5.7; Livy, 22.52.4.

67. Livy's figures (22.49.15) are the most convincing and consistent in this regard.

68. Livy, 22.51.5–9.

69. Again, this is Lazenby's compilation (*Hannibal's War,* p. 84) using Livy's figures.

70. Polybius (3.117.6) puts Carthaginian losses at four thousand Gauls, fifteen hundred Spaniards and Libyans, and two hundred cavalry, while Livy (22.52.6) places the losses at around eight thousand total.

71. Lancel, *Hannibal,* p. 108.

72. There is considerable disagreement about whether the incident ever took place. John Lazenby ("Was Maharbal Right?" in Cornell, Rankov, and Sabin, eds., *The Second Punic War: A Reappraisal,* p. 39) argues that "like most good stories, this one is probably apocryphal." Lazenby maintains that because Polybius does not mention Maharbal in his accounts of Cannae, Maharbal was probably not there. On the other hand, Dexter Hoyos ("Maharbal's Bon Mot," pp. 610–11) points out that Livy did have Maharbal commanding the Numidians at Cannae, and that Maharbal may well have urged Hannibal to march on Rome after Trasimene and possibly again after Cannae, because, after all, it was good advice.

73. Shean, "Hannibal's Mules," pp. 167–73.

74. B. L. Hallward, "Hannibal's Invasion of Italy," in *Cambridge Ancient History,* vol. 3 (Cambridge: Cambridge University Press, 1930), p. 55.

75. Hoyos, "Hannibal: What Kind of Genius," *Greece and Rome,* pp. 176–7.

76. Daly, *Cannae,* p. 46; Lancel, *Hannibal,* pp. 109–10.
77. Bernard Montgomery, *A History of Warfare* (London: World Publishing Co., 1968), p. 98.
78. The story is contained in Livy (22.53). Some modern authorities question its veracity. R. J. Ridley ("Was Scipio Africanus at Cannae?" pp. 162–3) calls it a "romantic story" and cites Scullard, Scipio's biographer, as casting doubt, since Polybius didn't mention it. Yet Scullard himself (*Scipio Africanus,* p. 30) points out that this section of Polybius is not completely preserved, and that Canusium later struck a coin almost certainly depicting Scipio, apparently as a tribute to the incident.
79. Livy, 22.57.2–6; Appian, Han, 27; Goldsworthy, *The Punic Wars,* p. 220.
80. Lazenby, *Hannibal's War,* p. 91.
81. Livy, 22.61.14–15.
82. Ibid., 22.57.9–11.
83. Ibid., 22.58.1–4.
84. Ibid., 22.60.
85. Appian, Han. 28.
86. Livy, 23.16.15.
87. Livy, 23.24.6–13; Polybius, 3.118.
88. Livy, 23.31.1–3.
89. This interpretation is most clearly evident in Silius Italicus, 10.649–658.

CHAPTER VII: AFTERSHOCKS

1. Lazenby, *Hannibal's War,* p. 89.
2. Lancel, *Hannibal,* p. 113.
3. Livy, 23.7.1–2; Lazenby, *Hannibal's War,* p. 90.
4. Livy, 23.10.1–2.
5. Lancel, *Hannibal,* p. 115; Livy, 23.18.10–15.
6. Livy, 23.45.4.
7. Lazenby, *Hannibal's War,* p. 92; Lancel, *Hannibal,* p. 115.
8. Goldsworthy, *The Punic Wars,* p. 223.
9. Livy, 23.11.7–12.
10. Ibid., 23.13.2.
11. Livy, 23.41.10–12; Lancel, *Hannibal,* p. 112; Goldsworthy, *The Punic Wars,* p. 226.
12. Goldsworthy, *The Punic Wars,* pp. 220–1.
13. Lazenby, *Hannibal's War,* pp. 94–5; Prevas, *Hannibal Crosses the Alps,* p. 212.
14. Lancel, *Hannibal,* p. 115; Cornell, "Hannibal's Legacy: The Effects of the Hannibalic War on Italy," p. 102.
15. Plutarch, Fabius Maximus, 20.
16. Delbrück, *Warfare in Antiquity,* p. 340
17. Goldsworthy, *The Punic Wars,* p. 358. The highest figures are Lancel's (*Hannibal,* p. 145).
18. Lancel, *Hannibal,* p. 122.
19. Scullard, *Scipio Africanus,* p. 226.
20. Livy, 23.33.5 and 23.34.4–5.
21. Polybius, 7.9.
22. Lancel, *Hannibal,* pp. 117–8. See also E. J. Bickerman, "An Oath of Hannibal," *Transactions and Proceedings of the American Philological Association,* vol. 75 (1944), pp. 87–102; E. J. Bickerman, "Hannibal's Covenant," *American Journal of Philology,* vol. 73 (1952), pp. 1–23.
23. Goldsworthy, *The Punic Wars,* p. 253.
24. Livy, 26.24.
25. Information about the raid comes from Polybius 11.7; information about Mantinea comes from Polybius 11.11–18.
26. Livy, 29.12.2.

27. Livy, 23.32.7–12, 23.34.10–15, 23.40–41.7; Lancel, *Hannibal,* p. 120.
28. Lazenby, *Hannibal's War,* p. 98.
29. Livy, 24.6.4; Polybius, 7.2.1–6.
30. Livy, 24.29–30. The killing of the two thousand Roman deserters is discussed in Livy, 24.30.6–7.
31. Lazenby, *Hannibal's War,* p. 35.
32. See Plutarch, Marcellus, 13.
33. Livy (25.6) devotes an entire chapter to a moving recitation of their grievances. The senate's reply is at Livy 25.7.2–4.
34. Goldsworthy, *The Punic Wars,* p. 263.
35. Polybius, 8.3–7.
36. Ibid., 8.5.6.
37. Plutarch, Marcellus, 17.
38. Lazenby, *Hannibal's War,* p. 107.
39. Livy, 24.36.
40. Polybius, 8.37.1–13; Plutarch, Marcellus, 18.
41. Goldsworthy, *The Punic Wars,* p. 265.
42. Lazenby, *Hannibal's War,* p. 118.
43. Plutarch, Marcellus, 19. Actually, Plutarch gives three versions of the story, all with the same result.
44. Ibid., 21; Livy, 25.40.1–3.
45. Livy, 26.1.10.
46. Lazenby, *Hannibal's War,* p. 119.
47. Livy, 26.21.14.
48. Livy, 26.29–30.
49. Lazenby, *Hannibal's War,* p. 172.
50. Ibid., p. 50; Daly, *Cannae,* p. 11; Polybius, 3.97.1–5.
51. Scullard, *Scipio Africanus*
52. Goldsworthy, *The Punic Wars,* pp. 246–7.
53. Polybius, 3.76.8–11.
54. Ibid., 3.96.
55. Livy, 22.20–21.
56. Goldsworthy, *The Punic Wars,* p. 249.
57. Scullard, *Scipio Africanus,* pp. 32–3.
58. Livy implies that it was late in 216, but this seems unlikely given the onset of bad weather in the Alps.
59. Lazenby, *Hannibal's War,* p. 128. Goldsworthy (*The Punic Wars,* p. 250) argues against this comparison, maintaining that there is no sign that Hasdrubal deliberately thinned the Spanish center. But Livy (23.29.8) makes it clear that the Spanish troops were irresolute, something Hasdrubal probably understood and was clever enough to exploit, especially in light of his brother's success at Cannae.
60. Lazenby, *Hannibal's War,* p. 129.
61. Livy, 25.32.3; Rawlings, "Celts, Spaniards, and Samnites: Warriors in a Soldier's War," pp. 91–2.
62. Hoyos, "Hannibal: What Kind of Genius," pp. 174–5.
63. Livy, 25.33.
64. Ibid., 25.34.
65. Ibid., 25.35–6.
66. Lazenby, *Hannibal's War,* p. 131; Goldsworthy, *The Punic Wars,* p. 253.
67. Livy (26.17.1) gives the figure as six thousand Roman infantry and three hundred cavalry, plus an equal number of allied foot soldiers and eight hundred cavalry. Appian (*History of Spain,* 17) reports ten thousand foot soldiers and a thousand horse.
68. Livy, 26.17.3–16.
69. Ibid., 23.43.4.

70. Ibid., 25.13–14; Lazenby, *Hannibal's War,* pp. 112–3.
71. Livy, 25.16–17, 25.20.4; Lazenby, *Hannibal's War,* p. 113.
72. Livy, 25.19.9–17.
73. Ibid., 25.21.
74. Goldsworthy, *The Punic Wars,* p. 237.
75. Livy, 26.1.9–10.
76. Lazenby, *Hannibal's War,* p. 174; Livy, 27.7.12–13.
77. Lazenby, *Hannibal's War,* p. 121.
78. Livy, 26.4.4–10.
79. Ibid., 26.5–6.
80. For the alternative versions, see Polybius 9.3–7 and Livy 26.7–11.
81. Livy, 26.11.6.
82. Ibid., 26.11.4.

CHAPTER VIII: THE AVENGERS

1. Lancel, *Hannibal,* p. 138.
2. See for example Lazenby, *Hannibal's War,* p. 133, and H. H. Scullard, *Roman Politics, 220–150 B.C.* (Oxford, UK: Clarendon Press, 1973), pp. 66–7.
3. Livy, 26.19.3–9.
4. Polybius, 10.2–3.
5. Livy, 26.19.10.
6. Scullard, *Scipio Africanus,* p. 40; Lazenby, *Hannibal's War,* p. 133.
7. Polybius, 10.9.3.
8. Ibid., 10.7.5. Mago's location "on this side of the Pillars of Hercules," according to Polybius, is confusing and may have been a copyist's error.
9. Polybius, 10.8.4–9.
10. Ibid., 10.11.5–8.
11. Ibid., 10.14–15, 1–2.
12. Polybius's description of the sack of New Carthage is frequently used as a typical example of Roman behavior in such circumstances, a sequential process beginning with indiscriminate slaughter. Polybius, 10.15.5–8, says "They do this I think to inspire terror, so that when towns are taken by the Romans one may often see not only the corpses of human beings, but dogs cut in half and the dismembered limbs of other animals. . . . After this, upon the signal being given, the massacre ceased and they began pillaging." Polybius then goes on to describe a very methodical and orderly process by which loot was accumulated and distributed equally to the legionaries. (10.15.4–16). Adam Ziolkowski "Urbs Direpta, Or How the Romans Sacked Cities," in John Rich and Graham Shipley, eds., *War and Society in the Roman World* (London: Routledge, 1995), pp. 69–91, argues that the process was likely to have been a lot less orderly, with soldiers grabbing any goods they could get, and raping those citizens they didn't kill.
13. Polybius, 10.17.6–14.
14. Livy, 26.51.1–2.
15. Polybius, 10.19.1–6; Livy, 26.50.
16. Polybius, 10.20.1–4.
17. Lazenby, *Hannibal's War,* p. 140.
18. Livy, 26.51.10; Polybius 10.35.6–8.
19. Polybius, 10.37.4–5.
20. Goldsworthy, *The Punic Wars,* p. 277; Lazenby, *Hannibal's War,* p. 141.
21. Scullard, *Scipio Africanus,* pp. 73–4.
22. Ibid., p. 74.
23. Livy, 27.19.1–3.
24. Ibid., 27.19.8–12.
25. Lazenby, *Hannibal's War,* p. 142.

26. Plutarch, Marcellus, 9.
27. Livy, 27.9.1.
28. Ibid., 27.10.10.
29. Ibid., 27.12.1–3.
30. Ibid., 27.12–14.
31. Ibid., 27.16.12–16.
32. Lancel, *Hannibal*, p. 143; Livy, 27.16.8.
33. Plutarch, Marcellus, 27; Scullard, *Roman Politics*, pp. 20–1; Lazenby, *Hannibal's War*, pp. 176–7.
34. It is probably telling that, despite Fabius Maximus's success at Tarentum, for the year 208 his imperium was not renewed.
35. See Livy, 27.26–7, and Polybius, 10.32.1–6.
36. Polybius, 10.32.7.
37. Lazenby, *Hannibal's War*, p. 179.
38. Ibid., p. 178; Livy, 27.24.
39. Livy, 27.36.1–4, 27.39.1–2, 27.39.5–11.
40. Silius Italicus, 15.513–21.
41. Lazenby, *Hannibal's War*, p. 180.
42. Livy, 27.34–35.
43. Ibid., 27.39.11–14; Lancel, *Hannibal*, p. 146; Goldsworthy, *The Punic Wars*, p. 239.
44. Livy, 27.46.6; Lazenby, *Hannibal's War*, p. 184.
45. Lazenby, *Hannibal's War*, p. 183.
46. Livy, 27.43.1–12.
47. Dodge, *Hannibal*, pp. 547–8.
48. Livy, 27.44.9.
49. Polybius, 11.1.1.
50. Livy, 27.46.1–4.
51. Ibid., 27.46.7ff.
52. Ibid., 27.47.1–5.
53. Ibid., 27.47.10–11; Dodge, *Hannibal*, p. 551.
54. Ovid, *Fasti*, 6.770.
55. Scullard, *A History of the Roman World*, note 6, p. 502; Walbank, *A Historical Commentary on Polybius*, vol. 2, p. 270.
56. Livy, 27.48.8.
57. Lazenby's explanation (*Hannibal's War*, pp. 188–90) of the course of the battle is lucid and logical.
58. Polybius, 11.3.1.
59. Ibid., 11.2.1; Livy, 27.49.3–4.
60. Livy, 27.50.1; Lazenby, "Was Maharbal Right?" p. 40.
61. Livy, 27.49.5–6.
62. Lazenby, *Hannibal's War*, p. 191.
63. Polybius, 11.3.6.
64. Livy, 27.51.12.
65. Ibid., 28.1.4.
66. Ibid., 28.2.12.
67. Polybius, 11.20.2. Livy (28.12.13–14) places the Carthaginian numbers at fifty thousand infantry and forty-five hundred cavalry. Lazenby (*Hannibal's War*, p. 145) argues convincingly that Scipio's tactic of extending his wings indicates that he was outnumbered considerably in infantry.
68. Goldsworthy, *The Punic Wars*, p. 279.
69. Polybius, 11.21.1–5.
70. Ibid., 11.22.1–5.
71. Lazenby, *Hannibal's War*, p. 146.
72. Livy, 28.14.12–14, 28.15.3.

73. Polybius, 11.22.11–23.2.
74. Goldsworthy, *The Punic Wars*, p. 282.
75. Scullard, *Scipio Africanus*, pp. 94–5; Goldsworthy, *The Punic Wars*, pp. 282–3; Lazenby, *Hannibal's War*, p. 150.
76. Polybius, 11.24.1.
77. Goldsworthy, *The Punic Wars*, p. 283.
78. Livy, 28.15.11; Polybius, 11.24.7–9.
79. Livy, 28.16.6.
80. Ibid., 28.16.15.
81. Lancel, *Carthage*, pp. 396–7.
82. Livy, 24.49.1–6; Lazenby, *Hannibal's War*, p. 151.
83. Livy, 28.17.13–16. An analogous situation occurred in A.D. 1914 during the early stages of World War I when German admiral von Spee's squadron, featuring the two cruisers *Scharnhorst* and *Gneisenau*, sailed up to the Falkland Islands. There the Germans found anchored in Port Stanley harbor a much more powerful British fleet with two capital ships, the new dreadnought battle cruisers *Inflexible* and *Invincible*. Like in Scipio's case, von Spee's best bet was to close—in this case to fight before his adversaries could raise a head of steam and while they were still sitting ducks. Instead, the German tried to flee and was run down and annihilated.
84. Lazenby, *Hannibal's War*, p. 152.
85. Livy, 28.22.2ff.
86. Goldsworthy, *The Punic Wars*, p. 284.
87. Lazenby, *Hannibal's War*, p. 153.
88. Livy, 28.25–29; Polybius, 11.25.30.
89. Livy, 28.36.1–2.
90. Ibid., 28.37.4.
91. Ibid., 28.38.5.
92. Ibid., 28.40.3–42.22.
93. Lancel, *Hannibal*, p. 162.
94. Livy, 28.44.1–2.
95. Goldsworthy, *The Punic Wars*, p. 286.
96. Livy, 28.45.8.
97. G. de Sanctis, *Storia dei Romani* (Florence, Italy: La Nuova Italia, 1968), vol. 3, 2, p. 645ff; M. Gelzer, *Kleine Schriften* (Wiesbaden, Germany: F. Steiner, 1964), vol. 3, p. 245ff; cited in Lazenby, *Hannibal's War*, p. 195; Livy, 25.45.13; Appian, Lib 7.

CHAPTER IX: RESURRECTING THE GHOSTS

1. Livy, 28.46.7–10; 28.46.13.
2. Scullard (*Scipio Africanus*, fn 81, p. 266) argues that the story should probably be rejected since an almost identical story is told by Plutarch about Agesilaus (9). Nevertheless, it remains true that Livy (59 B.C.–A.D. 17) predated Plutarch (A.D. 46–120), so unless the story is based on an earlier tradition, it seems possible to accept it.
3. Livy, 29.1.15.
4. Ibid., 29.24.12.
5. Ibid., 29.24.14; Lazenby (*Hannibal's War*, p. 203) argues that the number is too large, since it was not until the Third Macedonian War, thirty years later, that the Roman army had legions this big. Goldsworthy (*The Punic Wars*, p. 287) counters that this argument "denies the essential flexibility of the Roman military system," and Goldsworthy says that "it was normal to increase the size of legions when faced by an especially dangerous enemy." Certainly, this was the case at Cannae.
6. Lazenby, *Hannibal's War*, p. 202.
7. Livy, 29.1.13–14, 26.1.10.
8. Ibid., 29.24.12.

9. Scullard, *Scipio Africanus,* p. 111.
10. Livy, 29.9.4–7.
11. Ibid., 29.9.9–11.
12. Plutarch, Cato the Elder, 3.5–6.
13. Livy, 29.19ff.
14. Ibid., 29.22ff.
15. Livy does not state a date, but Lazenby (*Hannibal's War,* p. 204) thinks the June-July time frame is a good guess.
16. Livy, 29.25.12.
17. Ibid., 29.28.
18. Appian, Lib 9; Lancel, *Hannibal,* p. 165.
19. Livy, 29.34.1–6.
20. Ibid., 29.34.7ff.
21. Lancel, *Hannibal,* p. 164.
22. Livy, 29.28.7.
23. Ibid., 29.35.10–11; Polybius, 14.1.14; Goldsworthy, *The Punic Wars,* p. 292; Lazenby, *Hannibal's War,* p. 206.
24. Polybius, 14.1.3.
25. Livy, 30.3.1–7.
26. Ibid., 30.4.9.
27. Polybius, 14.4.10.
28. Livy, 30.6.8; Lazenby, *Hannibal's War,* p. 208.
29. Polybius, 14.5.15.
30. Livy, 30.7.6–9.
31. Ibid., 30.7.8–9; Polybius, 14.7.6.
32. Goldsworthy, *The Punic Wars,* p. 295.
33. Polybius, 14.7.9; Lazenby, *Hannibal's War,* p. 209; Lancel, *Hannibal,* p. 203.
34. Lazenby, *Hannibal's War,* p. 209.
35. Scullard, *Scipio Africanus,* p. 129.
36. Polybius, 14.8.8; Livy, 30.8.7.
37. Lazenby, *Hannibal's War,* pp. 209–211.
38. Livy, 30.8.7.
39. Goldsworthy, *The Punic Wars,* pp. 295–6.
40. Livy, 30.8.12–13.
41. Polybius, 14.10.7–9.
42. Goldsworthy, *The Punic Wars,* p. 297.
43. Polybius, 14.10.9.
44. Livy, 30.10.12.
45. Ibid., 30.11.5.
46. Lazenby, *Hannibal's War,* p. 212.
47. Livy, 30.12.11ff.
48. Diodorus (27.7) claims that before Hasdrubal Gisgo's condominium with Syphax, Sophonisba had been the wife of Masinissa. But this seems unlikely, given the prince's extensive time in Spain. According to Zonaras (9.11), Sophonisba was betrothed to Masinissa before marrying Syphax.
49. Livy, 30.13.12–14.
50. Ibid., 30.15.1–8.
51. Lazenby, *Hannibal's War,* p. 213; Scullard, *Scipio Africanus,* p. 134.
52. Livy, 30.16.4.
53. Lancel, *Hannibal,* p. 170.
54. Livy, 30.16.10–11.
55. Ibid., 30.16.12.
56. Appian, *The Punic Wars,* 32.
57. Livy, 30.16.14–15.

58. Lancel, *Hannibal,* p. 155.

59. Lazenby, *Hannibal's War,* p. 214.

60. Livy, 30.19.1ff.

61. Cicero (*On Divination,* 1.24.48) says the story came from Silenos, Hannibal's resident historian.

62. Delbrück (*Warfare in Antiquity,* p. 380) in particular draws attention to this time lag.

63. Hoyos, "Hannibal: What Kind of Genius," p. 179.

64. Lancel, *Hannibal,* pp. 156–7.

65. Appian, *The Punic Wars,* 134.

66. Livy, 30.20.7–8.

67. Goldsworthy, *The Punic Wars,* pp. 299.

68. Appian, *The Punic Wars,* 34.

69. Livy, 30.25.1ff; Polybius, 15.2.3–13.

70. Lancel, *Hannibal,* p. 171.

71. Polybius, 15.4.2.

72. Polybius, 14.5.1–2.

73. Lazenby, *Hannibal's War,* p. 218.

74. Appian, *The Hannibalic War,* 59.

75. Polybius, 15.3.5–7; Scullard, *Scipio Africanus,* p. 141.

76. Polybius, 15.5.4–7; Livy 30.29.2–3. Some doubt the story, since an almost identical tale exists in Herodotus (7.146.7), but it makes good tactical sense and Scipio was plainly capable of all manner of deception. He also knew Greek and may have actually gotten the idea from *The Histories.*

77. Polybius, 14.6.4–8; Livy, 30.30–31.

78. Polybius does not specify the size of the opposing armies. Appian (*The Punic Wars,* 40), who is generally good with numbers, gives Hannibal 50,000 total, while Lazenby (*Hannibal's War,* pp. 220–1) estimates his infantry at thirty-six thousand.

79. Polybius, 15.11.1; Lancel, *Hannibal,* p. 175.

80. Lancel, *Hannibal,* p. 175; Goldsworthy, *The Punic Wars,* p. 302. Livy (30.26.3 and 30.33.5.) may have been trying to use this as a justification for Rome's very aggressive behavior leading up to the Second Macedonian War.

81. Goldsworthy, *The Punic Wars,* p. 303.

82. Polybius, 15.11.1.

83. Goldsworthy, *The Punic Wars,* pp. 202–3; Scullard, *Scipio Africanus,* pp. 150–1.

84. Polybius, 15.9.6–10.

85. Scullard, *Scipio Africanus,* pp. 149–50. See also J. Kronmayer and G. Veith, *Antike Schlachtfelder,* vol. 3 (1912), p. 599ff, and vol. 4 (1931), p. 626ff.

86. Polybius, 15.12.8; Livy, 30.34.2.

87. Livy, 30.34.3.

88. Dodge, *Hannibal,* pp. 604–5.

89. Polybius, 15.13.6–7.

90. Ibid., 15.14.2.

91. Polybius, 15.14.9. Appian (*The Punic Wars,* 48) maintain that twenty-five hundred Romans plus some of Masinissa's men died at Zama.

92. Polybius, 15.19.5.

93. Lancel (*Hannibal,* p. 177) states that one Euboic talent was equivalent to twenty-six kilograms of silver, or 57.2 pounds. Thus ten thousand talents equaled 572,000 pounds of silver, or 9,152,000 ounces, at $13.25 per ounce spot price on March 5, 2009, which amounts to $121,264,000.

94. Appian, *The Punic Wars,* 54.

95. Scullard, *Scipio Africanus,* p. 159.

96. Goldsworthy, *The Punic Wars,* p. 317.

97. Toynbee, *Hannibal's Legacy,* vol. 2, pp. 277–81.

98. Livy, 31.14.1–2, 32.3.1–5.

99. Scullard, *Scipio Africanus*, p. 185.

100. Goldsworthy, *The Punic Wars*, p. 320.

101. Livy, 33.25.6–7.

102. Plutarch, *Flaminius*,13; Livy, 34.50.

103. Delbrück, *Warfare in Antiquity*, pp. 340–1.

104. Scullard, *Scipio Africanus*, p. 179.

105. Livy, 33.48; Lancel, *Carthage*, pp. 402–4.

106. E. Badian, "Rome and Antiochus the Great, a Study in Cold War," *Classical Philology* (1959), pp. 81–99.

107. Livy, 34.60.4ff, 36.7.1ff.

108. Pliny the Elder, *The Natural History*, 5.148.

109. Lancel, *Hannibal*, pp. 206–7.

110. Plutarch, *Flaminius*, 20.

111. Lancel, *Carthage*, pp. 404–5.

112. Goldsworthy, *The Punic Wars*, p. 331.

113. Charles-Picard, *Daily Life in Carthage*, p. 165; Lancel, *Carthage*, pp. 505–6.

114. Appian, *The Punic Wars*, 69.

115. Appian, *The Punic Wars*, 132.

116. Arnold J. Toynbee, *Hannibal's Legacy: The Hannibalic War's Effects on Roman Life*, 2 volumes (London: Oxford University Press, 1965).

117. Cornell, "Hannibal's Legacy: The Effects of the Hannibalic War on Italy," p. 104.

118. Victor Davis Hanson, *Warfare and Agriculture in Classical Greece* (Berkeley: University of California Press, 1998).

119. T. J. Cornell, *Cambridge Ancient History*, second edition (London: Cambridge University Press, 1980), pp. 334, 413; M. I. Finley, *Ancient Slavery and Modern Ideology* (London: Chatto and Windus, 1980), p. 81; Goldsworthy, *The Punic Wars*, p. 364.

120. Cornell, "Hannibal's Legacy: The Effects of the Hannibalic War on Italy," p. 105.

121. Goldsworthy, *The Punic Wars*, p. 362.

122. Lancel, *Hannibal*, pp. 212–3.

EPILOGUE: THE SHADOW OF CANNAE

1. See for example Daly, *Cannae*, p. ix ("The battle of Cannae may be the most studied battle in history; it has almost certainly had the most important effect on the development of military tactics."); Dodge, *Hannibal*, p. 379; Lancel, *Hannibal*, p. 107 ("it is not surprising that Hannibal's military masterpiece has influenced the ideas of war theorists, as far as Clausewitz and even beyond.").

2. Ed. and transl. George T. Dennis, *Maurice's Strategikon* (Philadelphia: University of Pennsylvania Press, 1984), p. 27.

3. Charles Oman, *A History of the Art of War in the Middle Ages* (New York: Burt Franklin, 1924), vol. 2, pp. 265–7.

4. Niccolò Machiavelli, *The Prince*, trans. Luigi Ricci, chs. 31, 53, and 44.

5. Machiavelli, *The Prince*, ch. 17.

6. Niccolò Machiavelli, *The Art of War*, transl. Ellis Farneworth (Indianapolis, Ind.: Bobbs-Merrill, 1965), p. 120.

7. Ibid., p. 112.

8. Geoffrey Parker, "The Limits to Revolutions in Military Affairs: Maurice of Nassau, the Battle of Nieuwpoort (1600), and the Legacy," *The Journal of Military History*, vol. 71, no. 2 (2007), pp. 338–9.

9. Ibid., pp. 345–6.

10. This conclusion is based in part on a personal correspondence with John A. Lynn and Geoffrey Parker, neither of whom recalled any further discussions of Cannae in the military writings of the enlightenment.

11. Parker, "*The Limits of Revolutions in Military Affairs*," pp. 357–8.

12. Terence M. Holmes, "Classic Blitzkrieg: The Untimely Modernity of Schlieffen's Cannae Program," *The Journal of Military History*, vol. 67, no. 3 (2003), p. 744.
13. Terence Zuber, "The Schlieffen Plan Reconsidered," *War in History*, vol. 6 (199); Terence Zuber, *Inventing the Schlieffen Plan* (New York: Oxford University Press, 2002).
14. Holmes, "Classic Blitzkrieg," pp. 757–9.
15. I owe these observations to Bruce Gudmudsson, personal correspondence March 31, 2009.
16. This phrase was suggested by Dennis Showalter; Holmes, "Classic Blitzkrieg," pp. 764–70.
17. Holmes, "Classic Blitzkrieg," pp. 769–71.
18. Wolf Heckmann, *Rommel's War in Africa* (London: Doubleday, 1981), p. 113.
19. Antony Beevor, *Stalingrad: The Fateful Siege: 1942–1943* (London: Penguin, 1999), p. 297.
20. Carlo D'Este, *Patton: A Genius for War* (New York: HarperCollins, 1995), p. 704.
21. Carlo D'Este, *Eisenhower: A Soldier's Life* (New York: Henry Holt, 2002), p. 594.
22. Martin Blumenson, *The Patton Papers: 1940–1945* (Boston: Houghton Mifflin, 1974), p. 594.
23. Cited in Goldsworthy, *Cannae*, cover page.

GLOSSARY OF LATIN, MILITARY, AND TECHNICAL TERMS

ala—Literally "wing." The allied operational equivalent of a Roman legion. Its configuration and armament are uncertain but are presumed to have been similar to that of a legion. Such units were accompanied by cavalry numbering nine hundred, or triple the size of the Roman horse units assigned to a legion.

aristeia—A Greek term for a serial display of heroic behavior.

as—The basic Roman bronze currency at the beginning of the Second Punic War.

augurs—Those who interpreted the signs and portents. Augurs were not career priests but came from the leading families and had normal career patterns.

auspicia—Those phenomena that were believed to reveal the will of the gods and were derived from a number of sources, including the internal organs of sacrificed animals.

Barca—Derived from the Punic word for "thunderbolt," this was a nickname given to Hamilcar, father of Hannibal, and was subsequently used by historians to designate members of the family line and their supporters. "Barcid" is also used as a noun and adjective to refer to the Barca family.

campus Martius—The Field of Mars. An area outside of Rome used for ceremonial purposes including meetings of the Comitia Centuriata.

censors—Two Roman magistrates normally elected at five-year intervals to hold a census and assign men to the various assemblies, including—most critical—the senate.

centurion—A key leader of the infantry ranks. Roughly equivalent in function to noncommissioned officers in the U.S. military.

century—Half a maniple, and also a voting unit in the Comitia Centuriata, since the origin of the century was the people at arms.

Cisalpine Gaul—That part of northern Italy inhabited by Gallic tribes south of the Alps.

clients—Those dependent in one way or another upon a Roman patron. Clients could include local farmers or workers, citizens defended in court, former soldiers, and even foreigners.

Comitia Centuriata—The assembly responsible for electing consuls, praetors, and censors, and for voting on war or peace.

Comitia Tributa—A tribal assembly that voted for lesser magistrates, such as quaestors, along with passing legislation.

Concilium Plebis—The council of plebs. Its functions were basically the same as those of the Comitia Tributa, except that patricians were not included. This body elected plebeian tribunes and passed legislation.

consul—Foremost magistrate of the Roman republic; two were elected annually. The role was largely a military one, and a consul had the power to make life-and-death decisions outside of Rome.

contubernium—A squad of eight Roman soldiers who ate and slept together. The smallest and most intimate unit in the army structure.

council of elders—A key body of Carthaginian notables, it represented the oligarchic element of the government. Continuity was probably maintained by a control element of either 104 judges or 30 key councilors, or possibly both.

Cunctator—"The Delayer." The nickname applied to Fabius Maximus by the Romans.

cursus honorum—Literally the "course of honors." This is the sequential order of elected office for men of the senatorial class, the highest being consul.

denarius—Silver coin circulated by Rome for the first time during the Second Punic War.

dictator—A single Roman magistrate chosen in emergencies to assume supreme power for a term not to exceed six months. During this time his imperium trumped all other magistrates', with the exception of tribunes of the plebs.

equites—Literally "horsemen." This was a group of wealthy Romans that during the Second Punic War was made up mostly of senators. This group occupied the eighteen centuries of horsemen in the Comitia Centuriata, and each was entitled to a state-supplied mount for service in the cavalry. Each man wore a gold ring as an insignia.

extraordinarii—A detachment of picked allied troops at the personal disposal of a Roman general.

gens—A clan or group of families sharing a common (second) name (e.g., "Cornelius" in the name Publius **Cornelius** Scipio). The Roman republic was dominated by a relatively few key gens, such as the Aemilii, Claudii, Fabii, and Cornelii.

gladius—The characteristic Roman cut-and-thrust short sword, likely adopted from the Spanish, thus the term *"gladius hispaniensis."*

hasta—The traditional Roman thrusting spear. By the time of Hannibal's invasion, the *hasta* was probably still employed only by the *triarii.*

hastati—Heavy infantry of the first line of maniples in the *triplex acies.* While these troops originally carried the *hasta,* the traditional Roman thrusting spear, by the time of Cannae, they were armed with the *pilum* and *gladius.*

imperium—A generalized power to rule, on the order of the Chinese Mandate of Heaven, except it was divisible and rotated yearly. Among magistrates who held it, the imperium was virtually without limit, subject only to certain rights held by all Roman citizens.

imperium pro—The extension of the imperium through the process of prorogation, usually at the end of a yearly term of office. A consul or praetor (occasionally others) might receive this extension so that he could continue operating as a proconsul or propraetor after new magistrates had been elected. This proved a useful instrument for overseas governance and military operations.

legion—The primary operational element of the Roman army, normally with a strength of forty-two hundred (twelve hundred *velites,* twelve hundred *hastati,* twelve hundred *principes,* and six hundred *triarii*) plus three hundred citizen cavalry. In special circumstances, such as at Cannae, these numbers could be increased.

legiones Cannenses—Strictly speaking, these are the units organized around the survivors of the Battle of Cannae, but the term came to include other defeated troops who were sent to join the survivors of Cannae in disgrace and exile.

lictor—A bodyguard assigned to Roman magistrates (dictators got twenty-four, consuls twelve and praetors six). Outside of Rome, each lictor carried an ax wrapped in a bunch of rods. This insignia connoted the magistrates' right to inflict corporal and capital punishment.

maniple—Literally "handful." Maniples were at the time of the Second Punic War the basic tactical unit of a legion. Besides *velites,* a legion had ten maniples each of *hastati, principes,* and *triarii.* Each maniple of the first two elements had 120 men, but each maniple of the *triarii* had only 60 men. Each maniple was made up of two centuries.

master of horse—The junior associate of a Roman dictator. Like the dictator, the master of horse had a six-month term of duty.

nobiles—Members of a Roman family whose relative had achieved consular rank at some point in the past.

novus homo—A "new man" or one who is the first in his family to reach the consul-ship.

ovation—A kind of consolation prize for a commander who did something heroic but not sufficient enough to be granted a triumph. The commander and his sol-diers either marched or rode on horseback into the city of Rome, to the acclaim of the populace.

patrician—The higher of the two basic designations of Roman citizens (the other being plebeian). The term roughly equates to "first families." By the time of the Second Punic War patricians had lost much of their political potency, since a number of plebeian families had reached the consulship. Thus, "patricians" and *"nobiles"* were decidedly not synonymous.

patron—The other half of the client-patron relationship. A patron was a person who had a number of dependents and looked after their interests. In return he could demand their loyalty and support.

pectorale—A small plate worn on the chest of most Roman line infantry as a heart protector.

pilum—The heavy javelin or throwing spear used by *hastati* and *principes,* generally at the outset of combat.

plebs—All Roman citizens except patricians. At the time of the Second Punic War the connotation of "commoner" was belied by the fact that several plebeian families such as the Fulvii Flacci and Sempronii Gracchi were virtually as wealthy and influential as any patrician equivalent.

praetor—An important elected magistrate at the tier below consul. During the Second Punic War, four praetors were elected each year and received the im-perium, which enabled them to command in wartime in the absence of a consul.

principes—Heavy infantry of the second line of maniples in the *triplex acies.* They were armed in the same manner as the *hastati.*

Punic—From the Latin *punicus* or Phoenician, the term refers to Carthage and all things and people Carthaginian.

quinquereme—The standard Carthaginian warship during the Second Punic War. It was a ram-bearing galley, and the exact configuration of its oarsmen re-mains uncertain. Roman quinqueremes were probably similar to Carthaginian models, though they may have differed in details and features.

scutum—The heavy shield of the Roman legionary.

senate—A consultative council, and the only one of the Roman assemblies that met in continuous session. Senatorial authority involved advising consuls, gener-ally on foreign policy. Of all Roman governing elements, it was the most power-ful, but that power was shrouded.

senatus consultum—Strictly speaking, this was the "advice" arising from a senatorial discussion and vote; in a deferential society like Rome, it had nearly the force of law.

spolia opima—The most honorable spoil, refers to the armor that a Roman commander would strip off an enemy leader after killing him in single combat.

suffete—Senior executives of the Carthaginian government. Two suffetes were elected annually by the time of the Second Punic War.

triarii—The third line of troops in the *triplex acies*. At the time of Cannae they were likely armed with the *hasta*, the traditional Roman thrusting spear.

tribunes of the plebs—Officials originally elected to protect the interests of the plebs in the face of the patricians. Tribunes retained the power to veto legislation and acts of the magistrates.

tribunes of the soldiers (*tribuni militum*)—The six officers assigned to each legion. They were generally young men of senatorial rank with political ambitions.

triplex acies—The three-line checkerboard pattern into which Roman heavy infantry characteristically deployed.

triumph—The honor accorded to a commander who had won a victory over a foreign enemy. A personal parade would be held in the city of Rome, with the recipient in a chariot followed by his troops and sometimes by the defeated enemy leader on his way to execution. All were cheered by the Roman populace.

turma—The basic tactical unit of Roman cavalry.

velites—Roman light troops or skirmishers. Twelve hundred were attached to each legion and were apportioned equally over all thirty maniples.

INDEX

ABOUT THE AUTHOR

ROBERT L. O'CONNELL was a member of the U.S. Intelligence community for three decades. Upon retirement he became a visiting professor at the Naval Postgraduate School. He is the author of four histories: *Of Arms and Men, Sacred Vessels, Ride of the Second Horseman,* and *Soul of the Sword,* along with the novel *Fast Eddie.* He is married and has two grown children.

ABOUT THE TYPE

The text of this book was set in Janson, a typeface designed in about 1690 by Nicholas Kis, a Hungarian living in Amsterdam, and for many years mistakenly attributed to the Dutch printer Anton Janson. In 1919 the matrices became the property of the Stempel Foundry in Frankfurt. It is an old-style book face of excellent clarity and sharpness. Janson serifs are concave and splayed; the contrast between thick and thin strokes is marked.